Regional Economics

Regional Economics

Location Theory, Urban Structure,
and Regional Change

Harry W. Richardson

*Director of the Centre for Research
in the Social Sciences, University of Kent*

PRAEGER PUBLISHERS
New York · Washington

BOOKS THAT MATTER

Published in the United States of America in 1969
by Praeger Publishers, Inc.
111 Fourth Avenue, New York, N.Y. 10003

© 1969 by Harry W. Richardson

All rights reserved. No part of this publication may be
reproduced, stored in a retrieval system, or transmitted,
in any form or by any means, electronic, mechanical,
photocopying, recording, or otherwise, without the prior
permission of the copyright-owner.

Library of Congress Catalog Card Number: 78-92369

Printed in the United States of America

Contents

	PAGE
List of Tables	ix
Preface	xi

Chapter 1   Introduction
1 The neglect of spatial analysis 1
2 General approaches to regional and locational analysis 5
3 Scope and outline 7

Part A   Location

Chapter 2   Spatial price theory
1 Spatial equilibrium in geographically separated markets 13
2 Introducing patterns of spatial dispersion 18
3 Single producer surrounded by many buyers: the spatial monopolist 20
4 Two sellers at different locations surrounded by many buyers: the law of market areas 24
5 Many sellers concentrated, buyers dispersed 28
6 Buyers concentrated, sellers dispersed 29
7 Buyers and sellers dispersed with a central market 30
8 Buyers and sellers dispersed: monopolistic competition and spatial oligopoly 32
9 Alternative spatial pricing systems 37
10 Spatial price variations: a testable model 38

Chapter 3   Transport costs and location
1 Transportation as a locational factor: some general considerations 42
2 Weber's theory of location: the locational and weight triangles and minimisation of transport costs 45
3 Transport inputs 49
4 Labour and other forms of orientation: substitution between transport and non-transport costs 56

	PAGE
Chapter 4 The optimal location of the firm	
1 The space cost curve	59
2 Demand cones: towards a space revenue curve	69
3 Space revenue, space costs and the profit maximising location	77
4 Locational interdependence	81
5 Alternatives to profit maximisation as a locational objective	90
Chapter 5 The general theory of location	
1 Obstacles to a general theory	101
2 The general theory of location according to Lösch	105
3 The general theory of location: Greenhut	108
4 Lefeber's general equilibrium theory	111

Part B   The urban economy

Chapter 6 Urban spatial structure	
1 The minimisation of costs of friction hypothesis	119
2 Some observations on models of urban spatial structure	123
3 Locational equilibrium of an urban firm	129
4 Consumer spatial behaviour and the location of retail establishments	132
5 A model of urban residential equilibrium	137
6 Concepts of city structure	145
Chapter 7 Urban growth	
1 Introduction	156
2 Central place theory	156
3 The urban economic base and urban growth	165
4 The human ecological approach to urban growth	170
5 The communications theory of urban growth	175
6 City size and urban growth	176
Chapter 8 The urban public economy	
1 Economic trends and urban government activity	186
2 Local government and the triple budget function	188
3 Urban fiscal problems	193
A Fiscal implications of spatial dispersion	193
B Urban budget decisions	194

		PAGE
4	Scale economies and efficient urban government units	196
5	Consumer preferences and spatial mobility between urban communities	203
6	Methods of financing urban government expenditures	208
7	Summary	217

Part C   Regional economics

Chapter 9   The regional framework

1	The region as a concept	223
2	Regional accounts	231
	A Introduction	231
	B Regional income and product accounts: an example	234
	C Regional input–output accounts: an illustration	237

Chapter 10   Inter-regional income theory

1	The regional economic base	247
2	A model of income determination in a multiple regional system	254
3	The inter-regional multiplier	256
4	Balance of payments implications	259
5	Regional balance of payments: mechanisms of adjustment	262
6	The gravity concept and regional macroeconomics	270

Chapter 11   Regional business cycles

1	Approaches to cyclical analysis	275
2	An inter-regional multiplier-accelerator model	281

Chapter 12   Factor mobility

1	Factor mobility and general equilibrium	287
2	Labour migration	295
	A Internal migration and its role	295
	B Theoretical hypotheses	298
3	Mobility of capital	304
4	Spatial diffusion of innovation and technical progress	310
5	The mobility of managerial talent	316

Chapter 13   Regional growth

1	Introduction	321
2	Harrod–Domar models	323

	PAGE
3 Equilibrium growth in a neoclassical model	331
4 The export base theory of growth	336
5 The sector approach	340
6 Industrial structure and regional growth	342
7 Long-run convergence of *per capita* incomes	347

Chapter 14 Policy objectives and efficiency

1 A framework for policy	358
A Decision models	358
B Linear programming	361
2 The consistency of policy goals	365
A The national interest and regional objectives	365
B Aggregate efficiency and inter-regional equity	372
C Compatibility of inter-regional goals	376
3 Regional stabilisation policy	379

Chapter 15 The strategy of regional policy

1 Alternative strategies for problem regions	386
A Introduction	386
B The market solution	389
C Measures to stimulate migration	392
D Capital mobility and location of industry policy	397
2 Wage subsidies, resource allocation and employment	409
3 The growth-point concept	415
Bibliography	429
Name Index	443
Subject Index	447

List of tables

		PAGE
1	The central place hierarchy: how n goods are supplied by M centres	161
2	Regional accounts system with government in an open economy: matrix form	236
3	Inter-regional input–output accounts: 2 regions and 3 commodities (sectors)	242
4	A simple regional income model: equilibrium condition	273
5	Alternative regional stabilisation programmes	383
6	Relative efficiency of different types of subsidy	407

Preface

When I began my Regional Economics special subject course in Aberdeen in 1966 I found it very difficult to direct my students to a single volume introduction to the subject, particularly on its theoretical aspects. As the bibliography shows there is an extensive literature on regional economics and related fields; there are textbooks on quite narrow areas (such as location, urban land use and regional planning techniques) and some valuable research monographs, but there are few, if any, comprehensive texts. This book attempts to cover within one volume the main elements of the theory of location, urban and regional economics. I hope that it may be useful to students not only of economics but also of planning, geography, sociology and other disciplines interested in regional analysis. The use of mathematics has been kept to a minimum, but it would be an advantage, and may even be necessary, for the reader to have an appreciation of basic economic principles.

This is not really an orthodox textbook though it covers much of the ground that we should expect from a textbook in this field. My aim was not merely to present the models developed by others but to criticise them – to examine their assumptions and conclusions and to suggest how they might be made more operational. Moreover, in some neglected areas of the subject I have found it necessary to suggest the broad outlines for the development of relevant theories myself.

The contents of this book do not represent a single all-embracing theory. There are two reasons for this. Firstly, to select one theory rather than another we have to formulate hypotheses from the theories and test them. The appropriateness of a theory must be judged by its predictive value as well as by its inner consistency. Since this book does not take the final step of testing alternative hypotheses it cannot with confidence choose one theory as being definitely superior to all others. Secondly, regional economics is in an embryonic state and its theoretical framework is still rather loose. However, the time for a grand synthesis may be near. I believe, and I have hinted as much at several points in the text, that such a synthesis will combine emphasis of the nodal relationships within regions with inter-regional flow analysis and will simultaneously explain the spatial organisation of regions, cities, firms and households. This book is merely a prologue to such a task. My modest aim is to try to order the different strands of the subject into some kind of coherent framework.

I wish to thank Professor J.Parry Lewis for his useful criticisms of an earlier draft, and Bert Shaw, Peter Sloane and Joan Vipond for discussions on a number of points. Responsibility for errors is, of course, mine alone. I am very grateful to Miss Aileen Fraser, Miss Margaret Hay and Mrs Margaret King for typing various drafts.

August, 1968   HARRY W. RICHARDSON

Regional Economics

Chapter 1
Introduction

1 The neglect of spatial analysis

Although location studies have a long respectable ancestry stretching back, especially in central Europe, into the last century, rapid growth of interest in the economics of location and of regions is relatively recent – within the last twenty years. Even today it is still possible to take the view that 'location theory and regional economics are only stepchildren in the family of economics'.[1] The reasons for this underprivileged position are complex and unclear, but the following considerations provide a partial answer.

In the first place, traditional economic theory ignored spatial aspects. Although the classical economists wrote about the evolutionary sequence of economic activity, their formal analysis was related predominantly to a static, spaceless world (or what Isard calls a 'wonderland of no dimensions'). Many of their economic propositions were elevated into immutable eternal laws that were held to have universal validity. It is not surprising that this extreme position invited reaction from many quarters. One manifestation of reaction was the development of the German Historical School, the members of which stressed the point that theory had to be verified by reference to social reality. They explicitly recognised the significance of the time element in economic analysis, but their acknowledgement of space and distance factors was implicit. With some exceptions,[2] dynamic considerations and the role of time in economics supplied a vein so rich for economists to work in that analysis of spatial phenomena was neglected for many decades.

To some extent, therefore, the habit of abstracting from space is

---

[1] Thompson, W.R. (1966) Urban Economic Development. 81, in Hirsch, W.Z. (edit), *Regional Accounts for Policy Decisions*

[2] Launhardt's pioneering investigations of location theory were published in 1882

to be explained by the belief that time was considered the critical dimension in economic analysis. The theoretical implications of space appeared secondary relative to time in evaluating how the economy worked and its performance. The problem of the optimum location of economic activities and population seemed rather trivial compared with the questions relating to the growth and stability of the national economy. Moreover, many spatial problems could be handled within the framework of traditional analysis. If the costs of movement through space were required, these could often be incorporated in standard pricing theory. Since location advantages include economising on time to cut down delivery delays, some space aspects could be treated as time aspects.

In addition, time elements readily lent themselves to rigorous economic analysis, whereas economists generally believed that their tools of analysis would give them only a partial understanding of spatial factors. They tended to assume that non-economic factors had a dominant influence on the spatial pattern of economic activity. The location of many natural resources is given, while non-economic considerations are regarded as determining the decisions where to live, to work and even to produce. This belief gives rise to surprising assumptions in economic analysis; for instance, international trade is normally implied to take place in a world economy without distance or transport costs. Other disciplines developed stronger interests in spatial problems earlier than the economist – geography, sociology and demography. Indeed, the growth of a new field of study called 'regional science' reflects the advantages of an interdisciplinary approach in studying locational and regional problems. Many of these problems are not comprehensible in terms of economic analysis alone. Thus in Part B of this book which is concerned with the urban economy, we find it necessary to make explicit reference to the principles of urban sociology and human ecology. But the view that economics cannot supply *all* the answers to spatial questions is no argument for the economist to ignore space. As Bos has argued, 'there is no reason to disregard spatial phenomena as being outside the economists' field of specialisation as long as no serious attempts have been made to arrive at a pure economic theory explaining the spatial structure of economic activity and until such attempts have shown this to be impossible'.[3]

[3] Bos, H.C. (1965) *Spatial Dispersion of Economic Activity.* 2

Another reason for the relative lack of systematic study of locational problems (at least, outside Germany) before the last two decades is the long-established reliance on marginalist analysis in microeconomic theory. Marginalist assumptions are frequently, though not always, inapplicable to the spatial dimension. In location theory, for example, the movement of plants is discontinuous, that is, there will be either a long distance jump, say to a consumption or a material site, or no movement at all. Similarly, in spatial price theory, the price relationships between spatially separated markets have often to be stated as inequalities; for instance, the condition prescribing that A does not import a homogeneous commodity X from B, is that the price of X in B plus the unit transport cost between A and B must be no less than the local price of X at A. The existence of nodal centres, population clusters and transhipment points are further examples of discontinuity in the structure of spatial systems. Transport routes do not fan out in all directions from a given point but develop along a very limited number of axes. Although population density gradients become less steep with distance from the city centre, nevertheless at some critical distance (such as the suburban periphery) there will be a discontinuity in their slope. For these reasons, the smooth continuous functions characteristic of so many areas of economic statics and dynamics are often not applicable to spatial problems. With regard to the latter, therefore, linear programming techniques are frequently more relevant than neoclassical marginalism.

The adverse influence of classical economic thinking on the development of the economics of space and regions manifested itself in another way. If traditional classical assumptions are made (of which price and wage flexibility and factor mobility within a country are the most crucial), then regional problems are unlikely to be troublesome since differences in prices, costs, wages and incomes between regions cannot persist, apart from the constraints on equalisation imposed by transport costs. Moreover, the 'equality doctrine' (as Myrdal has called it) was so pervasive that it became a convention to assume zero transport costs even in spatial analysis in order to ensure complete price equalisation. But the space economy is characterised by many imperfections in competition, and distance itself confers monopolistic protection. There are both economic and non-economic resistances to the movement of factors. Market forces do not lead inevitably to equality of regional *per capita* incomes or to the optimal spatial allocation of resources, and in some circumstances may operate in a disequilibrating manner. In fact, the market economy may lead to a massive drain of population from certain areas and a heavy concentration of resources at a limited number of high density conurbations. Recognition of these factors gives rise to the planning problem of how to determine the optimal dispersion of economic activity according to policy objectives that balance efficiency and equity. The growth of planning has demanded greater comprehension of and revived interest in spatial problems.

Concern with regional policy lagged behind other aspects of government intervention even after many economists had become disillusioned with the market economy. It was natural that attention should be concentrated on the problems of full employment and extreme inequities in income distribution first. Only when these problems had been more or less solved, did it become reasonable for policymakers to look at questions of *inter-regional* equity and of how to raise the economy's production potential by absorbing resources underutilised in certain areas of the country. Thus, preoccupation with national issues delayed intervention in regional problems and made it certain that, for a time, they received low priority.

It is also true, however, that regional problems are less noticeable. Statistical data deficiencies mask many inter-area changes in economic activity, and symptoms of distress may fail to attract much notice until they are very serious. Moreover, the rates of change in activity observed in national economic problems such as inflation, economic fluctuations and aggregate growth are more startling than what Borts and Stein call the 'glacier-like movements of regional economic development'. Locational movements, both of groups of individuals and of firms, tend to be long drawn out, and are not recorded as quickly within a country as are those across international barriers. Finally, pursuit of a location of industry policy has been made easier by technological change which has freed much of manufacturing industry from its previous dependence on raw material and other natural resource locations. As industry becomes more market-oriented, planning the geographical distribution of population and construction of transport facilities and other kinds of infrastructure enable us to mould the spatial distribution of industry in a way that was not possible in a previous era.

In recent years the economist's sphere of inquiry has been

broadening into new fields, of which spatial analysis is merely one. The relative neglect of location, urban and regional economics in the past is not, therefore, an indication that the subject is of minor importance. It partly reflects the longevity of classical modes of thought and the belated development of techniques of analysis appropriate for regional analysis. The growing interest in locational and regional problems is undoubtedly due to its policy implications, but spatial problems are also worth studying for their own sake. Investigation into this field is justified unless we subscribe to the view that *where* economic activity takes place has no significant repercussions on growth or welfare.

2 General approaches to regional and locational analysis

There are at least three ways of analysing the economic implications of the spatial dimension, two of which take explicit account of the distance variable while the third treats it implicitly. Firstly, one type of analysis assumes that the location of population, industry and resources is fixed, as well as the channels of transportation, and conceives of space as a friction to the flow of commodities between fixed points. In particular, models of this kind are often concerned with determining the equilibrium patterns of commodity flows and of price relationships. The friction of space, as measured by transport costs, restricts spatial interaction.[4] Although transport costs reflect other variables such as the volume and weight of goods and the density of traffic, they vary directly with distance (though most transport rates are, in fact, 'tapered', varying less than proportionately to distance). Since transport costs limit the ability of goods produced at one location to compete with locally produced goods at another location, commodity flows are reduced by distance. The equilibrium theories that fall into this category discuss the space economy in a realistic manner in the sense that they recognise the existence of space and the impact of distance on the economic interrelationships between different areas of the national economy. They

---

[4] Isard has suggested an illuminating analogy between spatial and temporal analysis. He suggests that space preference is a concept analogous to time preference, and that by discounting over space we can compare the values of goods, yields or inputs which are spatially separated. The rate of discount over space, or the price of movement through space, is the transport rate, and this, too, is analogous to the price of movement through time – the interest rate (Isard, W. (1956) *Location and Space-Economy.* 83–5)

provide a sharp contrast to Walrasian general equilibrium analysis which assumes a one point, non-spatial economy and to Keynesian aggregate general equilibrium analysis which when applied to regions divides the national economy into several sectors, none of which has a geographical frame of reference. Indeed, this approach does not lead to general equilibrium analysis at all, since locations are given as data rather than determined within the model.

Secondly, we may adopt a much more generalised spatial analysis which includes the determination of the spatial structure itself within its scope, and treats space as 'a matrix for the placement of economic activities' (R.E.Kuenne). General location theory is, in effect, an application of the Walrasian system to an economy in which distance is included as a variable. It is concerned with why individuals live and work at particular places, why plants and service establishments are built at one site rather than another, and why population centres of different sizes develop at one location rather than another. In addition, it attempts to explain the commodity flows that form the basis of inter-regional trade theory. The locational approach emphasises the heterogeneity of the spatial system. Production, consumption and population are not scattered evenly and continuously over the economy. Instead, the space preference of most individuals to herd together, scale economies and other agglomeration advantages lead to a concentration of most productive activities and population clusters in a limited number of centres. Thus, cities and other urban units are a relevant object of study in the economics of location and regions because in a spatial continuum people conglomerate there, and because the growth of cities can be explained, to a large extent, by systematic economic and sociological forces. On the other hand, some activities tend to disperse to exploit the uneven geographic distribution of resources, to offset congestion costs and to minimise transport costs by serving small market areas. The balance of opposing forces will determine the locational structure of the economy, and from this structure it is relatively simple to derive optimal flow patterns.

A third type of analysis concentrates on the interrelationship between regions in the national economy. Although geographical factors are implicitly recognised in this kind of analysis in the sense that regions are defined as actual bounded areas, distance variables are normally ignored. Regions are treated as integral parts of a multi-sector economy, but because transport costs and other distance elements are regarded as having only a negligible influence on inter-regional relations the regional system is considered simply as a set of spatially separated points. Partly because of the neglect of spatial factors, and partly because of key problems in regional economics such as regional growth, fluctuations and stabilisation policy and income determination theory, much of the analysis can be categorised as 'regional macroeconomics'. A valid approach to many regional questions is simply to disaggregate national income and growth models to the regional level. This is quite feasible provided each region is treated as an open economy which enables inter-regional flow analysis to be grafted on to the regional income models.

The three different categories of spatial analysis cannot be sealed off into watertight compartments with no overlap between them. For instance, the second approach encompasses the first, but in addition makes allowance for changes in location. Furthermore, with the notable exception of investigations into inter-regional factor flows, most regional economic studies have ignored the distance variable and assumed that each region is a spaceless point, but there can be no doubt that the distances between regions and intra-regional spatial variations can add a great deal of insight into regional economic problems. Although most discussion of regional economics (as opposed to locational and urban economics) in this book follows the traditional approach of abstracting from space, there are exceptions. These include Chapters 9.1, 10.6, 12 and 15.3. These parts of the book appear to suggest that future developments in this field which demand a closer integration of regional economics, distance variables and location theory will make for greater understanding of regional economic problems.

3 Scope and outline

The book is divided into three parts referring to location, the urban economy and regional economics respectively. This trichotomy is arbitrary, since there is some overlap from one part to another. A fully integrated analysis of the economics of space would have to explain the location of individual firms, the spatial distribution of population and the structure of the system of regions simultaneously. Location theory, for example, is necessary to understand the spatial structure of cities as described in Part B, Chapter 6, the relationship between industrial structure and regional growth in Chapter 13.6 and certain aspects of regional policy as outlined in Chapter 15.1.

Chapter 12 which is concerned with the movement of productive factors through space could just as easily have been placed in Part A rather than in Part C, since although inter-regional flows are its dominant theme the analysis could be generalised to explain factor movements between any two points in space without requiring subdivision of the economy into regions. Moreover, certain basic techniques for distance analysis of which gravity models are the main example have been given applications in all three parts, A, B and C.

Part A is primarily concerned with location theory. Chapter 2, however, takes the location of production and consumption points as given and explores the implications of distance for the theory of price determination under different types of market configuration. Chapters 3 and 4 analyse location theory mainly at the single firm level. Chapter 3 concentrates on the problem of how transport costs affect location with particular emphasis on the location theories of Weber and Isard, both of whom stressed the crucial importance of transportation as a locational consideration. In the first three sections of Chapter 4 the concepts of space cost and space revenue curves are developed as one means of obtaining the profit-maximising location. This is followed by a discussion of the interdependence between the location decisions of individual firms that builds upon the Hotelling–Lerner–Singer tradition. Finally, the chapter discusses some of the consequences for location theory of the possibility that a firm's objectives may relate to goals other than profit maximisation. It is believed that future advances in location theory probably lie in this direction. Chapter 5 attempts to deal with the vexed problem of a general location theory with special reference to the contributions of Lösch, Greenhut and Lefeber.

Part B consists of three chapters on the urban economy, a vital aspect of spatial analysis stemming from the unevenness of population distribution over space. Chapter 6 explores the spatial structure of cities partly via analysis of the locational choices of firms, retail establishments and residents, partly by considering the stylised models suggested to explain the overall layout of a city developing in response to market forces. Theories of urban growth discussed in Chapter 7 include central place and urban economic base models as well as the sociological and human ecological explanations of urban development. Chapter 8 deals with the problems arising from the provision of urban government services and how they should be financed. Spatial problems enter into this analysis because of:

INTRODUCTION

(1) the separation of workplaces from residences; (2) the consequences of movement of population from the central city to the suburbs; (3) benefit and cost spillovers of urban government services across community boundaries; (4) scale economies in population concentrations; and (5) the fact that individuals may choose a community in which to live according to the level, mix and cost of public services provided.

Regional economics proper is the concern of Part C. Chapter 9 examines the meaning of the regional concept and discusses the usefulness of regional accounts. The chapter also includes a simplified description of two basic forms of regional accounts, income and product accounts and an input–output framework. Chapter 10 presents the elements of inter-regional income theory. The logic of economic base models is examined, a Metzler-type theory of income determination is outlined, and the regional balance of payments adjustment mechanism is contrasted to the international. In the final section, it is suggested how the parameters of a regional income and trade model might be treated as distance functions. Chapter 11 is concerned with regional business cycles, and represents an extension of the theories of regional income determination of the previous chapter to account for regional income fluctuations. Various techniques of analysing regional business cycles are discussed, culminating in an examination of how international trade and business cycle theory can be amalgamated to explain regional fluctuations. An inter-regional multiplier-accelerator model is constructed to illustrate this integration. Chapter 12 analyses inter-regional factor movements. The implications of factor movements for general equilibrium theory are examined, thereby creating a link between this chapter and Chapters 2 and 5. A discussion of the theory of labour migration is followed by briefer analyses not only of capital and managerial mobility but also of the spatial diffusion of innovation and technical change. Theories of regional growth are considered in Chapter 13. The first half of the chapter shows how aggregate growth models of the Harrod–Domar and neoclassical type can be adapted to a regional context. This is followed by theories specifically used to explain regional growth – the export base, sector and the industrial structure approaches. Finally, the question of whether regional *per capita* income levels will converge or diverge is explored at the theoretical level.

The final two chapters relate to regional policy. Chapter 14 outlines a framework for policy and shows how the policymaker may have to compromise between efficiency and equity goals and to balance the interests of the individual region with those of the nation. The principles of regional stabilisation policy are also discussed. Chapter 15 looks at the policy problem mainly from the point of view of a single region by examining the relative advantages and drawbacks of the broad lines of action which might be followed to improve the situation in a depressed region. The theoretical justification for wage subsidies as a regional policy measure is also outlined, and finally, an attempt is made to explain the meaning of the nebulous concept of the growth point and its implications for regional development policy.

Part A
Location

Chapter 2

Spatial price theory

1 Spatial equilibrium in geographically separated markets

The price of a homogeneous good will not necessarily be uniform over space. If markets are spatially separated, and if local demand and supply curves intersect at a higher price in one market than in others, then this higher price can persist so long as it does not pay producers located in other markets to tranship supplies into the high-price market nor pay consumers in the latter to obtain their requirements from elsewhere. Transport costs and/or restrictions on trade can insulate spatially separated markets from each other. If, however, price levels in two markets differ by more than unit transport costs and if trade is completely free commodities will flow from the low price to the high price market until spatial equilibrium is restored. The circumstances, the constraints on flows of the good and the conditions of equilibrium can be described in terms of a simple model.

Consider a number of regions where a homogeneous good is produced and consumed in each. Assume that each region constitutes a single competitive market, and is distinct (this is most easily met by assuming that no region is spatially differentiated, but rather that all regions are in effect points separated by distance). Assume that in each region without trade a different price level obtains in equilibrium, i.e. where regional demand equals regional supply. Will this be the ultimate spatial equilibrium? Not necessarily. The original intra-regional prices will persist only under certain special circumstances: first, if there are legal or other restrictions on trade so that no inter-regional trade is possible; or, secondly, if the margin between the price levels in every possible pair of regions is less than the unit transport cost between the two respective regions so that it does not pay to transfer goods from one of the regions to the other. At the other extreme, if there are no restrictions on trade and transport costs are zero, commodities will flow from low price to high price regions until prices are equalised everywhere in the system.

With positive transport costs and significant price differentials between regions, the final spatial equilibrium will be characterised by a narrowing of inter-regional price differentials but not complete equality as in the zero transport costs case. What will be the conditions of spatial equilibrium?

The two-region case
The problem may first be examined for the simple two-region case. Consider two regions, Regions 1 and 2, which are separated by distance. Let T_{12} represent transport costs per unit of goods shipped from Region 1 to Region 2, and T_{21} represent unit transport costs from Region 2 to Region 1. Transport costs are not necessarily the same in both directions as they do not have to be linear functions of geographical distance. Transport routes are not necessarily reversible, and transport costs may include such items as insurance, interest and capital tied up in transit and handling charges in addition to freight costs. However, let us make the simplifying assumption that unit transport costs are independent of the volume of goods shipped, thereby ruling out the possibility of reduced freight rates for bulk deliveries. Let A_1 and A_2 represent the price levels in each region which equate local consumption with production (i.e. without inter-regional trade), and again assume that there are no restrictions on trade between the two markets. The problem is: given T_{12}, T_{21}, A_1 and A_2 what will be the final spatial equilibrium, where P_1 and P_2 represent the post-trade equilibrium prices?

If $A_2 - A_1 > T_{12}$ goods will flow from Region 1 to Region 2, but if $A_2 > A_1$ yet $A_2 - A_1 < T_{12}$ there will be no trade. Conversely, if $A_1 > A_2$ and $A_1 - A_2 > T_{21}$ supplies will flow from Region 2 to Region 1, whereas if $A_1 - A_2 < T_{21}$ again there will be no trade. Thus, if intraregional prices differ by less than unit transport costs there will be no transfer of supplies from one region to the other, and $A_1 = P_1$ while $A_2 = P_2$. But if the pre-trade price margin is wider than unit transport costs, it will pay producers in the low price region to tranship to the high price market for so long as the price differential between the two markets more than covers transport charges. In spatial equilibrium the price levels in the two regions will differ by the unit transport cost in the direction of the trade flow, for only in this situation will it no longer pay producers to

SPATIAL PRICE THEORY

shift goods from one region to another. Both the spatial equilibrium price levels, P_1 and P_2, and the spatial flow of goods ($E_{12} = -E_{21}$ where E represents exports and $-E$ represents imports) are mutually determined by the specified demand and supply schedules in both markets and by the transport costs.

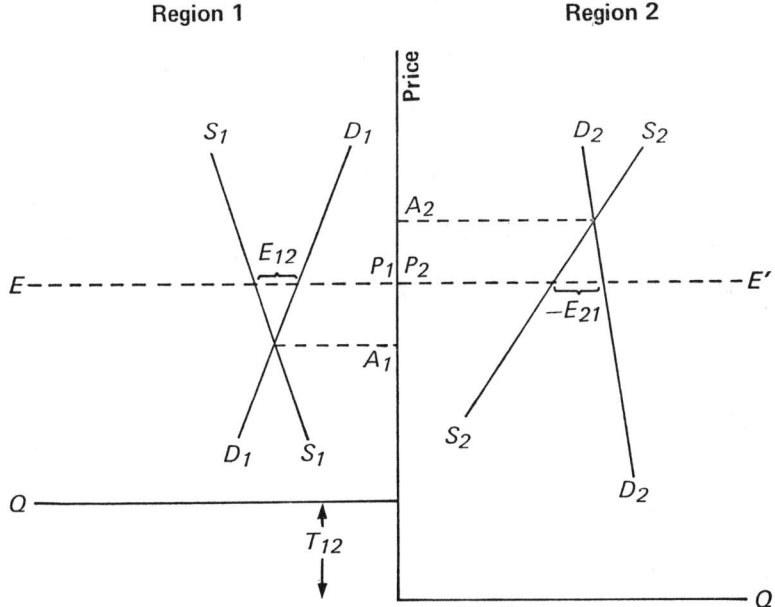

Figure 2.1

This is shown in figure 2.1, where the supply and demand diagrams for each region are placed back to back.[1] D_1D_1 and S_1S_1 represent the local demand and supply curves for Region 1 which yield the local equilibrium price A_1; likewise, the intersection of D_2D_2 and S_2S_2 yields the local price A_2. The left-side horizontal axis for the lower price region, Region 1, is raised above the right-side horizontal axis of the diagram for Region 2 by unit transport costs T_{12} so that we can determine whether supplies will flow from Region 1 to Region 2 before a spatial equilibrium is attained. It can be seen that because A_2 exceeds A_1 by more than T_{12}, Region 1 exports to Region 2. Because net supply is consequently reduced in Region 1 but increased

[1] See Samuelson, P.A. (1957) Intertemporal Price Equilibrium: A Prologue to the Theory of Speculation. *Weltwirtschaftliches Archiv*, Vol **79**

in Region 2, then $P_1 > A_1$ while $P_2 < A_2$. Equilibrium is attained where $E_{12} = -E_{21}$ and where $P_2 = P_1 + T_{12}$.

Multiple region situations

There are two basic conditions for general spatial equilibrium with a single good, and these conditions are sufficient to ensure equilibrium in an *n*-region model as much as in the two-region case:

(i) that $\Sigma E = 0$, where imports are regarded as negative exports;
(ii) that the price in each importing region equals the price in each region that exports to it plus the unit transport cost between them.

A The three-region case

The three-region case is also easy to solve if we make the simplifying assumption that exports (or imports) are a linear function of the difference between the final spatial equilibrium price and the original intra-regional price in any region.

Thus
$$E_1 = b_1 (P_1 - A_1)$$
$$E_2 = b_2 (P_2 - A_2)$$
$$E_3 = b_3 (P_3 - A_3)$$

where b_1, b_2, b_3 are constants for regions 1, 2 and 3.

We assume that the prices which equate local consumption and local production (A_1, A_2, A_3) and transport costs ($T_{12}, T_{13}, T_{21}, T_{23}, T_{31}, T_{32}$) are known. The problem is to obtain the final prices in spatial equilibrium (P_1, P_2, P_3) and the magnitude and direction of the trade flows.

The difficulty is that knowledge of A and T values alone does not directly yield sufficient information to show which regions will export, import or not trade at all. Thus, the first step in determining the equilibrium solution is to ascertain the trading roles of the individual regions, particularly the intermediate region with the middle A value.

Suppose $A_1 < A_2 < A_3$; then it follows that Region 1 will either export or not trade at all and Region 3, if it trades at all, will import. If there is some inter-regional trade then we know that $P_1 > A_1$, that $P_3 < A_3$, and that $P_3 = P_1 + T_{13}$. Region 2 has an A_2 value which is greater than A_1 and less than A_3, but will it be a net importer or an exporter? One answer is to consider Regions 1 and 3 together and to ascertain the consequent values of P_1 and P_3. Then when $E_1 + E_3 = 0$ and $P_3 = P_1 + T_{13}$, Region 2 will import if $A_2 > (P_1 + T_{12})$

while it will export if $P_3 > (A_2 + T_{23})$. But if neither condition is satisfied then Region 2 will not trade (i.e. $P_2 = A_2$, and $E_2 = 0$).

Once the role of Region 2 has been discovered, the solution is straightforward, for we can restate the trading functions of Regions 2 and 3 in terms of P_1. If Region 2 imports, then in equilibrium we may write $(P_1 + T_{12})$ for P_2 and $(P_1 + T_{13})$ for P_3. Also in equilibrium we may write:

$$E_1 = -(E_2 + E_3)$$

Substituting the trading functions in this equation, and expressing P_2 and P_3 in terms of P_1, we obtain:

$$b_1(P_1 - A_1) = -[b_2(P_1 + T_{12} - A_2) + b_3(P_1 + T_{13} - A_3)]$$

and this gives:

$$P_1 = \frac{b_1 A_1 + b_2(A_2 - T_{12}) + b_3(A_3 - T_{13})}{b_1 + b_2 + b_3}$$

Once P_1 is estimated, obtaining P_2, P_3, E_1, E_2 and E_3 presents no difficulty.

Conversely, if Region 2 had been an exporter, then in equilibrium $E_1 + E_2 = -E_3$ and $P_3 = P_2 + T_{23} = P_1 + T_{13}$.

In this case, the value of P_3 is found by solving the equation:

$$P_3 = \frac{b_3 A_3 + b_1(T_{13} + A_1) + b_2(T_{23} + A_2)}{b_1 + b_2 + b_3}$$

Again, the values of the other variables are then obtained quite easily.

B The *n*-region case

In the three-region example the volume of trade between each pair of regions was easy to calculate; for example, if E_2 and E_3 were both negative then $E_{12} = -E_2$ and $E_{13} = -E_3$. In a multiple region system, however, each region may export to or import from *several* other regions. Consequently, estimates of the total net trade for each region do not automatically give us the volume of trade between each *pair* of regions, and this complicates the computing procedure.

Several methods have been suggested to solve the spatial price equilibrium model for multiple markets. Enke's solution was to set up an electric circuit simulating the spatial system, representing all money values (i.e. final equilibrium prices and transport costs) by voltages and spatial flows by amperages. If the circuit is correctly constructed and the current is switched on, the system will immediately move into stable equilibrium and the relevant voltmeter and ammeter readings can be taken.[2] Samuelson showed that the model could be cast as a linear programming problem, where the objective was to maximise 'net social pay-off' (i.e. the sum of the algebraic areas under the excess supply curves in each market minus total transport costs).[3] A less artificial approach is to solve this problem via its 'dual'. For the system to maximise gains from inter-regional trade there will be an optimal flow of goods between each pair of regions (except autarchic regions) corresponding to the minimisation of transport costs.[4] In similar fashion, it has been shown more recently that the rent minimisation principle can be used to determine the conditions of spatial price equilibrium.[5] Finally, another study has shown how the problem can be solved by using quadratic programming techniques.[6]

The details of these procedures need not concern us for the general conclusions derived from the two- and three-region cases are unaltered. The flow of goods from low to high price markets will narrow inter-regional price differentials and improve the spatial allocation of commodities. The conditions of spatial equilibrium remain the same: that total exports equal total imports, and that the price in each region equals the price in all other regions plus or minus the intervening unit transport cost.

2 Introducing patterns of spatial dispersion

The spatial pattern discussed above seems, at first sight, a special

[2] Enke, S. (1951) Equilibrium among Spatially Separated Markets: Solution by Electric Analogue. *Econometrica*, **19** 40–7

[3] Samuelson, P.A. (1952) Spatial Price Equilibrium and Linear Programming. *American Economic Review*, **42** 283–303

[4] This is the well-known Hitchcock–Koopmans problem; see Hitchcock, F.L. (1941) The Distribution of a Product from Several Sources to Numerous Localities. *Journal of Mathematics and Physics*, **20** and Koopmans, T.C. (1949) Optimum Utilization of the Transportation System. *Econometrica*, Supplement, **17**

[5] Smith, V.L. (1963) Minimisation of Economic Rent in Spatial Price Equilibrium. *Review of Economic Studies*, **30** 24–31

[6] Takayama, T. and Judge, G.C. (1964) Equilibrium among Spatially Separated Markets. *Econometrica*, **32**

and highly abstract case. It assumes that buyers and producers are concentrated at a number of points (markets) which are separated from each other by what may be regarded as an economic vacuum, i.e. by empty space. It is true, as the alternatives outlined below suggest, that this case is only one of many quite different theoretical possibilities, but it would be wrong to accept that it is completely divorced from reality. If the homogeneous goods in question are industrial products, and if because of agglomeration economies these products are made at a limited number of industrial centres which attract population, then the spatially separated market model is useful for describing the influences on price levels over space in the individual industry. But other spatial patterns may be more relevant to an explanation of spatial price relationships for agricultural products, for material-oriented industrial goods and for manufactures produced at widely scattered locations.

In the following analysis, we retain the assumption of homogeneous commodities. This means that spatial differentiation is the only form of product differentiation, though identical goods which are separated in space are already imperfect substitutes for each other. We also assume that producers adopt f.o.b. factory pricing; this assumption will be relaxed towards the end of the chapter. We can identify and describe a number of quite different spatial patterns. The first case, in effect a spaceless situation, is where all producers and consumers are located at the same point. If there are large numbers of both producers and consumers, we obtain pure competition. There are no transport costs, there is only one price, and demand and supply will be infinitely elastic. The spatial problem does not exist. The simplest way of introducing space into this situation is to hypothesise two or more of these points, at each of which there are both buyers and sellers, separated by space. The models that result have been analysed at length above. Spatial equilibrium depends in such models on balanced trade flows and on price levels in spatially separated markets differing only by unit transport costs between them. Although these models may bear a reasonable approximation to reality especially in an industrialised economy with a heavily urbanised population and little agricultural activity, from a theoretical point of view the spatial separation of point markets is rather a special case. It does not admit spatial dispersion of either producers or consumers.

Spatial dispersion leads to departures from pure competition. A

REGIONAL ECONOMICS

critical assumption of pure competition is that demand is very great relative to the level of output that corresponds to the minimum point on the long-run average cost curve of the individual firm. But in the space economy the demand facing an individual firm is, more or less rapidly, whittled away by distance. The existence of transport costs shifts demand curves downwards, with the result that even if we assume that all consumers have identical tastes and incomes, 'the agglomeration of what otherwise would be identical demand curves becomes an aggregation of different demands when consumers are scattered over an area'.[7] The level of transport costs affects, therefore, not only the geographical area served by a firm (the boundary being determined by either high transport costs cutting demand to zero or by the competition of distant sellers) but also the volume of sales within the market area.

3 Single producer surrounded by many buyers: the spatial monopolist

A very simple model showing the effect of transport costs and the distance factor on demand is the spatial monopoly case. Here we assume that there is a single producer surrounded by many buyers. In the standard case of the discriminating monopolist it will pay him to discriminate against buyers with less elastic demands provided various buyers have different demand elasticities. The question is: are spatial factors conducive to spatial price discrimination?

a. *All buyers with identical demand curves of constant and equal elasticity*

This is the limiting case where transport costs are assumed not to affect demand. We assume: the monopolist charges a single price to all buyers at a given location, and discriminates only between different locations; T = transport costs per unit from seller's site to location of any buyer A; at his location A's demand is such that he will pay a price P for quantity Q of the product; elasticity of demand, E, is the same at every point on the demand curve of each buyer. The price paid by a buyer is reduced before the monopolist gets it by the freight charge, and the marginal revenue from sales to A will be:

$$MR = \frac{d(PQ)}{dQ} - T = \frac{P \cdot dQ + Q \cdot dP}{dQ} - T = P + \frac{Q \cdot dP}{dQ} - T \quad (1)$$

[7] Greenhut, M.L. (1963) *Microeconomics and the Space Economy.* 69

Since elasticity of Demand $E = -(P.dQ)/(Q.dP)$, we may rewrite (1) as

$$P - \frac{P}{E} - T = P\frac{(E-1)}{E} - T \qquad (2)$$

The maximising monopolist will equate marginal revenue and marginal cost from sales to all buyers. This means that (if we represent marginal cost by C) the price paid by any given buyer A can be obtained from the fact that

$$P\frac{(E-1)}{E} - T = C$$

$$\therefore \qquad P = \frac{E(C+T)}{E-1} \qquad (3)$$

The price charged by the seller at his own location (i.e. the f.o.b. factory price) is

$$P - T = \frac{E(C+T)}{E-1} - T = \frac{EC+T}{E-1} \qquad (4)$$

and the amount by which this f.o.b. price exceeds marginal cost is given by:

$$P - T - C = \frac{EC+T}{E-1} - C = \frac{C+T}{E-1} \qquad (5)$$

It is obvious from this that the f.o.b. prices charged by the monopolist at the factory (i.e. $P-T$) result in discrimination against more distant buyers. This is because $P - T = (EC+T)/(E-1)$, an expression which increases as T increases, that is with greater distances. However, buyers at the factory door (where $T=0$) pay a price exceeding marginal cost by an amount equal to $C/(E-1)$. However, if elasticity of demand (E) is very large, conditions approach Chamberlinian pure competition and the scope for spatial price discrimination is severely reduced, as is the divergence between price and marginal cost.[8]

This highly simplified model suggests that the profit maximising monopolist in a spatial market discriminates against more distant buyers. Observation of real world pricing practices, however, more

---

[8] Hoover, E.M. (1936–7) Spatial Price Discrimination. *Review of Economic Studies*, **4** 182–191; Singer, H.W. (1937–8) A Note on Spatial Price Discrimination. *Review of Economic Studies*, **5** 75–7

REGIONAL ECONOMICS

frequently suggests the opposite – discrimination against nearer buyers. How is this contradiction to be explained? The answer is twofold: distance and transport costs affect demand making the assumption of constant equal elasticity for all buyers heroic; and pure spatial monopoly is rare, since in most real world situations there are rival sellers.

b. *Distant buyers' demand curves lower but more elastic*
To illustrate this proposition and its effect on spatial price discrimination let us assume that demand curves are linear and that

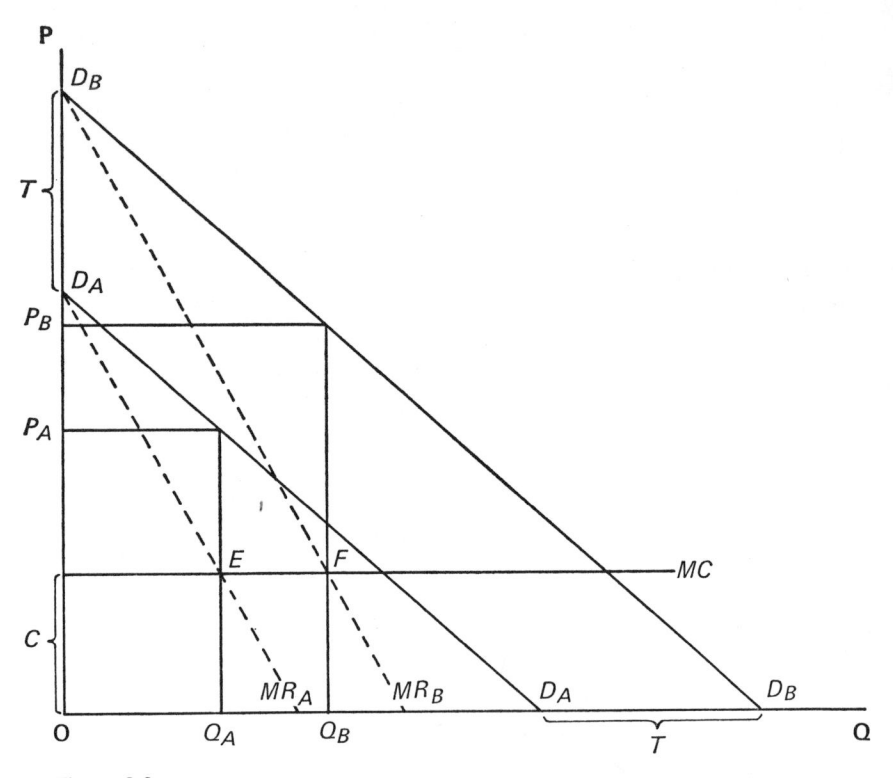

Figure 2.2

they join both axes. We also assume that buyers would have identical demands except for the effect of transport costs. Transport costs can be shown as a deduction from the demand curve, and therefore shift it downwards by an amount equal to these costs (in figure 2.2, D_B

22

becomes D_A, both curves having the same slope, when unit transport costs $=T$, assumed constant regardless of the quantity demanded). The demand curves of distant buyers, from the producer's point of view, are identical to the curves of the nearby buyer apart from this shifting down effect due to transport costs. Given demand curves like D_B and D_A, where B is the consumer at the factory door and A is a buyer at a distance, then within any specified range the demand curve D_A is more elastic. A given change in price will result in the same *absolute* change in the quantity demanded by both A and B (because the slopes of D_A and D_B are equal), but the proportionate change in demand, and hence elasticity, is less for B than for A because B's total demand is greater at any given price level. In this case, then, the remote buyers have more elastic demands than those nearby. It can be shown that if this is so, in order to maximise profits the monopolist will discriminate against the nearby buyers (who have relatively inelastic demands).

In figure 2.2, apart from the assumption that the demand curves of buyers A and B are straight lines of equal slope that differ only because the curve of buyer A is shifted downwards by unit transport costs T, we assume that the monopolist's marginal costs are constant (at level C) at all levels of output. The monopolist will equate marginal revenue and marginal cost for both buyers (at E and F), and f.o.b. prices charged to the two buyers are P_A and P_B. The nearer buyer is discriminated against to an extent $(P_B - P_A)$. This holds irrespective of the slope of the demand curves so long as they are straight lines of equal slope. Just as in non-spatial models, it pays the monopolist to discriminate against the consumers with the less elastic demands.

c. *Limitations on spatial monopoly*

Situations where a sole producer has monopoly control over his entire market area are rare, and this fact also explains why discrimination against nearby consumers is more common in practice. The seller has most control over his nearby purchasers; even in an industry containing many producers distance from alternative suppliers will give a producer a protected market around his plant unless firms in the industry are clustered together at the same location. Thus, there is scope for sellers to discriminate against nearby buyers. Discrimination against distant buyers is, however, normally severely constrained. Firstly, there is the possibility of resale. If a seller discriminated against distant buyers, then purchasers nearby could buy on behalf of those at a greater distance and resell the goods to them. Secondly, in many cases rival selling locations will limit the exercise of monopoly power. Towards the periphery of the seller's market area there will be a market area zone within which sales are shared between this particular seller and his rivals and where the scope for exploitation of monopolistic power is at a minimum. In this zone the nearest seller will charge a delivered price that is equal to marginal cost at the next nearest production site plus the transport costs from that site. If he charged more all sales in the boundary zone would be lost; if he charged less he would not be exploiting the maximum monopolistic advantage. The nature of market area boundaries is considered in more detail in the next section.

Thirdly, if the market being analysed is oligopolistic,[9] competition between sellers at different locations may be limited by price agreements. If the number of firms in the market was sufficiently small, the optimal policy for the producers would be to allow each firm to exploit its own market area monopolistically. The administrative difficulties involved in such a scheme probably result in a preference for price agreements, which are easier to operate, rather than market area agreements. The widespread frequency of agreements setting a uniform delivered price for the whole market and certain forms of basing-point price agreements involving freight absorption is another reason why actual discrimination tends to be against nearby buyers.[10]

4 Two sellers at different locations surrounded by many buyers: the law of market areas

The next step is to allow for more than one seller in the spatial market. The simplest case is to consider two geographically separated selling markets, X and Y. The Samuelson–Enke analysis outlined

[9] Greenhut argues that oligopoly is the typical spatial market form. Indivisibilities in the size of firms and transport costs severely limit the number of firms operating in any market area. Also, there is a general tendency in spatial markets to maintain a fixed price, as is frequently the result in normal oligopolistic conditions. In a spatial market, a price cut by a firm at the market centre invites reaction from other rivals whose market areas have been diminished; conversely, an increase in price could result in heavy losses in both nearby and distant markets (Greenhut, *op. cit.*, 209, 289)

[10] Of course, basing-point price systems can be devised with discriminatory zones that penalise the most distant regions

above showed that if goods could be shipped from one market to the other the prices in the two markets could not differ by more than transport costs between them. However, in contrast with the Samuelson–Enke case, we now assume that the space between X and Y and, indeed, surrounding X and Y is inhabited by many buyers, rather than the two markets being treated as economic enclaves in a vacuum. Furthermore, we assume that the location of the two markets X and Y is fixed; this allows us to ignore for the time being locational moves as envisaged in the location theories of Hotelling, Chamberlin, Lerner and Singer, and others.[11] We also ignore the price strategies and responses characteristic of many duopoly and oligopoly situations, and rule out price discrimination by assuming that the two f.o.b. prices are the same for all buyers at any one time.

The questions now arise as to the shape and size of the market area of each seller, and to how sales in the territory between the two markets are divided between the sellers concerned. This requires determining the boundary separating the market areas of the two sellers, a boundary which is unlikely to be a straight line except under the most restrictive assumptions. The delimitation of this boundary requires us to derive the economic law of market areas.[12]

We assume: the two fixed markets, X and Y, surrounded by external consumption points (Z_1, Z_2, Z_3 ... Z_n); a homogeneous good; freight charges equal to linear distance multiplied by the freight rate per unit distance between the market and any Z. Let the market price at X and Y be P_X and P_Y, the freight rate per unit between X and Z be T_{xz} and between Y and Z be T_{yz}, and let the respective distances be d_{xz} and d_{yz}. If the consumer at Z buys from X he pays $(P_x + T_{xz}d_{xz})$ per unit; if he buys at Y he pays $(P_y + T_{yz}d_{yz})$. When these two amounts are equal, the consumer is indifferent as to the market from which he purchases. The boundary line between the territories' tributary to markets X and Y will consequently be determined by the equation:

$$P_x + T_{xz}d_{xz} = P_y + T_{yz}d_{yz} \tag{1}$$

[11] These problems are treated in Chapter 4.4 below
[12] The analysis stems from Fetter, F.A. (1923–4) The Economic Law of Market Areas. *Quarterly Journal of Economics*, **38** 520–9. However, Fetter only outlined a special case. The more general statement was given by Hyson, C.D. and Hyson, W.P. (1949–50) The Economic Law of Market Areas. *ibid.*, **64** 319–27

Rearranging, we get

$$d_{xz} - \frac{T_{yz}}{T_{xz}} \cdot d_{yz} = \frac{P_y - P_x}{T_{xz}} \qquad (2)$$

Since T_{yz}/T_{xz} is always positive, while $(P_y - P_x)/T_{xz}$ may be positive or negative, the equation may be expressed in the form:

$$d_{xz} - t \cdot d_{yz} = \pm p \qquad (3)$$

where $\qquad t = T_{yz}/T_{xz} \quad$ and $\quad p = (P_y - P_x)/T_{xz}$

This equation describes a family of indifference curves, which we call hypercircles. The peculiar mathematical feature of this family is that any one curve represents the locus of all points the ratio of whose distances from two fixed circles is a constant (such curves are sometimes called Descartes' ovals). Equations (2) and (3) show us that the size of the tributary market depends not only on the relative prices at the two markets, but also on the ratio of freight rates (t or T_{yz}/T_{xz}) and on the ratio of the difference in prices to the freight rate (p or $(P_y - P_x)/T_{xz}$).

From this analysis we can state the **general law of market areas** as follows. The boundary between areas tributary to two geographically competing markets for homogeneous goods is a **hypercircle.** At each point on this curve the difference between freight costs from the two markets exactly equals the difference between market prices, whereas on either side of this line freight differences and price differences are unequal. The ratio of the difference in prices to the freight rate and the ratio of the freight rates from the two markets determine the location of the boundary line. The higher the relative price and the lower the relative freight rate, the larger is the tributary area.

The shape of the curve that marks the market area boundary, and the size of the tributary area attached to each market depends on economic circumstances. Three simple cases are illustrated in figure 2.3. Figure 2.3a shows the special case when both freight rates and market prices are equal; the curve degenerates into a straight line which is the perpendicular bisector of the line joining X and Y. In figure 2.3b freight rates from both markets are the same while selling prices are unequal; the curve becomes one branch of a hyperbola. In figure 2.3c the freight rates are unequal but the market prices are identical in both markets; the curve then becomes a circle. The right hand diagrams in figure 2.3, which replace an areal

(a) $P_x = P_y$; $T_{xz} = T_{yz}$

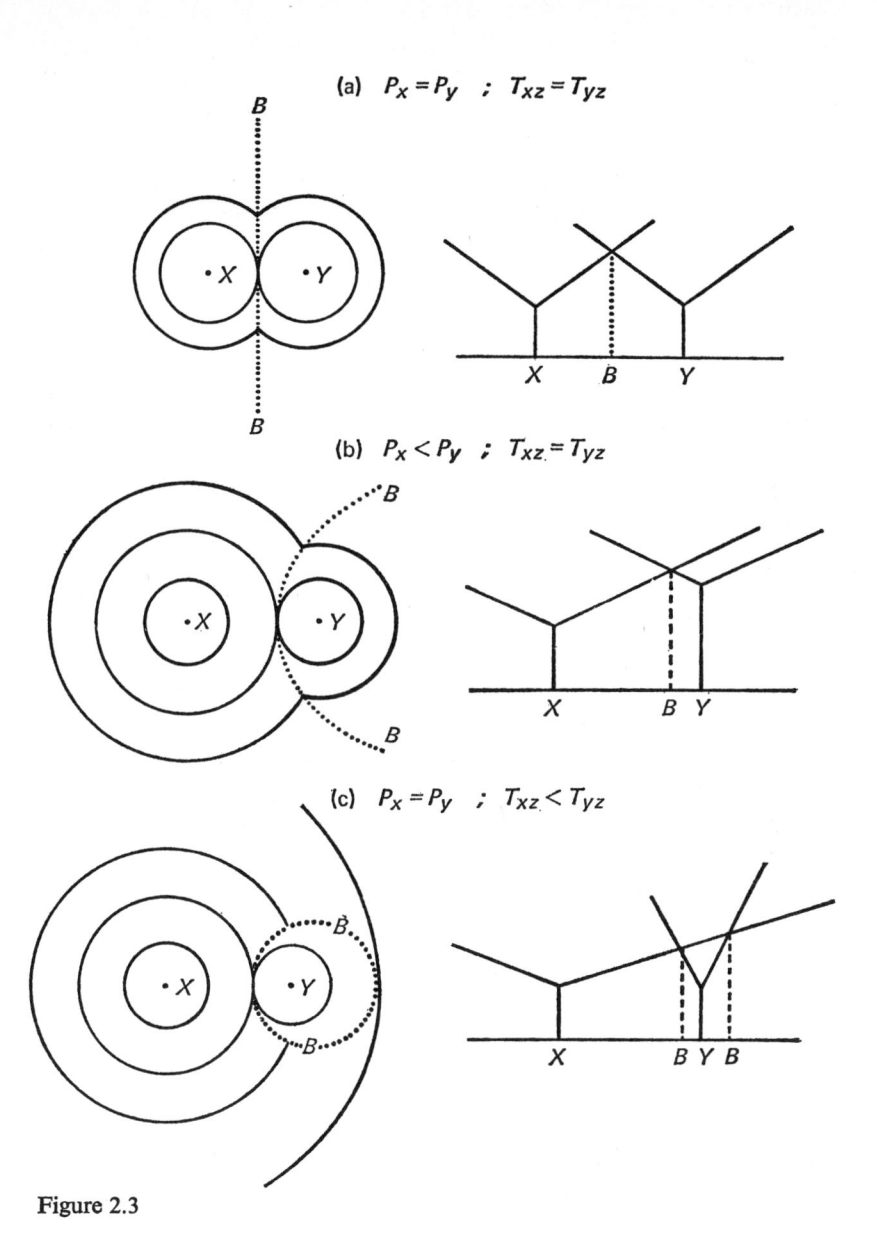

(b) $P_x < P_y$; $T_{xz} = T_{yz}$

(c) $P_x = P_y$; $T_{xz} < T_{yz}$

Figure 2.3

scattering of buyers by dispersion along a line, indicate the market price and freight rate differentials more clearly. Alternatively, these diagrams could be regarded as lateral cross-sections of the market areas illustrated in the left-hand maps. These cross-section diagrams are a less unwieldy device for exploring spatial price analysis, but they lack the mathematical precision of the indifference maps derived from equation (2). They cannot, for example, demonstrate how the market area of one of the sellers increases as the ratios T_{yz}/T_{xz} and $(P_y - P_x)/T_{xz}$ change in value.

5 Many sellers concentrated, buyers dispersed

The situation where a large number of sellers is concentrated in a small geographical space (in the limiting case, at a point) surrounded by a haphazard (or even) scatter of consumers does not lead to results other than those produced by conventional non-spatial theory. Given homogeneous goods and free entry, the firms at the centre will compete with each other, and competition means that the average revenue of all producers is the same.[13] The only difference from a spaceless economy assumption is that, provided we assume that prices are quoted f.o.b. at the sellers' location, individual demand curves are reduced by an amount equal to transport costs. The consequences for the f.o.b. price of this fact is obvious from figure 2.2: because of freight costs the profit maximising f.o.b. factory price will be lower than the price that would prevail in a spaceless economy.[14] But if freight rates do not vary with distance from the sellers' door, such as we find with postal rates or zonal freight rates, then consumers in the same zone may be regarded as, in effect, at the same location. However, in dynamic terms, it is important to note that the market is imperfect with dispersal of consumers over space. For instance, the expansion of a firm's output may involve a change in price. An increase in output may require the sales radius to be extended, and this extension results in a different price as the elasticity of demand alters. Although under competition all sellers obtain the same average revenue from sales to any one buyer, the profit to a seller from sales to one buyer differs from the profit obtained on sales to another buyer at a different location. Moreover,

[13] Enke, S. (1941–2) Space and Value. *Quarterly Journal of Economics*, **56** 627–37
[14] Greenhut, *op. cit.*, 114–15

there is a finite limit on sales at a particular price for any one seller when his sales radius is extended.

6 Buyers concentrated, sellers dispersed

The opposite set of circumstances to that in the previous example is where producers are scattered over a wide area while buyers are concentrated at a central point. This central point can be conceived as a city, if we make the simplifying assumption that there are no intra-city locational differences among buyers. This is the market type associated with J.H.Von Thünen. All buyers pay a given price, but net unit revenue varies from one producer to another according to his distance from the consumption centre. However, net unit revenues are the same for any one seller on sales to any buyer. With large numbers of sellers and a homogeneous product, a single price prevails in the market and the seller's average revenue curve is horizontal. It does not matter whether free delivery or f.o.b. pricing practices are followed, since price is unaffected whether transport costs are subtracted from demand curves or added on to cost curves. But the level at which demand is perfectly elastic may differ from seller to seller, according to their distance from the market.

If goods are sold at delivered prices, an increase in transport costs will shift the aggregate supply curve to the left, thereby raising the market price. On the other hand, a fall in transport costs reduces price and expands sales. The benefits of increased sales will be enjoyed by more distant sellers, perhaps beyond the former boundary of the supply area. Sellers near the consumption centre, with negligible transport costs, will be the main sufferers. A reduction in transport costs that enables more producers to serve a market tends, therefore, to intensify competition.

Figure 2.4 explains these points diagrammatically. We assume: continuous location of sellers along a line *LL*, all consumers concentrated at *M*, constant production costs, constant freight rates per unit of distance, *MZ* is the delivered price to buyers. The f.o.b. price for each seller is shown by perpendiculars from the sides of the triangle *XYZ*; thus, for a seller at a distance *NM* from the consumption centre the f.o.b. price is *PN*. The sellers at *X* and *Y* can barely serve the market; *X* and *Y* represent the outer limits of the supply area. However, if transport costs are reduced the arms *XZ* and *YZ* slope more gradually, and the outer limits of the supply area now become X_1 and Y_1. The delivered price to *M* is also lowered, from

REGIONAL ECONOMICS

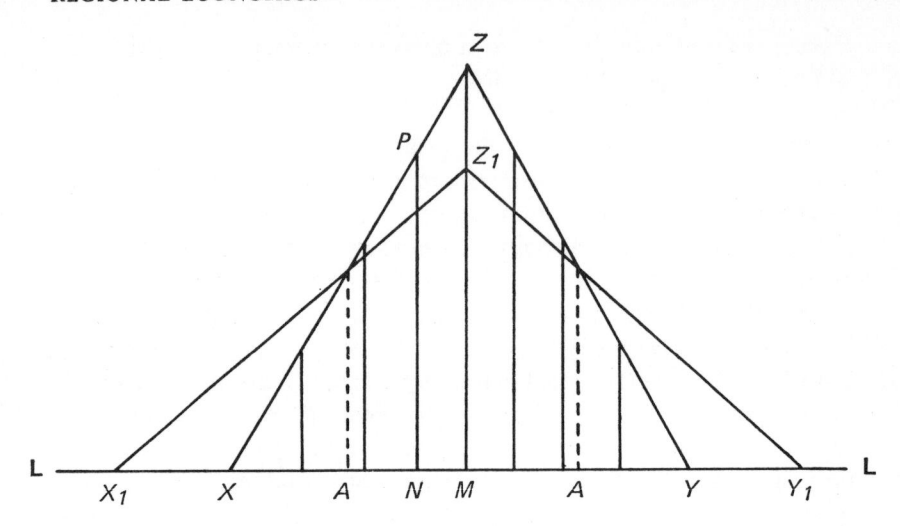

Figure 2.4

MZ to MZ_1. Nearby sellers suffer, i.e. those within AA. Sellers outside AA, on the other hand, benefit from the fall in transport costs.

7 Buyers and sellers dispersed with a central market

We may envisage a situation where buyers and sellers are scattered indiscriminately over an area, but where all exchanged units of the good pass through a central market, M. In this model, the price elasticity of demand and supply are infinite at M no matter where the buyers and sellers are located and despite the fact that the net revenue received and the price paid may vary for all concerned in trading.

However, if all trade passes through a central mart unnecessary cross-hauling will develop. Producers will transport goods to the market only for them to be transported back to consumers in the vicinity of the producer's establishment. The result is that, with active price competition between buyers and sellers, it is unlikely that all goods will pass through the market. As figure 2.5 shows there will be two cone-like price lines centring on the market M. With each unit of distance from M where the equilibrium price is attained, net unit revenue to sellers and price paid by buyers diverge by double the unit transport cost multiplied by distance from M. At V for instance, sellers receive a sum $P_V V$ net of transport charges,

30

SPATIAL PRICE THEORY

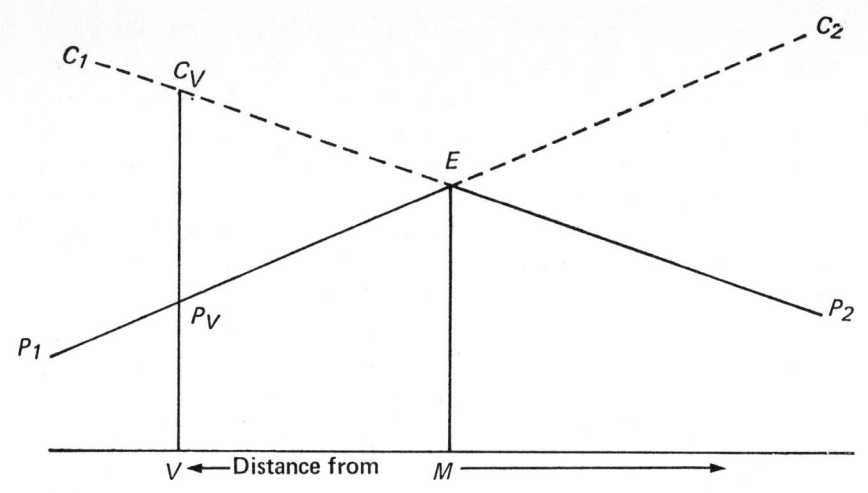

Figure 2.5

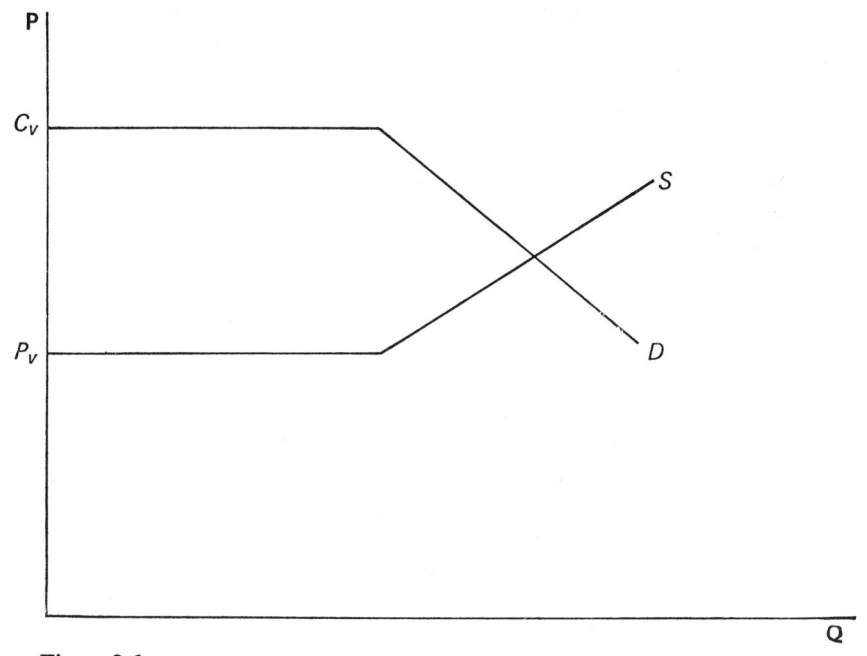

Figure 2.6

while buyers at V pay a unit price of $C_V V$. If buyers and sellers at V engaged in trade outside the market, price could range between $P_V V$ and $C_V V$. There is a strong incentive for such buyers and sellers, especially if located at a great distance from the market, to short circuit the market and engage in trade locally. Neighbouring buyers and sellers will bargain with each other until prices are established that represent a sharing between them of transport charges which would have to be paid if goods had been shipped to and from the market. The equilibrium price at the market ME does not determine the exact price over the area as a whole, it merely sets limits for it. Price at any point will depend on the relative force of supply and demand there, and a different price level may be established at every point. The demand-supply diagram of figure 2.6 illustrates the fact that the supply and demand schedules of each seller and buyer are horizontal at the price limits; though between these limits the schedules will be inclined. In local markets, the elasticity of supply and demand is infinite at prices $C_V V$ and $P_V V$ because below the price $P_V V$ sellers at V would prefer to send their goods to the market M, while at a price above $C_V V$ the buyers at V would prefer to buy at M and pay the return transport costs.

Although the monetary gains from 'short-circuiting' may be large, there are factors which could make for more goods being exchanged through the central market M. For example, there may be ignorance of demand conditions except at the central market. The market may offer special marketing facilities, such as credit or packing services, that are unobtainable elsewhere. Finally, a scarcity of hinterland transport routes may induce goods to flow through M.

8 Buyers and sellers dispersed: monopolistic competition and spatial oligopoly

First, we may consider the situation when buyers and sellers are evenly dispersed. Let us suppose that sellers are sparsely distributed. Then, in the absence of nearby competition, firms will establish the profit-maximising price and sell to everyone who intend to buy at this price. The resulting sales area would be circular, the most profitable market area. But with free entry, firms will continue to enter the industry as long as there exists some pattern of market areas that will allow a greater density of sellers with all firms making at least zero profits. Lösch argued that the effect of free entry would be to compress the ideal circular market areas into hexagons, with market areas covering all space like a net.[15] But since the circle is the most profitable market area, it must be possible for an industry to be sufficiently unprofitable for the circular market area to be the only one in which sellers can break even.[16] If this happens, there may be gaps between market areas in which buyers are not served by any seller. With such gaps sellers' prices are unrelated to each other, and any one firm is independent of its geographical counterpart in price policy. Despite product homogeneity, sellers are not in close competition with each other because of space and transport costs; instead, they compete more closely with the prices of differentiated goods that are very imperfect substitutes for their own, but which are produced at adjacent locations. This model resembles monopolistic competition. Free entry results in tangency between the negatively sloped average revenue and the average cost curve. Since the f.o.b. price equals average cost, the f.o.b. price exceeds marginal cost and the delivered price exceeds marginal cost plus transport costs. In long-run equilibrium, the price level in each market area is determined by the average costs of production of the firm operating in that area.

However, it can be argued that monopolistic competition is not the most prevalent spatial market form. With locational inertia due to high mobility costs, a long-run equilibrium may be established with a smaller number of sellers and excess profits compared with the position outlined above. This is represented by a situation where there is not enough room between established locations of sellers for a new seller to enter the market at a profit, even if more sellers could have been accommodated without incurring losses had different locations been selected in the first place. In other words, the original pattern of selling locations may not have been even dispersion. In more general terms, homogeneous distribution of buyers and sellers is a special case, and even if it existed originally it is unlikely to persist. Instead, agglomerating advantages will develop, resulting in concentration of sellers.

The growth of population centres will similarly result in clusters of buyers. Such concentration leads to irregularly shaped market areas, and this irregularity, in turn, may be conducive to long-run non-zero profits, interdependence between sellers and struggles for

[15] See Chapter 5.2
[16] This is the argument of Mills, E.S. and Lav, M.R. (1964) A Model of Market Areas with Free Entry. *Journal of Political Economy*, 72 278-88

market area control. This suggests not long-run monopolistically competitive equilibrium but oligopolistic markets. Since agglomeration economies lead to an even dispersion becoming uneven, the appropriate market type will be the same regardless of whether the initial distribution was regular or not. There will be a market area potentially common to sellers naming minimum prices, and here we have the makings of an oligopoly problem.

Although sellers and buyers can be assumed to be scattered over a wide area, the dispersion will not be regular and there will be interspersed clusters of sellers and/or buyers. Each seller might find several buyers and rival sellers in his neighbourhood. Further away there will be more buyers and sellers but their influence will be reduced by transport costs. Demand and supply schedules are not infinitely elastic. Any seller can increase his sales by cutting his price, either extending the boundary of his market or by absorbing freight. Similarly, a large buyer may increase his supplies by offering a higher price or by shipping in goods from a greater distance. Unless there is organised price collusion, the price levels established are indeterminate and may be different from seller to seller, since apart from when sellers are located next to each other they will receive some shelter from competition due to space and transport costs. Although there may be considerable opportunities for price variations, presence of a kinked demand curve may lead to price stability. In fact, spatial considerations magnify the importance of kinked demand functions because discontinuities develop when competition arises from distant sources of supply.

The demand curve facing the spatial oligopolist is, however, not so much the standard kinked demand curve as a three-section curve. The top section is highly elastic; attempts to raise price would lose all the markets if the prices of rivals remained low. The bottom section of the curve may be highly elastic or, alternatively, very inelastic depending on the reactions of rivals to price cuts. If the prices set by rivals could be assumed constant, a reduction in price towards the bottom end of the demand curve would gain him the complete market. On the other hand, prices set at this low level might provoke sharp price reactions from some rivals. In this case, low prices would yield very little increase in sales. The uncertainty of competitors' responses at these price levels is the primary reason why the spatial oligopolist will tend to operate only on the middle section of his demand curve. This middle section will have a moderate slope, similar to the typical demand function facing the monopolist or monopolistic competitor. Over this middle range the oligopolist has a certain freedom to act without regard to reactions from rivals. Slight upward changes in price do not lead to substantial declines in sales, and minor price cuts do not lead to price wars. The explanation of this freedom is either that the oligopolist has no near rivals therefore distance gives him a certain degree of protection or, at the other extreme, the agglomeration advantages at his location are so large due to high density of buyers that his share of the market is too small to provoke reactions from his rivals at the same location.

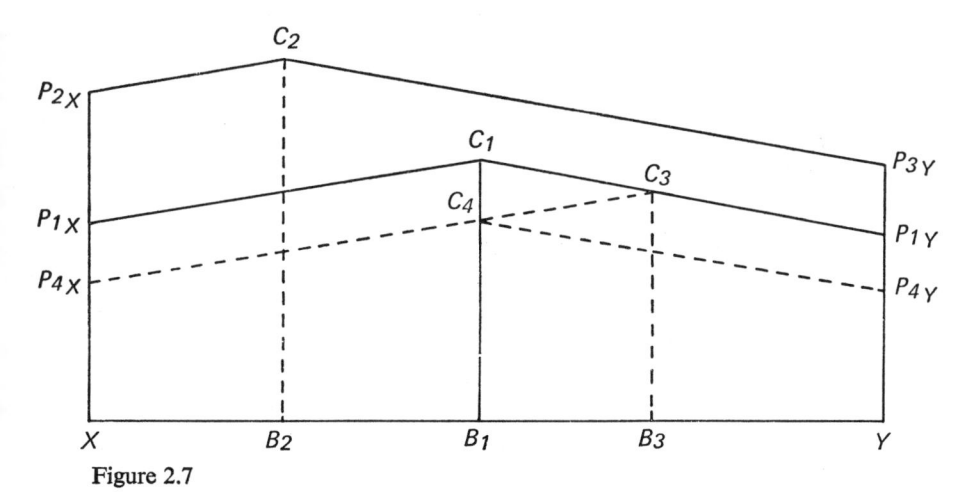

Figure 2.7

Some simpler aspects of spatial oligopoly relations can be illustrated with a duopoly analysis. In figure 2.7, we assume that two sellers, X and Y, located at opposite ends of a market set identical f.o.b. prices, P_{1X} and P_{1Y}. The market area boundary occurs midway between them at B_1, assuming that transport rates are identical on goods sold by either seller. Delivered price at the indifference boundary is B_1C_1. Now suppose firm X, in view of a cluster of nearby buyers with relatively inelastic demands, increased its price to P_{2X}. Firm Y, however, decides that a price P_{3Y} is now worthwhile, where $P_{2X} > P_{3Y}$. Since transport rates remain constant, the slopes P_2C_{2X} and $P_{3Y}C_2$ are the same as $P_{1X}C_1$ and $P_{1Y}C_1$. The market area boundary shifts to the left, to B_2. Its higher price has led to firm X forfeiting sales within the area B_2B_1 which are now taken over by firm Y. In this particular situation, firm Y is quite happy with X's

35

price rise, since it boosts Y's demand and enables it to increase its own prices and profits.

However, the results are less clear-cut when one of the firms attempts to reduce its price and take over the outer limits of the market area served by the other seller. Suppose firm X reduced its price from P_{1X} to P_{4X}. Firm Y could surrender some of the market area previously controlled by making no price change. In this case the new market area boundary will be B_3, maximum delivered prices will fall from B_1C_1 to B_3C_3 and firm X will have compensation for its reduced prices in increased sales within the area B_1B_3. However, firm Y might decide to respond to X's move by reducing its price to meet X's price cut, from P_{1Y} to P_{4Y}. In this case, the market area boundary remains the same at B_1, but delivered price to this boundary falls from B_1C_1 to B_1C_4. Unless demand over the market area, but particularly near the boundaries, is highly elastic, the profitability of both sellers will be reduced by X's move and Y's countermove.

This summary of moves and reactions shows only one or two of the many possibilities that arise in duopoly, and more so in oligopoly, situations. The many uncertainties, and fears of incurring losses, explain why price stability is so common, apart from price changes involving discrimination against nearby buyers over whom a seller may have a certain degree of monopolistic control. The encroaching attempts on a rival's market area, analysis of which points to the application of games theory, probably develop only when the boundary zone contains large clusters of buyers sensitive to price changes or whose custom is necessary for the attacking firm to break even. A further complication is that a high density cluster of buyers may attract entry of new firms, even if cost conditions do not favour location near the boundary zone.

Another possibility in spatial oligopoly situations is that there will be collusion among sellers to keep up their profits at the expense of buyers. Such collusion could take many forms: tacit collusion where firms follow the actions of a dominant price leader; geographical market division, an obvious form of agreement in spatial relations but difficult to operate unless the geographical border decided upon approximates to the market area boundary itself; price agreements, such as equalised delivered price or basing-point systems. Of course, the effectiveness of such collusion depends upon whether or not new entry can be blocked.

9 Alternative spatial pricing systems

Except when the contrary was explicitly stated, most of the analysis in this chapter has assumed that prices are quoted f.o.b. factory by sellers. A brief mention should be given of alternative pricing methods that occur in spatial oligopoly, particularly free delivery and basing-point pricing. Free delivered prices will normally be determined by the addition of sellers' anticipated *average* transport costs to the profit maximising f.o.b. price. Free delivery of goods throughout the market area obviously involves discrimination between buyers. Buyers located in the vicinity of the seller's site bear some of the conveying charges to peripheral areas. Sales volume and prices to the consumer vary under a free delivery system from the levels resulting from f.o.b. pricing, except for two situations: when transport costs are constant to all points in the market area; or when buyers are concentrated at one centre while sellers are dispersed.

If sellers are scattered indiscriminately, free delivery may operate without equalised delivered prices established by all sellers. Each seller will discriminate among buyers within his market area, but will be able to set a free delivered price different from those of other sellers since there are no great gains from engaging in active price competition. However, if sellers are located so close to each other that large portions of their market areas overlap, free delivery pricing can be maintained only with collusion requiring identical free delivered prices. In the absence of such collusion, it would be open to a firm locating near the free delivery competitors to sell f.o.b. to buyers in the vicinity, thereby depriving them of almost all nearby customers and breaking down the free delivery price system. The free delivery pricing method is most appropriate in conditions where the demand of nearby buyers is inelastic while the demand of distant buyers is elastic. In certain, probably rare, circumstances, free delivery might, by extending the market area boundary under decreasing costs conditions, result in a lower net price to *all* consumers. Finally, although free delivery practice could be applied to the country as a whole, in most cases it will be limited to a zone. It would be irrational to expand the outer boundary of the market area within which free delivery operates to an extent which reduced net profits; this means that the amount of freight absorption to distant customers will never be allowed to exceed the free delivered price.

Also common are basing-point pricing methods, where prices are quoted f.o.b. at a given centre, the basing point, and freight charged from that centre to the buyer's location, regardless of where the good is produced or the actual freight cost involved. Basing-point prices have certain characteristics: every seller's price at any destination is identical regardless of where the product is sold or who sells it; there will be price discrimination among buyers, since delivered prices to buyers situated near to the seller will contain 'phantom freight', while prices to buyers further away from the seller than from the basing point will reflect freight absorption; where prices contain either phantom freight or freight absorption they will result in varying f.o.b. factory prices. Basing-point pricing will lead to distortions in the spatial pattern of economic activity.

Firstly, it may lead to unnecessary cross-hauling. Some of the demands of buyers situated on the periphery of the market area will be satisfied by purchases from sellers near the basing point when they could be more efficiently supplied by sellers in their own vicinity. Secondly, it distorts the optimal location pattern. Large firms supplying goods over the whole market area tend to concentrate near the basing point, even if other agglomeration economies are non-existent there. Small firms, on the other hand, aiming for sales to small groups of buyers will tend to locate towards the periphery of the market, and boost their profits out of phantom freight gained from sales to nearby buyers. Multiple basing-point systems, and other complex pricing methods, do permit an element of price competition between sellers located at a considerable distance from each other. Distortion is reduced as compared with a single basing-point system, but price discrimination between buyers remains.

10 Spatial price variations: a testable model
Much of the analysis in this chapter rests on highly abstract assumptions, and is presented in terms of formal models. It is possible, however, to devise an approach to the study of spatial prices which can be tested empirically. Such an approach has been suggested by W. Warntz.[17] His analysis has the virtue that it is not dependent upon some predetermined spatial figuration of buyers and sellers, but can accommodate dense population centres and sparse rural

---

[17] Warntz, W. (1959) *Toward a Geography of Price: A Study in Geo-Econometrics*

SPATIAL PRICE THEORY

settlements, highly concentrated localisation of firms or even dispersion. It can also take account of dynamic influences on price by recognising that it takes time for supplies from a distance to be brought to a given destination. The limitation of the technique is that it is applicable only to competitive conditions, and indeed Warntz uses it solely for studying geographical variations in the price of agricultural commodities.[18]

The model is a very simple one, representing a return to the basic proposition that price is determined by supply and demand, but making explicit allowance for spatial factors. The price of a given commodity varies over space as a result of spatial variations in the intensity of supply and demand. Warntz's contribution is to suggest methods by which demand and supply intensity can be measured. His methods rely on gravity potential analysis. To measure demand, he draws on the concept **population potential**.[19] Any population concentration exerts an influence that varies directly with its size, but this influence is reduced by distance. A force field surrounds each population cluster, and at any point within the field its intensity can be measured by dividing the size of the population by distance. The total population potential at any point within an economy (region, market area, etc.) can be computed by dividing the economy into a large number of areal units, then dividing the population of each by its average distance to the point of reference. The resultant quotients may be aggregated to give the total population potential at that point, expressed in terms of persons per mile. Population potential estimates can be computed for a very great number of points.

Demand, of course, is not a function of population alone. Each individual should not be given unitary weight, but should be weighted by his income. An approximation to this is to weight the population of each areal unit by the average annual *per capita* income within the area. The resulting potential, called **gross economic population potential** (GEPP) takes into account numbers of people, their

---

[18] However, the technique can be used for estimating the degree of distortion from competitive pricing. The comparison of estimated prices from the model with actual prices at a given point might show the effects of intervention with market forces, such as the impact of an agricultural subsidy policy or of monopolistic transport rates

[19] This concept, developed if not discovered by J.Q.Stewart, recurs again and again in this book; see, for example, Chapter 4.2

location and their incomes. Lines can be drawn through points of equal value (equi-potential lines) and the resulting GEPP map can be viewed as showing the geographical distribution of effective demand.[20] It is from the GEPP map that the spatial pattern of demand for a given commodity is derived. Such a derivation involves adjusting for consumer tastes, the income elasticity of demand for the product and the prices of its substitutes etc. as some of the main factors modifying the overall economic effect of population and income over space. The adjusted values may be called **product demand space potential** (PDSP) measuring the spatial variation in demand for a given product. Similarly, there will be temporal variations in demand reflecting seasonal and cyclical factors, and giving rise to a parallel concept, **product demand time potential,** measured in terms of demand per time unit.

The influence of the distance factor has also to be taken account of on the supply side. Maps of potential of product availability can be drawn in the same way as maps of potential of human population. Areal variations in the intensity of **product supply space potential** (PSSP) indicate variations in the accessibility of places to the aggregate output of the product in question. The point with the highest space potential is the point of greatest accessibility to the output of the commodity, and at this point the influence of supply on price is greatest. Contour maps can be drawn for product supply space potential. Whereas product demand space potential varies only moderately from product to product, product supply space potential may differ tremendously from commodity to commodity because of wide variations in the geographical location of production of individual goods. The time dimension is also of some significance, especially for agricultural products with their seasonal variations in output. Prices will reflect supply influences over time: past production (because of the possibility of goods being stored), current output and expectations of future output. The intensity of supply over time can be measured by a concept, **product supply time potential** (PSTP), computed in terms of production units per time unit.

Spatial variations in the intensity of supply and demand will tend to produce geographical variations in the price of a commodity. A rough testable hypothesis to be drawn from this proposition is that

[20] This assumes that total income payments to individuals can be equated with effective demand. In practice, some allowance for leakages through taxes and savings would have to be made

price tends to vary directly with demand space potential and inversely with supply space potential (and supply time potential, where products with widely fluctuating outputs are being considered). Suppose the price of a product is considered as the dependent variable, while PDSP, PDTP, PSSP and PSTP are considered as independent variables, and estimates for each variable are obtained for a large number of points in space are obtained. Assume that there is a functional, quantifiable relationship between the dependent variable and the independent variables. Then a multiple linear regression equation may be applied to the data to obtain net regression coefficients. These computed coefficients can be used to yield an estimating formula which enables us to estimate the price levels ruling at particular points in space, and to show how price at each point is determined by the interaction of the independent variables, spatial and temporal variations in the intensity of supply and demand.

There is considerable scope for further analysis of spatial price variations. We might explore, for example, the effects on price of increasing or reducing the supply available at different locations. The universal impact of an increase in supply will be to lower price, but the price falls at given locations will depend upon the spatial relationship of each point analysed to the specific location where the increase in supply occurred. A more ambitious possibility is to extend the Walrasian general equilibrium theory of price (a model that is basically without dimensions, i.e. static *and* spaceless) by including supply and demand time and space potentials for goods and factors in its functions.

Chapter 3

Transport costs and location

1 Transportation as a locational factor: some general considerations
Transport costs, as the money costs of moving over space, obviously have a special place in locational analysis. Early theories of location often regarded the location that minimised transport costs as the optimum location. Such theories were too partial in that they ignored the possibility of spatial variations in production costs and spatial variations in demand explained by factors other than the cost of transporting factors on the one hand and finished goods on the other. However, even though the minimum transport cost point cannot give a general answer to the problem of the best location, transport costs may be a critical force in locational analysis under certain conditions.

If we ignore personal and subjective considerations, and if processing costs and the location of competitors (the demand factor) are held constant, then the choice of location depends upon transport costs. The maximum profit location for a plant is the one where transport costs are minimised. Even if these assumptions are relaxed, transportation may still be an important locational influence especially when the freight/total cost ratio is high, and when this ratio varies widely between different sites. Consumer goods producers will in such a situation be pulled towards the market, while earlier stages of production (processing stages) will be attracted towards raw material supplies. If the consumer market and the raw material source are spatially separated, the result will be a **vertical dispersion** of locations. The greater the transfer costs, the greater the degree of locational dispersion, especially in an industry making a homogeneous product and in purely competitive conditions. Demand influences too will tend *ceteris paribus* to make for dispersion, since high transport costs act as a form of protective tariff for local industries. Indeed high transport costs may even make it pay for a monopolist to set up branch plants in order to obtain raw materials and/or intermediate inputs closer to their source and to be able to sell in the markets located nearby.

Material-oriented industries will tend to share one or more of the following characteristics: overall transport costs will vary more widely than other costs at alternative sites; the raw materials lose weight during conversion to finished products; the transport rate on raw materials exceeds or equals the rate on the final product (unless the rate differential is offset by the weight factor). The second and third characteristics are very often subsumed in the first. On the other hand, a market-oriented location will tend to be preferred when one or more of the following conditions obtain: when the finished product is more expensive to transport than the raw material; when the finished good is perishable; when consumer demand fluctuates markedly, since in this case location near to buyers will keep inventory costs at a minimum; when close contacts with consumers increase sales. This last point applies particularly to service industries, and to industries producing intermediate goods the main consumers of which are other industries; for these industries nearness to their markets facilitates speed of delivery, quality control by buyers, etc.

The relative pull of the material source and the market can be illustrated with a simple example of finding the optimum location for a firm selling to one market and using one material. Consider such a firm using a raw material produced at M, and converting it into a finished product via a single stage production process to sell at the market, city C. The costs of production are assumed the same at all locations, so the firm's objective if it wants to maximise profits is to minimise total transport costs. These consist of assembly costs (i.e. bringing the raw material from M to the plant) and distribution costs (i.e. the cost of sending the final product from the plant to C). Let D be the distance from M to C, and d represent the distance from M to the factory. Thus the distance from the factory to C is $(D-d)$. If the cost per mile of carrying enough raw material to make one unit of the finished product is t_M, then assembly costs per unit $= t_M d$; while if the cost per mile of transporting a unit of the finished product is t_C, then unit distribution costs $= t_C(D-d)$. Total unit transport costs, represented by T, can be shown in the following equation:

$$T = t_M d + t_C(D-d)$$

or

$$T = (t_M - t_C)d + t_C D.$$

The firm will locate at that value of d that minimises T. If $t_M > t_C$, the firm will want to keep d as small as possible; it will consequently locate at the raw material source M where $d=0$. On the other hand, if the transport rate is higher on the final product ($t_C > t_M$), then the coefficient of d will be negative, and the firm will locate at the site which maximises d, at C where $d=D$. Finally, in the case where $t_C = t_M$, the coefficient of d is zero and transport costs per unit $= t_C D$ wherever the plant locates. Under the assumptions of the examples, the firm may then locate at M, or at C, or at any site between.

Apart from the assumption of a single market and a single raw material, the model is oversimplified because of its transport cost assumptions. The notion that transport costs increase in direct proportion to distance covered implicit in the assumption of a constant transport rate requires modification. Firstly, there are terminal costs to be considered, representing such factors as loading and handling costs. These terminal costs may arise at both ends of the haul. Their effect is that total transport costs $= X_M + t_M d$, where X_M are terminal costs, t_M is the transport rate per mile, and d equals the number of miles carried. Secondly, in most transport rate structures the rate per mile is lower for longer hauls. Thus, the slope of the transport curve declines with increasing distance representing the economies of longer hauls. Thirdly, the transport curve's curvature may be increased by allowing for alternative means of transportation. For example, road transport may have low terminal costs but higher carriage rates per mile than trains, while trains may be placed similarly relative to ships. The shipper will choose the carrier which has the lowest average costs for the particular distance to be traversed.

Modification of the transport structure to take account of the existence of terminal costs and curvilinear rather than a linear transport curve reinforce the attractiveness of endpoint locations (that is, either M or C) which were normally preferred even in the simplest model outlined above. Because the transport curve flattens out with increasing distance it pays to maximise the length of the haul by locating at an end point. Even if assembly and distribution costs are symmetrical, a midway site is often the costliest. Similarly, leaving aside the curvature problem, the elimination of one set of terminal costs will also induce location at the raw material site or the market. Transportation influences of this kind are one element in explaining why a given industry may be concentrated at either the market or the raw material source rather than spatially dispersed.

Another qualification is the possibility that alternative transportation means will not be available everywhere. For part of the distance the good is carried one form of transportation may have to be used, and then a change may be necessary to another means of carriage. The points where transport systems converge are usually called transhipment points. Costs are involved in transferring goods from one form of transport to another, and these costs can be evaded by locating a plant at the break in the transportation network. Transhipment points are therefore very desirable locations as well as raw material and market locations, particularly for plants engaged in intermediate stages of production, such as working up raw materials into semi-finished goods.

Although these elementary considerations illustrate some of the main points, they fail to do full justice to the role played by transport costs in location theory. It is desirable to discuss briefly this role by referring to the writings of Alfred Weber and, more recently, Walter Isard, two location theorists who have treated the transport costs factor systematically.

2 Weber's theory of location: the locational and weight triangles and minimisation of transport costs

If we ignore until Section 4 the complications introduced into Weber's theory by taking account of the possibilities of substitution between transport costs and labour costs (therefore recognising that cheap labour may have a locational pull) and the influence of agglomerating and deglomerating tendencies, then within the Weberian context transport costs alone influence the choice of location. The determination of the optimum location is reduced to finding the point which minimises transport costs.

In a simplified case the minimum transport location may be obtained by geometric means with the aid of Weber's locational triangle. If materials are divided into, to use Weber's terms, **ubiquities** and **localised raw materials,** ubiquities being obtained everywhere will have no locational pull but localised raw materials available at some locations but not others will influence the choice of site. In some cases, it is unnecessary to resort to the weight triangle concept. Weber coins the term **material index** defined as the ratio of the weight of the used localised materials to the weight of the final product. He also uses the concept **location weight** defined as the weight of the product plus the weight of the localised materials per unit of product. The locational weight (L) has the minimum value 1 when the material index (M) is zero, i.e. where ubiquities only are used, and rises parallel to the material index ($M=\frac{1}{2}$, $L=1\frac{1}{2}$ or $M=1$, $L=2$, etc.). In general terms, industries with a high L are attracted towards materials, while those with a low L are attracted to the market. Industries with $M<1$ will locate at the place of consumption. As for material orientation, only weight losing (as opposed to pure) materials can exert a locational pull. For if materials do not lose weight in production, M will never be greater than 1. For production to be located at a material source, the material concerned must be weight-losing, i.e. $M>1$ while $L>2$, *and* the weight of that material must be equal to or greater than the weight of the product plus the weight of all other localised materials. In these limiting cases, location is determined at either the place of consumption or at a raw material source and resort to the weight triangle is unnecessary.

In intermediate cases, where $M>1$ but a weight-losing material source is not dominant, the weight triangle is a useful device for solving the locational problem. Assume that we have a product composed of two materials which are found in scattered deposits, and that the most advantageous sources of these two materials relative to a single consumption centre C are represented by M_1 and M_2. This case of two material sources and one consumption point can be solved quite easily geometrically. Where the material sources >2 and/or the consumption centres >1 we obtain polygons. With polygons the net resultant of the different locational pulls can still be obtained from finding the equilibrium of forces in which relative weights and relative distances are the relevant components, but the solution is most easily obtained by analogies in applied mechanics.

A locational triangle is seen in figure 3.1a, where C, M_1 and M_2 represent the place of consumption and the two raw material sources and the sides of the triangle represent the relative actual distances between the three points (d_1, d_2, d_3). We now assume that a_1 tons of material m_1 produced at M_1 and a_2 tons of material produced at M_2 are required to produce a_3 tons of the finished product (it is easiest to assume that $a_3=1$). Thus $(a_1+a_2)/a_3$ equals the material index. If any one of the three variables (a_1, a_2, a_3) exceed the other two, then location is determined at the site associated with that particular variable. If no variable predominates in

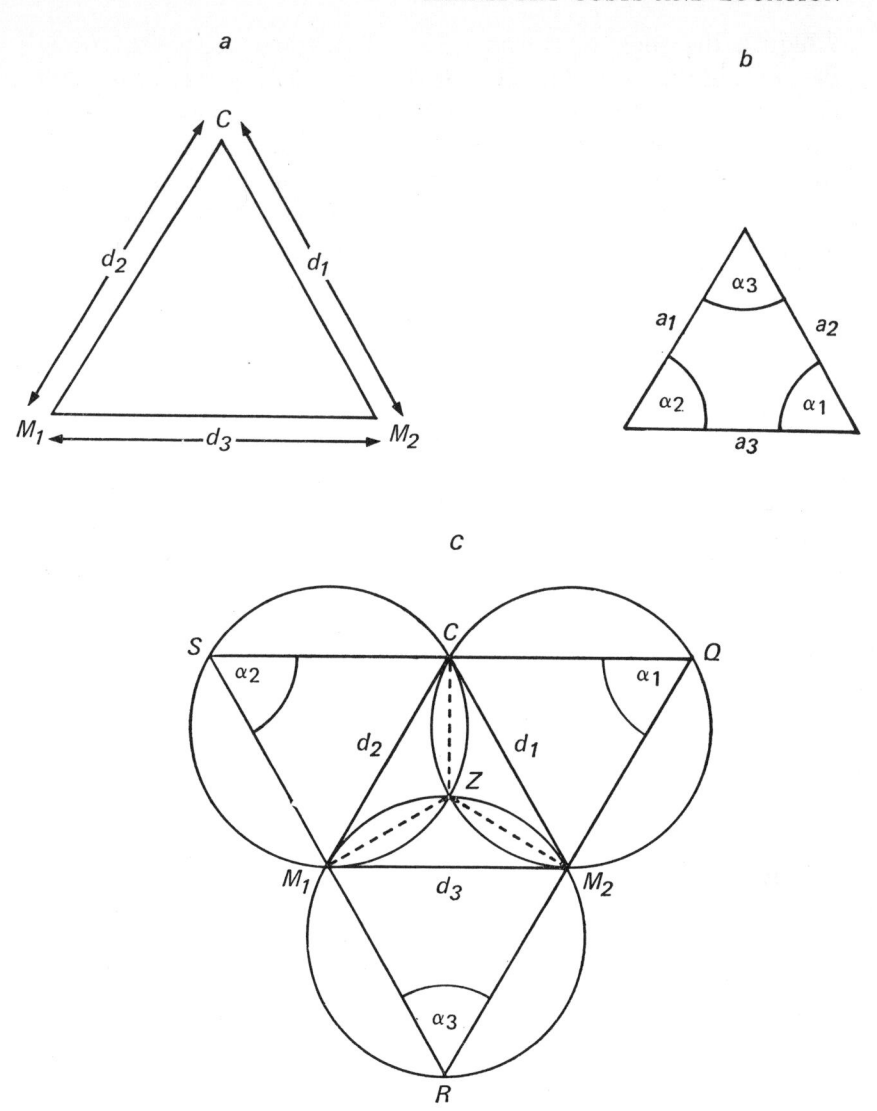

Figure 3.1

this manner we can construct a triangle having the sides a_1, a_2 and a_3; this may be called the *weight triangle* (figure 3.1b). Since the weight triangle is uniquely determined by a_1, a_2, a_3, we can measure the angles of the triangle and call these α_1, α_2, α_3 as in figure 3.1b. We now erect triangles similar to the weight triangle upon each of the three sides of the locational triangle (see figure 3.1c), where

47

REGIONAL ECONOMICS

α_1 equals the angle of the quadrilateral CM_1M_2Q opposite M_1, α_2 the angle of the quadrilateral CM_2M_1S opposite M_2, etc. The circles described around these triangles determine the production site Z which minimises transport costs (in fact, two of these circles suffice to locate Z). Z represents the point where the three locational forces exerted from M_1, M_2 and C are in equilibrium, since these forces (a_1, a_2, a_3) at Z have been weighted by the distances from M_1, M_2 and C respectively to Z. Total transport costs per ton of finished product are at a minimum and equal $a_1 M_1 Z + a_2 . M_2 Z + a_3 . CZ$.

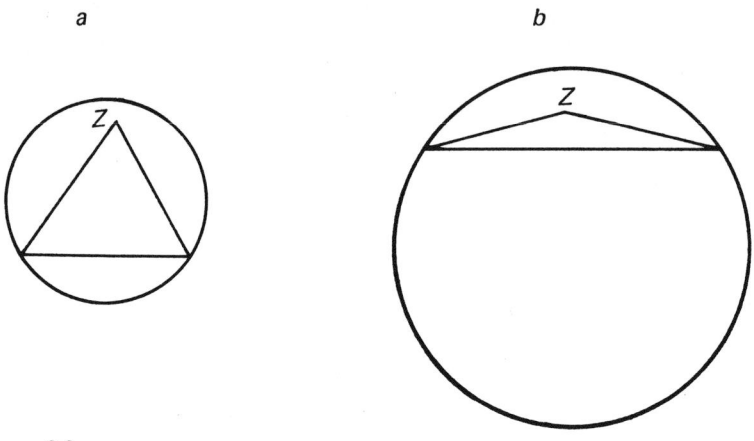

a   b

Figure 3.2

However, the condition $M > 1$ does not necessarily mean that the location of production cannot be at a corner of the locational triangle or even at a raw material source which does not lose weight in production. If the circles described around the similar triangles intersect outside the locational triangle, the point of equilibrium occurs outside the locational triangle. This point ceases to be the solution of the locational problem since transport costs could always be reduced by moving to one of the corners of the locational triangle. This case can always be recognised by the fact that one of the circles constructed on each side of the locational triangle includes the third corner that does not lie upon its base. The included corner is always the minimum transport cost site. This occurs either when the weights of the other two corners are small relative to the third (figure 3.2a), or when the included corner lies near the connecting line of the other two corners (figure 3.2b).

48

The application of this geometric technique depends upon the assumption of linear transport functions. If transport rates decrease with distance then the locational triangle (polygon) technique no longer works. Weber suggested that rate structures of this kind could be accommodated by substituting fictitious distances for geographical distances where the fictitious distances reflected the decreasing transport scale. The longer the actual distance, the more it would have to be shortened for geometric representation. The trouble is, of course, we do not know how much to shorten the distance from any corner of the triangle to the production site until we can locate the production site, and we cannot locate the production site until we know these distances. Thus for realistic transport rate structures the triangular technique is impossible. However, this does not affect the validity of the model since although geometry has to be dropped the problem can still be solved mathematically if the non-linear transport functions are given.

3 Transport inputs

Isard's work on location theory, particularly in its transport orientation aspects, is very much in the Weberian tradition.[1] Like Weber, Isard outlines a simple model where the search for the optimum location involves the minimisation of transport costs, though his technique is rather more flexible since it can accommodate more realistic transport rate structures.

The basic concept used in Isard's analysis is the *transport input*. This is defined as the movement of a unit weight over a unit distance; thus transport inputs could be expressed in ton-miles. Transport inputs correspond to the exertion of effort (cf. man-hours) required to overcome the resistance encountered in movement through space. Just as we discount over time, we may discount over space. Space discounting allows comparison of values of two or more goods (materials) spatially separated from any given geographical point of reference. The rate of discount over space, or the price of a transport input, is the transport rate. In the real world there are many different transport rates reflecting length and character of the haul, type of product transported, degree of competition in the transport sector, topography of the territory over which goods

---

[1] Isard, W. (1956) *Location and Space-Economy*, especially Chapters 4–6 and 10–11, 77–142 and 221–87

Figure 3.3

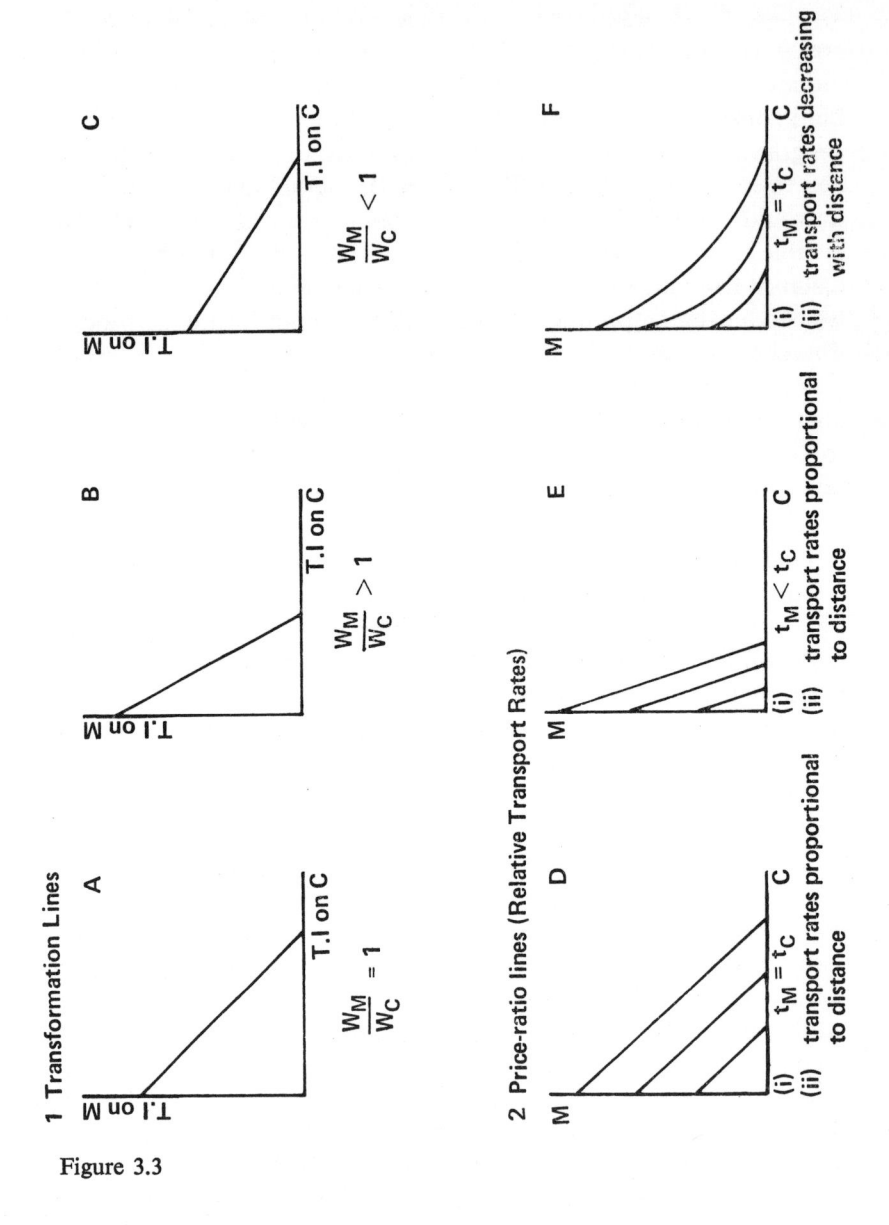

1 Transformation Lines

A: T.I on M / T.I on C; $\frac{W_M}{W_C} = 1$

B: T.I on M / T.I on C; $\frac{W_M}{W_C} > 1$

C: T.I on M / T.I on C; $\frac{W_M}{W_C} < 1$

2 Price-ratio lines (Relative Transport Rates)

D: M — C; (i) $t_M = t_C$ (ii) transport rates proportional to distance

E: M — C; (i) $t_M < t_C$ (ii) transport rates proportional to distance

F: M — C; (i) $t_M = t_C$ (ii) transport rates decreasing with distance

TRANSPORT COSTS AND LOCATION

3 Locational Equilibrium

	D	E	F
A	Indeterminate	C	M or C Indifferent
B	M	M or C depending on slopes of T.L and P–R.L	M
C	C	C	C

Figure 3.3 (*continued*)

are carried, etc. But we can still think of *the* transport rate as a hypothetical representative rate, just as in discounting over time we speak of *the* interest rate although there are in fact several interest rates varying between regions, and according to degrees of risk and the length of the loan.

Let us first consider the simplest case. We assume a single consumption centre C and let a point M be the only source of raw material indispensable for production of a given good. All other productive factors are taken to be available everywhere as required, and at the same cost. The raw material is considered mobile (i.e. the industry considered is not an extractive industry), and a straight line road connects points M and C. The only variable cost factor is transport inputs on the raw material and the finished product. If we assume that one ton of raw material is used to make one ton of the commodity (i.e. $W_M/W_C = 1$), transport inputs become distance from M and distance from C. If we plot these two variables we obtain

51

a straight transformation line with the slope of -1, as in figure 3.3.1A. If there is weight loss in the production stage, location at the consumption centre would absorb more transport inputs (ton-miles) in bringing the material to the place of production than if the plant was sited at M and the finished product transported from M to the market. So where W_M/W_C exceeds unity, the transformation line has a slope less than -1 algebraically as in figure 3.31B. Finally, where there is weight gain in production the converse situation applies, the negative slope of the transformation will be shallower, that is, will be algebraically greater than -1 (figure 3.31C).

The transformation line shows us how by changing location we can substitute transport inputs on one good (say, the material) for transport inputs on the other (the finished good). To find the spatial equilibrium position we need a set of price-ratio lines reflecting the relative prices of the two sets of transport inputs. If we assume that the transport rate per ton-mile is the same on both raw materials and final goods and that this transport rate is proportional to distance, then the various price-ratio lines are straight lines with a slope of -1, as in figure 3.3.2D. If we retain the assumption of proportionality to distance, but assume that the transport rate on finished goods is higher than on raw materials (which is often the case in practice) the price-ratio line becomes steeper as in figure 3.3.2E. In figure 3.3.2F we revert to the assumption of the same transport rate on materials and final goods but instead we relax the assumption of proportionality allowing for the fact that, especially in advanced countries where modern transportation media involve heavy overhead expenditures and high terminal costs, tariff structures are normally graduated with the transport rate falling off with increasing distance. This gives us a set of price-ratio lines which are convex to the origin but which cut both axes symmetrically.

With the aid of the transformation lines and the price-ratio lines considered together it is possible to obtain the point of locational equilibrium for the plant. The condition of equilibrium is directly parallel to the normal equilibrium condition in substitution analysis in the theory of production. This is that the point of production corresponds to where the transformation line is tangential to the price-ratio line. This means that the marginal rate of substitution between any two transport inputs equals the reciprocal of their prices (the corresponding transport rates). Thus, the equilibrium site corresponds to the point on the transformation line which lies on the lowest price-ratio line, therefore incurring the least total transport costs. To find this equilibrium point all we need to do is to superimpose price-ratio lines on the transformation diagram. If we consider in figure 3.3, 1A, 1B, and 1C, together with 2D, 2E and 2F we arrive at nine different combinations. The results are set out in the matrix in figure 3.3.3.

These results are rather obvious, so it is unnecessary to comment on them in detail. Combination A–D is indeterminate because the slopes of the transformation line and the price-ratio line both equal −1, and any location (M, C or anywhere on the road between them) incurs the same overall transport cost. With A–F the symmetry of the price-ratio curve convex to the origin ensures that the lowest of these curves touches the transformation line A at both axes, therefore the producer is indifferent between location at either end point, M or C. In the bottom horizontal row of the table location at the consumption centre results in every case; this is because the transformation line 1.C, representing weight gain in production, dominates over all the price-ratio lines considered (D, E and F) because in all these cases the transport rate on the finished product $\geqq$ the transport rate on the material. With the transformation line B where there is weight loss in production, location at the material source follows in cases (B–D, B–F) where the transport rate is the same on the material as on the finished good. Combination B–E is the most difficult; here a weight-losing raw material influence is offset by a higher transport rate on finished goods. However, the location of the plant is fully determinate depending on the relative slopes of the transformation line and the price-ratio line. If these slopes were completely specified then we could determine whether equilibrium occurs at M or C.

A final important point to notice about the results of figure 3.3.3 is that the equilibrium location is always an end point. The equilibrium point is almost always an end point where the locational polygon reduces to a line, e.g. when only one raw material is used in production. In this case, the transformation line is a straight line or a number of feasible points (sites) lying on a straight line. The only exception to an end point location in examples of this kind would be if the price-ratio line was concave to the origin; this would require the most unlikely condition of transport rates increasing with distance. In fact, the convexity of modern transport rate structures is a potent factor increasing the likelihood of end point locations. On the other hand, it must be stressed that end point solutions are only possibilities not probabilities in more complex situations with multiple raw material sources and/or multiple consumption centres.

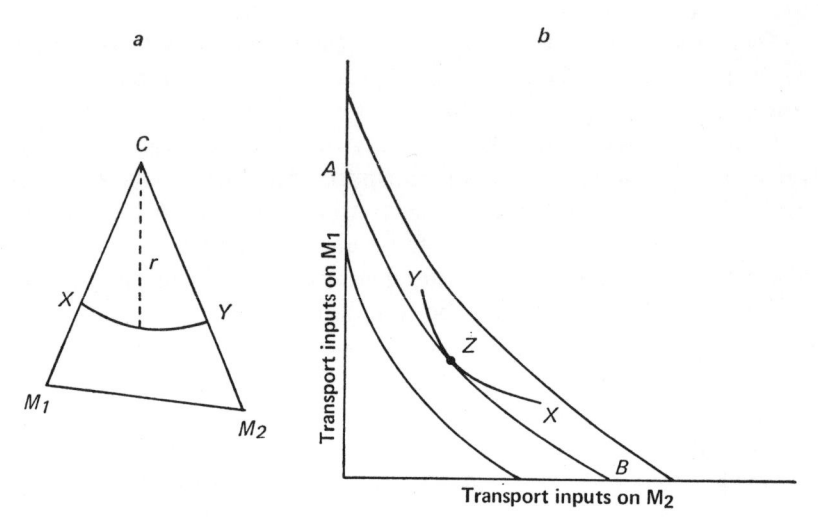

Figure 3.4

The models discussed above are, of course, highly oversimplified. If we consider locational polygons Isard's technique then becomes rather cumbersome because the final equilibrium location cannot be found immediately. The problems can be illustrated with the two raw materials (M_1 and M_2) and single consumption centre (C) case. Once more we retain the assumptions about uniformity over space in labour and other costs, so that if the plant's location is changed only transport inputs are altered. We can draw up a locational triangle as in figure 3.4a where the corners of the triangle represent the raw material sources and the consumption point. The only difference between this and the Weberian locational triangle is that here the sides of the triangle are not actual distances but measure transport inputs (ton-miles) so that the weights of raw materials used to make each ton of the finished good are already accounted for and do not have to be considered as in Weber's analysis as weights pulling from each corner.

The procedure is to assign a value, say r, to the variable transport inputs to C, and this gives us the arc XY of radius r which is the locus of all production sites for that particular value of transport inputs to C within the locational triangle CM_1M_2. This locus can be expressed in terms of quantities of transport inputs from M_1 and from M_2 which gives us for these two variables a transformation curve YX in figure 3.4b. If we know the transport rates on raw materials M_1 and M_2 we can draw up a set of price-ratio lines. AB represents the lowest of these lines which is tangential to the transformation curve YX. This point of tangency is Z which stands for the partial equilibrium set of quantities of the two variable transport inputs which determines location under the given assumptions.

However, Z is only a partial equilibrium point because it depends on the assumption that the site is r transport inputs from C. But the transport inputs to C must be allowed to vary if the overall equilibrium site is to be found. Thus, the next step is to take the transport inputs from M_2 consistent with location at point Z, and to construct a transformation curve for the variable transport inputs from M_1 and from C. We superimpose the price-ratio lines reflecting the relative transport rates on M_1 and the finished good. Again a partial equilibrium position is obtained. This will probably be consistent with a value of transport inputs to C other than the assigned value r. Consequently, the transformation curve between M_1 and M_2 changes, and it may be necessary to find a new partial equilibrium position for these two variables. The process continues until we get an overall equilibrium position. This is attained where the partial equilibrium positions corresponding to three pairs of variables (transport inputs on finished product and on raw material M_1; transport inputs on finished product and on raw material M_2; transport inputs on M_1 and on M_2) coincide.

The technique is equally applicable to cases of four- or more-sided polygons, and to more realistic assumptions about transport networks and transport rate structures. For example, if we assume that instead of radiating out in all directions transport facilities connect a finite number of points, then the transformation curve itself becomes discontinuous and degenerates into a number of points. Moreover, despite the ponderous task of finding locational equilibrium in this analysis, its main advantage over Weber's more elegant approach is that it can accommodate much greater realism in relation to transport rates. Isard shows how by substituting iso-outlay lines (for transport costs) for price-ratio lines, it is possible to take account of the zonal character of many transport rate structures, high terminal costs, and increased costs due to breaks at transport junctions in addition to dealing adequately with non-proportional transport rates.[2]

One result of Isard's approach is that it links analysis of location due to transport orientation with traditional production theory. The inclusion of transport inputs in the firm's transformation function adds a spatial dimension to the theory of production. This advantage is not without its drawbacks: the possibility of marked discontinuities in both transformation curves and transport iso-outlays lines indicates the limitations of marginalist substitution analysis for solving the location problem.

4 Labour and other forms of orientation: substitution between transport and non-transport costs

Both Weber and Isard recognised that transport costs alone were not the decisive determinant of location, and both conceived of the least cost location as resulting from a substitution between transport and non-transport costs.

Weber accepted that fuel and raw material costs could vary over space but he simplified the analysis by linking such variations with transport costs. Thus if the cost of a raw material is higher at one location than at others this is assumed to be due to this location being more remote. However, labour may exert its own locational pull and induce location at a site other than the minimum transport cost point provided that higher transport costs are more than offset by labour savings. There are therefore two main forms of orientation – transport orientation and labour orientation. A third type of orientation may be the dominant locational influence whenever transport and labour differentials at alternative sites are negligible. This is the **agglomerating** or **deglomerating** factor which tends to result in either spatial concentration or dispersion. Agglomerating forces include nearness to service industries, easier access to marketing outlets and economies of scale (including scale economies in public service facilities ancillary to production). The main deglomerating factor is higher rent which offsets the tendency to industrial concentration.

[2] Isard, *op. cit.*, 104–12

Isard's discussion of these locational factors other than transport costs went little further than Weber's. This no doubt reflected his judgment that transport costs alone, as distance functions, can impart regularity to the spatial ordering of economic activity.

We may illustrate Isard's analysis with the example of substitution between transport and labour outlays. We relax the assumption of uniform costs over space, and allow sites to differ in their access to labour reserves. The result is that labour costs vary from one location to another. We assume other costs and demand to be the same at every site. Thus we have two variables, labour costs and transport costs. We cannot, however, speak of substitution between transport inputs and labour inputs. The units of measurement (ton-miles and man-hours, for example) have no common denominator. But the main point is that location at a cheap labour site does not normally involve more inputs of one kind and less of the other. When the cheap labour site and the transport-cost-minimising location do not coincide, and the plant is located at the cheap labour site, more transport inputs are consumed and transport outlays increased while the firm holds constant (or even increases) its labour inputs but reduces, thanks to low wages, its labour outlays. It follows that the correct formulation is that of substitution between transport outlays and labour outlays.

Figure 3.5 illustrates this kind of substitution. We take a number of cheap labour sites *I, J, K, L, M, N, O* where the labour outlay per ton of product is measured on the vertical axis. For each of these sites, we estimate the transport outlay involved on raw materials and the final good from the relevant transformation curves showing substitution possibilities between each pair of transport inputs. We obtain a transport outlay estimate for each site, measured on the horizontal axis. As a result, we obtain a line *IJKLMNO* which Isard calls an *outlay-substitution line*. It demonstrates the substitution feasibilities between transport outlays and labour outlays, just as the transformation curve does for two inputs. But marginal substitutions may not be possible, since the relationship between cheap labour sites and distance may be random. If substitution is best regarded as discontinuous, we have a number of outlay-substitution discontinuous points rather than the continuous curve shown in figure 3.5. We may also construct a set of iso-outlay lines, representing transport plus labour outlays. These iso-outlay lines are straight and have a negative slope of -1 if the same scale is used

REGIONAL ECONOMICS

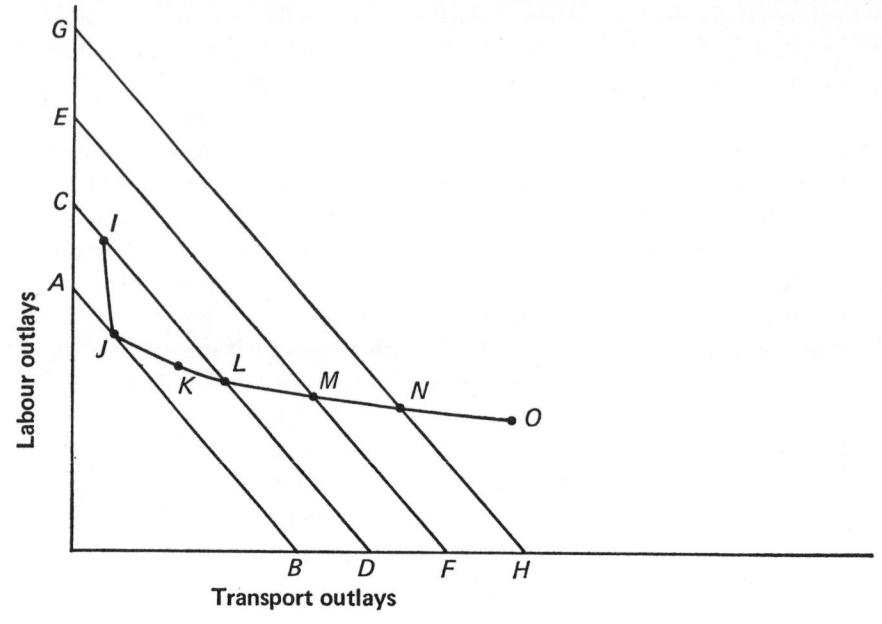

Figure 3.5

on both axes. *AB*, *CD*, *EF*, *GH* are examples of such lines in figure 3.5.

Of the outlay-substitution points in figure 3.5, point *I* is the least transport outlay point while point *O* is the cheapest labour site. Neither is the least-cost site since low outlays on one cost element are outweighed by heavy outlays on the other. Of the several cheap labour sites, *J* represents the equilibrium location because it stands on the lowest iso-outlay line *AB*. Labour costs at *J* are in fact higher than at *K*, *L*, *M*, *N* or *O*, but the relatively high labour outlays are more than offset by very low transport outlays. It is apparent that this procedure is not confined to consideration of labour outlays. If power costs varied markedly over space, we could determine the optimum location from outlay-substitution lines between power outlays and transport outlays with the aid of appropriate iso-outlay lines. Similar analyses are possible between transport outlays and rent outlays, transport outlays and raw material outlays (at source), and for any other production outlay where costs differ substantially among alternative sites.

Chapter 4
The optimal location of the firm

1 The space cost curve
The traditional cost curve of the firm shows how average costs vary with the level of output. It implicitly assumes that the firm's location is given. The transfer costs involved in moving a plant from one location to another may be so great that the firm will not move its location instantaneously in response to spatial variations in cost. Admittedly, if in the very long run changes in costs move persistently against the firm's location in favour of another, the plant may migrate but within such a long time horizon all the ancillary assumptions made before drawing up a firm's cost curve will have ceased to hold anyway.

In location theory, where we are greatly interested in low-cost locations, we obviously cannot ignore spatial variations in costs. Just as the normal cost curve in effect holds location fixed and indicates how costs vary with the level of output, we can devise a very different cost curve which in essence hold the firm's output fixed and shows how costs of production vary over space. Such a curve might be termed a *space cost curve*.[1]

To isolate the effects of locational influences on costs we can adopt either of two procedures. We may draw up our space cost curve as an iso-output curve, showing how the average unit costs of producing a given level of output vary over space. In this case, we might well need a separate space cost curve for each possible level of output. Such curves might vary markedly in shape, in their minimum *level* of average costs, and in their indications of the least cost

---

[1] This concept was suggested by Smith, D.M. (1966) A Theoretical Framework for Geographical Studies of Industrial Location. *Economic Geography*, **42** 96–113. As a geographer Smith's analysis was suggestive rather than formal. I have tried to develop the concept a little more rigorously than he conceived it

location. Alternatively, we may assume constant costs so that each point on the space cost curve indicates the average costs of producing *any* output at that location. In effect, this assumes that inputs are in perfectly elastic supply. This assumption is rather restrictive for locational analysis, since spatial differences in the supply of productive resources are one of the main reasons why some locations are preferable to others. Indeed, the assumption of inputs in perfectly elastic supply is incompatible with an uneven spatial distribution of such inputs since (unless transport costs are zero) costs will be incurred in moving, say, raw materials from a point A to the least cost location B.[2] Moreover, travel-to-work limits restrict the supply of labour at any site. Consequently, we prefer to use multiple iso-output space cost curves rather than the single space cost curve based on constant costs assumptions.

There is another parallel between the familiar average cost curve showing how costs vary with output and the space average cost (iso-output) curve showing how costs vary over space. Just as average costs can be split up into two components, average fixed costs and average variable costs, where the terms 'fixed' and 'variable' relate to the level of output, so average costs over space can be divided into average **basic costs** and average **locational costs.** By basic costs we mean the minimum costs of producing a given output irrespective of the location of the plant; for example, we count the cost of raw material at source and the cost of labour at its cheapest point. By locational cost, we mean spatial premiums in the costs of productive factors over the basic minimum and/or the additional costs (i.e. transport costs) incurred in bringing factors, such as raw materials, to the factory location. Locational costs include geographical differences in homogeneous labour costs above the minimum point, variations in capital costs between areas, differences in raw material, machinery and power costs from place to place primarily to be explained by transport costs, workers' commuting costs, salary differentials necessary to induce managers to unattractive locations, and so on. Basic costs represent the minimum costs of producing a given output when all inputs are valued at their least-cost source; thus, they are a fixed constant regardless of location. Locational costs represent the additions to these minimum costs, and vary according to location. In this sense, basic and locational

[2] Unless all the inputs necessary for production are located at B

costs are directly analogous to fixed and variable costs except that they have reference to space rather than levels of output.

On the other hand, the space cost curve is unlike the normal cost curve in certain important respects. In the first place, its shape is much more indeterminate. With the traditional cost curve it is common to make it U-shaped, on the grounds that costs will fall steadily with increasing output up to a certain level after which costs will start to rise steadily again, primarily reflecting economies and ultimate diseconomies of scale as output expands. The possibility of reversibilities in this pattern so that there might be two minimum average cost points is considered so rare as to be ignored. With the space cost curve, however, the assumption that costs will rise continuously on all sides of the least cost point is less soundly based. Instead there might be multiple low cost locations which are separated by distance, with the possibility of a multiple solution to the problem of finding the least cost point. There are many reasons why costs should not necessarily vary *regularly* with distance. Raw materials may occur in isolated pockets distributed over space. Also, population concentrations will be distributed unevenly.[3] Such locations may be low-cost points because pools of labour are readily available there and/or because of other external economies attached to urban locations.

Another reason for multiple solutions of the least cost problem arises from the fact that the space-cost curve is an iso-output curve. There will be an isoquant relating to the output produced on this space cost curve, and assuming two inputs, each point on the isoquant will represent how the output may be produced with a given combination of the two resources.[4] The least cost combination will be where the isoquant is tangential to the appropriate isocost line the slope of which equals the price ratio of the two inputs. However,

---

[3] The theories discussed in Chapter 7 stress the hierarchical structure of urban centres, indicating to a greater or lesser extent a definite pattern in the distribution of towns and cities

[4] Let A and B represent inputs measured on the horizontal and vertical axes respectively. The slope of a given isoquant at any point equals the marginal rate of technical substitution of A for B = ratio of the marginal physical products of A and B. If T represents total outlay available to the firm, the slope of the isocost curve = $(T/p_B)/(T/p_A)$ where p represents price. So where the isocost curve is tangential to the isoquant $MPP_A/MPP_B = p_A/p_B$, or $MPP_A/p_A = MPP_B/p_B$. Thus, the costs of producing the given output cannot be lowered by substituting one factor for the other

since the price ratio of the two inputs will tend to vary from place to place because of spatial differences in the cost and availability of productive resources, the slope of the isocost line will change according to location. It follows that the least cost combination of resources producing a given level of output will also vary between locations. Now this does not necessarily affect the existence of a unique least cost location since the absolute costs of factors will be lower at some locations than at others. On the other hand, even if input costs are nowhere the same, the probability that the least cost method of producing a given output at any one location involves a different combination of inputs from that at another location opens the door to the possibility of multiple least cost locations. These may occur if in comparing two (or more) locations having different input price ratios and a different least cost combination of inputs, the elasticity of substitution between the two inputs is equal to unity. In this situation, the costs of production will be equal at both sites, so that if one is a least cost location then so is the other.

A second important dissimilarity between the space cost curve and the traditional cost curve is that while the latter is two dimensional, comparing quantities of output on one axis with money costs on the other, the former is not. This is because space really needs to be treated areally,[5] so that a three dimensional diagram is required to cope with money costs and location. Thus the space cost curve should strictly be drawn as a concave surface (which may be like a regular or an irregular 'saucer' or alternatively a cone, depending on the assumptions). However, the clumsiness of three dimensional diagrams suggests the desirability of treating location either as a linear problem or as a mathematical formulation.

Let us draw a hypothetical space cost curve on the simplest set of assumptions. Consider a number of possible production sites along a straight line, thus assuming away the areal problem mentioned above. Assume that all productive resources are uniformly distributed along this line and are available at each location at the same cost with the exception of an essential raw material whose sole source is at Z. If production is started at any site other than Z, therefore, it will be necessary to transport this raw material to it. Let the trans-

[5] Strictly speaking, space has three dimensions in itself, two over area and one referring to height. However, it is customary in the economics of location to ignore topographical distortions and to assume a uniform flat plain thereby enabling one to concentrate on area alone

THE OPTIMAL LOCATION OF THE FIRM

port cost for this raw material be constant at £t per ton-mile, where t = slope of *FH* (*FG*) in figure 4.1 divided by the quantity of the raw material required per unit of output (assumed to be invariable). £*CZ* represents the average *basic cost* of producing one unit of the commodity. However, even at *Z*, the raw material source, average

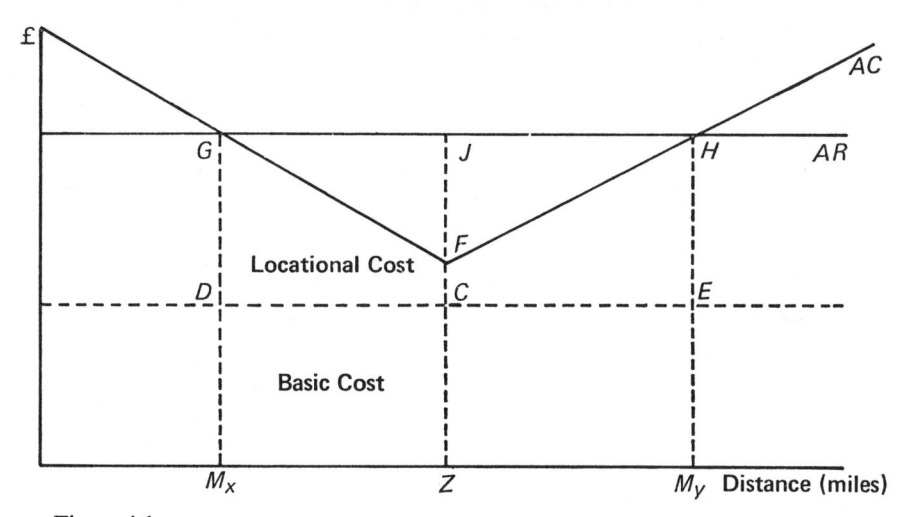

Figure 4.1

costs = £*FZ*, reflecting the fact that even though all other inputs are uniformly distributed and have the same price at each location it is necessary for a plant to bring some inputs from nearby locations in order to produce the level of output under consideration. Finally, to simplify as much as possible let us assume a perfectly competitive market for the commodities, that the ruling price is the same at every location and that the good is either consumed on the spot or that transport costs for the finished product are zero. Thus, the average revenue (demand) curve can be drawn as a horizontal line.

On these assumptions, the space cost curve representing the way in which unit costs of producing a given output vary with distance from the raw material source may be plotted as in figure 4.1 *CZ* (DM_x, EM_y) = average basic costs which are constant irrespective of location. Locational costs are at a minimum at $Z = FC$, and rise proportionately with distance from *Z*. Given a horizontal demand curve *AR*, the marginal locations are M_x and M_y where locational costs = *GD*(*HE*), and where average cost = price. Location further

63

away from Z than M_x (M_y) would involve the plant in losses, therefore M_x and M_y represent the spatial margins to profitability. The least cost site is at Z, defined as the location where total locational costs (i.e. the sum of location costs of all inputs required to produce the given output) are at a minimum. With a horizontal demand curve, the least cost location also yields maximum unit profits of £JF which equal the cost of transporting the raw material requirements per unit of output ZM_x (ZM_y) miles.

Generalising from a simplified space cost curve of this kind, two broad conclusions may be drawn. Firstly, spatial variations in average production costs impose limits to the locations at which production can be undertaken at a profit. In figure 4.1 production is profitable only between M_x and M_y. Along this line profits will vary, though firms are free to locate at any point between M_x and M_y. Secondly, the steeper the gradient of the cost lines,[6] the more localised the plants are likely to be. If the gradients of the cost curve are shallow, on the other hand, costs will not vary significantly with location and the distribution pattern of plants may be well dispersed.

Once we relax the assumptions which enabled us to plot this V-shaped space cost curve, however, the shape of the curve becomes much more indeterminate. There is no inherent reason why a location which has the lowest costs for one resource should also be low cost for others. For example, a city location may be low cost as far as labour costs are concerned because of the access to large metropolitan labour pools,[7] but congestion may lead to heavy terminal transport costs. A raw material location may drastically cut down on transport costs especially if there is weight loss in production, but if the area is isolated it may be difficult to attract enough labour for industry in addition to that required for raw material extraction. If we were developing a theory of industrial location in relation to an uninhabited plain where natural resources were uniformly distributed these problems would not trouble us, but if instead the background is that of an advanced industrial economy they cannot be ignored.

The possibility of irregularities in a space cost curve plotted with reference to empirical observations is therefore very great. Low cost

---

[6] In terms of our set of assumptions, this means the higher the transport costs

[7] On the other hand, compared with a rural location which has a trainable reserve of labour, labour costs in a city may be considered high. But rural areas may in general be regarded as high labour cost areas because of sparse population and the unsuitability of the labour which is available

locations may appear discontinuously, and multiple solutions of the least-cost problem are not impossible. For the purposes of location theory, however, these questions are not critical. If we relax the assumptions of uniformly distributed productive factors with no spatial cost variations and of linear transport functions, and instead assume that there is only one least cost location and that costs at other sites are a function (though not a linear function) of the distance from the least cost point, then the space cost curve can be drawn as approximately U-shaped like the traditional cost curve.[8] There is no reason why the U should be regular, and instead it is quite possible for it to be 'skewed'. Once we rule out discontinuous low cost locations, a U-shaped space cost curve is probably more realistic than a V-shaped curve, partly because actual unit transport costs tend to vary with the length of hauls partly because it is consistent with locations being low cost for some inputs but high cost from the point of view of others.

The space cost curve is essentially an iso-output curve. If the level of output changes a new space cost curve is required, and the least cost location may change. If there are economies of scale in the production of the commodity, a space cost curve for a higher level of output will be represented by a downward shift in the curve and an extension to the spatial margins of profitability. It may or may not be associated with a change in the least cost point, depending on whether or not scale economies are neutral between locations. It is quite possible for plants of different size in the same industry to have different least cost locations. Broadly speaking, a change in the basic cost of a productive resource will alter the spatial margin of profitability without affecting the optimum least cost location; but if a fall in locational cost follows from scale economies this will tend to affect both the marginal and the optimal location. Differences in managerial efficiency will similarly be reflected (even for plants of constant size) in upward and downward shifts in the space cost curve; again, the least cost point may change because certain managers may operate more effectively in some geographical environments than in others.

Two illustrations of changes in space cost curves deserve a little more detailed treatment. The first shows how changes in the profitability of locations can be affected by taxes and subsidies. Secondly,

---

[8] Or, in three dimensional terms, as a saucer-shaped surface

REGIONAL ECONOMICS

we may illustrate how the replacement of an input with considerable locational cost by one which is available at a constant cost at every site could alter not only the margins to profitability but also the least cost location. For both these demonstrations it is convenient to retain our assumption of a horizontal demand curve.

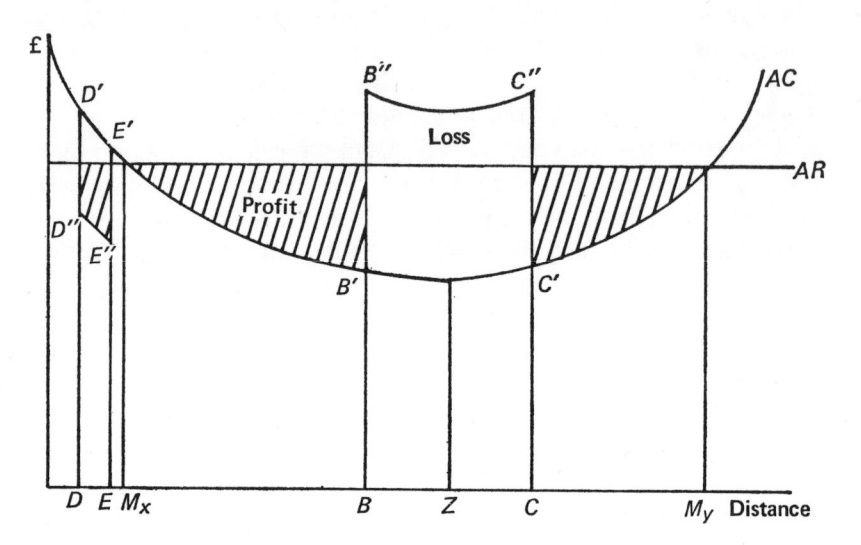

Figure 4.2

The effects of taxes on congested and/or highly favoured locations and of subsidies to unattractive locations are shown in figure 4.2. AC is a space cost curve (measured in terms of average costs per unit) for an optimum site plant with a single least cost location Z. AR is the average revenue curve (assumed to be a horizontal line), and therefore M_x and M_y represent the spatial margins to profitability. The objective of policy is considered to be a need to attract industry to the area DE outside the spatial profitability margin, M_x. This area can be made profitable by provision of a subsidy which has the effect of shifting the cost curve downwards below the price line between D and E, from $D'E'$ to $D''E''$. There may be coupled with this an attempt to restrict expansion in a congested or very prosperous location, say the area BC around the least cost location Z. If a tax is imposed this would shift the cost curve within that area upwards from $B'C'$ to $B''C''$, making the area no longer profitable for new firms. The least cost locations would then become

66

THE OPTIMAL LOCATION OF THE FIRM

B and *C*, but it would be possible with the aid of very heavy subsidies to make an area originally outside the spatial profitability margin the least cost location. This example shows the effects of the most simple form of tax and subsidy which raises and lowers average unit costs evenly over given areas specified for restriction and expansion respectively. But the effects of more complex fiscal measures could be illustrated without much difficulty with the same technique.

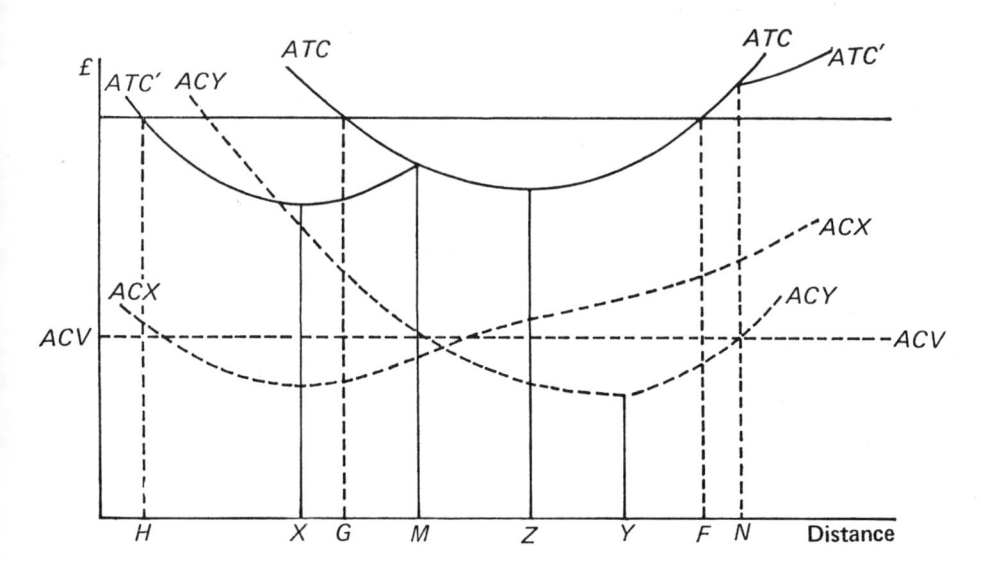

Figure 4.3

The influence of the replacement of an input with considerable locational cost by one whose locational cost is zero can be demonstrated in figure 4.3. *ATC* is the original space cost curve for a plant of given size for production of a good requiring two inputs, X^9 and *Y*, both of which vary considerably over space as shown by the curves *ACX* and *ACY*. The least cost location is *Z*. Factor *Y*, let us say it is coal, is very bulky and its cost increases steeply from source (*Y*) because of high transport costs. Now let us assume that electricity is made available to the area covered by the curve, and that either the transmission costs of the new factor *V* are zero or alternatively

[9] It is perhaps more realistic to call *X* a composite input, referring to all productive factors required other than *Y*

that the pricing policy of the new power is so arranged that the cost of electricity is the same at all locations, as shown by the horizontal line ACV. It is assumed that producers can substitute one form of energy for the other without incurring any additional costs. What will be the consequences of the availability of the new source of power? The new cost curve for power will follow the horizontal line ACV as far as M, then it will dip down to follow ACY to N. This will be reflected in a new space cost curve ATC' which follows the original (ATC) between M and N. Thus, the general effect of making available a substitutable input with zero (or low) locational cost alongside another input the costs of which vary considerably over space is to reduce total costs over a wider area, thereby broadening the spatial profitability margins from FG to FH. As can be seen in figure 4.3, the margin is extended in one direction only, as the cheapness of factor Y near its source (i.e. on the coalfield) leaves the original cost situation unaltered between M and N. A change in locational costs of this kind is likely to affect the least cost location as well as the margins. The least cost point shifts from Z to X, the source of factor X.

What are the virtues of the space cost curve approach compared with the more traditional analysis of the least cost location problem? It has the advantage of clear and simple geometrical representation in a form closely analogous to the tools used in standard microeconomic theory. Although this parallelism has its dangers[10] and it is easy to confuse the two curves, the techniques developed to deal with traditional cost curves are to some extent applicable to this type of treatment as well. Secondly, as we shall see, the space cost curve can be combined with diagrammatical analysis of spatial variations in demand if we relax the simplified assumption of constant demand everywhere. This provides a simple method of determining the profit-maximising location, and enables a direct comparison to be made of the maximum profit, least cost and sales maximising locations.

Thirdly, the space cost curve concept lends itself more readily to empirical application than the more abstract and formal Weberian

[10] For example, because the space cost curve is an iso-output curve the scope for a marginal cost/marginal revenue approach is extremely limited unless we use multi-dimensional curves dealing with variations in output as well as changes in location to solve the problems of optimum location and optimum output simultaneously

approach. It should be possible, given certain assumptions, to construct a space cost curve from actual data for a given output in an industry (say, the output equal to the capacity of an optimum sized plant). Since the locations tested would have to be limited in number, it may be necessary to assume that costs vary regularly with distance from the examined sites to allow us to join a series of discontinuous points into a continuous curve. Of course, because costs vary over an area rather than along a line the cartographical technique of iso-cost contours may be more appropriate than a linear curve. However, if it is assumed that urban sites are potentially the best locations for industry an approximation may be achieved by drawing a line through a number of representative towns and cities and plotting the variation in space costs along this line.

2 Demand cones: towards a space revenue curve

The Löschian demand cone

An obvious starting point to an analysis of demand factors in location is the derivation of a market area as outlined by Lösch. His preliminary assumptions greatly simplified the analysis. Firstly, he abstracted from costs by assuming no spatial differences in resources, including labour and capital, over a homogeneous plain. The assumption of no spatial variations in costs is valuable since it allows us to isolate the influence of demand alone. Secondly, by assuming uniform population densities and constant tastes and ignoring income differentials, he was able to assume that demand varied directly with distance and found it possible to obtain aggregate demand by summing the homogeneous demand curves of individuals. As will be seen, these assumptions leave the location of a firm trying to maximise demand indeterminate. Thirdly, he assumes that the firms faced with locational decisions are so geographically spread apart that their market areas and the demand available to them are not affected by the locations of rival firms. This is all very well if the problem being considered is that of a firm in a new industry or of a firm locating in a non-industrial region, but not very relevant to a firm deciding on a site in a highly developed industrial area where the locations and actions of existing firms in the industry may predominate as an influence on its decisions. However, for the more limited analysis of geometric representation of spatial demand variations, this assumption of no locational interdependence may be necessary since the complexity of actions and responses between competitors cannot adequately be incorporated in such a simplified framework.

Given these assumptions, the demand for a commodity is a direct function of its factory price, which is initially assumed to be given, and an inverse function of the transport costs required to carry the good over space. This is obvious. Unless demand curves are infinitely inelastic there are two ways in which by reducing its price a firm may increase its demand: by raising the demand of each individual consumer and by extending the boundary of its market area. The complications arise because the factory price is not usually independent of the firm's level of output and is consequently not determined independently from the level of demand. The influence of transport costs is also clear, for we have assumed away the difficulties arising from the fact that in a multi-commodity economy the relative prices of goods will vary from place to place with the result that the demand curve for a product will usually differ for consumers near the factory relative to those at a distance. In our oversimplified picture, the good in question has a maximum transport distance beyond which it cannot be sold. Distant consumers have to pay the factory price plus the freight cost involved in carrying the good to them,[11] and given that the demand curve of each consumer is the same they will obviously consume less than the individuals in close proximity to the factory site. As freight costs increase with distance, there will be a finite limit to the boundary of the market area, since the cumulative total of factory price plus freight will eventually reach a limit where the amount consumed by the individual at this distance is zero.

How the market area and the demand curve are obtained is clear from figure 4.4.[12] An individual demand curve is shown in figure 4.4a. If OA is the price at the factory which is located at A, then consumers living at A will purchase AB units. At a distance from A price will be higher than OA by the amount of freight and demand will consequently be lower. At C where freight costs $= AC$, no units at all will be sold. AC is the extreme sales radius of the plant. Total sales over the market area equal the volume of the cone obtained from rotating ABC on AB as an axis (figure 4.4b) multiplied by a

[11] We rule out the possibility of uniform delivered prices and other means of absorbing freight

[12] See Lösch, A. (1954) *The Economics of Location.* 105–8

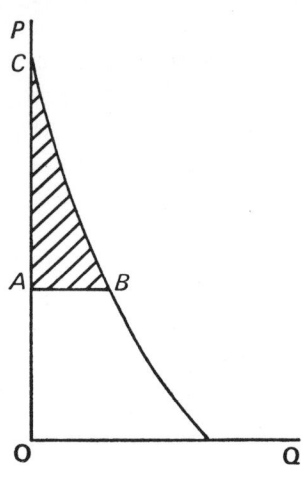

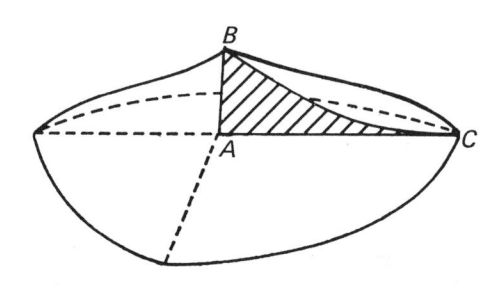

Figure 4.4

constant given by population density. The result is therefore total demand D at the factory price OA.

Algebraically, $$D = b \cdot \pi \int_O^R f(p+t) t \cdot dt$$

where D = total demand as a function of f.o.b. net mill price, p
$b = 2 \times$ population density of a square in which it costs 1 money unit to ship 1 unit of the good along one side
$d = f(p+t)$, individual demand as a function of price at place of consumption
p = f.o.b. net mill price
t = freight costs per unit from the factory to the consumer
R = maximum possible transport cost (AC).

The demand cone not only tells us what the level of demand will be as a function of the net mill price it obviously also shows how this demand is distributed over space. If the sales at each location are multiplied by the given factory price then we can plot the revenue earned by the firm at each point in space (aggregated together these separate spatial receipts equal the volume of the demand cone multiplied by the factory price).

The Löschian demand cone, however, provides little guide as to where a firm should locate to maximise demand. If, as Lösch assumed, costs are the same everywhere then, with the additional assumptions of evenly distributed population and homogeneous individual demand curves, the firm can locate anywhere. For a given factory price, provided there are no irregularities in transport costs between different areas, profits are the same at any location which the firm decides to choose, though once sited the firm's sales at that location will obviously be higher than at a distance (reflecting the fact that the demand cone simply shows the space distribution of demand for a given net mill price and a given structure of transport costs). The assumptions of the Löschian demand cone therefore make location indeterminate. If costs are allowed to vary over space, the plant will be located at the least-cost point and this point will also form the peak of the demand cone. But in this case cost factors not demand determine location.

A modified spatial demand cone

The trouble with the demand cone is that the assumptions made in deriving it far from highlighting the importance of spatial variations in demand assume most of them away. These limiting assumptions are uniform population density, homogeneous individual demand curves and the lack of spatial differences in transport rates.[13] An evenly distributed population rules out the probability that a major demand influence governing locational decisions is access to customers. For consumer goods industries[14] the size of the population within a commodity's market area can be a primary determinant of whether the firm locates at site A or B; with a uniform spatial costs assumption it is likely to be the most important single factor. The constant $b/2$ as a measure of population density used in Lösch's demand cone formula is unsatisfactory because although it enables the total population of the market area to be taken into account it does not weight this population according to distance from the plant site. If, for example, with a market area of 50 miles radius 80% of

---

[13] A further restrictive assumption is no locational interdependence, but in the analysis which follows this assumption will be retained

[14] Capital goods industries are likely on demand considerations alone to locate near firms in industries which buy their products. But if the purchasing industries are market-oriented the locational influences are virtually the same but one stage removed

the population lived within five miles of the factory the total demand would be, unless infinitely inelastic, much greater than under conditions of uniform population density. Thus, it may be inferred that a demand-determined locational choice would strongly favour population concentrations, that is, location in or near large towns and cities. But the size and the distribution of the population within the market area as a whole must also be taken into account. We must not only allow for the total population to which the firm has access but also estimate the influence of different population clusters within the market area by weighting them with distance, since nearer consumers will buy more than distant customers who pay higher prices because of transport costs. The population potential concept[15] will be useful for this purpose. Peaks in total revenue over space will tend to be points of high population potential. Population potential estimates can be used to help us locate the centre of the market area. In the Löschian demand cone function we must then adjust the population density coefficient ($b/2$) to take account of the higher population densities near the centre and the fact that near buyers require more weighting than distant buyers. The new coefficient will therefore be a weighted rather than a single average value and, because population will be denser near the factory site, will have a rather higher value than the unweighted coefficient.

Other refinements are desirable in order to develop the space revenue concept. Lösch's assumption of homogeneous individual demand curves is too restrictive. Although we can let the assumption of constant tastes pass, his assumption of constant incomes must be relaxed. Average incomes may vary widely among locations, and in the choice between market areas of similar population size higher income levels in one of the markets may govern the location decision. Given variations in income, Lösch's assumption of homogeneous demand curves makes sense only if the income elasticity of demand for the good in question is zero. The easiest way to accommodate spatial variations in income into the framework is to incorporate them in the population potential estimate by using the concept Gross

---

[15] See Chapter 2.10 and Stewart, J.Q. (1949) Empirical Mathematical Rules Concerning the Distribution and Equilibrium of Population. *The Geographical Review*, **37** 461–85; (1948) Demographic Gravitation: Evidence and Applications. *Sociometry*, **11** 31–8; (1950) The Development of Social Physics. *American Journal of Physics*, **18** 239–53; Potential of Population and its Relationship to Marketing in Cox, R. and Alderson, W. (edits) (1950) *Theory in Marketing*. 19–40

Economic Population Potential.[16] Treating the spatial influence of population and income together is more acceptable if the two variables are positively correlated. The degree of correlation should be high *within* regions since income levels and population density will both tend to vary positively with proximity to urban centres.

Transport costs influence how revenue varies over space by determining how fast, with a given demand curve, the amount bought by an individual consumer falls off with distance from the factory site. Measuring the sales radius of the spatial demand cone in distance units (rather than, as Lösch did, in transport costs) the higher the transport costs the steeper the gradient of the cone and the smaller the market area. The influence of transport costs on the shape and size of the cone will be determined by the nature of transport rates and by spatial differences in price elasticity of demand. Assuming substantial terminal costs and transport rates varying inversely with the length of the haul, the slope of the spatial demand cone will tend to start steeply from the factory site but flatten out considerably as the economies of long haul exert themselves. However, the tendency could be offset by spatial differences in elasticity of demand. For example, if demand near the site was completely price inelastic but became elastic at a distance (perhaps because of nearness to the boundaries of the market areas of other firms), then the gradient of the cone would probably be more regular. But unless transport rates varied dissimilarly with distance in different areas of the economy these considerations will have no independent effect on location.

On the other hand, *inter-regional* differences in transport rate structures may induce location on demand grounds in one region rather than another, at least for goods where freight charges are a high proportion of the market price. These inter-regional variations could arise for several reasons: topographical differences; imperfectly developed transport networks in some areas leading to roundabout freights and too many transhipment points; inter-regional variations in the degree of competition within the transport sector. Where transport costs are important for an industry firms will tend to locate in regions where transport rates are lower, because *ceteris paribus* minimisation of transport charges will enable demand to be

[16] Again see Chapter 2.10 above, and Warntz, W. (1959) *Toward a Geography of Price: A Study in Geo-Econometrics*, especially 30–42

expanded via an outwards extension of the market area. However, this factor may not help to pinpoint precisely the optimal demand location *within* the selected region. Low transport rates will mean a gently sloping spatial demand cone and therefore a slight locational shift in the vertex of the cone would result in only moderate losses in terms of revenue sacrificed. In regions with costly transport structures, on the other hand, the more necessary it will be to locate at the point where demand in close vicinity to the site is greatest, therefore the more likely is the location to be uniquely determined.

A final, and obvious, factor in the spatial demand cone is the factory price. Although factory price will not be determined independently from demand in conditions where costs vary with output, under our assumption here of abstracting from costs we may treat the net mill price wholly as an influence operating on demand and unaffected by it. A low price will clearly increase the quantity of output consumed and extend the market area, except under conditions of infinite inelasticity, but whether or not it raises total revenue depends on the elasticity of demand. However, there is not a single elasticity involved, since total receipts over space will depend on the elasticity of demand over the whole range of locations between the factory site and the boundary of the market area. Consumers at separate locations may have different demand curves of varying elasticity. Even if we assume a homogeneous demand curve common to all consumers its elasticity will vary over the length of the curve. For instance, such a demand curve may be very elastic within the range of prices likely to be set by the firm, but very inelastic at higher prices reflecting the possibility that distant customers who pay the factory prices plus the freight costs will not alter their purchases very much as the factory price is changed. In such circumstances a reduction in the factory price will tend to increase total revenue earned in the vicinity of the factory site considerably, offsetting the smaller loss in revenue earned at a distance (resulting from little expansion in purchases by distant consumers in response to the fall in price). Examples of this kind could be multiplied several fold. The important point is that any change in price, except under the strictly defined condition of homogeneous demand curves of unitary elasticity throughout their length, will alter the volume of the demand cone and may well have uneven effects on the revenue earned at different locations within the market area.

Having relaxed some of Lösch's restrictive assumptions we can now construct a representative modified spatial demand cone. In contrast to the Löschian cone, we shall here measure revenue earned at each location on the vertical axis and distance on the horizontal axis, and to simplify we will draw the cone in two dimensions, though it must be remembered that this is a cross-section of a three dimensional cone. Although the volume of the cone varies over space, drawing up a single cone does not show us the location where demand is maximised; it merely indicates that the vertex is the factory site and how, given this location, revenue varies at different points in the market area. Thus, we either arbitrarily assume the centre of the market area or, alternatively, we use one measure of high demand locations, say population potential, to pinpoint a potential site. The total revenue earned at the factory site and at all other locations between the site and the boundary of the market area where sales fall to zero depends upon several variables: (i) the f.o.b. factory price; (ii) the elasticity (within the relevant range) of the demand curves of all consumers within the market area; (iii) unit freight costs, particularly how these vary with the distance of the haul and whether transportation is possible in all directions radially from the site; (iv) factors differentiating the demand curves of consumers at separate locations, of which we have expressly considered average incomes and how these are distributed over space; (v) population density, and its distribution over space as indicated by measures of population potential.

A typical spatial demand cone reflecting some of these variables is shown in figure 4.5. This indicates the way in which revenue earned from sales with a given f.o.b. factory price falls off with distance from the factory site Z which we have assumed to be within a city. We have assumed no gross differences in the demand curves of consumers at separate locations,[17] and therefore the shape of the cone is primarily explained by population densities, the spatial distribution of average incomes and the characteristics of the transport rate structure (though we assume transportation possible in all directions). Although the revenue obtained at a single location is maximised at the factory site Z, it does not fall off very much in the surrounding zone AB. The high revenue obtained over this zone may be regarded as indicating that AB represents the boundaries of the city,

---

[17] Apart from the effect of differences in average incomes shifting the curves either to the left or to the right

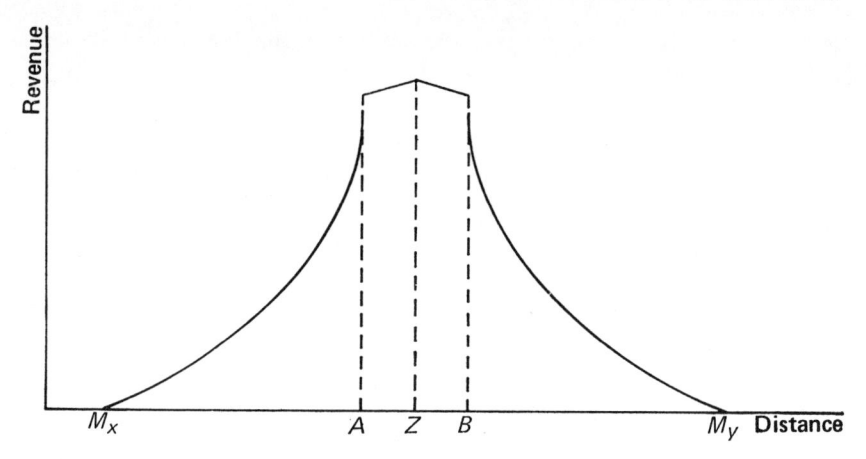

Figure 4.5

which is assumed too extensive to be represented by a point. This zone will have the highest population density found within the market area, average incomes are higher than in the surrounding (rural) hinterland, and if we assume that terminal costs are associated only with long distance transportation and that distribution of output within the city can be achieved cheaply and efficiently then demand within the zone AB is not reduced substantially by freight costs. Outside the zone AB revenue falls off sharply. This reflects declining population density and lower average incomes, but most of all it is explained by freight costs and their structure. High terminal costs drastically reduce demand in the area immediately surrounding the zone AB. With increasing distance, however, these terminal costs are spread over longer hauls and, in addition, unit freight costs per mile may fall because of other economies of longer hauls, so that the slopes of the sides of the cone decline with distance from the site Z. Ultimately, the addition of rising freight costs to the f.o.b. price will choke off demand at M_x and M_y. These points are the limits of the market area.

3 Space revenue, space costs and the profit maximising location

If we take a large number of possible sites within an area we can construct a spatial demand cone for each potential location. These cones will vary in volume depending on the demand accessibility of each site and will, if a sufficient number of sites are considered, overlap each other. The shape of any one cone may also vary

REGIONAL ECONOMICS

considerably from the others: the peaks of the cones will be of dissimilar heights due to marked variations in population and income potential between points over space, and the slopes of the cones will be affected by uneven population densities, the spatial distribution of income, differences in transport rates and in the degree of development of transport routes, dissimilar individual demand curves, and other factors.

However, the large number of overlapping, often irregularly shaped spatial demand cones which result from this procedure are too cumbersome for inquiry into the optimum location. It is clear, of course, that if the objective of the firm were to maximise revenue then the site associated with the spatial demand cone of the greatest volume is the optimal location. This point can be more easily observed if instead of setting down a set of overlapping cones we cumulate all the locational receipts emanating from given market area centres to yield the total revenue earned at each of these potential sites (=the aggregate of all receipts earned at each point within the market area). If we plot the total receipts earned at a very large number of locations over space we may construct a *space revenue curve*. This curve enables us to pick out the high demand and low demand locations, which represent the net effect of all the variables which mould the size and shape of the demand cones. Since access to numbers of consumers and their incomes is likely to be a major determinant of maximum demand locations, peaks in the space revenue curve are likely to occur within cities and large towns. If we consider a large area of space covering several regions there will probably be several peaks in the curve with, as with the space cost curve, possibilities of multiple solutions to the problem of the optimal location.

In figure 4.6 we have drawn a space revenue curve on the assumption of a given factory price, P, for a firm producing a given commodity.[18] It is too unrealistic to rule out the possibility of more than one high demand location so we have included three peaks (Z_1, Z_2, Z_3), each of which represents a site within a high income, high

[18] We could, of course, allow the factory price to be a variable subject to a lower limit set, say, by the firm's average costs. In this case, complete allowance could be made for spatial differences in the elasticity of demand and their effects on total receipts obtained at a given site. However, this introduces considerable complications into the derivation of the space revenue curve since average costs themselves are not constant in the face of variations in demand

THE OPTIMAL LOCATION OF THE FIRM

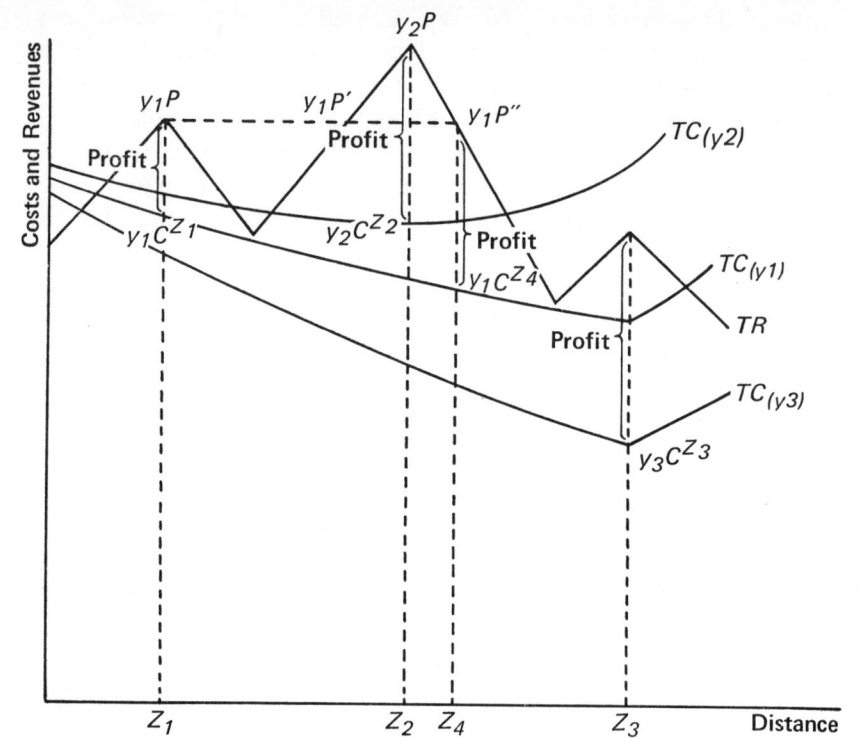

Figure 4.6

density city. We assume, for the purposes of simplification not realism, that revenue falls off with distance from each city down to some level between two cities where their influence in terms of income, population, etc., is equal. In this way, we ignore minor peaks in space revenue caused by pockets of high density population concentration such as smaller towns and villages. Again, we simplify to two dimensions; the space revenue surface itself would really be rather like a mountain range. The space revenue curve alone will permit us to obtain the maximum demand location. To find the profit maximising location, however, we need to compare space revenue with space costs. Since the space revenue curve is a total revenue curve[19] while the space cost curve developed earlier was formulated as an average cost curve, it is necessary to translate the

[19] The firm charges the same price at all locations therefore an average revenue curve would have no meaning

79

latter into total cost terms. This is a straightforward conversion since the space cost curve is an iso-output curve. The space total cost curve therefore follows exactly the same path as the average cost curve yielding the same least cost point multiplied by the quantity of output. However, simply because the space cost curve is an iso-output curve while the space revenue curve by its very nature indicates how revenue (sales, output) varies at different locations, we require (if we assume output = demand)[20] a separate space cost curve corresponding to each point (or points) of equal sales volume on the space revenue curve. In this case only three space cost curves need to be considered, those relating to the three peaks in the space revenue curve. These three space cost curves $TC(y_1)$, $TC(y_2)$ and $TC(y_3)$ correspond to the peaks in space revenue, y_1P, y_2P and y_3P. As in the previous section, we assume a unique least cost point on each space cost curve with production costs rising steadily with distance from the least cost site.[21] This least cost point may vary for different levels of output; thus in figure 4.6, Z_3 is the least cost location for plants with capacities y_1 and y_3, but for a larger plant of capacity y_2 the least cost site lies at Z_2 perhaps because of external economies available there (e.g. access to a large metropolitan labour pool). One obvious difference between the space average cost curve and the space total cost curve is that while economies of scale mean that the space average cost curve often shifts downwards with increasing output, the curves used here since they refer to total costs usually shift upwards as the scale of output increases.

In figure 4.6 profit is represented by the gap between total revenue and total costs on the appropriate space cost curve. Thus, at location Z_1, revenue $= y_1P$, cost $= y_1C^{z_1}$ and profits $= y_1(P - C^{z_1})$; at Z_2 revenue $= y_2P$, costs $= y_2C^{z_2}$ and profits $= y_2(P - C^{z_2})$; and at Z_3 revenue $= y_3P$, costs $= y_3C^{z_3}$ and profits $= y_3(P - C^{z_3})$. The revenue maximisation location is to be found at Z_2 since the maximum demand obtainable on the space revenue curve TR is y_2P. We can only identify the least cost location with respect to a plant of given capacity: as stated above Z_3 is the least cost point for outputs y_1 and y_3 whereas Z_2 is the least cost location for output y_2. The maximum profit location, however, is at Z_3 for a plant of capacity y_3, and this is the optimum plant size. The profit maximising location

---

[20] We ignore therefore production for inventories
[21] This assumption may easily be relaxed

differs therefore from the maximum demand location. However, if a site for a plant of capacity y_1 is being considered, neither the location Z_1 nor the least cost point Z_3 is the optimum site. Sales of y_1P are obtained not only at the first peak in the space revenue curve, but also on the slopes of the second peak at y_1P' and y_1P''. Since costs for producing output y_1 are lower at Z_4, profits are maximised at Z_4, where profits are $y_1(P'' - C^z{}_4)$, rather than at Z_1.

This approach to the problem of the profit maximising location is less abstract and probably less elegant than the traditional analyses of Lösch and others. On the other hand, its assumptions are more realistic. Although it gives rise to quite formidable data problems, it offers hope of empirical application.

4 Locational interdependence

A Introduction

A serious weakness in the above analysis is its neglect of locational interdependence. In effect, it assumed either monopoly conditions or that the industry concerned was new to the region (regions) under consideration. The locating firm had not to meet the problems resulting from the optimum site already being occupied and/or the danger of its market area at certain sites being nibbled away by nearby rival firms. If we take account of interdependence, however, we accept that there may be several firms in an industry within each region and that their location and the policies they pursue may affect the locational decision of an incoming firm. We must also consider that relocation of existing firms is feasible. In some cases, the net effect of these additional variables is to induce agglomeration; in other cases, dispersion is the most likely location pattern.

B Duopoly: the Hotelling case[22]

The essence of the locational interdependence approach can be illustrated with the duopoly situation first outlined by Hotelling. We make the following simplifying assumptions. Buyers, who each purchase one unit of the product in each time period, are uniformly

---

[22] The analysis stems from the classic article by Hotelling, H. (1929) Stability in Competition. *Economic Journal*, 39 41–57. For discussion and criticism see Lösch, A. (1954) *The Economics of Location*. 72–5; Chamberlin, E.H. (7th ed., 1956) *The Theory of Monopolistic Competition*. Appendix C, 260–5; Ferguson, C.E. (1966) *Microeconomic Theory*. 273–6; Greenhut, M.L. (1966) *Plant Location in Theory and Practice*. 38–40 and 141–3

distributed along a line of length, L.[23] There are two producers, A and B, producing a homogeneous product. Production, including material, costs are the same everywhere. Marginal costs for competitors are constant, and in fact we may assume not only that average and marginal costs are equal but that they are zero. The good produced is differentiated in the eyes of buyers only because of the locations of A and B. Each producer charges the same f.o.b. factory price to all buyers, but the price paid by each buyer differs because he has to go to the site and transport his purchases home at a cost of C per unit bought per distance carried, and transport costs are assumed to be the same over all the linear market. Demand for the product is infinitely inelastic. Relocation is possible, and is instantaneous and costless. The producers are willing to compete in price and location, and if permitted each producer is capable of supplying the whole market.

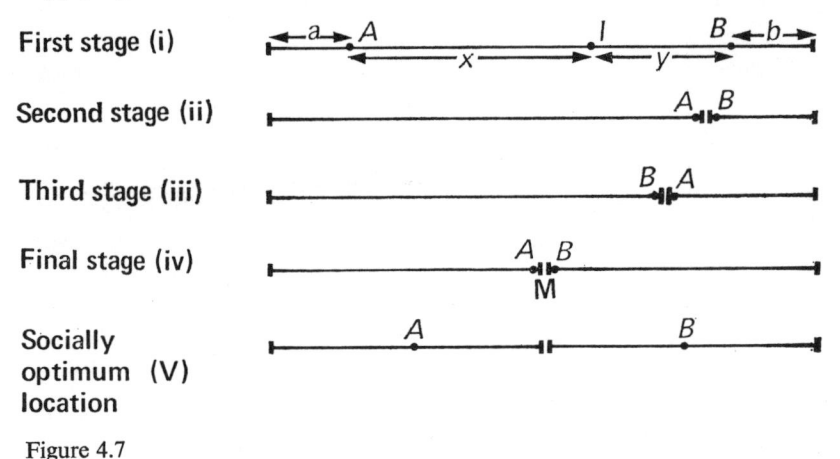

First stage (i)

Second stage (ii)

Third stage (iii)

Final stage (iv)

Socially optimum (V) location

Figure 4.7

In figure 4.7 (i) the two producers are located at points A and B along the line L. There are a buyers to the left of A and b buyers to the right of B, with $x+y$ buyers located between them. If one buyer lives in each unit of the line, L units in length, then total sales in each time period amount to $L = a + x + y + b$. We can allow the two producers some latitude in setting their prices subject to the proviso that each charges the same f.o.b. price to all buyers. But B, for

---

[23] The linear market assumption instead of an area market is for simplification purposes. The original Hotelling analysis was in terms of ice-cream sellers along a finite stretch of beach

example, never sets his price so high that the b buyers find it cheaper to buy from A. In setting his price, each producer assumes that of his rival fixed. Since products are identical to consumers, the market boundary between the two producers will be where delivered prices are equal.[24] Let A's price be P_A and B's price be P_B, set in such a way as to leave A with the 'sheltered' market a and B with the 'sheltered' market b. The $x+y$ buyers located between A and B will for any set of prices be divided by a point such as I. I is the location where the delivered prices are equal, thus where $P_A + C_x = P_B + C_y$. Because of the zero costs assumption, A's profit $= P_A(a+x)$ and B's profit $= P_B(b+y)$. Maximising these two profits always yields unique and determinate prices.

However, these locations are not equilibrium locations. Since the two producers are free to move, A has an incentive to move as far towards B as possible, thereby expanding the sheltered market to his left. Thus, as shown in figure 4.7 (ii) A will shift his site until he is next to B. B, however, has a similar incentive, and he maximises the number of consumers that he monopolises by hopping over A and locating the other side of him, thus taking over A's formerly sheltered market and leaving A with the market to his right only. This is seen in the third stage, figure 4.7 (iii). The 'hopping over' sequence will continue until the two producers are located beside each other at the centre of the market, M (as in figure 4.7 (iv)). M alone is the stable equilibrium location for both A and B, for if either producer located away from M it would pay the other to locate just on the side of him which ensured the relocating firm the largest market. The ultimate location M would, in fact, be achieved in the first place if one producer had entered the market prior to the other. Thus, if B was the initial firm it would locate at the centre of the market, M, where it could supply the entire market and minimise transport costs to consumers. Then if A invaded the market it would locate at the site closest to B, since any other location would decrease A's sheltered market.

At M, the location of the producers is therefore stable. Also, the prices set by the two producers will be equal, for if they were unequal the higher price producer could not guarantee his control over his

---

[24] This is the basic condition governing the economic law of market areas. See Fetter, F.A. (1923–4) The Economic Law of Market Areas. *Quarterly Journal of Economics*, **38** 520–9, and Hyson, C.D. and Hyson, W.P. (1950) The Economic Law of Market Areas. *Quarterly Journal of Economics*, **64** 319–27

'sheltered' market. Thus, the Hotelling case illustrates the tendency of firms to agglomerate. It is also notable that the median solution which results from price competition is not the solution which maximises social welfare. From the standpoint of the public interest, A and B should locate at the quartile points of the market as in figure 4.7 (v). The quartile locations minimise freight costs and consequently minimise delivered prices to consumers. The median location, on the other hand, involves maximum transport costs.

C Criticisms and extensions

Hotelling's analysis has been criticised on a number of grounds. He assumed that each firm acts as if its rival will not react. But if both producers choose symmetrical locations at the same time anywhere along the line and quote identical prices, neither producer would move towards the centre because he would realise that his rival would respond by jumping over him. Moreover, agglomeration only follows if the firms assume in fixing prices that the market has to be shared. A duopolist threatened by his rival moving towards him to corner a larger part of the stretch may retaliate by price cuts, possibly with the aim of crowding his competitor out of the market altogether. In the end, price competition will be best avoided by dispersion.

Furthermore, if we drop the assumption of completely inelastic demand the rationality of central location by duopolists no longer exists. With elastic demand curves transport costs are a limitation on sales. Central location by duopolists would maximise not minimise freight costs. The first and third quartiles are the most profitable sites because by minimising transport costs they maximise sales. Finally, Hotelling's results are altered if the assumption of a finite line is replaced by that of an endless stretch or that of a circle on a sphere. With an endless stretch, the duopolists would gain by moving apart until an area not supplied developed between them. With a circle, a relocation by one of the firms to a site next to the other would certainly increase his 'sheltered' part of the market, but since it would increase equally his rival's sheltered part agglomeration would serve no purpose.

A recent analysis by Devletoglou[25] argues that two sellers of the same commodity will be dispersed in equilibrium. He examines an

---

[25] Devletoglou, N.E. (1965) A Dissenting View of Duopoly and Spatial Competition. *Economica*, **32** 140-60

areal rather than a linear market, and assumes that population is evenly distributed. Clustering ensures that each seller will, at best, have potential access to all customers but is guaranteed the exclusive patronage of no one, while an inadequate dispersal means that neither seller can be sure that he will gain the allegiance of half the total customers at minimum cost. The key assumption in his analysis is that though consumers consistently behave so as to minimise travelling distance (i.e. transport costs) there is a constraint of indifference influencing their actions. Some positive minimum exists where the difference between the distance involved in patronising one seller or another is inconsequential. This assumption is compatible with the fact that most people recognise that to behave like economic robots involves substantial material and psychic costs. This assumption manifests itself as discontinuity in utility functions. It implies that customers will not change their allegiance in order to reduce marginally their transport costs; consequently, sellers will not necessarily gain by making marginal jumps in their location. Other factors reinforcing a dispersal tendency stressed by Devletoglou include the improbability of zero price and income elasticities of demand, the possibility that sales for the industry are likely to vary as the two firms change their locations, and the realisation by a seller contemplating a change in location that his rival may adjust symmetrically.

The assumption of two producers is also restrictive; if three or more producers are allowed the conclusions are different. Hotelling himself argued that provided demand was infinitely inelastic more than two producers would tend to cluster in the same way as two, but he was wrong. With three producers, concentration by all three is not possible as an equilibrium position because the firm caught in the middle would always gain by moving to the outer edge of the group, and a sequence of moves of this kind, always by the man in the middle, disperses the group. Chamberlin argued that two firms would locate at the quartiles with the third somewhere between them. In this case if either of the outside firms moved towards the centre in an attempt to increase its market it would be replaced by the middle man.

Lerner and Singer[26] suggest, assuming that each competitor acts

---

[26] Lerner, A.P. and Singer, H.W. (1939) Some Notes on Duopoly and Spatial Competition. *Journal of Political Economy*, **45** 145–86 but especially 176–9

on the presumption that the location of the others are fixed, that there will be no equilibrium solution but instead complete instability in location. The escape by the middle firm from imprisonment on either side by the other two will continue, in their view, until two firms are located at one quartile and the third is at the other. The middle man has now no incentive to go outside since he supplies a quarter of the market from his inside position, just as he would if he moved outside. However, this is not equilibrium. The sole occupant of the other quartile will move closer to the other two firms gaining control of up to three-quarters of the market instead of one-half. This again provides an inducement to the middle firm to jump outside again, and the instability continues. This analysis is, however, unsatisfactory although consistent if we keep the assumption that each firm acts on the understanding that the location of his rivals is fixed. But the point is that after a bout of relocating the firms are almost certain to cease holding this view. When this happens, the lucky firm having a quartile location, and hence half the market, to itself is not going to be greedy and risk disturbing the equilibrium by trying to obtain three-quarters of the market. He will realise that the middle firm will not allow itself to be squeezed out.

The Chamberlin assessment of two firms at the first and third quartile with the third somewhere between them (possibly at a site next to one of the others as in the Lerner–Singer quasi-equilibrium case) again illustrates the possibility of divergence between the competitive solution and that which is optimal from the point of view of consumers. With quartile locations no buyer has to transport his purchases more than a quarter of the length of the line. But the ideal solution for consumers is for the three firms to locate at the first sextile, the centre and the fifth sextile. In such a case no purchase needs to be carried more than one-sixth the length of the line. Although this solution will not result under the Hotelling assumptions, it is quite likely if these assumptions are relaxed. For instance, if marginal costs are not zero but high, if transport costs are heavy, if demand is highly elastic rather than infinitely inelastic and the firms are willing to discriminate against nearby consumers by charging higher f.o.b. prices as freight charges fall, then sextile sites may be more profitable than quartile locations.

Where there are more than three producers, they may either tend to disperse or to cluster in pairs, but any group of three or more will be broken up by the firms trapped in the centre seeking a more profitable location. Whether complete dispersion or clustering of pairs develops depends on the existing location pattern as new firms enter the market. Consider, for instance, the entry of a fourth firm to the market. If the three firms already in the market were dispersed, the final result of the new firm's entry would be a perpetuation of the dispersed pattern. But if two of the firms were located at the first quartile with the third firm sited at the third quartile, the fourth firm would also locate at the third quartile, resulting in clustering by pairs. Similar analysis can be applied to n firms. If L = the length of the line, for n firms the distance between the last seller at either end and the end of the line can never exceed L/n (or with an odd number, $L/(n+1)$). Thus, the distance a commodity has to be transported to any buyer can never exceed L/n. However, this is twice the distance resulting from an ideal dispersion, where it could not exceed $L/2n$. With nine firms, for instance, the competitive solution would be either location at intervals of $\frac{1}{10}, \frac{2}{10} \cdots \frac{9}{10}$ of the line or a clustering of pairs type of dispersion. The optimal distribution would be at intervals of $\frac{1}{18}, \frac{3}{18} \cdots \frac{17}{18}$. The larger the number of firms involved, the more likely is the actual dispersion to approximate to the ideal. Finally, as in the three firm case, where demand is highly elastic and/or freight charges are costly and/or marginal costs are high, an ideal dispersion will result.

D General considerations in locational interdependence: a summary
Although the Hotelling case presents only a highly simplified illustration of the locational interdependence problem it serves to emphasise the fact that in making a locational decision a firm has to take into account in estimating demand potential the existence of other firms in the industry, their locations and their possible responses to actions taken by the incoming firm. The analysis above allowed for a large number of locational shifts the feasibility of which depended on the unrealistic assumption, in most circumstances, that producers were free to move their locations instantaneously and without costs. But even if we assume that plants are completely immobile and can be relocated only when they wear out and need replacement, locational choices still have to take account of interdependence between the incoming and the existing firms in the industry. Our aim here is to give a brief summary of some of the main factors in locational interdependence that influence whether firms will tend to agglomerate

or disperse.[27] Some of these influences have already been mentioned in the previous section in the criticism of the Hotelling analysis.

As is clear from the discussion above, the elasticity of demand curves is a critical factor in locational interdependence. The more inelastic the demand for an industry's product the greater is the tendency to concentrate; conversely, the more elastic are demand curves the greater the probability of perfect dispersion. Where demand is elastic the need to minimise freight costs becomes more important in seeking the profit-maximising location, and this need will tend to result in a dispersed location pattern. For example, under conditions of elastic demand it might even pay a monopolist to set up two plants at quartile locations rather than to operate a single plant at the centre. Secondly, the relationship between the freight rate and the selling price will affect the tendency to concentration or dispersion. The lower the freight rate, the greater the tendency of firms to agglomerate, and vice versa. This is obvious. Costly freight charges will severely limit the distance over which goods can be sold. If firms hope to maximise sales they must disperse.

Once the assumption of zero marginal costs is dropped, the shape of the marginal cost curve influences the tendency to disperse or to agglomerate. If marginal costs are decreasing over the relevant ranges of output and a f.o.b. factory pricing system is adopted, adding freight cost to the marginal cost curve causes a large increase in the net mill price (thus, freight absorption is slight). Why does this happen? With falling marginal costs, adding freight costs to marginal costs results in an intersection of marginal revenue and the marginal cost plus freight curve at a high point on the latter curve. This means a high factory price. In consequence, sales to consumers at the market area boundaries are, if there are any at all, very low. This fact encourages dispersion. The prediction is not so clear when marginal costs are rising. In this case, adding freight cost to marginal cost does not increase the factory price as much, and the quite heavy absorption of freight cost in price points to a relatively wide market area. The advantages accruing to firms from dispersion are much more uncertain, and this very uncertainty is conducive to concentration.

If instead of assuming that costs of production are equal at all

[27] This section benefits considerably from a study of Greenhut, *op. cit.*, especially Chapter II, 23–83, Chapter VI, 140–62 and 257–63

locations, we take cognisance of the fact that costs will be unequal between different sites, not only do we introduce more realism but we affect the conditions governing concentration or dispersion. Let us assume that a firm locates at the centre of the market which is also the least cost location. Production costs are heavier at other locations. Where will other firms locate? If the higher production costs at alternative sites exceed the transport savings to nearby market segments gained from being at such sites, no location other than the least cost site is possible. If, however, plants located at the least cost site leave some of the spatial market untapped, then distant high cost locations are feasible, since freight charges will protect producers at these sites from competition by least cost producers. The untapped portions of the market will tend to be small, and therefore these higher cost locations are practicable only for small plants. In an industry characterised by large firms and wide spatial variations in costs, these firms will often agglomerate at or near the least cost location.

Moreover, where costs are unequal the situation becomes characterised by uncertainty. Producers have only imperfect knowledge about each other's costs. The possibilities of price competition increase, and the rivalry from substitutable products becomes more of a threat than formerly. The greater uncertainty following from unequal costs means that the measurement of gains and losses involved in locating at, say, a quartile point becomes much less precise. In a duopoly situation, a firm will only go directly to the quartile site if he is convinced that his rival will locate symmetrically. The losses involved in locating at a high cost site, that is, the higher production costs themselves, are certain; the gains, such as an anticipated increase in sales, are nebulous and unclear. On the other hand, little is lost and something may be gained by locating at the central least cost site. Once again, these considerations weigh more heavily for a large plant than for a small firm which may find itself a small niche on the fringe of the spatial market. Thus, it may be concluded that spatial differences in production costs favour concentration of producers at one least cost centre, or at a few centres, rather than dispersal over the market.

Other factors which on the whole provide support for the concentration hypothesis may be treated cursorily. Uncertainty about competitors' location policies may make a firm unwilling to risk a site at a distance from the centre of the market area. Secondly, if the reasons for a least cost location are general rather than specific to a particular industry, firms producing heterogeneous goods may cluster at such a point. If some of these products are substitutable for those of the locating firm, it is much more likely to locate at the same site for if it located at a distance this would mean higher delivered prices in the vicinity of the sites occupied by the firms producing the substitutes, and hence additional losses resulting from a high cross-elasticity of demand in the area. Thirdly, the Hotelling type of analysis is invariably based on an assumption of uniform population distribution. If we accept that population distribution is in fact uneven, then high density population centres have because of their demand potential special appeal as selling locations. This factor will induce firms to concentrate there.

Fourthly, personal contacts between firms and their customers, suppliers and financiers will lessen the importance attached to location of rivals; this may result in either concentration or dispersion according to circumstances. Finally, alternative pricing systems to that of f.o.b. net-mill pricing assumed throughout the above discussion have their impact on agglomeration or dispersal tendencies without distorting beyond recognition the other basic forces in locational interdependence. With non-discriminatory prices, there is an advantage in being nearer to certain consumers than one's competitors. But uniform delivered pricing policies, particularly attractive to industries with heavy fixed costs and facing severe competition near market area boundaries, reduce the significance of buyers' locations to some extent. Under such a system firms are much more likely to locate on cost grounds leading, where there is a location with significantly lower costs than alternatives, to agglomeration. Spatial price discrimination against near consumers, uniform delivered prices and single basing-point pricing systems[28] all, to a greater or lesser extent, discourage dispersion by diminishing the importance of distance. The location pattern may therefore depend in part upon the type of pricing policy pursued.

5 Alternatives to profit maximisation as a locational objective

The preceding analysis has been based on the assumption that the

[28] Multiple basing-point systems are of course more decentralising in their effect than the single basing-point system. They therefore permit greater dispersion

THE OPTIMAL LOCATION OF THE FIRM

primary objective of firms is to maximise profits. Particularly in recent years, it has become widely recognised that firms may pursue objectives other than profit maximisation. For reasons outlined below, the latter may be less appropriate than other goals when it comes to location decision-making. The evolution of location theory has followed a course which has only made it possible to develop a fully-fledged profit maximisation model in the post war period. The first stage in the development of locational analysis was to argue that the optimal location was at the site that minimised transport costs, on the grounds that these were the most obvious costs to vary over space. It was later realised that many other costs, particularly wages, site costs and raw material costs other than the freight charges on them, differed substantially at alternative sites. This gave rise to location theories that minimised total costs. However, total cost minimisation is deficient as a basis for location because it neglects spatial variations in demand. The next stage was, therefore, to construct a model that determined the profit-maximising location. This was the Löschian approach, but as argued above Lösch's analysis had severe limitations in this respect. He adopted uniformity assumptions which, in effect, abstracted from spatial cost differences, and these assumptions also led him to ignore some of the critical aspects of spatial variations in demand. We have constructed a profit-maximising theory of location earlier in this chapter which requires less restrictive and more realistic assumptions, and an alternative formulation has been put forward by Greenhut.[29]

Even so, profit-maximising location theories still require many simplifying assumptions. The location decision lends itself more than most managerial decisions to interpretation in terms of 'psychic income' influences and other personal factors which are not *automatically* consistent with notions of economic rationality. Moreover, theories based on alternative assumptions to profit maximisation may provide a superior explanation of business behaviour in the sense that they may be more compatible with empirical observations on location decisions. Of the many possible sets of assumptions those required by sales maximisation and 'satisficing' theories seem quite appropriate to location analysis. Thus, just at a time when location theory had developed to where it was possible to construct

---

[29] Greenhut, M.L. (1956) *Plant Location: In Theory and Practice*, especially 263–9

a concrete profit-maximising model, microeconomic theorists in general were beginning to display grave doubts about the value of profit maximisation as a rationale for entrepreneurial behaviour.

Traditional location theory has many limitations which, if account is taken of them, reduce the value of profit maximisation as a basic assumption.[30] In the first place, the theory usually assumes that each plant produces a single product. But multi-product plants are increasingly prevalent in an advanced industrial economy. Possible variations in 'product mix' ought to be considered since the best location for the production of one good in a firm's range is not necessarily the best for all its products. Unless the 'product mix' is fixed by technological considerations, future changes in the 'mix' because of the changing structure of demand may be impossible to predict. In such a situation, the profit-maximising location may change considerably over time, and decisions based on the present may turn out incorrect in the long run.

This, of course, is merely one aspect of a more general problem – the uncertainty of the future. Technical change, variations in input costs, demand for final output and the institutional framework (e.g. the fiscal system) will all tend to vary over time, and not necessarily in a predictable manner. Location decisions based on present data and/or on assumptions that the present can be extrapolated into the future will be unlikely to maximise profits in the long run. New theoretical advances could attempt to formulate a dynamic profit maximisation model, based on estimation of the costs and benefits of alternative decisions in the light of the probabilities of different future courses of events. But it is unlikely that many firms will make sophisticated calculations in conjunction with crystal-gazing. It is much more probable that firms, in full recognition of the unpredictability of future changes in spatial costs and prices and the difficulties of measuring external economies, will not go to extreme lengths to find the most profitable location, but instead will opt for a location that seems viable in the long run and rely on increasing efficiency in other respects to raise their profitability.

Moreover, as far as the relocation of existing plants is concerned, profit maximisation in conditions of uncertainty is a poor criterion.

---

[30] There are, of course, other objectives to profit maximisation independent of location factors, such as the probability that technical and institutional considerations may prevent the marginal adjustments that profit maximisation demands

Firms are not free to move instantaneously and without incurring costs. If the profit maximisation principle is adhered to, relocation costs must be accounted for in total costs. But relocation costs, involving the scrapping of an existing plant and the erection of a new one, will normally be very heavy, and can only be recuperated over a long period. Managers will need to feel certain of the long-term advantages of a new site before deciding to relocate, for transition costs will have to be recovered from the difference in profits between the new site and the old. The more uncertain the future, the less existing plants are likely to relocate.

Even if changes in production methods, transport costs, consumer tastes and demand could be predicted with complete certainty, time elements would still pose a problem. In dynamic analysis, there is no single optimal profit-maximising location, since the optimal location depends on the time preference of firms, which may vary from one set of decision-takers to another. Each firm faces the choice of whether to try for early profits or for larger later ones. Both alternatives may be rational, and may result in quite different location decisions. Thus, in a dynamic analysis the time period over which profits are to be maximised must be clearly stated.

Firms may also differ in the importance they attach to the security motive. Entrepreneurs may decide not to locate at the theoretically optimal location if it is new for industrial enterprise because of greater risks. It may be much safer to locate at existing industrial centres where costs of error are lower than at isolated sites, because information can be gained from the experience of existing firms. This may help to explain why industrial agglomeration tendencies are more common than dispersion. Clearly, risk premiums must enter into revenue-cost calculations, but if the risk premium varies from firm to firm then the profit-maximising location for a plant of a given scale for one firm may not maximise profits for another.

Simon has argued that managers recognise the complexity of calculations required and imperfections of data used in any optimality calculation, and for this reason make no attempt to maximise profits, or indeed anything else.[31] Moreover, it is widely believed that non-economic considerations help to determine location

---

[31] Simon, H.A. (1959) Theories of Decision Making in Economics. *American Economic Review,* **49**

decisions. The assumption of economic rationality may be reasonable for most managerial decisions – for instance, all firms will tend to prefer high profits to low profits – but is not necessarily justifiable when applied to the location decision. It is an empirically tested fact that many firms prefer to be sited in Region A rather than Region B, or near a given city rather than at an isolated rural location, regardless of the congestion costs incurred and no matter where the theoretically optimal site is to be found. Space preference is an undeniable fact of life. It may vary from firm to firm, but broadly speaking the majority of industrialists will prefer to concentrate at established industrial centres even if production costs are higher than at alternative sites with few market access disadvantages.

Moreover, empirical studies suggest that personal considerations may be important in the location decision. An entrepreneur may obtain non-pecuniary satisfaction from working and living in a particular area, and may locate his plant there if the 'psychic income' derived from the site outweighs the profits sacrificed through not locating at the maximum profit point. Apart from environmental preferences, an entrepreneur may wish his firm to remain small enough for him to retain control and a psychic income element may be related to the size of plant. The scale of operation chosen may be below that which maximises long-run profits, and this possibility may have locational significance since the optimal site may vary for plants of different size. If psychic income is included as a locational factor, and accepting that the difficulties of assigning a monetary value to psychic income are insuperable, then in order to retain the maximisation principle we must argue that industrialists locate to maximise satisfactions not profits.

Another fact of observation is the tendency in an advanced industrial economy for market orientation to be the dominant feature of most location decisions. Since this factor seems to prevail even in cases where much lower production costs (including transport costs on finished goods) exist at distant sites, it casts some doubt on the relevance of the profit maximisation criterion. It is just possible that persistent market orientation for industries with marked cost differentials at alternative sites could be made compatible with profit maximisation on the grounds that access to and direct contact with markets is a vital influence in a dynamic economy for profit growth in the long run. But market orientation may be more easily explained by the hypothesis that firms pursue a different objective, the maximisation of revenue. Short-run revenue maximisation may be consistent with long-run profit maximisation,[32] but this need not be the case.

This leads us on to consider alternative objectives for decision-making to the traditional emphasis on maximising profits. This takes us from the area of normative prescriptions into a field where it is regarded as very important to explain how business firms actually behave, in other words, into the realm of behavioural theory.[33] Although there are many possible objectives for a firm (such as profit maximisation, sales maximisation and cost minimisation), an enterprise cannot pursue multiple goals at the same time. It must either compromise amongst goals or decide upon one. Apart from an overall objective, in regard to the specific spheres in which managers are required to make decisions, Cohen and Cyert have pointed out that a firm probably has at least five goals, relating to production, inventories, sales, market share and profit. From the locational standpoint, different sites may be optimal depending on which goal is given priority. If the production goal is dominant, for instance, a firm may prefer a location which offers proximity to raw material supplies or which can draw upon a considerable labour pool of the desired quality. This may conflict with the location that is best for fulfilling the sales goal or the market share goal. If these latter goals are uppermost, firms may choose the location which is nearest to large population centres or if the product is an intermediate good they may select sites next door to their customers' plants. These contradictions will have to be resolved by an ordering of the goals. Here, however, we shall limit comment to overall objectives, and in particular to two hypotheses which appear to have great relevance to location analysis in the sense that they make it easier to understand many of the location decisions which are taken in the real world. These are: firstly, that firms choose production

---

[32] Baumol, W.J. (2nd ed., 1967) *Business Behaviour, Value and Growth*. 52, is now somewhat sceptical on this point

[33] Apart from Baumol, *ibid.*, and Simon, *loc. cit.*, important references include Cyert, R.M. and March, J.G. (1963) *A Behavioural Theory of the Firm*; Cohen, K.J. and Cyert, R.M. (1965) *Theory of the Firm: Resource Allocation in a Market Economy* and Baumol, W.J. (2nd ed., 1965) *Economic Theory and Operations Analysis*, Ch. 13. None of these sources explicitly considers location decisions, but their hypotheses can easily be adapted to location theory

sites that maximise revenue; or, alternatively, that concrete location decisions are explained much better in terms of 'satisficing' behaviour than by profit maximisation.

How reasonable is revenue maximisation as a criterion for locational choice? If we abstract from cost differences as, in effect, Lösch did, then revenue maximisation is equivalent to profit maximisation. This follows from the identity: profit = revenue − costs. But if production costs vary, the results of the application of the two principles will be different. The factors usually held responsible for explaining why sales maximisation may be a firm's dominant goal are as valid in the space economy as in an assumed spaceless economy. These include: aspects of a firm's competitive position such as pressure to preserve market leadership; managerial salaries and promotion prospects may be related more to size than to profitability; the market share may be accepted as the main indicator of a firm's success, at least in oligopolistic markets, and the highest market share may be a matter of prestige.

The implementation of the revenue maximisation principle, however, will vary between situations where location is the primary variable and situations where location is held fixed. In the latter case, if a firm aims to maximise short-run revenue then, with a given scale of plant, it will produce that level of output which will yield the greatest money revenue. This output will correspond to the peak of the total revenue curve, where marginal revenue = 0. Normally, the pursuit of this objective will be subject to a profit constraint which may be determined arbitrarily but is more likely to be governed by considerations of the capital market, i.e. the profit level that will satisfy shareholders and enable the firm to obtain its external capital requirements in the future. It will be necessary for the firm to identify its total cost curve as well as total revenue if the profit constraint is to operate. The sales-maximising output will still be at the peak of the total revenue curve provided that the gap between total revenue and total costs is not less than the minimum profit level. If this condition is not satisfied, the optimal output will be below the peak in total revenue, where the gap between revenue and cost is equal to the required profit.

In a locational context this procedure, which requires a firm to estimate its total revenue and total costs at all feasible levels of output, cannot be followed. When the locational decision has to be faced, a firm will not have had the experience of operation which simplifies identification of total costs and revenues.[34] Its attempts to estimate these costs and revenues will therefore be subject to greater degrees of error. Moreover, since various sites will be under consideration, costs and revenues would need to be estimated at each site. An additional complication stems from the fact that the time horizon relevant to a location decision is very long because of heavy relocation costs. This means that in site selection the relevant objective will have to be long-run rather than short-run sales maximisation. The scale of plant will have to be considered as a variable rather than taken as given. A firm whose primary goal is sales maximisation obviously intends to expand, and the estimation procedure would have to take account of revenues and costs at each location of plants larger than the one initially to be established. These additional variables rule out the precise calculations which may be possible for a firm's decision makers when its location is fixed and the plant size is given.

Nevertheless, it is still practicable for a firm to retain the goal of long-run revenue maximisation when it makes its choice of location, provided it is accepted that the basis on which the decision is taken will be much more rough and ready than is possible in the static, spaceless model. If any attempts are made to estimate total costs and revenues (and profits, in order to see whether or not a profit constraint can be met), these will be used as supplementary data rather than the main criteria for the decision. The firm will locate at that site which offers the maximum long-run growth of sales at a 'reasonable' profit (which may be defined in terms of the profitability of other firms in the industry and/or be dictated by capital market considerations). Isolated locations will be ruled out immediately, regardless of any potential cost advantages, because distance hampers contact with the market, and because the danger of future increases in freight charges on finished goods (whether absorbed by the firm or paid by customers) may interfere with the long-run sales maximisation objective. Knowledge of the market, including the supply of market research information and close personal contacts with the market, may be one of the most vital determinants of potential sales expansion. Firms pursuing this goal will consider only market-oriented sites, except in cases where there is another

[34] Even if the firm is not newly established but is relocating from another site it will clearly not have had the benefits of experience at the new sites under consideration

powerful locational lever such as control of an important raw material source, or where there are heavy transport costs on raw materials and production results in considerable weight loss. However, the existence of a profit constraint will inhibit firms from choosing automatically the site which offers the greatest market access. Of the sites under consideration those with very high production costs will be excluded on the grounds that they may fail, if not now possibly in the future, to satisfy the profit constraint. The desire to avoid high cost sites explains why new plants will not normally locate at or near a city centre where, even if land is available, site costs and congestion costs are heavy. Instead, the firm will choose the most favourable location from the demand point of view once the high cost sites have been rejected. For consumer goods industries, the optimal site will tend to be found near to, but not at the core of, a large population centre.

Another consideration for a revenue-maximising firm arises from the fact that given a long-run time horizon the scale of plant is a variable. The chosen location will therefore need to offer scope for extending the plant, and for this reason room for potential site extension will also act as a constraint on the choice of the maximum market-oriented location. This analysis has been phrased in generalised terms, but it would not be too difficult to construct a determinate model. The advantage of the sales-maximisation hypothesis as a locational objective is that it explains the strong observable tendency for most modern industry, other than basic industry tied to raw material sources, to be market-oriented in the absence of industrial development controls.

As an alternative, there is much to be said for the hypothesis that firms do not attempt to maximise anything. Indeed, when competition is very imperfect (and Greenhut has argued persuasively that oligopoly is the characteristic spatial market[35]), maximising can be a very ambiguous goal. The reason is that the optimal course of action for one firm depends on the actions of other firms, as the earlier analysis on locational interdependence shows. In oligopolistic situations, of course, each firm can influence the market by its behaviour so that a behavioural theory is not only especially applicable but is necessary in order to understand how such markets operate. If firms reject maximisation criteria because of lack of data

---

[35] See Greenhut, M.L. (1963) *Microeconomics and the Space Economy*

and the uncertainty of what will happen in the future (due to lack of faith in forecasting and recognition of the interdependence of the decisions taken by different organisations), they may choose more limited objectives. Simon has suggested that they may set some minimal standards of achievement which they expect will ensure the firm's long-run viability and achieve a reasonable level of profits. If these standards are consistently exceeded, then the firm's goals may be revised by a raising of the standard; conversely, if the firm falls below the set standard goals may be revised downwards. Firms which are happy to aim at limited objectives are said to 'satisfice'. The behaviourists believe that 'satisficing' explains how firms really act.

With regard to the location decision, the implications of 'satisficing' are fairly obvious. Firms will avoid risky locations particularly in relatively non-industrialised areas; they will also tend to avoid sites which involve high congestion costs even if a precise calculation might reveal that such sites have market potential high enough to offset these disadvantages. They will tend to select sites which offer a safe location, preferring, say, centres of industrial agglomeration to dispersed locations. Broadly speaking, they will choose sites where future cost increases are not expected to rise above an assumed level (hence their avoidance of locations with increasing congestion costs where the rate of increase may be highly conjectural) and where minimum levels of sales are guaranteed, provided that they believe that a satisfactory profit level can be earned at such sites. Critics of the 'satisficing' hypothesis may argue that locations meeting these requirements may be difficult to select without going through the rational calculations called for if firms pursued maximising goals. This objection is not very convincing. Provided the organisation is confining itself to locational choices *within* a region[36] and the industry to be entered has sound secular demand prospects, likely locations almost suggest themselves. They tend to be found near existing or planned transport routes and/or near raw material sources or labour pools and/or near nodal points and major population centres. Having ruled out the highly congested core sites, the managers may decide on one of the list of possible locations on personal grounds, such as strong environmental preferences.

[36] The 'satisficing' firm is most unlikely to attempt inter-regional cost comparisons

The weakness of 'satisficing' as a hypothesis relevant to location theory is that it results in indeterminacy in location, a fact which severely limits the chances of constructing an operational model. Its advantage is that such a theory can take into account 'psychic income' which in addition to monetary rewards is considered an important element in the location decision. There is no doubt that by manipulating the concept of psychic income, 'satisficing' behaviour can be made compatible with maximisation criteria. If an entrepreneur (or a group of managers) balance a loss of profits against an increase in psychic income, the notion of 'satisficing' can be translated into the hypothesis that managers maximise utility or satisfaction. However, a utility-maximising theory is no more operational than the original satisficing theory.

Despite its operational limitations, 'satisficing' hypotheses have the compensating advantage that they offer a rational *a priori* explanation of location decision-making. In particular, they enable us to accommodate the environmental preferences, such as access to the metropolis or to a favoured cultural and social milieu, which are widely regarded as influencing managerial decisions in preferring sites in particular regions even in the face of evidence of lower costs and higher potential profitability elsewhere. 'Satisficing' also helps to explain why new entrants to an industry, especially where plant size is relatively small, more often than not set up business in the areas where the founders live rather than seeking out more profitable locations. Above all, the hypothesis is consistent with the evidence of considerable locational inertia in the modern industrial economy and with the reluctance of established firms to relocate even if they are offered large monetary incentives or if their expansion plans are held back by negative controls on new industrial development.

Chapter 5
The general theory of location

1 Obstacles to a general theory

The locational problem as it faces the individual firm in an industry is much less complex than general location theory which is concerned with all economic activities in space and needs to explain production locations and inter-regional flows of inputs and commodities simultaneously. As yet, no fully satisfactory general theory of location has been developed. It is not difficult to outline some of the main factors affecting spatial economic activity and to demonstrate their influence in a broad unsystematic fashion, but such an approach fails to develop any rules for explaining the structure of the space economy. One of the main troubles is that the simplest methodology for development of a determinate theory is that of general equilibrium analysis, yet the concept of general equilibrium is not very appropriate to an understanding of the geographic basis of production, consumption and trade. Simon has argued that: 'Economics has been moving steadily into new areas where the power of the classical equilibrium model has never been demonstrated, and where its adequacy must be considered anew. In these areas the complexity and instability of his environment becomes a central feature of the choices that economic man faces.'[1] A meaningful general location theory must be dynamic rather than static, since one of its main purposes will be to explain the impact of changes in techniques, transport costs, income levels and tastes, etc., on locational patterns of consumption and production. The addition of the time dimension to the already substantial complications arising from considering spatial aspects of production problems multiplies the range of possibilities several-fold. The increase in complexity and

[1] Simon, H.A. (1959) Theories of Decision Making in Economics. *American Economic Review*, **49**

uncertainty is not easily made consistent with the notion of rational decision-taking tending towards an equilibrium.

Even if some kind of equilibrium was assumed to exist, it would be difficult to predict the consequences of a disturbance of that equilibrium. If marginalist assumptions are made, each disturbance will give rise to a chain reaction of locational readjustments throughout the space economy. Not only do continuous marginal readjustments conflict with empirical observation, but these readjustments take time because space presents a barrier to the transmission of economic information. Before the repercussions of one autonomous disturbance have worked themselves out, other disturbances originating at different locations are likely to have come into play. At any given time, the situation may be more disequilibrating than equilibrating. If, more realistically, we allow for immobilities, discontinuities and frictions in space, it becomes necessary to make a distinction between disturbances that are too small to involve locational adjustments and those that have sufficient impact to alter locational patterns. A model capable of doing this requires great precision in setting up its assumptions and specifying the constraints within which it operates. It would demand quantification and would, therefore, need to be operational. Moreover, even if disturbances calling for readjustments could be identified, space frictions would limit the extent to which the consequences of such a disturbance could be predicted. Not only does it take time for knowledge (for instance, of changes in market behaviour or, more likely, of technical advances) to travel from firm to firm through space, locational factors may prevent knowledge from reaching some areas at all. Thus, the dilemma is that it is difficult to formulate a determinate general theory of location without adopting the pedagogic device of the equilibrium concept, yet if this concept is adopted complications arise from the probability that general equilibrium is inconsistent with the implications of the space economy.

In attempts to deal with the complications resulting from time and space elements without abandoning completely the idea of a general theory, economists have simplified the problem by constructing what Kuenne calls 'inter-regional trade models'.[2] These models take the spatial structure of the economy as given, that is, they assume constant production and consumption locations, fixed

[2] Kuenne, R.E. (1963) *The Theory of General Economic Equilibrium.* 398–9

resource patterns and transportation networks and unchanging technology. In effect, they freeze the spatial aspects of the economy, and seek to determine the equilibrium patterns of prices and flows of goods over the given space economy. In other words, these models abstract from locational influences. They do not try to show how the spatial structure of the economy has evolved, and they do not pretend to predict how it will change in the future. Such models can scarcely pose as general theories of location. In a sense, however, they are special cases of such a theory, in that they are consistent with a location theory in which transport costs are zero and all inputs and outputs are perfectly mobile (Walrasian general equilibrium analysis) or a theory with zero transport costs, factor immobility but free trade in commodities (international trade theory).[3] But the former assumptions are consistent with a one-point economy, while the latter although ostensibly relating to an international economy ignore the facts of distance and transport costs.[4] It is sometimes argued that trade and exchange models of this kind implicitly contain transport costs within production costs, thereby justifying analysis of the single-point economy. Against this view may be urged the argument that the particular effects of transport costs and other spatial frictions in separating one producer from another and in separating points of production from points of consumption cannot be ignored.

If this latter proposition is valid, it follows that locational considerations have to be treated explicitly in a general spatial model. A truly general theory will not only explain the location of production but also interdependence between producers and consumers and the patterns of trade which follow from this. Thus, such a theory may be best attempted by grafting locational aspects on to an inter-regional trade model rather than by abandoning the latter. However, most attempts at formulating a general location theory have concentrated on explaining the pattern of production to the exclusion of inter-regional trade. This is usually achieved by assuming that each firm (or regional industry) has its own regular market area with only limited terrain open to competition from rivals. Lefeber's analysis[5]

---

[3] Isard, W. (1956) *Location and Space-Economy*. 53–4

[4] A typical example of the inter-regional trade model paying lip-service to, but in reality devoid of, spatial considerations is that of Ohlin (Ohlin, B. (1933) *Inter-regional and International Trade*)

[5] See below, Section 4

is a notable exception since he attempts to integrate production and trade (in goods and factors).

Adding location theory to an inter-regional trade model in order to yield a truly general theory is made more difficult by the fact that locational models are so often concerned with partial equilibrium analysis. Lösch, for example, failed to encompass the interdependence of demand for different commodities in his attempt at a general theory; instead, he assumed that the demand functions for a particular good were functions of its price alone. Even Lefeber, because his was a programming model, had to specify final product prices in advance whereas a truly general theory would include these prices as part of the solution. An ideal general theory would recognise the existence of differentiated regions, nodal points and transport channels within each region, and the spatial interconnections of production and consumption within and between regions. It would locate all points of production and consumption in the space economy, the inputs and outputs at each production site, all flows (intra-regional and inter-regional) of factors and goods and their prices, and the relationship of the output and price of transportation services to all other economic activities.

The contributions of Weber, Predohl, Weigmann and other pioneers in the development of a general theory of location have been assessed by Isard.[6] In this chapter we shall deal with three more modern formulations. None of these is fully satisfactory, and they suggest that the development of a general theory has still some way to go. Lösch's model was based on highly simplified assumptions (neglecting cost differences), concentrates heavily on production and equilibrium within a given industry, can be classified as a general equilibrium theory only in a one-good economy, and contains a major inconsistency by deriving nodal production (and demand for labour) points in a model postulating uniform spatial distribution of consumers. The assumptions of Greenhut's model are less restrictive than those of Lösch, yet his analysis applies only to the location of production and he ignores the critical importance of transport costs in the space economy. Lefeber's model has much greater generality and represents a worthwhile attempt to incorporate space in a Walrasian general equilibrium framework. Its major weakness

[6] Isard, W. (1949) The General Theory of Location and Space Economy. *Quarterly Journal of Economics*, **63** reprinted as Chapter 2 of his book, *Location and Space-Economy, op. cit.*

stems from the fact that it is a programming model bound by linear maximisation assumptions and by an inability to handle demand relationships. Prices have to be specified arbitrarily rather than determined within the general theory itself.

2 The general theory of location according to Lösch

The Löschian theory of general locational equilibrium requires the standard assumptions maintained by Lösch throughout his main analyses: uniform distribution of industrial raw materials and ubiquitous transportation possibilities, and hence equal costs at all points over a homogeneous plain; an even distribution of population; identical consumer tastes and preferences; and production opportunities open to all. Equilibrium is the net resultant of two tendencies: firstly, producers aim at maximising individual profits and consumers try to gain access to the cheapest market; secondly, a competitive struggle between producers when firms in an industry multiply sufficiently to compete spatially eventually wipes out excess profits. When all supernormal profits have disappeared equilibrium is attained, the struggle for space dies down and locations are determined.

The conditions for equilibrium in the Löschian scheme can be summarised by five equations:

$$\frac{\Delta R^m_q}{\Delta x^m_q}=0; \quad \frac{\Delta R^m_q}{\Delta y^m_q}=0 \qquad (1)$$

$$\sum A^m_1 + A^m_2 + \ldots + A^m_q = A \qquad (2)$$

$$P^m(Dq) = C^m(Dq) \qquad (3)$$

$$\frac{\Delta P^m_q}{\Delta A^m_q} = \frac{\Delta C^m_q}{\Delta A^m_q} \qquad (4)$$

$$B^m_q = P^m_q + t^m_q \sqrt{(x-x^m_q)^2 + (y-y^m_q)^2} = \\ P^m_{q-1} + t^m_{q-1} \sqrt{(x-x^m_{q-1})^2 + (y-y^m_{q-1})^2} \qquad (5)$$

where m = number of products 1, 2 ... m.
  q = number of sites 1, 2 ... q, thus q and $q-1$ may be regarded as representative locations.
  R = profit.
  x, y = co-ordinates of location.
  A = size of entire area, while $A_{1, 2 \ldots q}$ represent market areas associated with individual sites, 1, 2 ... q.

105

P = factory price.
C = average cost.
D = demand.
B = boundary of market area expressed in money terms (as a delivered price).
t = freight rate.

The above equations can be interpreted as follows:

(1) The location for the individual producer should be optimal, so that each producer maximises profits (and, as a corollary, consumers maximise gains) insofar as the restrictions imposed by equations (2), (3) and (4) permit. If this equation is met, a shift in location cannot increase profits.

(2) The number of firms (and hence their locations) should be so numerous that all space is occupied. This condition is a critical one for the validity of the equations which follow depends upon it. It means, for example, that the market areas of all the sites for each good must when multiplied by the number of sites exactly equal the area of the system. If this condition were not fulfilled so that there was some space left over unoccupied by any firm then some of the plants in existence would compete for this space and could earn excess profits.

(3) This condition states that factory price must equal average cost, both of which are a function of demand. If this condition obtains there are no excess profits earned, all firms instead earn normal profits and consequently equilibrium rules. (Again, there is a corollary on the consumer side: that net advantages of consumers are equalised.)

(4) This condition states that the market area must be at the minimum necessary to justify continued production. If market areas were greater than this the minimum price would be in excess of average costs, and there would be scope for firms to enter the industry, compete spatially with existing firms and reduce their market areas until price equalled average cost. This equation must hold in equilibrium. If a change in the size of the market area was associated with a price change greater than the change in average costs, there would still be scope for spatial competition and disequilibrium would reign until the equality was restored. If the price change was less than the average cost change then clearly the firm would not voluntarily alter the size of its market area, while if the

change was forced by outside competition the firm would go out of business in the long run.

(5) This condition states that on the boundaries of market areas it must be a matter of indifference to consumers from which of two neighbouring locations (q and $q-1$) they purchase their supplies. Thus there are indifference lines which in fact divide the market areas associated with particular sites. For any given point on the boundary of the market area the factory price plus the freight rate multiplied by the radius of the market area must be the same for the consumer whether he buys from location q or from location $q-1$. If these values were not equal the consumer would always purchase from the cheaper delivered price plant and the market area of that plant would expand until its delivered price did equal that of the neighbouring plant.

With these five conditions of general locational equilibrium together with Lösch's initial assumptions, all firms in a given industry have the same costs whatever their location, their market areas will be identical, freight rates will be constant over the entire area of the system, and all firms in each industry will charge the same f.o.b. factory price. The equations enable us to estimate the size and the limits of the market areas, the location of production sites within each market area and within the area of the system as a whole, and the f.o.b. prices charged for each product. Finally, given the spatial uniformity of freight rates, equations (4) and (5) together enable us to deduce that the market areas have an hexagonal shape.

Although Lösch's general theory has many limitations, its path-breaking nature should be recognised. It was the first attempt to describe general spatial relations in a set of simple equations, and by presenting a model of the space economy operating under conditions of monopolistic competition Lösch avoided the difficulties arising from the assumption of perfect competition. The limitations of the model stem largely from its highly unrealistic simplifying assumptions, yet without the uniformity assumptions (ubiquitous raw materials, uniform spatial population distribution, equal costs at all locations) the analysis would become very difficult to handle. But these assumptions result in inconsistencies, such as between uniform population distribution and the hierarchical pattern of concentrations of economic activities as a consequence of superimposing nets of hexagonal market areas upon each other, often around a common core. Such concentrations will lead to the expansion of population at these centres, and clusters of buyers may give rise to irregularly shaped market areas. Löschian analysis underestimates agglomeration economies in industrial production, particularly *within a single industry*, and does not provide a comprehensive explanation of the existence of nodal points in the space economy. Nodal points only arise in Löschian analysis when the centres of market areas for different commodities or services coincide. One aspect of this neglect of agglomeration economies is the assumption of uniform raw materials available everywhere. This means that the analysis is much more relevant to activities, such as service sectors, with negligible raw material needs than to basic industry oriented towards localised raw materials.

Lösch's general theory can be criticised for not being general enough. It assumes independence of production, sales and prices of separate commodities, so that the space economy is conceived as being composed of several independent sectors rather than as a united whole. Commodity and factor markets are not interrelated via utility and production functions, for instance the price of a good is assumed a simple function of its demand, and the analysis consequently fails to reveal a true general equilibrium system. Moreover, the stability of equilibrium depends upon the existence of hexagonal market areas which are necessary to ensure that all space is used up. But the circular area is the most profitable market area shape. Lösch argued that circles would be compressed into hexagons under the force of competition. However, some industries may be so unprofitable that only the circular market area will allow firms to break even. If market areas are circular, there will be gaps between market area boundaries. These gaps will be too small to permit new entrants, but their existence interferes with Lösch's concept of a general equilibrium. Finally, the assumption of uniform production costs and the resulting spatial configuration of evenly spaced production plants clearly conflicts with reality in the space economy. The theory fails to explain the strong real world tendency for firms in the same industry to conglomerate together, because of agglomeration economies or locational interdependence. Despite its deficiencies, however, it would be wrong to underestimate the value of Lösch's pioneering analysis.

3 The general theory of location: Greenhut

Greenhut's general location theory does not, unlike that of Lösch, abstract from costs. Instead he attempts to determine the conditions of locational equilibrium when firms aim at maximising profits, but where costs are allowed to vary and where demand influences are affected by the possibility of locational interdependence. In his theory of individual location Greenhut laid some stress on personal factors, psychic income elements and the value of a satisfaction-maximising theory. He ignores these factors when it comes to presenting a general theory on the grounds that the gain in generality would be outweighed by the indeterminacy of such a theory. However, he believes that the formulation of his theory does not specifically exclude personal gratifications since these may be considered as cost deductions or demand additions.

We assume a well developed economy, and that at a given point in time a new product is innovated. Under the simplifying assumptions of zero costs everywhere and identical demands the innovating firm locates at the centre of the market area. Under the profit-maximising non-discriminatory f.o.b. factory price system, the innovator will deliberately limit his market area – at the point where the marginal revenue curve intersects the horizontal axis, where $MR = MC = 0$. Over this restricted market area the factory price will exceed zero, its value depending upon the ratio of the freight rate per unit of distance to the highest price consumers are willing to pay. In the limiting case, if we assume a population infinite in size, the profit-maximising price would in fact be zero plus the smallest increment.

As firms enter the industry they will locate either in the areas not previously supplied, at the side of the innovator, or at a site distant from him, depending upon demand influences. If the assumption of zero costs is relaxed, cost differentials will also exert their impact on the ultimate locations. Each new entrant will seek the location from which its sales to a given number of buyers (whose purchases are needed for maximum profits) can be supplied at the lowest total cost. As more and more competitors arrive both costs and relative demands at each site will change. Eventually, the successful attempts of competitors to locate at the maximum profit site will so reduce the market areas of firms as to cut profits, ultimately leading to a state of locational equilibrium. This equilibrium will be characterised by:

1 marginal revenues = marginal costs.
2 average revenue (i.e. the factory price) tangential to the average cost curve.

3 clustering and dispersion of plants in such a way that relocation by even a single plant would involve losses.

Equilibrium can be disturbed either by changes in demand or by changes in costs. Demand changes will not simply affect the number of firms in the industry, but will also lead to direct changes in sites. In this way, demand becomes an active determinant of each location. Cost changes may result in multiple disequilibria, and may have indirect repercussions on demand through locational interdependence. Finally, even if demand and cost are constant this is insufficient to perpetuate equilibrium. Although Greenhut ruled them out of detailed discussion, variations in psychic income may lead to different values being placed on cost data and thereby may distort equilibrium.

From the point of view of the individual firm its location is stable when the site is chosen which maximises the gap between total revenue (R) and total cost (C). But general equilibrium will not exist if the profit-maximising f.o.b. factory price (p) $\neq$ average cost exclusive of freight (Ca). Thus for equilibrium both conditions must be satisfied: profits must be maximised for each firm, therefore $\Delta R = \Delta C$; there must be no excess profits earned by firms in the industry, thus $p = Ca$. If initially $p = Ca$ equilibrium could be disturbed by several dynamic factors: for example, tastes could change leading to variations in demand and a new p; an innovational change in transportation could occur, again affecting p since the profit maximising f.o.b. factory price includes the seller's absorption of freight; technological developments could reduce Ca again resulting in spatial disequilibrium.

If V represents sales, generalising we may write:

$$\sum_{i=1}^{n} p_i V_i = p_1 V_1 + p_2 V_2 + p_3 V_3 + \ldots + p_n V_n \tag{1}$$

and
$$\sum_{i=1}^{n} Ca_i V_i = Ca_1 V_1 + Ca_2 V_2 + Ca_3 V_3 + \ldots + Ca_n V_n \tag{2}$$

In locational equilibrium

$$\sum_{i=1}^{n} p_i V_i - \sum_{i=1}^{n} Ca_i V_i = 0 \tag{3}$$

Although this formulation of a general theory of location has certain similarities to that of Lösch, in that individual firms aim to maximise profits and equilibrium requires the elimination of excess profits via the tangency of the average revenue to the average cost curve, it has a greater degree of generality. It permits costs to vary from site to site, and allows the entry of new firms to alter cost situations. Perhaps even more significant it takes account of alternative locational patterns in an industry consisting of many firms by inclusion of the locational interdependence element. By recognising that profit maximisation may, because of agglomeration economies and uncertainty about future demand and cost conditions, induce a new firm to locate as close as possible to an existing firm, it does not necessarily require the ideal but unrealistic locational pattern of even dispersion of firms producing homogeneous goods as outlined by Lösch. The main weakness of Greenhut's attempt at a general theory of location is that transportation was not integrated into his general equilibrium framework, a defect which was also common to Lösch. Thus in the model above, the main variables are the profit-maximising f.o.b. factory price which includes freight absorption but not the overall freight costs and average costs specifically excluding freight. It is unclear how transportation fits into the picture. It was left to L. Lefeber[7] to make transportation a major element in his general equilibrium theory.

4 Lefeber's general equilibrium theory

A distinctive feature of Lefeber's approach to general equilibrium theory was his attempt to integrate the transportation element into it. Firstly, Lefeber criticises both Lösch and Isard for assuming a continuous transport plane with uniform transport rates. Under these assumptions a straightforward objective in a non-zero transport costs model is to minimise the number of ton-miles involved in spatial movement of products. But Lefeber argues that these assumptions prevent a theoretical assessment of the problems of optimal transport networks. Secondly, he criticises Isard's treatment of transport inputs as intermediate goods and his analysis of the location problem in terms of substitution between transport and other inputs. As a result, transportation services were not identified among his output variables. This meant different production functions for each plant, since the production function had to vary

[7] Lefeber, L. (1958) *Allocation in Space: Production, Transport and Industrial Location*

with the firm's location, its market and its sources of raw materials. Lefeber, however, suggested that the output of transportation services could be regarded as a necessary social sacrifice, in the sense that for transportation to be provided inputs had to be withdrawn from the production of final goods. Within the context of general equilibrium analysis this social sacrifice can be deducted from the total bill of final goods. The theoretical advantage of this approach is that production functions of identical goods produced in diverse locations remain constant despite changes in location.

Lefeber's model is essentially a programming model. His objective is to show simultaneously the optimal locational pattern and how this pattern maximises the production of final goods for consumers. The 'dual' of this objective is to minimise the deduction from final output required for transportation services. In Lefeber's terminology, the sum total of **location rents** has to be minimised. This comes to the same thing. If we compare the returns to a homogeneous factor at different locations the differential between the return at any location and that location where the return is lowest can be regarded as a location rent, that is a rent earned by virtue of the factor being at a particular location. In equilibrium, it is clear that the location rent must equal the marginal cost of transportation of the factor.

Linear programming models have a serious weakness for general equilibrium analysis. This is their failure to cope with demand considerations with the result that the prices of final goods, which ought to be part of the solution, have to be specified as data. This requirement also applies to transportation rates over space. Thus, Lefeber shows what, with a given set of prices, the optimal locational pattern will be and specifies the conditions under which equilibrium will be preserved. But this is scarcely a fully fledged general equilibrium theory since such a theory would have to determine the set of final product prices as well.

In his analysis Lefeber makes a distinction between **transportable** and **non-transportable** factors of production. In the short run, flows of transportable factors may be utilised locally or, with the help of the transport system, at other spatially distant locations. In the long run, the source of flow may be transportable to a different location. Non-transportable factors can only be used at locations of their origin, and are immobile both in the short and the long run. Thus, to take one of Lefeber's own examples, a mine is not transportable but an electric generator is. The distinction is not so clear cut, however, since some factors may be non-transportable in the short run but transportable in the long run. Labour, for example, is non-transportable in the sense that it can be employed only within commuting distance from its source. In the short run, therefore, homogeneous labour at a given location will receive identical wages in all occupations, but the wages paid at any two locations may differ since the returns to non-transportable factors do not have to be linked through the cost of transportation. In the long run, on the other hand, labour is transportable, either by movement of the whole labour pool, or, more generally, by individual migration to high wage locations. If the costs of migration (monetary and subjective) are assumed zero, and labour is indifferent between places of residence, then the process of long run adjustment will make the marginal product of labour equal for all workers. If migration costs are positive, then the return to labour at different locations will differ by the marginal cost of migration. Since the Lefeber model aims at maximising output, it is clear that wage equalisation (with the qualification introduced in the previous sentence) is a necessary but not sufficient condition for long-run equilibrium. The absolute condition is that there should be no alternative spatial distribution of labour which could result in a higher output.

Lefeber initially assumes two goods, each of which is produced at a different location, and two factors. Each location is endowed with a given amount of transportable factors. He also assumes that the transformation curve that he derives is convex, that there are constant returns to scale, and that transport costs for final goods are zero. Different combinations of the two commodities may be produced by the transfer of transportable factors from one location to the other. For each possible pair of techniques (each representing different factor proportions) we can draw up a transformation function corresponding to the most efficient patterns of factor movements required to redistribute factors from one location to the other in order to produce different combinations of the two goods. We can obtain a series of such transformation functions, and from them derive a transformation surface which takes the form of an envelope composed of segments of particular transformation functions. The transformation curve will be a smoothly curved surface if all production functions are continuously differentiable and of first order homogeneity, but will take the form of a polyhedron if production functions are linear. In both cases the feasible portion of the curve will be convex. This enables a maximum to be established.

The transformation envelope permits us to determine the optimal outputs of each good to be produced. Given a set of final product prices (which is uniform for identical goods, since transport costs on final goods have been assumed zero), then the optimal product mix corresponds to the point on the transformation surface where the marginal rate of transformation = the price ratio. Thus, where the price line is tangential to the transformation curve represents the combination of the two goods which maximises the total value of output. Given any set of constant prices for final goods, we obtain a unique optimal combination of the two final goods, the most efficient factor combinations used in the production of each good and the associated factor price ratio. A homogeneous set of shadow prices or rents for productive factors are yielded, and the existence of these ensures stable equilibrium in allocation.

The conditions of spatial equilibrium are as follows:

(1) The value of the marginal product of a factor originating from a given location must equal its rent in local employment. If the same factor is employed at the other location its marginal product must equal its rent in local employment plus the marginal cost of its transportation. The latter is represented by the rate of change in demand for transportation due to the variable under consideration multiplied by the shadow price of transportation.

(2) Factors employed in transportation must receive the same rent as in local employment. In turn, this implies that if a factor is taken from the two locations for use in the transport sector, its rent must be uniform at both locations.

(3) If a factor is idle at one location its locally received rent must be zero, while if it is employed at the other location its rent there must equal the marginal cost of its transportation.

Lefeber then broadened the analysis by explicitly introducing consumption locations as well as production locations, and by allowing transport costs of final goods from the latter to the former to be positive. He found that the spatial distribution of final goods does not interfere with the existence of spatial equilibrium. The shadow price of a final good at the production location can be derived by subtracting from the market price the marginal cost of shipping one additional unit of the good to the market. Similarly, the rents that assured the optimal stable allocation of a factor were found to be related to the values of the marginal product of that factor in different sectors, estimated in terms of the shadow prices of the different goods.

The model is generalised still further by assuming divisible locations. This means that more than one industry could settle at the same production point. Also, we now permit the production of identical goods to take place simultaneously at several locations. By maximising the value of all final goods shipped to different markets, optimal production locations are obtained. The optimal locations and the quantities produced at each location for different sectors are determined by several variables: market prices; the prevailing level of technology; the local endowment of factors at each production point; the parameters of the transport demand function, which depend on the distances factors and goods have to be carried and on their weight. All these influences act together, and considered in isolation each is insufficient to determine the choice of location. Relaxation of the earlier assumption of indivisible locations permits a stable optimal solution even with the presence of intermediate good flows. The introduction of intermediate goods has no disequilibrating effect, provided that their rent if used locally is identical to the f.o.b. factory price, and if used at another location is equal to the f.o.b. factory price plus the marginal cost of transportation. Finally, even though Lefeber's analysis is restricted to two consumption points, two production locations, two factors and two goods, the generalisation of the system presents no special difficulties.

The optimal locations and maximisation of the value of output are obtained only under conditions of pure competition, with perfect knowledge and no institutional rigidities. Relaxation of the assumptions, however, results in departures from the optimum. For example, consumer discrimination and preferences may demand more factors for production of transportation services than would otherwise be required. Institutional rigidities may interfere with the long-run process of equalisation of factor rents, particularly wages. If transportation services are produced under conditions of increasing returns, then marginal cost pricing (which is required in this sector for equilibrium) is not feasible without some assistance from a subsidy. Finally, entrepreneurs may suffer from lack of knowledge or from inertia. Even if entrepreneurs are aware of opportunities, the risk of investing at a new location may be too strong a deterrent because the costs of error are normally much smaller at sites of agglomeration than at scattered locations.

To sum up, the Lefeber analysis as a basically programming model is not fully determinate. It demonstrates the equilibrium locations and spatial allocation of factors and distribution of goods that follow from a given set of market prices, but it fails to explain the determinants of these prices themselves. On the other hand, the theory incorporates the transportation sector into the equilibrium framework more adequately than in some other analyses. Transportation services are regarded as a part of final output, and their production requires productive factors which have to be diverted from other potential uses for transportation to take place. Transportation can therefore be deducted from the final goods bill, rather than being treated (as by Isard) as a variable input in the production function of the individual firm. A major advantage of the former approach is that one can as a result assume identical production functions for homogeneous goods, an assumption which greatly simplifies the general equilibrium analysis. Moreover, Lefeber's distinction between transportable and non-transportable factors is illuminating in showing how output and factor rents can vary over space.

Finally, Lefeber's theory is much broader than a pure location theory. Not only are the optimal locations determined, but also the value of total output is maximised, the optimal allocation of productive factors and the spatial flows of final goods to each market are found. In effect, his theory is a pure Walrasian general equilibrium model modified to take account of the existence of space. Most earlier contributions to general equilibrium theory considered an economy where all factors, commodities, producers and consumers were, in effect, located at a single point. The only radical addition by Lefeber to the customary Walrasian production assumptions was the existence of spatially separated but divisible production and consumption locations. However, this extension in itself enables him to attempt to embrace the two major spatial aspects, the spatial flows of goods and factors and the locational problem, within the same general framework.

Part B
The urban economy

Chapter 6
Urban spatial structure

In this chapter we are interested in the economic theory of urban spatial structures. Thus we are concerned with how the spatial organisation of cities and towns is determined by economic forces. Their influence is shown most clearly in the conflict between cost minimisation and the desire for accessibility. It must be recognised, however, that a complete understanding of the structure of modern cities may require us to relax free market assumptions and to take explicit account of urban planning and public policy decisions. The economist cannot be expected to provide all the answers to a problem which really needs an interdisciplinary analysis.

1 The minimisation of costs of friction hypothesis

Of the different principles suggested to give order and regularity to spatial urban structure, the minimisation of costs of friction has been one of the longest held and has probably received most attention. The first definitive statement was made by R. M. Haig in the 1920s, but followers include Dorau and Hinman, Ely and Wehrwein, Ratcliff and, more recently, in a much modified form, Guttenberg.[1] The basic element in the theory is that the organisation of the city reflects the attempts by households and firms to overcome 'the friction of space'. Transport costs are the obvious item in the costs of friction. Transportation is a means of overcoming the friction of space, and the more efficient the transportation network the lower will be transport costs and the less the friction. However, rent also is included in the costs of friction. This is because rent offers accessibility,

[1] Haig, R.M. (1926) Toward an Understanding of the Metropolis. *Quarterly Journal of Economics*, **40**. Dorau, H.B. and Hinman, A.G. (1928) *Urban Land Economics*. Ely, R.T. and Wehrwein, G.S. (1940) *Land Economics*. Ratcliff, R.V. (1949) *Urban Land Economics*. Guttenberg, A.Z. (1960) Urban Structure and Urban Growth. *Journal of the American Institute of Planners*, **26**

and therefore represents savings in transport costs. Haig is here taking over a much older view advanced by R.M.Hurd at the beginning of the century, and implicit in Von Thünen's analysis when he anticipated the extension of his agricultural model to an urban context.[2] Hurd suggested that the value of land depends upon proximity, while Von Thünen argued that rent increased near the centre of the town because the greater convenience of being there saved labour and time. Thus, the 'costs of friction' consist of transport costs and site rent (regarded as negative transport costs). Haig's contribution was to link these two elements explicitly together. However, the sum of the two items is not regarded as a constant.[3] Instead, it varies with the site. In theory, the optimal site for an activity is that which furnishes the desired degree of accessibility at the lowest costs of friction. The layout of the city is, it is argued, determined by this principle. Thus, in competition and with perfect knowledge, the urban land market is held to operate in a way that results in minimum aggregate land rents and transport costs for the city as a whole. Later formulations suggested that the costs to be minimised should include the disutility of travelling. This refinement makes the hypothesis more realistic but weakens it from the point of view of operational capabilities, largely because of the problems involved in assigning a monetary value to disutility.

Considering the original formulation, the theory contains a number of weaknesses. Haig failed to clarify how the minimising of friction costs by the household or firm would lead to a minimisation of aggregate costs throughout the city. His view that urban firms and residents locate to minimise costs of friction does not fully explain their behaviour. If revenue potential varies from one site to another, and firms aim at maximising profits (or sales), the costs of friction would comprise only one element among many in their revenue-cost calculations. Thus, the hypothesis is more applicable to manufacturing in perfect competition[4] than to a retail shop. The minimisation of the costs of friction as a location criterion works

---

[2] Hurd, R.M. (1903) *Principles of City Land Values* and Hall, P.G. (edit) (1966) *Von Thünen's Isolated State*

[3] This may be contrasted with the more formal model elaborated by Wingo where costs of friction are regarded as a constant sum, see section 5 below

[4] In Chapters 2, 4 and 5 we showed that perfect competition is an assumption generally inconsistent with the determinants of economic activity in the space economy

only in the special case where revenues and all other costs are held constant. The hypothesis also fails to explain satisfactorily the behaviour of households. Households locate to maximise their satisfaction rather than to minimise friction costs. A household could reduce the rent component of friction costs by taking a smaller residential site. If preferences for site size are excluded, and minimisation of friction costs was the sole determinant of residential location, dwellings would tend to be clustered around the centre of the city at very high densities.

Haig intended that the principle could be applied to city planning. The planner's function is consequently to offset the effects of market imperfections, which increase friction, and to plan in a way that minimises friction costs. But do the assumptions of a free market and perfect knowledge inevitably result in minimum aggregate costs of friction? A few examples will show that this is not necessarily the case. If a landlord had imperfect knowledge he might charge lower rents than would rule in a free market, thereby reducing friction costs. Alternatively, if zoning restrictions prescribed larger minimum sites than would result in a free market, the price of land would be lower than the free market price. This is because bidders failing to comply with the site-size regulation are ruled out from the market. On the other hand, prices will tend to rise in sections of the city where the zone restriction does not operate. Aggregate friction costs may be increased or reduced depending on the price elasticity of demand. A maximum site regulation throughout the city, however, would inevitably reduce friction costs. Finally, the effects of lags in the rate of adjustment to changed conditions may also affect friction costs. If A is a higher bidder for a given site, but this has already been pre-empted by B who holds a long lease, A must be satisfied with some other site. He will choose between central or distant locations and between a small or large plot, and depending on his choice his friction costs may be greater or smaller in either case. However, let us suppose that his costs of friction are greater than if he had obtained the location held by B. Then, aggregate costs of friction would increase only if A's higher friction costs exceeded the savings accruing to B (whose rent is less than A would be willing to pay) under the terms of the lease. Aggregate friction costs may fall rather than rise.[5]

[5] These arguments are pointed out by Alonso, W. (1964) *Location and Land Use*. 103–5

If pushed to the extreme, the minimisation of costs of friction hypothesis would lead to very odd situations. For instance, a city planner aiming at minimising these costs alone might crowd all residences to their maximum physical density around the city centre and make by-laws forbidding all industrial and commercial developments thereby reducing friction costs in this sector to zero. But would a spatial configuration of this kind be compatible with maximising (or even 'satisficing') behaviour by individuals? The friction cost minimising principle may be an important element in explaining a city's spatial structure, but as a single-factor determinant it explains and predicts nothing.

Urban ecologists have also a version of the minimum costs of friction hypothesis, modified to take account of non-economic variables as well as land values. This states that the spatial distribution of ecological units tends to be such that the total costs of gaining maximum satisfaction are minimised. However, costs in their statement were given a broad meaning, including all kinds of disutility as well as economic and other measurable costs.[6] Clearly, because disutility cannot be measured in monetary terms the hypothesis in this form cannot be tested.

A recent reframing of the friction costs minimisation theory has been attempted by Guttenberg,[7] but he stresses the importance of transport efficiency in determining the spatial structure of the city and also formulates his model in dynamic terms. He sees the organising principle as 'a community effort to overcome distance'. Guttenberg divides the locational possibilities of urban activities into two components, 'distributed facilities', i.e. those that are dispersed over the city, and 'undistributed facilities', i.e. those that are concentrated at one major centre. The degree of emphasis on a distributed or undistributed structure depends on the efficiency of the transportation system. Transport costs are the primary determinant of the level of friction costs, so an efficient transport system represents a successful attempt by the community to overcome distance and permits an undistributed structure of activities. If transportation is poor, on the other hand, workplaces, service centres, commercial and public institutions may have to assume a distributed pattern.

Changes in transportation efficiency alter the pattern of urban

[6] Quinn, J.A. (1950) *Human Ecology*   [7] Guttenberg, *loc. cit.*

spatial structure by permitting substitution between peripheral and central locations. However, there is probably a capacity limit on the ability of a single major centre to absorb the increased activities associated with urban growth. Growth will result in structural adjustments to overcome distance. These adjustments may be manifested in the development of new centres and/or improved transport facilities. Population movements accompany these adjustments, and areas within the city grow or decline according to the degree of accessibility they offer. The density gradient of households and firms changes with the city's expansion. For example, if transport efficiency improved in a way that favoured the substitution of distant for central locations, the slope of the density gradient will decline. Although Guttenberg accepts that variables other than the time-distance factor will influence urban location decisions, he argues that given certain *ceteris paribus* assumptions accessibility as measured by time-distance tends to distribute activities spatially. Although his theory is dynamic in intention, and stresses the continuous interaction between the location of urban activities and transport efficiency, it is phrased in very general terms and lacks the analytical elegance of, say, the Wingo model discussed below.

2 Some observations on models of urban spatial structure

Apart from treatment of the minimisation of friction costs hypothesis above, and detailed analysis of three models (one each for households, business firms and the spatial relationship between consumers and shopping locations) outlined later in this chapter, space forbids more than a brief mention of other theories and models explaining spatial distribution within a city.

Many analysts, especially those based in sociology rather than economics, have concentrated on the theory of residential land values. Hawley, for example, argued that households are distributed with reference to land values, the location of other activities and the cost and time spent in transportation to centres of activity, and suggested that these three factors are combined in a single measure, rental value for residential use. Hawley offered an explanation of the paradox of low income families living on high priced land and wealthy families on cheap land. Residential property on high priced land is normally in a deteriorated condition, because since it is close to industrial and commercial areas it is held speculatively in anticipation of being put to more profitable use. Owners of such property are not willing to spend much on maintenance hence low rents. Low rents also result from nearness to objectionable uses and distance from family amenities, offset to a limited extent by accessibility. New houses, however, are built on low value land with few alternative uses. They command high rents because they are new and of high quality, and they are near to utilities but distant from objectionable uses; again, these tendencies are offset by reduced accessibility to the city centre and to places of employment. This means that 'while land values, in the main, grade downward with distance from concentrations of associational units, rental values for residential buildings grade upward. That is, rental values for residential property tend to vary inversely with land values'.[8] This paradox is the consequence of city growth, real or anticipated. It is growth which leads to speculative activity in the deteriorated areas potentially ripe for it, and population growth which results in new houses being built on the city's periphery.

Alonso suggests an alternative explanation which does not rely on the dynamics of city growth or on assigning a crucial role to speculators. He argues that the desire for land is strong and not easily satisfied. Consequently, the size of site demanded varies greatly with income. The wealthy are affected relatively less by commuting costs. The rich are price-oriented while the poor are location-oriented. Since less accessibility is bought with increasing income, accessibility behaves as an inferior good. Thus, the income elasticity of demand for land is high but the income elasticity of demand for access to the city centre is negative; these propositions become increasingly true when we consider the upper income ranges. If this hypothesis holds, luxury flats near the city centre would satisfy the demands of only a small proportion of the wealthy.[9]

A similar model is presented by Beckmann.[10] His basic assumptions are: in the choice of residential location, every household maximises the amount of living space it can obtain for its housing expenditure; average expenditure on housing and commuting is a function of income; a linear commuting-costs function. Given these assumptions Beckmann obtains a market solution for the spatial distribution of households, which shows the wealthier households settling on the periphery of the city.

[8] Hawley, A.H. (1950) *Human Ecology*. 281   [9] Alonso, *loc. cit.*, 105–9
[10] Beckmann, M.J. On the Distribution of Rent and Residential Density in Cities. Paper presented at Yale University, Feb. 1957

Operational models

The brief discussion above refers either to general observations on land values and urban spatial structure or, in Beckmann's case, to a mathematical model based on simplifying assumptions. Another stream of analysts of the spatial structure of cities has attempted to construct less abstract models that offer some hope of being made operational.

Wendt, for example, has criticised the simplifying assumptions of the land economists, such as their treatment of the city as having a single central core and their overemphasis on transport costs. Instead, he formulates a generalised model where the aggregate value of urban land is defined as the difference between gross revenue and expected costs divided by the amortisation rate. More precisely, the model can be stated as:[11]

$$V = \frac{f_x(P, Y, S, P_u, PI) - \Sigma(T + O_c + I_{im} + D_{im})}{f_x(i, R, C_g)}$$

where V = aggregate value of urban land.
f_x = expectations.
P = population.
Y = average income.
S = supply of competitive land.
P_u = competitive pull of area.
PI = public investment
T = local taxes.
O_c = operating costs.
I_{im} = interest on capital invested in improvement.
D_{im} = depreciation on improvements.
i = interest rate.
R = investment risk.
C_g = the possibility of capital gains.

The operational potential of this model stems from the fact that it aims at predicting secular and cyclical variations in aggregate land values rather than attempting to analyse static equilibrium conditions. Wendt does make a critical distinction between factors affecting aggregate land values and those influencing the land value of a

---

[11] This formulation is to be found in Wendt, P.F. (1958) Economic Growth and Urban Land Values. *The Appraisal Journal*, **26** 427. See also Wendt, P.F. (1957) Theory of Urban Land Values. *Land Economics*, 33

particular site. In regard to the latter the revenue and cost components in a function of the above type would vary from user to user: users in service industries would base their revenue component on the volume of expected sales at alternative sites, and costs of business operating expenses at these sites; industrial users would compare product sales potentials to costs of production; for households the comparison would be between the monetary value of benefits anticipated from alternative residential locations and the costs as measured by commuting costs, taxes, improvement costs, etc. The Wendt model would require much more detailed specification before it could be properly tested.

Another approach is the Herbert-Stevens linear programming model of residential development.[12] This model shows how households may be distributed to locations when they maximise their aggregate rent-paying ability. They assume that households seek to satisfy their housing needs and wants in the market, and that location decisions are reached in the light of a comparison of the costs of obtaining housing requirements with the household budget available. Assuming that households have perfect knowledge, the model is designed to optimise locations for households in different income groups, subject to the constraints of a capacity limit in each residential zone and a given number of households in each group. The model recognises four explicit location factors – a type of house, an amenity level, an accessibility preference, and a site size. The difficulties in application arise from the need to know in advance the ordering of preferences for these location factors. This calls for sampling surveys to establish preferences of households at different income levels for housing type, amenity level, and site size. Moreover, if such a model were to be used for predictive purposes, we would either need to assume unchanging tastes or make estimates of future preferences.

Lowry attempts to forecast the structure of comprehensive land use with the aid of a linked series of models.[13] His main assumptions are that the locations of 'basic' employment centres are given and that economic activity levels are exogenously determined. His first model distributes households relative to these employment centres subject to constraints such as the availability of land suitable for

[12] Herbert, J.D. and Stevens, B.H. (1960) A Model for the Distribution of Residential Activity in Urban Areas. *Journal of Regional Science*, **2**
[13] Lowry, I.S. (1964) *A Model of Metropolis*

residential use, and set maximum density levels. The key device used in distributing households spatially is **trip distribution indices,** which can most easily be developed from an area-wide urban or regional transportation study. He constructs around each of 13 residential zones a set of 11 concentric rings of one mile radial width. He computed the percentage of all work trips originating in each zone which can expect to find terminals in each successive ring outwards, assuming an even distribution of employment opportunities in each ring. Indices obtained by this method are applied to estimates of employment at workplaces so as to arrive at the residential distribution of this employment and its equivalent in population, with the result forming various overlapping patterns of population densities generated from different work centres. A second model is based on trip indices for four types of retail establishments and other service trips. The computed indices are then applied to the population distribution generated by the first model in order to obtain a distribution of retail and service activities on the basis of access to markets, in this case households, subject to the constraint of a specified minimum market size.

Artle suggested two operational models for estimating the spatial distribution characteristics of retail and service establishments in the city, an income potential model and a regression model, and evaluated the results against a probability distribution of establishments.[14] In his income potential model Artle divides the city into a number of equal squares. The basic notion is that the income of people living in a particular square (or zone) has a potential influence on all other squares, but with the influence declining with distance. The income potential produced by any square j on square i is given by:

$$_iV_j = \frac{G_{ij} Y}{d_{ij}} \qquad (i=1, 2 \ldots n)$$

where G_{ij} = a constant.
Y_j = income of residents of square j.
d_{ij} = distance between squares i and j, measured for purposes of simplification as the distance between their central points.
n = total number of squares.

Artle obtained conditional forecasts of spending on particular

[14] Artle, R. (1959) *Studies in the Structure of the Stockholm Economy.* 123–38

services from input-output data[15] and applied these to his aggregate income-potential estimates for each square, and from this procedure estimated future demand for the services concerned as relating to all individual squares. If future demands per square can be accepted as estimates of future receipts, it is then possible to distribute to different parts of the city area a total number of retail and service establishments of appropriate types. The procedure required certain simplifying assumptions: that the average propensity to consume particular services was the same in each square; that places of residence alone can be used as a basis for computing income potentials, neglecting the tendency for some consumption spending to occur near places of work; that receipts obtainable per square are the only factors influencing spatial distribution of establishments, neglecting the possibility of high rents in some squares determining location.

The data requirements of this model are very heavy. If the necessary information is impossible to obtain, Artle suggested as an alternative a simple regression model using the size of the resident population and size of the working population per zone as the independent variables influencing the number of service establishments in each zone. Thus, we may write the following regression equation:

$$N = a + bP_r + cP_w + z$$

where N = number of establishments per zone.
P_r = size of resident population per zone.
P_w = size of working population per zone.
a, b, c = constants.
z = residual.

A more sophisticated model would have to take account of rent levels prevailing in each zone and of some measure of travel costs as an influence on the location of retail and similar centres. It is important to note that the theoretical implications of the two models are quite different: in the income potential model it is assumed that there are no barriers between zones from the point of view of site selection, but the regression model implies that interzonal trade is negligible.

[15] The information was obtained from an input-output table constructed by Artle for the Stockholm economy

3 Locational equilibrium of an urban firm

How will a business locate itself in a city in relation to the city's core? The model which follows depends on certain simplifying assumptions. The city is assumed to be completely centralised, and that the more central the chosen location the greater is the access to consumers. We ignore locational interdependence problems by taking the price of the firm's product as given. Thus, sales volume and total revenue increase the nearer the firm locates to the core. We further assume that the firm is faced with a given structure of prices for land varying inversely with distance from the city centre, described by the function P_d, where P_d = price of land at a given location, d, measured as distance from the centre. We assume that this price function is determined by supply and demand; all urban land is regarded as of equal quality and is freely bought and sold in a perfect market free from institutional restraints. We ignore a host of factors which might influence the rent of an urban site, such as the type of business most suitable for a particular location and the effects of agglomeration and deglomeration economies. Finally, we assume that firms aim at maximising profits.

As the firm moves away from the centre of the city its revenue will tend to fall and its operating costs will increase (primarily due to the increased transport costs necessitated by a less accessible location), but this will be compensated for by a fall in the site costs (rent). At each location there will be some rent which the firm will be prepared to pay which will exactly compensate for the change in operating costs and the change in revenue compared with the total costs and revenues obtained at any other location. Thus, as the firm moves away from the centre of the city, it will substitute increased transport and other costs and falling revenue for reduced rent costs. If the substitution is exact the firm will attain a constant level of profits regardless of where it is situated, and accordingly will be indifferent between locations. At all locations between the city and the boundary where total revenue is equal to the required level of profit plus operating costs there will be some rent which the firm will be prepared to pay without involving any sacrifice in terms of profits. There will also be a large number of possible paths traced by these bid price (or rent) functions, each of which corresponds to a certain level of profits. We have assumed that the actual price function of land, P_d, is given. The firm will locate at the point where the actual price of land is equal to the price the firm is prepared to pay to assure itself the highest possible profits.

The location choice can be demonstrated most easily with the concept of **bid price curves.**[16] The bid price function is not necessarily related to actual prices. Rather it is a hypothetical function showing how the price of land must vary with distance for the firm to obtain the same profits regardless of location; thus it is an iso-profit curve. The function may be denoted by $p_d(\bar{X})$ which may be read as the price (p) bid by a firm at each location d, such that when the size of site is optimised, the firm will achieve a constant level of profits $\bar{X}$.[17] Since the level of profits is constant, the firm will be indifferent as to its location. The bid price function enables us to define the bid price, p, in terms of the single variable of distance from the city centre, d.

Bid price functions have certain properties:

(1) **A bid price function is single-valued.** For any given level of profits, $\bar{X}$, there is only one value of p possible at any given d.

(2) **Bid price curves,** representing different levels of profits for the same firm, **do not intersect each other.**

(3) **The lower bid price curves represent higher profit levels,** and are preferred by the firm. Since profits are a residual after payment of operating and site costs, the lower the price of land the higher the profits. Curves above that corresponding to zero profits ($X=0$) can be ignored, since to bid such prices for land would involve the firm in losses.

(4) **Bid price functions normally slope downwards.** The slope is such that the savings in rent are exactly equal to the revenue lost plus the increase in operating costs. Since revenue tends to decrease and operating costs to increase with distance, bid prices fall with distance for profits to remain constant.

These properties suggest that a family of bid price curves is analogous to a set of indifference curves. Both form preference maps, but in contrast to indifference curves a lower bid price curve is preferred to a higher one.

Having derived bid price curves we can use them to show the

[16] This concept is coined by Alonso, W. (1964) *Location and Land Use: Towards a General Theory of Land Rent.* Especially 42–58

[17] Henceforth we let P stand for the actual price of land while p is the bid price. Note that we define the bid price function in a way which takes account of the site size that maximises profits at a given location

URBAN SPATIAL STRUCTURE

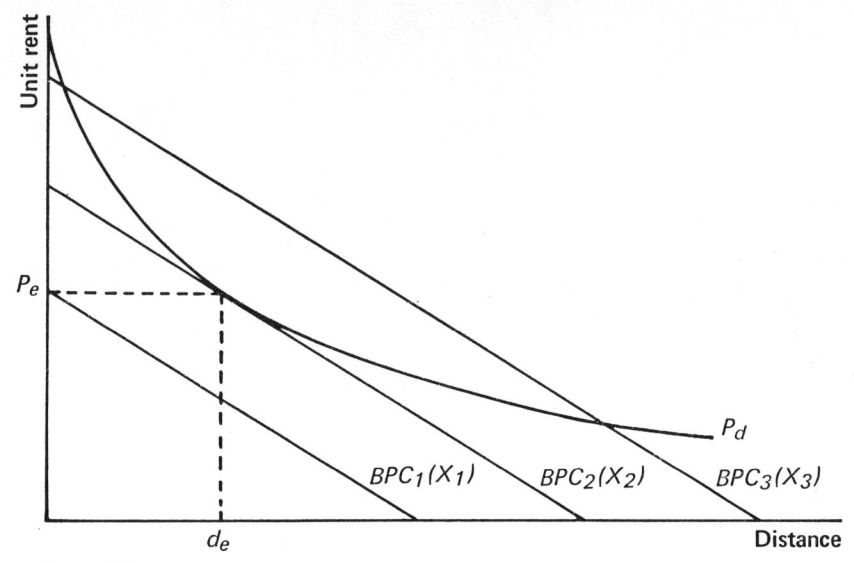

Figure 6.1

equilibrium location of the firm. In figure 6.1 a family of bid price curves is drawn.[18] BPC_1 refers to level of profits X_1, BPC_2 to X_2 and BPC_3 to X_3, where $X_1 > X_2 > X_3$. Thus BPC_1 is preferable from the firm's point of view to BPC_2, which is in turn preferable to BPC_3. The firm is faced with a given structure of land prices P_d. The actual price function is drawn in a way which assumes that the price of land falls with increasing distance from the city centre; this is an equilibrium requirement as well as being true in most cities. In figure 6.1 the bid price curves map the firm's preferences, while the price structure, P_d, illustrates the opportunities available to it. The firm will locate at the point where the price function is tangential to the lowest possible bid price curve. P_d is tangential to BPC_2 in figure 6.1, so that d_e represents the location where profits are maximised (X_2).[19]

[18] Although the bid price curves in figure 6.1 are drawn as straight lines this is by no means necessary

[19] If the highest BPC, for which $X = 0$, is at all parts below the price function, the firm will not enter the market since this would mean losses. Another point to notice is that if the price function is more concave from the origin than the bid price curves, this would yield end point solutions, that is, location at the city centre

At the point of tangency the slopes of the price function, P_d, and the profit maximising bid price curve, BPC_2, are equal. At locations nearer the city centre than d_e, P_d is steeper than BPC_2. Since the slope of the bid price curve is the change in the price of land required to offset revenue losses and higher costs, where P_d is steeper the savings in site costs exceed the losses in revenue and increased operating costs associated with increasing distance, and the firm would increase its profits by moving farther out. Conversely, to the right of d_e, BPC_2 is steeper than P_d, meaning that savings on land are insufficient to offset reduced sales and higher costs. The firm would move towards the city centre and settle in equilibrium at d_e.

4 Consumer spatial behaviour and the location of retail establishments

With regard to retail activities, we can make broad empirical generalisations about their spatial structure, especially in the context of a metropolitan region. *Per capita* sales are higher in the central city than in nearby suburban zones. Beyond a certain radius (perhaps twenty miles, often more) sales per head will start to rise again with distance, reflecting the influence of other retail centres. This pattern confirms the drawing power of the large city which tends to attract shoppers from contiguous zones. At greater distances, however, the friction of space operates to discourage longer trips to the centre, and acts as a barrier to protect other centres from the competition of the central city. Distance factors therefore ensure higher sales for peripheral suburban zones and for smaller outlying towns and cities that form retail trade centres for their own hinterlands. Observation also shows regular variations by distance in individual trade categories. The main centre specialises in general merchandise, and completely dominates nearby suburbs in most durable goods, clothes, jewellery, etc. For food sales, newspapers and tobacco and goods of this kind, sales are much more evenly distributed.[20] A sound conceptual analysis of the distance factor must, at least, help to explain this broad spatial pattern of retail activity.

A promising approach to this problem is by way of gravity potential models. Indeed, one of the earliest uses of what are now known as gravity models was in studies of retail trade. This is Reilly's Law

---

[20] For a classic discussion on these lines see Isard, W. and Whitney, V.H. (1949) Metropolitan Site Selection. *Social Forces*, **27**

of Retail Gravitation,[21] which states that a city attracts retail trade from an individual customer located in its hinterland in proportion to its size (as measured by population) and in inverse proportion to the square of the distance separating the individual from the city centre. The boundary separating the market areas of two centres x and y competing for shoppers in a hinterland is delimited as the locus of points for which

$$\frac{P_x}{d_{bx}^2} = \frac{P_y}{d_{by}^2} \quad (1)$$

where P stands for population, and d_{bx} and d_{by} are the distances of centres x and y respectively from any point b on the boundary.

Reilly's Law is a special case of a more general gravity model. A generalised model can be expressed in the following terms:

$$F_{ij} = K \cdot \frac{A_j^\alpha}{d_{ij}^\beta} \quad (2)$$

where
F_{ij} = expected frequency of interaction between point i and destination j.
A_j = attraction of the jth destination.
d_{ij} = distance between i and j.
K = a constant.
α and β = exponential parameters, the values of which have to be estimated.

In a retail context, this states that the potential interaction between a consumer and various retail sources (an individual store or, more likely, a shopping centre) within an urban area varies directly with the attraction (or size) of each source, inversely with distance separating them from the consumers' point of origin. A gravity model of this kind could, therefore, be used for explaining the fact that large retail centres attract more customers than small centres, and showing how the drawing power of each centre is reduced with increasing distance.

The value of such a model would depend on its predictive power. This in turn would depend on how well the model is applied – that

---

[21] Reilly, W.J. (1929) Methods for the Study of Retail Relationships. *University of Texas Bulletin.* No. 2944. For a recent discussion see Parry Lewis, J. and Traill, A.L. (1968) The Assessment of Shopping Potential and the Demand for Shops. *Town Planning Review,* **38**

is, on empirical problems such as how to measure A and d and how to estimate α and β. As these are primarily questions of research methodology they need not greatly concern us here. Nevertheless, it is desirable to comment briefly on some of the problems. How should the size or attraction of a centre be measured? In many cases population size is used, occasionally weighted; for example, a study of luxury travel patterns might justify correction of the population of an area by multiplying it by the area's *per capita* income. In considering the attraction of a retail centre, an obvious indicator to use would be the volume of retail sales. In many cases, the attractive power of a centre should take account of the range of choice it offers. The index would need to allow for the number of items available within each major retail category with weights attached for brand varieties, with different weights assigned to each category according to several factors (such as whether perfect substitutes were available at a nearer source and shopping habits for different kinds of goods). The overall index would measure the range and quality of consumer choice offered at each locational source. Measurement of d may give rise to similar if less taxing, problems. For example, should it refer to physical distance, or travel time, or a measure of 'economic distance', such as transport costs plus a monetary value of time lost in travelling and of the inconvenience of travelling?

More troublesome is the question of what values should be assigned to the exponents. The exponent for the distance variable is very often assumed to be 1 or 2 (as in Reilly's Law); there is no inherent reason why it should take these values, and empirical tests have confirmed this. One series of studies failed 'to justify either the inverse linear or the inverse square "law" which previous investigators had suggested for the distance function'.[22] Finally, whether an exponent should be applied to A has also to be considered. This, again, will vary according to the character of the study. In most models no exponent is applied or, rather, there is an implicit assumption that its value is unity. For many purposes, however, agglomeration economies may be so significant that the exponential variable applied will be a function of A. This means that the exponents of different sizes of A will vary in value.

The value of gravity models as an aid to understanding consumer

---

[22] Hammer, C. and Iklé, F.C. (1957) Intercity Telephone and Airline Traffic Related to Distance and the 'Propensity to Interact'. *Sociometry*, **20**

spatial behaviour and retail location has been criticised by Huff.[23] His first criticism is that the gravity concept is primarily an empirical notion with very little theoretical content. Gravity models describe and predict a pattern of spatial interaction, but they do not explain why this pattern develops. It is probable that the theory behind the gravity concept could be explained in terms of optimising behaviour, such as attempts by individuals (or society) to minimise cost (or effort) or to maximise utility (or satisfaction). But few gravity analysts have tried to probe the existence of such a link by exploring the nature of the theoretical base, if any, of their models.

Secondly, Huff argues that gravity models have a low predictive power. This is because, in his view, a gravity model would point to a greater probability of interaction taking place in a large city, and could not easily explain a trend towards retail decentralisation as urbanisation intensifies. This is in line with a view held by some analysts that agglomeration diseconomies (high population densities, high land values, traffic and other forms of congestion, parking problems, managerial difficulties in controlling large establishments) cannot be encompassed in gravity models. Some go further and argue that the gravity concept is inconsistent with the existence of these diseconomies, since one of its main propositions is that interaction between any point and a centre varies directly with the size of the centre.

Although there is something in this view, it does not justify rejection of the gravity technique. Modifications can be made to a gravity model that improve its predictive power. Thus, an exponent of less than unity can be applied to A, if it exceeds a certain size, thus accounting for agglomeration diseconomies. Congestion costs can also be included in the measure of d; d will not be measured in physical units of distance but in economic distance terms. Within a large congested urban area, the friction of distance will be much greater than an actual distance measure would suggest. With these refinements, the drawing power of a large centre (reduced by a low exponential variable) over consumers located at a distance (properly measured) would fall off so much that at a certain distance the low intensity of interaction might justify the development of a new retail centre (or persuade existing firms to transfer from the central core

[23] Huff, D.L. (1961) Ecological Characteristics of Consumer Behaviour. *Papers and Proceedings of the Regional Science Association,* **7** 19–29

to outlying areas). In other words, a gravity model developed
explain retail location patterns is capable, when correctly specifie
of predicting trends in retail decentralisation.

The Baumol–Ide model

A different model has been proposed by Baumol and Ide.[24] It stat
that a consumer will shop at a locational source when his demai
function is such that

$$F(N, D) = wp(N) - v[C_d D + C_n \sqrt{(N)} + C_i]$$

is positive.

(1) $F(N, D)$ measures the expected net benefit of the consum
from going to a store at a particular source. It varies with ,
his distance from the store, and N, the number of items offere
for sale at the store.

(2) Assumed costs are C_d = a cost of transport assumed propo
tional to distance, $C_n \sqrt{N}$ = assumed costs of actual shoppin
and C_i = opportunity cost of other shopping opportuniti
foregone.

(3) $p(N)$ = the probable satisfaction function.

(4) w, v = subjective weights assigned by the consumer.

Certain general implications can be drawn from this model. Th
minimum number of items required to induce a consumer to sho
at a given store will increase with D. The maximum shoppir
distance is where the consumer's expected net benefit from shoppir
at a given store is zero. This is found by fixing $F(N, D) = 0$, an
solving for D. This yields

$$D = \frac{w}{vC_d} p(N) - \frac{1}{C_d} [C_n \sqrt{(N)} + C_i]$$

Finally, since the probable satisfaction function $p(N)$ takes int
account the numbers and types of goods offered at each centr
while the opportunity cost function C_i allows for the location c
other retail establishments and the variety of goods each has t
offer, this model results in consumers discriminating between particu
lar items according to their location (distance from the consumer
and according to the categories of goods available at each source

[24] Baumol, W.J. and Ide, E.A. (1956) Variety in Retailing. *Managemer Science*, **3** 93–103

In other words, a theory of consumer spatial behaviour of this kind can help to explain why retail establishments of a given type may be located optimally at sites different from those that are optimal for other types of store.

However, the Baumol–Ide model gives rise to serious empirical difficulties: the problems of estimating the probable satisfaction function, of how to measure opportunity costs and how to deal with the subjective weights, w and v. When correctly specified, gravity models are much easier to test empirically and have greater predictive power in forecasting likely trends in retail location.[25] These advantages more than compensate for gaps in their theoretical foundations.

5 A model of urban residential equilibrium

The most systematic economic model of urban spatial structure has been presented by Wingo.[26] His theory relates to residential development, though with modifications it could be applied in other spheres. It is an equilibrium theory where the organising force is provided by the market mechanism, that is, urban land is allocated in terms of site size and accessibility (nearness to the city centre) according to supply and demand relationships, and equilibrium is achieved because the resulting spatial organisation conforms to least cost principles. The theory builds on ideas suggested by other urban researchers. As we shall see, Wingo's analysis retains the assumption of complementarity between rent and transport costs advanced more than three decades earlier by R.M. Haig, which in turn provides an urban parallel to Von Thunen's agricultural model. In addition, following M.J. Beckmann and anticipating W. Alonso, Wingo allows for the fact that the size of site is an important variable, and uses a consumption function expressing how the quantity of land demanded by the individual household varies inversely with price. At the same time, he treats the locations of households as a variable rather than simply assuming them fixed. But the theory is also original and elegant, and Wingo demonstrates how households of particular rent-paying abilities are spatially distributed to sites

---

[25] On the other hand, gravity models have only a limited value for forecasting the sales of a new shopping centre. The use of such a centre may involve extensive changes in journey patterns and breaks in old shop loyalties, and consequently its growth is difficult to predict from present and past experience

[26] Wingo, Lowdon, Jr. (1961) *Transportation and Urban Land*

with a particular structure of rents in a way that achieves equilibrium. Locational equilibrium is achieved by substitution by households between transportation costs and rent costs. The possibility of such substitution enables households to distribute themselves so that they take up the total supply of land available for use within the city. On the demand side, if the prices of other goods are held constant, rents that households are willing to pay are assumed to be consistent with utility theory so that the greater the unit rent, the fewer the units of land consumed. This means, of course, that the density of settlement is higher in the more accessible (i.e. the high rent) locations.

The model assumes: a city with a population homogeneous in regard to income and tastes; a given location of employment centres; a given transportation technology; the marginal value the worker places on leisure is known, as is the marginal value households place on residential space; prices other than the price of urban land are taken to be constant. Transportation costs are a major element in the model. Monetary costs are a function of distance travelled and terminal costs which depend on congestion at the city centre. In addition, transport costs include commuting time to work, regarded as an extension of working hours and priced according to the marginal value of leisure.[27] These elements make up transport costs, t, which are a function of distance from the home to the city centre, d. Therefore, transport costs in money terms equal t_{d_j}, where j represents the location of the household. In the diagrammatical exposition given below we assume that transport costs are a linear function of distance, but there is no need for this simplification. The rent for a site is defined simply as the price per unit of land multiplied by the quantity of land occupied, i.e. pq where p = price per unit of land, and q = quantity of land. Since, as we shall see, the price of land is assumed to be zero at the margin of settlement on the city boundary, it is clear that rent is conceived only in terms of accessibility to the city centre and specifically excludes opportunity cost elements measuring the alternative uses to which land on the periphery of urban settlements might be put. Land near the city centre is valued more highly than land at a greater distance because it offers greater accessibility; the price of land thus varies inversely

---

[27] On the other hand, no allowance is made for the disutility and inconvenience of travelling

with distance from the city centre. Rent payments and transport costs are linked together for the urban resident. It is assumed that, regardless of location, each household spends a constant sum on land rent *plus* transport costs. This constant is assumed equal to transport costs to the most distant, i.e. the marginal, residential location, d_m, where the price of land is zero. We may write:

$$p_j q_j + t_{d_j} = t_{d_m} \qquad (1)$$

Rearranging:

$$p_j q_j = t_{d_m} - t_{d_j} \qquad (2)$$

Rent for land is equivalent to costs of transport *not* incurred. Wingo calls this 'position rent' defined as 'the annual savings in transportation costs compared to the highest cost location in use'.

Households prefer more land rather than less land, but the higher the price of land the fewer units of land will be consumed. The size of site a household occupies is, therefore, inversely related to the price of land; in other words, the demand curve for land is downward sloping from left to right. Algebraically,

$$q_j = \frac{a^b}{p_j} \qquad (3)$$

where a and b are parametric constants and $b > 0$.

At any given location within the city area, equation (2) fixes the amount of money spent on position rent while equation (3) determines the size of site occupied and the price of land when the equations are solved simultaneously. The functions p_d and q_d may thereby be derived. This provides the equilibrium solution for the individual household.

Market equilibrium requires that the demand for land at each distance from the city equals the supply at that location given the structure of position rents consistent with individual equilibrium, and in such a way that the total land available is allocated between households. From equation (3), we know that the spatial distribution of households which permits equilibrium will result in a population density gradient, with the slope declining from the centre to the city boundary. If we assume that the city is circular in shape and that all land is available for residential use, then the supply of land function is as follows:

$$\sum_{}^{j=1} S_{d_j} = \pi d_m^2 \qquad (4)$$

REGIONAL ECONOMICS

Market equilibrium is then determined by

$$n = 2\pi \int_{d_o}^{d_m} \frac{d}{q_d \partial d} \qquad (5)$$

where n = total population, i.e. the number of households, in the city, and d_o represents the city centre. The equation states that the city population is equal to the integral of the density of population, $1/q_d$, over the area of the city. If equations (2), (3) and (5) are solved simultaneously, d_m, p_d and q_d are obtained, and this is the solution to the problem.

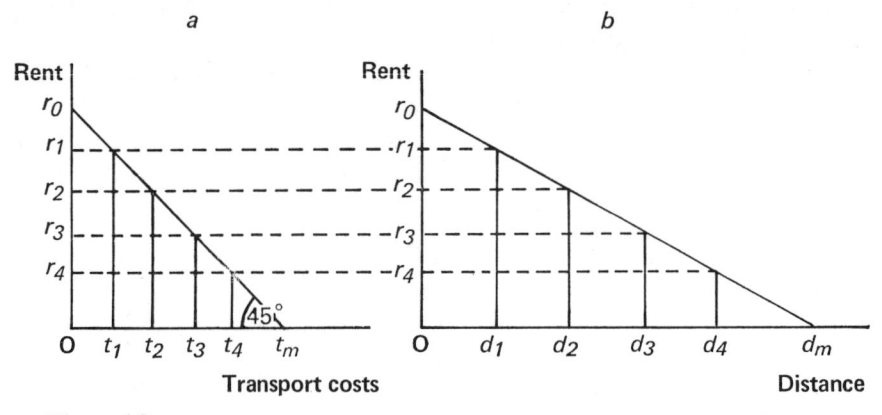

Figure 6.2

The model may also be illustrated diagrammatically. Figure 6.2 enables us to derive the total rent payment for land per household at each location between the city centre and the margin of settlement, d_m. Figure 6.2a reflects equation (2) showing that the sum of rent and transport costs equals a constant. Thus, the function relating rent to transport costs consists of a straight line having a 45° slope. At the city centre there are no transport costs but rent = r_0; at the city boundary rent is zero but transport costs are at a maximum, t_m. At intermediate locations the summation of the two elements equals t_m; for example, $t_m = r_1 + t_1$. From figure 6.2b we may read off the locations associated with each position rent as given by the expenditure constraint, that is, the budget line in figure 6.2a. We thereby obtain the *fixed* position rents per household paid at each location measured in terms of distance from the city centre.

URBAN SPATIAL STRUCTURE

This leads on to figure 6.3a. No matter how high or how low the price of land each household pays the same amount in rent at a given location. This fact can be shown by a set of rectangular hyperbolas on the graph that relates price of land to quantity consumed. Locations increasingly distant from the city centre are

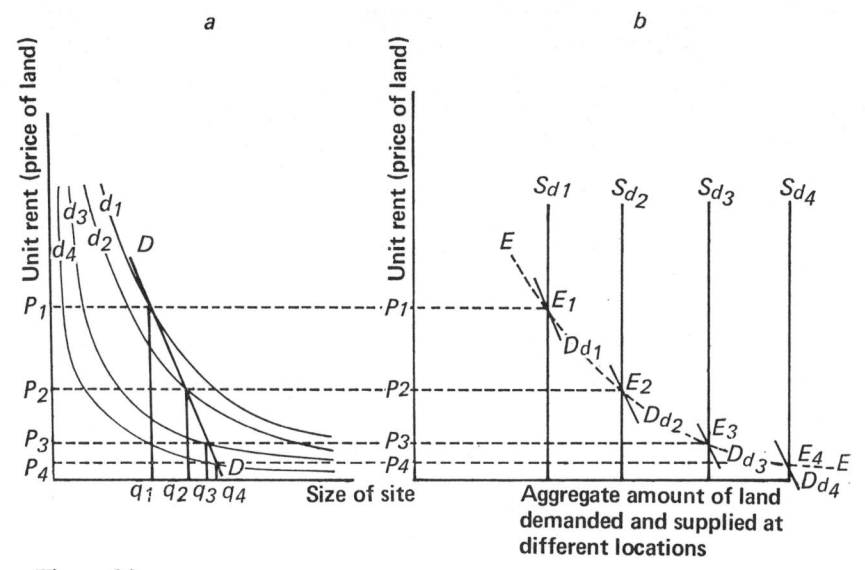

Figure 6.3

reflected in lower rectangular hyperbolas, since as households move out towards the city boundary more and more of their constant expenditure available for rent and transport costs is absorbed in transport costs leaving less for rent. Thus, the rectangular hyperbolas d_4, d_3, d_2 and d_1 are associated with rent payments r_4, r_3, r_2 and r_1 and locations d_4, d_3, d_2 and d_1.[28] The point on each rectangular hyperbola that denotes the price of land and the actual quantity of land occupied will depend on the nature of individual demand functions. Equation (3) tells us that demand curves will slope downwards from left to right. Since households have the same income and the same tastes the demand curve DD is the same for all households. Figure 6.3a shows us, therefore, that the nearer the city centre a household is situated the higher will be the price of land and the

---

[28] We assume that each location represents a concentric ring of equal width around the city centre

141

smaller the site occupied (i.e. the greater will be residential densities). Given the individual household's demand curve and the position rent paid in each concentric ring (d_1, d_2, d_3 and d_4), we can determine the price of land in each ring and the amount of land occupied by each household. Thus households near the city centre at d_1 will pay a relatively large rent r_1 which will reflect a high unit rent p_1 but a small site q_1; households near the boundary at d_4 will pay a very low rent r_4, but because land is very cheap, unit rent being p_4, they will each consume a relatively large amount of land, q_4.

The market solution requires that the total supply of land within each ring should equal aggregate demand for land within that ring at the ruling price of land. The requirement for market equilibrium is clear from figure 6.3b. The supply of land within each concentric ring is fixed, so that we get a set of infinitely inelastic supply curves where $S_{d_4} > S_{d_3} > S_{d_2} > S_{d_1}$. This reflects the fact that if each concentric ring is of the same width, the supply of land available within each ring increases as we move outwards from the city centre. Since the price of land for the market solution must be consistent with individual equilibrium, it follows that the demand curve for land within each ring must intersect the relevant supply curve where the position rent at each location meets the supply curve, in other words, at E_1, E_2, E_3 and E_4. Thus, for equilibrium to be achieved the total number of households must distribute themselves spatially over the city in such a way that the ruling land prices equate demand and the fixed supply of land within each ring. If the available land in the city were divisible into a very large number of concentric zones we would have a large number of supply functions and of equilibrium points. These points could be joined to obtain what may be called a **household demand spatial equilibrium schedule** (*EE*) which shows how households must be distributed over space so that demand and supply are equated at all locations, representing the spatial adjustment of demand to the overall supply of land as given in equation (4). It is important not to confuse this schedule with an aggregate demand curve; aggregate demand is not found from one point on the household demand spatial equilibrium schedule but from the integral of this schedule in the case of perfectly divisible locations.

A disturbance of equilibrium is easily handled in the diagrammatical solution. For instance, consider the effects of an increase in the number of households. The aggregate demand for land must increase and if the supply of land remains constant the price of land must rise. This may show itself in a leftward shift in the demand curve *DD* reflecting a willingness by households to live at greater densities and to tolerate smaller residential plots. In figure 6.3*b* the demand curves for land within each ring will shift upwards so as to restore equilibrium between demand and supply at the now higher unit rents. Another possible result might be an extension of the margin of settlement. This will raise the maximum level of transport costs t_m and will consequently involve a higher budget line in figure 6.2*a*. This, in turn, will shift the rectangular hyperbolas associated with specific locations outwards in figure 6.3*a*, a change which in itself will tend to raise the price of land. This effect will be moderated, however, by the fact that extension of the margin of settlement will increase the supply of land available for residential occupation. It is conceivable that the household demand curve could shift to the right sufficiently to maintain the formerly held living densities within the original city limits. Urban land prices will still increase in this latter case, unless the increased supply of land is so great and marginal transport costs so low that spatial densities throughout the city actually fall. We leave it to the reader to work out the effects of other departures from equilibrium.

The key element in this model is the complementarity of rent and transport costs as expressed in equation (1). The preferences for access to the city centre and for residential living space are described in separate equations and are not interrelated. Without the fixed budget constraint of equation (1) there would be no solution. Equation (1) has other important consequences for the model. The constant expenditure constraint on rent plus transport costs along with the assumptions of the same unchanged income for all households and no changes in expenditure on other goods and services ensure that we can draw up a single individual demand curve that applies to *all* households regardless of their location.[29] Equation (1)

---

[29] This is to be contrasted with the expenditure function adopted by W. Alonso which admits variations in spending on land, transport costs *and* other goods and services. In his theory, as transport costs change not only will the amount of money available for spending on land and other goods vary but also the allocation of this variable sum between land expenditures and other expenditures may alter as well. This means that, according to Alonso, the demand curves for the same individual will vary with his location. (Alonso, W. (1964) *Location and Land Use*. 36–7)

also tells us something about the character of individual demand curves. The fixed budget line means that as households move out from the city centre, and as transport costs increase, total rent payments must fall. In addition, the model presupposes that the price of land decreases with increasing distance from the city centre, partly because land near the centre will command a higher price because of its greater accessibility value, partly because in a city of circular shape the supply of land within each concentric ring increases with distance from the centre. It follows that the elasticity of demand for land is less than unity; a fall in the price of land with increasing distance from the city centre also involves a fall in total household rent payment. That the household's demand curve for land has less than unitary elasticity is, in fact, a condition of equilibrium. Assuming that the price of land falls off with distance from the city centre, this equilibrium condition is guaranteed by equation (1). If, on the other hand, the price elasticity of demand was equal to unity, then the household demand curve would also be a rectangular hyperbola, and there would be no solution. Finally, if elasticity exceeded unity an individual equilibrium solution is possible only if land is dearer near the city boundary than near the city centre; market equilibrium would in such a case be impossible since the amount of space occupied by households would vary inversely with distance from the city centre, and this is obviously at conflict with the supply of land function.

This model explains and illuminates some observed regularities in the allocation of urban space among households and in the structure of city living densities and rents. The assumption of identical incomes and tastes for all households would obviously need to be relaxed if the model was to be made more realistic. This might be achieved by dividing the total number of households in the city into different income-classes, and drawing up separate expenditure functions and land demand curves for each class. Thus, in figure 6.3a we would need a set of rectangular hyperbolas and a different demand curve for each class of households. As a consequence, the revised model may be able to explain such observed statistical associations as the tendency for site-size and location distance from the city centre to increase with income, and the fact that although the income elasticity of demand for land is positive for all income groups it probably exceeds unity for the rich but falls well below unity for the low income households. Even so, the model would not be able to accommodate the tastes of those households that might require a large residential site near the city centre and/or those households demanding only a small residential plot in the distant suburbs. A quite different model would have to be used to show how marked variations in the demand for land at a given location could result from households having different relative preferences between living space and other goods and services.[30] Another difficulty is that the supply of residential land will not be equal to the area of the city. Substantial modifications are necessary to take account of land uses (by industry, commerce and the community) other than residential land use. Topographical irregularities within the city may also alter the available supply of land. Employment locations may be scattered indiscriminately or clustered at one end of the city so that accessibility cannot be measured solely in terms of distance from the city centre. The urban transport network may vary in density and efficiency in different sectors of the city, and technical changes in transportation may have to be allowed for. As we introduce more and more realism, elegance, simplicity and internal consistency may be lost. Nevertheless, the model offers some operational possibilities.

6 Concepts of city structure

In discussing some of the economic principles underlying the urban spatial structure, we have said nothing about the overall layout of the city. A few inferences could be drawn from the above analyses: a marked tendency for residential living densities to decline with increasing distance from the city centre; a systematic relationship between the location of retail shops and consumer service units and the spatial distribution of households; a tendency for the structure of land values, itself largely the result of competitive forces, to mould the pattern of urban land use; considerable spatial differentiation within the city by types of activity. From these, occasionally contradictory, tendencies it was not possible to elicit an impression of the pattern of the city as a whole. We must now refer to three classic attempts to describe city patterns. These are generalisations, partly based on observation, partly reflecting some of the economic principles outlined above, partly reflecting other principles drawn from sociological and human ecological theory. They represent ideal patterns in that they express views of how cities have developed under

---

[30] Alonso's theory, already referred to, is more adaptable in this direction

the operation of market forces in an institutional environment limiting, if not ruling out, intervention by city planners, and they also ignore inter-city differences in the composition of urban activities, topographical irregularities, constraints imposed by irregularly developed transportation networks, and so on.

The three systems to be discussed are: the **concentric zone** theory (elaborated by E.W. Burgess); Homer Hoyt's **radial sector** theory; and the **multiple nuclei** concept developed by Harris and Ullman from a suggestion by McKenzie.[31] The first two themes can be used to describe, and possibly predict, changes in the basic structure of land use patterns, while the multiple nuclei theory was intended as a summary of the urban land use pattern at a given point in time. However, there is no reason why the latter theory should not be made dynamic so that it can deal with urban growth and expansion; the analysis of Guttenberg briefly discussed earlier suggests ways in which this might be achieved. Another difference is that the radial sector concept was developed mainly to explain urban residential patterns, while the other two hypotheses refer to the structure of all urban land use. A characteristic common to all three theories, making them particularly relevant to the scope of our study, is that although they require interdisciplinary analysis for a complete explanation they rely heavily on the operation of economic forces in a market environment. Post war developments in land use theory have criticised this very narrow approach. Firey, for example, has stressed the importance of cultural values and the social behaviour of city residents, and this readily leads on to the view that group values will be reflected in urban planning decisions and controls which will mould the physical pattern of the city.[32]

The concentric zone hypothesis
This states that any city tends to expand radially from the centre so as to form a series of concentric zones, as shown in figure 6.4. The

[31] Burgess, E.W. (1925) The Growth of the City, in Park, R.E. *et al.* (edits) *The City*; Hoyt, Homer (1939) *The Structure and Growth of Residential Neighbourhoods in American Cities* and Weimer, A.M. and Hoyt, H. (1960) *Principles of Real Estate*; Harris, C.D. and Ullman, E.L. (1945) The Nature of Cities. *Annals of American Academy of Political and Social Science*, **242** and Ullman, E.L. (1962) The Nature of Cities Reconsidered. *Papers and Proceedings of the Regional Science Association*, **9**; McKenzie, R.D. (1933) *The Metropolitan Community*
[32] Firey, W. (1947) *Land Use in Central Boston*. For a typical expression of the revised approach see Willhelm, S.M. (1962) *Urban Zoning and Land Use Theory*

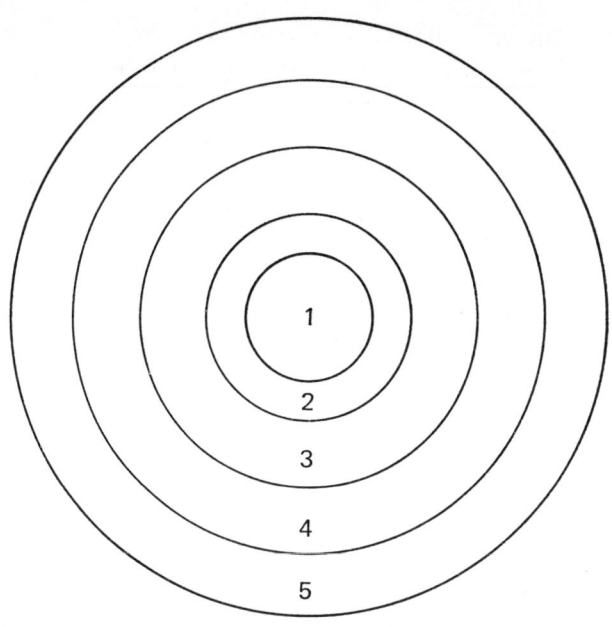

Figure 6.4

hypothesis may be present in either sociological/human ecological or economic terms. According to the former view, the circular zones show that the influence of a large city over the surrounding area of settlement wanes with distance outward. Social differentiation is present in the city area as a whole, but instead of being homogeneous it is polarised towards the city centre. Results of this differentiation may be presented by comparing averages of circular zones in regard to particular social phenomena (delinquency rates, tax ratios, indicators of poverty, etc.), and the trend line of these averages is sometimes called the 'gradient'. The gradient pattern reflects a spatial structure of land use within the city, which is determined by the preferences and needs of firms and households in respect to accessibility. Thus, a five-ringed city may typically be divided into the following zones: (a) the central business district; (b) a transitional zone, characterised by property in poor condition and rundown areas being invaded by business and light manufacturing; (c) a workers' housing and factory zone, with residences and plants in close proximity; (d) a high class residential zone; (e) a commuters' zone of residential suburbs and satellite commercial and shopping areas within accessible time-distance (say, varying between 30 minutes and an hour depending on city size) from the city centre. The main feature of the theory is the tendency, as growth occurs, for each inner zone to extend its area by invading the next outer zone, following a sequence known as 'invasion-succession'. The rate of this process depends on the rate of the city's economic growth and on population expansion. On the other hand, if a city's population tends to decline the outer zones tend to remain stationary while the transitional zone recedes into the central district. This contraction of the centre may mean the creation of commercial and residential slums, resulting in 'urban blight' problems.

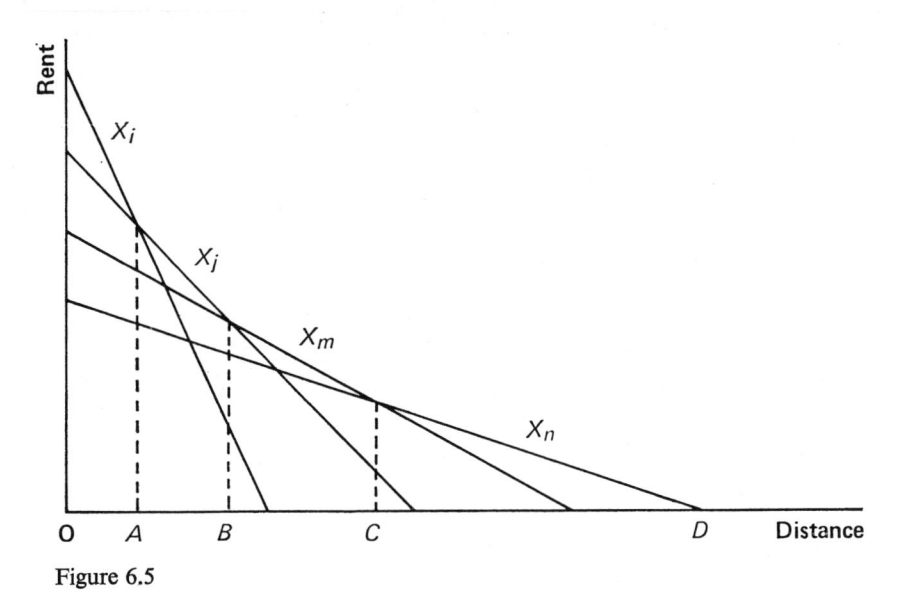

Figure 6.5

The economic interpretation of the concentric zone theory draws attention to a land values gradient from the city centre and land use functions reflecting this. The theory of land use on which this stands is a very simple one, already implicit in Haig's work in the 1920s. Since friction costs consist of transport costs plus rent (defined as negative transport costs) the dual of minimisation of the friction of distance is the maximisation of rent. Consequently, rent varies directly with accessibility. Each economic activity has a utility from a piece of land, measured by the rent which the activity is willing to pay for the land. The greater the utility obtained, the higher the rent an activity is willing to pay. In competitive conditions, bidding for land will in the long run ensure that each site is occupied by its highest and best use. The result is an orderly pattern of land use in which rents are maximised throughout the system. In a simple model, this results in a concentric circular pattern. If utility is measured by rent (under competition any surplus above costs will accrue to the landlord) and utility falls with distance from the city centre, we can draw up for any set of activities a set of rent functions which show how the rent each is willing to pay diminishes with distance. For simplicity, let us assume that there are only four uses competing for the available land and that rent-distance functions are linear. In figure 6.5, rent functions are shown for four activities, X_i, X_j, X_m and X_n derived from a set of potential uses of land. Since competition ensures that the highest and best use occupies any given piece of land, the rent functions may be arranged in a spatial pattern from the function with the steepest slope down to that with the flattest slope. Thus, at all distances from the centre to point A, X_i outcompetes all other activities, X_j dominates between A and B, X_m between B and C, while X_n uses the peripheral land CD. If the system is generalised from linear to areal terms by a rotation of OD about O we obtain a concentric circle system of land use, with activity X_i concentrated in the central zone, X_j in the next outer zone, X_m in the third zone, and X_n located in the peripheral zone.

At first sight, there appears to be inconsistency between the human ecological analysis and the economic interpretation of the concentric zone hypothesis. The two can be reconciled only if the poor families who inhabit the transitional zone and the workers' housing and factory zone live on relatively high value land. But this paradox is in agreement with actual observation, and rational explanation may be put forward to resolve it, for example, on the lines suggested by Hawley or Alonso above.[33] The concentric zone theory in both forms has been subject to several criticisms, most of which reduce to the argument that actual cities do not conform to the concentric pattern. Kish pointed out growth tends to be uneven in different parts of a zone,[34] and this leads on to the sector theory discussed below – the idea that expansion may tend to take place out from a limited sector of a concentric zone rather than throughout its circumference. Others have drawn attention to the existence of more than one focal

[33] In Section 2, 123–4
[34] Kish, L. (1954) Differentiation in Metropolitan Areas. *American Sociological Review*, **49**, reprinted in Gibbs, J.P. (edit) (1961) *Urban Research Methods*

point in a city with rent gradients around each point, and to the possibility of foci other than rent peaks, and this fact of observation is more consistent with the multiple nuclei concept. It has also been argued that the assumptions of the theoretical economic model may not hold: that special site characteristics may affect the competitive bids for land; that restrictions on competition, such as local authority regulations or factors inhibiting free entry, may result in distortions of the rent gradient; some types of business tend to conglomerate together while others tend to locate at a distance, and if this is so it suggests that a firm's rent function may not be determined independently of the locational pattern of firms already in the industry.

Finally, the concentric circles may have to be modified by topographical considerations and by the transportation network pattern. For instance, if a city has a limited number of main radial roads and other transport routes outwards from the city centre, high value land uses tend to develop near these routes, and as city growth proceeds land use and population tend to push out along the main roads. The result is that the ideal circular shape is distorted into a star-like formation. These criticisms do not invalidate the concentric zone hypothesis as an underlying principle of organisation rather than as a precise reflection of the structure of the city. The sector theory, as can be seen from figure 6.6, is a modification of the concentric zone hypothesis to take account of differential rates of increase in different segments of a zone; the multiple nuclei hypothesis may also employ the concentric circle concept to indicate diminishing rent gradients around each nucleus. Allowance for topographical factors and transport nets merely means a recognition of the fact that physical and economic characteristics vary from city to city, and in no way destroys the possible usefulness of the concentric zone hypothesis.

The radial sector theory
This theory, associated primarily with the work of Homer Hoyt, concentrates on the areal pattern of and shifts in residential locations. Different income group classes in a city tend to live, it is argued, in distinct areas describable in terms of sectors of a circle around the city centre. High rent or high price residential areas can be identified in particular sectors by the prevailing rents and/or prices, and there is a rent gradient downwards from each high rental area in all directions. Middle rental areas tend to adjoin the high rent area on one or

more sides, but low rent areas occupy completely different sectors (apart from when they are clustered near the city centre itself) quite often at the opposite end of the city. Areas which develop initially as low rent or low price areas tend to remain such as urban growth takes place, and there is a similar tendency with middle quality residential areas. This is not necessarily true of high class residential areas. The best houses tend to be located on the outward edge of a high grade zone. As growth proceeds and the boundary of the high class residential zone is extended, the inner areas of this sector may be abandoned by the upper income groups and lower rental groups will then filter into them.

In dynamic terms, the theory holds that similar types of residential land use originating near the city centre will normally migrate within the same sector and further away from the centre. High quality areas are conceived as the main propulsive force in this process, and exert a dominant influence on the direction of residential area growth in that it is the movement of such areas (defined on the basis of rent and/or price levels) that pulls city growth in a given direction. The characteristics of the extension of the high quality zone have been summarised by Hoyt as follows: it tends to proceed along the fastest existing transportation lines, and either towards another existing nucleus of buildings or trading centres, or towards the section of the city with open country beyond its boundary and away from dead-end sections which are limited by barriers to expansion; trends in the location of new office buildings, banks and shops within the city tend to pull the high grade residential zone in the same general direction; the growth of the zone continues in the same direction over long periods of time, but the direction of its path may be bent by the activities of property developers.[35] A qualification to the movement of the centre of gravity of the high grade zone outwards as growth proceeds is the possibility that luxury flats may be established in older residential areas near the business centre, especially in large metropolitan cities.

A hypothetical city structure embodying the radial sector concept is illustrated in figure 6.6. The central zone (1) refers to the city centre and the central business district. Sector (2) contains wholesale and light manufacturing activities, located at the opposite end of the

---

[35] Hoyt, H. (1939) *The Structure and Growth of Residential Neighbourhoods in American Cities*. 117–19

city from high quality residential areas. The areas labelled (3) are low class residential areas; these are mainly found at the opposite end of the city from the high grade zone or close to the manufacturing zone. The exception is a small inner ring around the city centre which may be territory at one time occupied by upper income groups

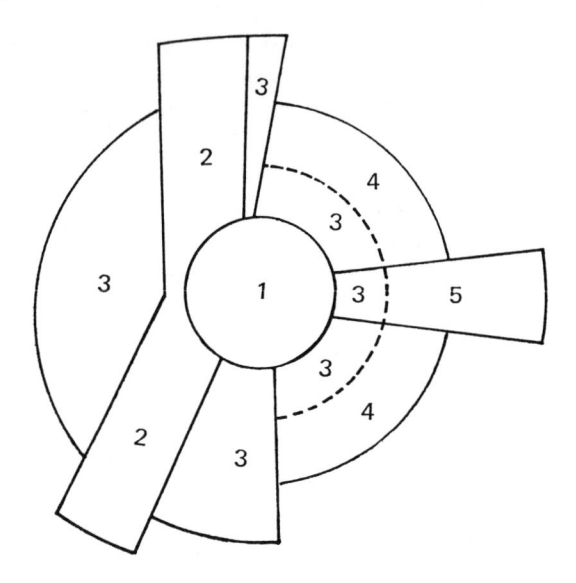

Figure 6.6

but long abandoned by them. The areas marked (4) are medium class residential zones which are found next to the high class zone (5). The latter proceeds radially outwards but only over a fairly narrow sector. According to the hypothesis, the trend of expansion will be in the general direction indicated by zone (5).

The radial sector concept has been criticised, by Rodwin among others.[36] The most damaging of these criticisms would appear to be: its reliance on an oversimplified view of the class structure; overemphasis of upper class attraction as a criterion for explaining and predicting shifts in residential location; dependence on the notion of residential trends in a free market without taking account of planning decisions and regulations by urban governments. This last point is not a damning criticism if a free market is an assumption of the theory; it is relatively easy to show how city planners may alter the

[36] Rodwin, L. (1950) The Theory of Residential Growth and Structure. *The Appraisal Journal*, **18** 295–317

city's residential structure once this assumption is relaxed. Many of the differences between actual observation and theoretical prediction are explicable as the consequence of planning controls; for example, low density high grade sites may be cleared, usually through public intervention, for high density low and medium class dwellings. The other defects of the theory are rather more serious. For instance, if the city population expands rapidly as a result of attracting manufacturing industry, are the housing demands of the new industrial workers likely to result directly or indirectly in expansion of the high-grade residential zone?

The multiple nuclei hypothesis
The basic idea of this approach is the view that cities develop around several distinct nuclei rather than around one centre of origin. Sometimes these other nuclei were distant centres, established in an earlier rapid urbanisation phase, which persist as centres as city growth fills in the space between them. Sometimes, nuclei emerge as new centres as the city expands. The number of nuclei and their functions will vary from city to city; generally speaking, the larger the city the more nuclei it will contain. The origins of a nucleus may vary considerably: a village cluster, a dock area or railway facility, an industrial estate, a suburban shopping centre or commercial district, a beach or other leisure facility. Once developed, each nucleus provides a focus for a hierarchical pattern of land use and a rent gradient around it.

The emergence of separate nuclei reflects, according to Harris and Ullman, four main factors; the interdependency of some types of activity that have to be close to each other because of dependence on specialised needs (for example, access to a trunk line transhipment point); the tendency for some kinds of like or complementary activities to agglomerate, such as retail shops and office buildings;[37] conversely, there is locational antagonism between dissimilar activities, for example factories and high class housing; finally, high rents and high land costs may attract or repel particular kinds of land use, and some service activities (especially standardised functions that can assume a distribution pattern similar to that of population) not able to afford the high rents of the main dominant centre will tend to locate at another nucleus.

[37] An example of complementary activities is given by the tendency for restaurants to be located near theatres

REGIONAL ECONOMICS

A representative city structure, following Harris and Ullmann, is shown in figure 6.7. No particular significance is attached to the shapes of each zone. Zones 1–5 inclusive are the same as in the radial sector model. Zone 6 is a heavy manufacturing area, and the nearby but separate Zone 9 is an industrial suburb. At the other end of the

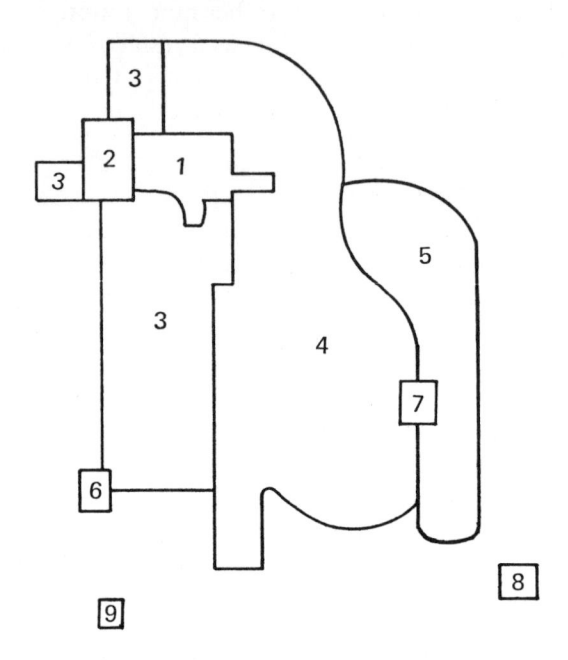

Figure 6.7

city near the high grade residential area is to be found the outlying business and commercial district (Zone 7) conveniently situated to the homes of executives and a residential suburb (Zone 8). The shapes of areas and the functions of nuclei may vary considerably between cities, but the structure and land use pattern will tend to reflect the same basic underlying principles.

The multiple nuclei explanation of urban structures takes into account more real world factors than the two other approaches. However, as Harris and Ullman conceived it, it merely gives a snapshot of a city at one point of time. In its original form, it did not amount to a comprehensive theory of land use. To become operational, it needs to be translated into dynamic terms and given predictive power. The original hypothesis offered no clues as to how this might be achieved. A new nucleus may emerge as the result of the operation of market forces **or** as a planned unit, perhaps in response to central congestion; it could develop around an existing facility or because of a nucleation of new service units. As Guttenberg suggested, the efficiency of the transportation network may determine whether growth occurs at the city centre or via the creation of a new nucleus. But if the multiple nuclei concept is to be more than mere description, it will need considerable refinement to explain the conditions under which new nuclei will develop and to indicate their probable locations.

These three concepts of city structure are not diametrically opposed to each other. Each concept probably has some relevance in explaining the structure of any city. The main difference between them is that the concentric zone and radial sector theories assume one dominant centre in the urban growth process while in the multiple nuclei theory various nuclei function as minor foci for growth. The radial sector and multiple nuclei concepts obviously take account of more complications than the concentric zone interpretation, but they modify the latter rather than refute it. As we have seen, expansion according to the radial sector hypothesis *does* take place outwards concentrically although only within sectors; in the multiple nuclei model the same basic tendencies are found around each minor nucleus as around the city centre (rent gradients, differentiation in land use, etc.) in the concentric zone theory. The same general theoretical notions, such as the attempt to minimise friction costs as an organising principle, are applicable in varying degrees to all three concepts of a city's structure.

Chapter 7
Urban growth

1 Introduction
The theory of urban growth is an underdeveloped area in the field of urban and regional economics. This is partly a consequence of the great diversity of urbanisation experience which does not easily lend itself to generalisation. It also reflects the complex character of the urban growth process and the fact that the city is probably more of a social and cultural phenomenon than an economic entity, so that its development cannot be explained solely in economic terms. Moreover, there is a dearth of detailed empirical studies on urban growth from which meaningful and testable generalisations might be drawn to build a theoretical framework. For these reasons, this chapter outlines several different approaches to studying urban growth rather than works out a detailed formal model.

The most intensively studied theory of urban growth is central place analysis, and examination of the scope and limitations of this approach takes up a substantial part of this chapter. Some attention is given to human ecological and sociological interpretations of urban growth, partly because of our acceptance of the necessity for urban growth to be treated in interdisciplinary fashion but also because these interpretations have considerable economic implications. Economic theories, such as the urban economic base concept, consideration of the city as an industrial location, and analysis of the relationship between scale and urban growth, are also discussed. This chapter presents less a theory of urban growth than a prologue to the development of such a theory.

2 Central place theory
Central place theory, introduced by Christaller in the 1930s,[1] is the

[1] First published in 1933 Christaller's classic is now available in English. Christaller, W. *Central Places in Southern Germany* (1966, translated by C.W. Baskin)

most widely known theory of urban growth. Although geographers have given it most attention, it is economic in content. According to the theory, the growth of the city depends upon its specialisation in urban service functions, while the level of demand for urban services over the service area determines how fast central places grow. Moreover, it is a general theory in the sense that it not only explains growth in the individual city but also the spatial ordering of urban centres over the regional and national economy.

The city's primary function is to act as a service centre for the hinterland around it (called the **complementary region**) supplying it with central goods and services such as retail and wholesale trade, banking, business organisations, professional services, administrative services, educational facilities and entertainments. These central services can be ranked into higher and lower orders, and we obtain a hierarchy of centres graded according to the orders of services they supply. Cities and towns grow because economic development and rising incomes lead to a more than proportionate expansion in the demand for central goods and services, and hence in the net income received by urban residents engaged in their provision.

The two key concepts determining why certain goods and services are offered only centrally and the factors affecting the size of the central place offering a particular service are the **demand threshold** and the **range** of a good. The threshold is defined in terms of the minimum level required to support a service and can be expressed in terms of population and/or income.[2] The threshold occurs when sales are just sufficient for the firm supplying the service to earn normal profits. It reflects economies of scale in the provision of certain services and agglomeration advantages accruing from locating centralised service establishments near to each other.[3] The range over which a service is supplied is affected by many

[2] Warntz's Gross Economic Population Potential (see Chapter 2.10) is a relevant measure here

[3] Services for which there is a large generalised demand (grocers' shops, primary schools, doctors in general practice, etc.) will be found in small as well as large central places whereas more specialised services (model fashion shops, colleges of commerce, specialists and surgeons) will only be provided in larger centres such as cities. External economies include the savings from avoiding duplication of commuting trips as a result of establishments such as department stores and technical institutes being sited near the business and commercial centre

factors[4] but its main determinant is economic distance (i.e. geographical distance converted into freight costs and other monetary costs involved in transportation). The range of central goods may be extended by technical progress and its impact in reducing transport and/or production costs. If we assume transportation is possible in all directions from the central place at the same cost, the threshold of a central good can be represented by the smallest concentric ring containing the demand necessary to make supply viable while its range can be shown by the concentric ring forming the outer boundary.

This outer ring will delimit the complementary region. It will vary in size for different goods and services, and its size will be regulated to a considerable extent by the distance from a neighbouring central place of similar or greater size. Demand within the hinterland will vary inversely with distance from the central place because of transport costs, even if we assume constant incomes and identical tastes. The growth of consumption of central services and the development of central places may be stimulated by several forces: high population density makes for more frequent social contacts boosting demand through a form of 'demonstration effect'; rising incomes; the level of cultural development and the region's social structure, since many central services are of a cultural nature; the degree of competition among establishments supplying central goods and services.

The central place hierarchy results not from accidental or arbitrary factors but from definite relationships between the size and functions of central places and inter-urban distance. There is an inverse relationship between the size of a given class of centre and the number of centres to be found in the class. Moreover, because the size of service areas varies directly with the size of centres, the complementary regions of small centres must be contained in those of large cities. Service areas of centres of dissimilar size overlap, but the service areas of equal-size centres do not. In the latter case, if the whole area of the system is to be covered service areas must be hexagonal rather than the ideal circular market area shape. A honeycomb of hexagonal complementary regions will develop with each enclosed centre in contact with the boundary of six equal

[4] These include the price of the service of the central place, the size of the place, population density in the hinterland, income distribution, and the distance of other central places supplying the same service

ranking and approximately equidistant centres. Because there are many different sizes of central place, there will be several honeycomb lattices with varying size hexagons superimposed upon each other.[5] The number of centres in each size-class will bear a constant mathematical ratio to each other following the sequence 1—2—6—18—54 ... Since each high order central place contains the characteristics of successive lower order centres, the number of complementary regions will increase in the ratio 1—3—9—27—81 ... Centres in the same size-class will tend to be equidistant, but larger centres will be further apart than smaller ones. This ideal structure represents the **marketing principle,** i.e. the association between each central place and its service area. It may be distorted by the **traffic** and **administrative principles.** The spatial distribution of towns will be influenced by the structure of the transport network. If economic development radiates out along a limited number of main traffic routes this will be the main determinant of central places, leading to a nesting of central places in multiples of four. The administrative principle reflects the need for centres where institutions exist to carry out administrative functions. It shows itself particularly where the administrative divisions of a region and their centres are planned ahead of settlement, giving rise ideally to a sequence of centres in sevens.

Departures from the pure theoretical scheme follow from interregional differences in economic development, income levels and tastes and from the fact that urbanisation takes place slowly over time leading to differences between the predictions of central place theory and observed real world structures. For instance, consider the consequences of economic expansion and population growth in an elongated area originally supporting two central places. Now a third central place becomes justified. According to theory it should be located at a point mid-way between the two original centres. However, many sites may satisfy the condition of having a sufficient service area, and there may be competition between rival locations to try to become the new central place. Which location triumphs could depend on many factors: the availability of transport facilities, the presence or absence of manufacturing or mining, the characteristics and distribution of population, whether entrepreneurial skills are on tap or not, and chance factors.

[5] For a more detailed description see Christaller, *op. cit.*, 58–80

The Christaller pure model of central place development can be generalised if we make certain assumptions.[6] Firstly, that population is evenly distributed over a homogeneous area. Secondly, that central places provide goods and services for a surrounding hinterland of fixed sizes, so that any two central places supplying the same centralised services will be surrounded by hinterlands of equal size.[7] Thirdly, that central places are sited in a pattern which maximises the spacing of places, subject to the constraint that all available space is swallowed up in at least one market area. Fourthly, the central places form a hierarchy. Thus, a central place provides the bundle of central goods and services associated with the function n if, and only if, the place also supplies the goods and services associated with the function $1 \rightarrow (n-1)$.

Given these assumptions we obtain hexagonal market areas, a central place in the centre of each market area, and a hierarchy of central places in which each place with the function n dominates M places (where M represents the number of size-types of central places in the system) including itself. The development of hexagonal markets results from the assumption that market areas soak up all the plane, since when this happens firms in each central place earn only normal profits and the complementary region of each central place is at its minimum possible (the threshold). Obviously, in the absence of free competition this result will not materialise. But even under conditions of free competition it is possible, and more realistic, for some of the plane to be left untouched by threshold market areas, for market areas other than of an hexagonal shape to emerge, and for some firms to earn excess (i.e. supernormal) profits. This modification permits the abandonment of one of the more restrictive of the original assumptions, and to this extent generalises the central place model.[8] At the same time, we can relax the implicit assumption of uniformly distributed purchasing power, since we are not tied to this assumption unless we need to obtain hexagonal areas.

---

[6] See especially Berry, B.J.L. and Garrison, W.L. (1958) Recent Development of Central Place Theory. *Papers and Proceedings of the Regional Science Association*, **4** and Dacey, M.F. (1966) Population of Places in a Central Place Hierarchy. *Journal of Regional Science*, **6** 27–33

[7] In considering dynamic factors Christaller in fact relaxed this assumption

[8] Berry and Garrison, *loc. cit.* See also Mills, E.S. and Lav, M.R. (1964) A Model of Market Areas with Free Entry. *Journal of Political Economy*, **72**

Even if threshold market areas do not use up the whole area and no matter what the distribution of purchasing power, provided we retain the concepts of the **range** and the **threshold,** so that there is an upper and a lower limit to the hinterland which for each central good can be serviced by a given central place, a hierarchical spatial structure still emerges. This can be demonstrated in the following way.

Assume an area supplied with n types of central goods, ranked in ascending order from 1 to n. Then the central place which supplies n (let us call it A) needs the largest market area. As many A centres will exist as there are threshold sales levels to support firms supplying good n. If total sales levels are an exact multiple of thresholds for good n, market areas will be bounded by the lower limits to the range of A centres. In such a case firms will earn only normal profits and even this performance requires locating to minimise costs, either by minimising distribution costs if the product is delivered or minimising commuting costs if the consumer comes to purchase the product. In the simplest model, this means that central places have to be sited at the centre of the market area. If total sales exceed a multiple of the threshold but are not great enough to justify another A centre, then excess profits are possible. All other central goods and services ($n-1, n-2 \ldots 1$) will also be supplied by A centres, and excess profits are possible in the supply of these.

Table 1

The central place hierarchy: how n goods are supplied by M centres

centres	$n^*, n-1, \ldots$	$n-i^*, n-(i+1), \ldots$	$n-j^*, n-(j+1), \ldots$	...	$k^*, k-1, \ldots 1$
A	x	x	x	...	x
B		x	x	...	x
C			x	...	x
.					.
.					.
M				...	x

However, there will be some good, let us call it $n-i$, where purchasing power located in the interstices between the threshold market areas of A centres supplying good $n-i$ will justify further threshold market areas in these gaps. It will be more efficient for these gaps to be plugged by a second set of centres, which may be named B centres, supplying the good. As before, if the market areas are exactly threshold size only normal profits will be earned, whereas the existence of part-multiples of the threshold will allow some firms to earn excess profits. The central good $n-i$ is called a **hierarchical marginal good;** the number of hierarchical marginal goods determines the numbers of orders of central places in the hierarchy. B centres will, of course, also supply lower threshold goods from $n(i+1)$ down to good 1. Similarly, if $n-j$ (where $j>i$) is also a hierarchical marginal good, a third set of central places designated C centres will also emerge. The hierarchy will consist of a number of types of central place equal to the number of hierarchical marginal goods; if there are M marginal goods ranging from n to k, there will be M sets of central places. Some firms supplying each central good may earn excess profits, depending on whether threshold areas absorb the whole plane. All central places will be located at points from which they can most efficiently serve their complementary regions with central goods. The marginal firm will probably earn only normal profits, but the supra-marginal firms can compete spatially for subthreshold purchasing power existing between the threshold market areas of the spatial system. The hierarchy is shown diagrammatically in Table 1; the asterisks (*) indicate hierarchical marginal goods while x indicates the set of goods supplied by a particular centre.

Criticisms of central place theory
The theory has by no means been generally accepted, and has had to face a battery of criticisms from various quarters. Whatever the force of these, central place theory remains one of the most fruitful theoretical and operationally feasible approaches to the study of urban growth. Its value is multiplied in a regional economics context because no other theory stresses as much the interdependence between a city and the region within which it is situated.

Some of the criticisms need not be taken very seriously, because they are either unjustified or irrelevant to assessment of the theory as a theory. Some critics have argued that central place theory predicts urban location patterns which can be distorted out of recognition by transport developments which affect accessibility in different directions or by variations in local administrative patterns.[9] But, as we have seen, the qualifications resulting from consideration of the traffic and administrative principles were fully admitted and analysed

[9] For example, see Boskoff, A. (1962) *The Sociology of Urban Regions*

by Christaller himself and far from detracting from the theory increase its value by making it more realistic. Other criticisms, though not without weight, stress the difficulties of its empirical application rather than question its theoretical importance. Thus, it is argued that it is sometimes difficult to identify what are central goods and services, particularly since (as Christaller himself recognised) the division between central and dispersed goods changes over time, and, because of spatial differences in the level of technology, over space. Similarly, there have been criticisms made of the measures used to determine the centrality of a place. Christaller himself, probably because of lack of data on retail trade and other activities, used telephone connections as an approximate indicator of centrality. The defects of this indicator are obvious, particularly at a time when a country's (or a region's) telephone system is being extended, especially if at uneven rates over space. For a more precise indicator we would need to estimate the net income received from the supply of central goods and services, which runs into the difficulty of identifying central goods mentioned above.

Central place theory predicts that large cities will specialise in goods with broad market areas. But as cities grow services are supplied which have very little to do with supplying large non-local market areas. For example, living and social conditions in large cities generate needs which are not typical of small urban centres, such as car parking facilities. Secondly, as city size increases some services performed by households or business units for themselves are demanded in large enough quantities to support specialised units supplying them. Economies of scale may account for the growth of launderettes, copying services, and so forth. Thirdly, as cities grow, services which were performed by generalised units or by units engaged in 'sales and service' functions are taken over in part by units specialising in a more restricted line of services. This development of new functions is not necessarily associated with an increase in the volume of services performed or in an extension of market areas.

These hypotheses have received some empirical support from **urbanisation indices** measuring the *per capita* importance of an industry or service in large cities relative to smaller centres. An index of this kind can be represented by a Lorenz curve where the abscissa shows the cumulated proportion of receipts by a specified service industry while the ordinate indicates the cumulative proportion of resident population by urban centres. Such indices help us to separate central goods and services into higher and lower orders and to discover specialised non-central services which are supplied primarily in large cities. Empirical research referring to the United States showed that 'the differentiation and specialisation of service trades with increasing city size can be explained to only a small degree by principles stemming from the central place scheme or from notions of an urban hierarchy'.[10]

The theory is more relevant to agricultural than to highly industrialised regions. According to the theory, the role of the city is to act as a service centre for its hinterland. This function is most clearly visible when there are no urban centres of any size in the hinterland. Where large urban centres of similar size are found in a region, there is a greater possibility of specialisation in functions between them and a probable distortion of Christaller's urban size hierarchy. Moreover, in a densely populated and highly industrialised area there will be many urban centres, often leading to quite large centres being in close proximity to each other. In a case of this kind, social and commercial interaction between the two centres is likely to promote growth by a mechanism not directly related to the provision of central goods and services. Again, the common phenomenon of suburban development in relation to a central city and the growth of industrial estates cannot be fitted easily into a central place framework.

Large urban centres are often very important manufacturing locations, due to agglomeration economies and the existence of metropolitan labour markets. To the extent that urban growth is the result of the expansion of manufacturing within the boundaries of the city or town, particularly if the plants concerned cater for national and world markets, then this growth cannot be predicted by central place analysis. In large countries such as the United States urban manufacturing plants often serve only regional markets, but in small countries such plants rarely serve the regional market alone. Moreover, the administrative headquarters of *national* commercial and financial organisations are usually located in large cities. Central place theory is more applicable to the supply of personal services than business services.

[10] Duncan, O.T. (1959) Service Industries and the Urban Hierarchy. *Papers and Proceedings of the Regional Science Association.* **5** 105–20

Central place theory also underplays the contribution which migration may make to increased urbanisation.[11] Although, of course, migration into urban centres may reflect increased employment opportunities associated with a growth in net income received from supplying central goods and services, not all or perhaps even the bulk of migration will take place for that reason. The growth of the labour market may be explicable by increased employment opportunities in manufacturing. In other cases, increased urbanisation may be the result of in-migration from rural areas where the migrants have been pushed off the land because of technical progress in agriculture or other factors making for declining employment in the agrarian sector.

For these reasons, central place theory is inadequate for a complete understanding of the process of urban growth and the evolution of the spatial urban hierarchy. But this implies a need to add to and reinforce the central place concept, not to supersede it. In fact, it would be difficult to draw up a theoretically consistent and plausible theory of urban growth which neglected the function of cities and towns as providers of central goods and services for their hinterlands.

3 The urban economic base and urban growth

The economic base concept may be employed for analysing either cities or regions. The application of the concept to regions is treated formally in a later chapter. Here we merely consider the value of the base ratio as a predictor of urban growth and change.[12] Some mention must be made of base theory because it provides one of the few purely economic explanations of urban growth, and considerable attention has been devoted to it. The idea behind urban base theory

---

[11] See Morrill, R.L. (1963) The Development of Spatial Distribution of Towns in Sweden. *Annals of the Association of American Geographers*, **53**

[12] Important sources on urban base concepts include: Hoyt, H. (1949) *The Economic Base of the Brockton, Massachusetts, Area*; Andrews, R.B. Mechanics of the Urban Economic Base, a series of articles in *Land Economics* (1953–6); Pfouts, R.W. (1957) An Empirical Testing of the Economic Base Theory. *Journal of American Institute of Planners*, **23**; Pfouts, R.W. and Curtis, E.T. (1958) Limitations of the Economic Base Analysis. *Social Forces*, **36**; Blumenfeld, H. (1955) The Economic Base of the Metropolis. *Journal of American Institute of Planners*, **21**; Tiebout, C.M. (1962) *The Community Economic Base Study*; Mattila, J.M. and Thompson, W.R. The Measurement of the Economic Base of the Metropolitan Area in Gibbs, J.P. (edit) (1961) *Urban Research Methods*

is simple, perhaps too simple. The structure of the urban economy is considered to be composed of two main categories: basic activities which produce and distribute goods and services for export outside a defined urban area; and service (or non-basic) activities whose goods and services are consumed at home within the confines of the city. Base theory assumes that basic activities are the key to the city's growth, and that expansion in the base sectors induces growth in service activities and hence in the urban economy as a whole. This is an oversimplified framework for analysing the complex phenomenon of urban growth.

There are three main criticisms that can be levied against the urban base approach. Firstly, there are serious difficulties involved in measuring the economic base, especially the problem of how to distinguish between basic and service activities. Secondly, the base concept appears to be a poor predictor of urban growth. Thirdly, urban base analysis suffers from theoretical drawbacks so weighty that one might argue that a division into basic and non-basic sectors ts meaningless. These three strands of criticism may be discussed in turn.

We cannot describe sales of goods and services outside a given area as exports or base activities until we define the area itself. In international trade, this presents few problems since national boundaries are fairly strictly drawn. At the urban level a satisfactory solution to the problem may be almost insuperable. If we delimit the city area at the boundary where the city government's political jurisdiction stops, we obtain a result very different from when we define the area in terms of the city's drawing power for particular kinds of retail sales and/or services. Possible criteria include labour catchment areas, retail trade areas for key commodities, or a 'consensus area' taken from the charting of market areas for several goods. A variant of this last suggestion is to draw the boundary at a series of 'breaking points', each of which is defined as 'a point up to which one city exercises the dominating retail trade influence, and beyond which the other city dominates'.[13] There is considerable choice in urban area delimitation for the purpose of base analyses, and the size of the base is obviously not determined independently of the boundaries selected.

---

[13] This concept was developed by Reilly, W.J. (1931) *The Law of Retail Gravitation*

Even if the area delimitation problem could be solved, there remains the question of how to classify basic and non-basic activities. Possible base sectors include manufacturing, mining, finance and banking services, distributive organisations catering for non-local markets, and activities supported by outside income such as tourism, central government offices, laboratories and other establishments, certain kinds of medical and educational institutions. Non-basic sectors include local government, shops supplying local demand, schools, lawyers, doctors and local service industries. But most categories cannot be sharply defined, and virtually all will produce for both outside and local markets. Moreover, the effect of an expansion in the urban base may be different in cases where goods and services are delivered to consumers compared with the consequences when consumers come to the city to purchase their goods and services. In the latter circumstances, consumption of non-basic output, for instance, travelling on local bus services and eating in the city's restaurants, may be ancillary to purchases of a commodity produced by the basic sector. Similarly, with regard to classifying non-basic activities a distinction must be made between sectors which import goods, services and capital for local output and those which do not. Finally, the larger and more complex the city's economic structure the less easy it becomes to make the division between basic and service activities. In a complex economy, a wide range of intermediate goods will be produced as well as final goods and their composition in terms of local, imported and exportable materials will vary. The urban economy becomes highly interdependent, and even considerable data on the inter-regional and inter-industrial commodity flows do not permit a simple division of total urban activities into basic and non-basic activities, especially since it may be quite common for a city to import as well as to export some quantity of a 'basic' commodity.

If an urban base model is to have operational value it will be necessary to employ a measure of basic and non-basic activities that enables a quantitative assessment to be made of each basic sector, and permits a separation of the total product of each sector into basic and service components. Possible measures include employment, wage bills, net output, gross output, physical production or money income and expenditure accounts for the whole urban area. Since social accounting analysis reveals capital transactions as well as goods and services transactions, the last measure is probably the best, but data cannot easily be obtained. In the absence of detailed information available on other possible measures, employment is the most commonly used measure. Its weaknesses are obvious: it is meaningless as a measure of capital exports; employment data fail to reflect changes in productivity, especially between basic and service activities; the base ratio varies widely from urban centre to urban centre, and even more significant, changes within a city over time; division of the employment of each firm or institution between basic and service employment requires costly and inaccurate survey methods (except possibly in a very small community). The deficiencies of the latter have resulted in the use of indirect methods, such as assuming that the employment associated with a location quotient greater than unity indicates basic activity.

The empirical difficulties attached to separating out basic from total urban activity mean that any base-service ratio constructed will only be an approximation, and its value as a predictor will be severely constrained by the deficiencies of the data, the imperfections of the measure used and the imprecision of the assumptions necessary to distinguish between base and service activity. Even leaving these problems aside, the base ratio will have low predictive power as a tool for forecasting urban growth. In some simple tests Pfouts found no relationship between basic activity (as measured by location quotient techniques) and growth (measured by population growth), and instead found a closer relationship between service activity and growth.[14] This finding, if supported by further studies, suggests that the proportion of basic to total activity will tend to fall as the city becomes larger. If true, this tendency would rule out the base concept as an explanation of long-term growth. If the base logic has any predictive value, it is more likely to be revealed in short-term forecasting when the structural composition of the urban economy will remain unchanged than in secular growth analysis. But base ratios may have serious shortcomings even as a short-run tool, because the base ratio may alter in value at different phases of the business cycle. In the long run, stability in the base ratio, if it existed, would probably be merely accidental. This is because in a secular growth context any causal relationship between the base sector and total urban activity will probably be obscured by the close interdependence between the base and service components.

[14] Pfouts, *loc. cit.*

The demand for local services may be derived indirectly from expansion in the export base, but at the same time non-basic industries will supply important inputs for export products and the efficiency of the local service sector may be a critical determinant of the competitiveness of urban firms engaged in exports.

This leads on to the conceptual weaknesses of base theory itself. It clearly overemphasises the role of exports, for can it be shown that a large proportion of basic industry will always result in urban growth and stability? A more satisfactory theoretical approach would be to substitute urban income analysis, a methodology parallel to national income models, for base theory. This would reduce the excessive dependence on exports and stress the significance of imports and savings as leakages from the income stream and also stress investment as an injection into the stream additional to exports.

The existence of imports has caused Blumenfeld to question the meaningfulness of the distinction between basic and non-basic activity. For example, a location quotient equal to unity for an industry may mean considerable imports cancelled out by exports. Attempts to quantify base activity inevitably lead analysts into urban input-output relationships, and when the city is viewed as an integrated unit of mutually interdependent activities the basic/non-basic distinction, in Blumenfeld's words, 'seems to dissolve in thin air'.[15] The same author notes that applicability of the base concept will tend to decrease with increasing city size and with the size of the flow of non-wage income into and out of the city; on the other hand, base theory becomes more relevant if there is increasing specialisation between cities. Blumenfeld's most extreme criticism is to invert base theory on its head by arguing that the local service sector is the primary determinant of long-run levels of urban economic activity and of the vitality, or otherwise, of the export base sector. Large cities prosper, it is argued, because their efficient local service sectors enable them to replace stagnating basic industries with new ones. The composition of the base sector in terms of industries and firms is variable, and subject to replacement. The service activities are the truly permanent feature of the urban economy, the key element in the attraction of export sectors and a vital factor in their continuing efficiency and competitiveness. In

---

[15] Blumenfeld, *loc. cit.*, 121

analysis of the growth potential of the urban economy Blumenfeld suggests the importance of **'criticality' studies,** which he conceives as being concerned with the vulnerability of local economic activity to outside competition and the potential capacity of the city's economic activities to expand into outside markets, and balance of payments analyses which are concerned with capital as well as current transactions and with imports as much as the export base. In short, the urban base methodology is a crude tool for analysis of the urban economy, and predictions based on the share of basic activities in total urban output are most unlikely to result in a sound forecast of long-run urban growth.

4 The human ecological approach to urban growth

Most theories of urban growth suffer from gross oversimplification. The city is not only an economic organisation, and its expansion is not solely explicable in economic terms. The city is also a physical structure of architectural units, an administrative institution, and above all a social organism. The process of urban growth is describable, therefore, from many perspectives. Sociological, especially human ecological, interpretations of this process have much to commend them, and since there are certain similarities between human ecological organisation and the phenomenon of economic competition a few brief general statements on this approach to studying cities are not out of place.

Human ecology may be defined as the study of movements and settlement of human populations as affected by their natural, social and cultural environments. To the human ecologists the city is a natural environment. Its development reflects the forces of economic competition, the counterpart to biological competition in the animal world. The struggle for survival induces human populations to aggregate in communities of different size and character as society becomes more complex; in a highly developed economy the appropriate community is the city. There are probably three main forces explaining how economic conditions operate within the city and urban communities in general. The first is the fundamental interdependence of men, the fact that they have to live in communities because they share the same basic condition. Thus, for instance, division of labour within urban communities is an adaptation for survival under the pressures of economic competition. Secondly, localisation has an economic function. Human beings locate their economic activities (and also their social and cultural activities) at certain places to help them to realise their objectives. Thirdly, the friction of space induces individuals to congest together in the central areas of the city. This tendency intensifies competition for central locations resulting in higher land values, higher rents and higher traffic congestion costs. Individuals have to weigh these higher costs against the strength of their functional needs for central locations.

A second major ecological concept, additional to economic competition, is dominance. In a market environment, before the introduction of zoning regulations and urban planning controls, the location of economic activities was the reflection of economic considerations alone. Industry and commerce tended to settle in the central city, partly because of the desirability of access to the market, partly because of the advantages of a large labour pool with a wide range of skills. Once located there, industry and commerce set the character of the city and the surrounding area and of the people living there. But as Reissman points out: 'The location, *per se*, of industry in a city is not a sociologically significant fact. When the location of a factory in a given neighbourhood, however, transforms it and the kind of population that lives near it, then we are, in effect, dealing with *social* space.'[16] Industry and commerce are, therefore, the dominants of an urban community, but their dominance in this context is not of an economic nature. Rather, they shape how people live in the city and in the space around it. One major aspect of this influence is the transformation of the city as a single point of agglomeration into the focal point within inhabited space which includes other 'subdominant' centres. Thus, Bogue[17] described his own work as 'a study in dominance and subdominance', in which he demonstrated a complex but systematic geographical division of labour between separate spatial units which were spread over an area far larger than the city itself. This analysis is a direct descendant of the thesis put forward by McKenzie in the 1930s.[18] He added to the concept of the city as a continuous densely settled area the view that there may develop a cluster of cities forming a

---

[16] Reissman, L. (1964) *The Urban Process: Cities in Industrial Societies*. 15
[17] Bogue, D.J. (1949) *The Structure of the Metropolitan Community*
[18] McKenzie, R.D. (1933) *The Metropolitan Community*. See also Schnore, L.F. Urban Form: The Case of the Metropolitan Community, in Hirsch, W.Z. (edit) (1963) *Urban Life and Form*; Sirjamaki, J. (1964) *The Sociology of Cities*; Boskoff, A. (1962) *The Sociology of Urban Regions*

'supercommunity' organised around a dominant central city and comprising several differentiated centres of activity. Moreover, the metropolitan community was a dynamic concept, and its growth was characterised by two main trends: an increase in aggregate population and an extension of the area within which local activities are carried on in common; an increased mobility of products, services and people opening up new choices for individuals, resulting in a higher degree of specialisation and making for a closer integration between the various centres within the metropolitan area.

Kish took the argument further. He demonstrated that the dominant centre was surrounded by bands of 'metropolitan influence' varying in width according to the size of the city. Subdominant centres nearer the central city displayed much greater internal specialisation of functions than those further away. This was explained by the theory that the power of the organising centre declines with distance, and that its influence over dependent units is reflected in various degrees of specialisation within these units.[19]

According to these theories stressing the dominance–subdominance relationship, urban growth manifests itself through the central city exporting specific functions (or groups of functions) to peripheral areas resulting in the development of new centres there, while at the same time 'encroaching' on areas and functions already in existence which lie in the path of regional expansion. These centres may be called **urbanised nuclei** that are located outside but accessible to the central city. They may have a degree of political independence but they are economically bound to the metropolis and rely on it for many services and facilities. These nuclei will have relatively high population densities, a non-rural occupational structure, and recognisably urban patterns of life. However, they cannot be considered separate communities, but rather a selection of urban 'fragments' which function more efficiently when segregated from the central city.

With industrial suburbs the mutual advantages of specialisation between the central city and the sub-centre are clear-cut. Central cities tend to intensify their commercial and service functions, but reduce their industrial character. The location of industry in the suburb reduces central congestion and physical nuisance costs, yet

[19] Kish, L. (1954) Differentiation in Metropolitan Areas. *American Sociological Review*, **49**

furnishes a continuous demand for labour and a supply of finished commodities; industrial firms in the suburb benefit from reduced pressure on space, lower costs of production, generally shorter journeys to work, without losing the advantages of access to urban services and to local markets. The functional role of residential suburbs speaks for itself. We also may find within the urban region satellite cities which are characterised by a more visible spatial separation but not independence, from the central city; these too may differ in function but their normal role would be to act as employing areas for the urban region. The **urban fringe** area, usually peripheral though it may be found in 'islands' or 'pockets' within the city limits, is recognised by the fact that the distinction between urban and rural characteristics within it is blurred. It is important in this scheme because it provides the major geographical source of urban expansion, within which residential and industrial suburbs may emerge during the growth process. Finally, since population densities tend to be higher in sectors containing roads to other major centres and to satellite cities than in other parts of the metropolitan area, another aspect of the central city's dominance is that it is the latent regulator of regional population distribution patterns.

The drawback to studying urban growth in terms of the dominance of a metropolitan city and its influence on the emergence of subdominant centres is that it treats the metropolitan area as a 'closed system' in isolation from broader regions and from the national economy as a whole. For this reason, ecologists have switched the emphasis of their attention from the economic dominance of central cities to examining the wider functions in the spheres of industry, transportation, marketing and finance performed by metropolitan cities in a broader regional and national context, i.e. in a generalised 'ecological field'.[20] In a comparison of factories located in Illinois with their spatially separated administrative offices located throughout the United States, Pappenfort found that Illinois factories were dissimilarly distributed according to where their head offices were located. Those factories with local head offices were distributed with reference to Chicago, the state's dominant metropolis, while those with head offices outside the region were located with reference to the influence of adjacent or more distant

[20] Pappenfort, D.M. (1959) The Ecological Field and the Metropolitan Community: Manufacturing and Management. *American Journal of Sociology*, **65**

regions. Pappenfort concluded: 'the consistency of the relationships suggests that they may reflect general principles of ecological organisation on the national level that the contemporary interpretation of the metropolitan community does not include'.[21]

In similar vein, Duncan and his associates argued that 'to understand metropolitan communities we must examine them in the context of a more inclusive system', a system which may be supraregional – sometimes the national economy.[22] Each metropolitan function may give rise to a distinctive type of sub-regional, regional or supra-regional relationship. Metropolitan influence or 'dominance' cannot be understood simply in terms of flows to each hinterland areal unit from a single metropolitan city, and the full scope and complexity of metropolitan relationships are revealed only in the context of an open system. The national and supra-regional functions of the metropolis are performed primarily through business corporations located in the city. The extent of these functions can be measured by net output data, wholesale sales, business service receipts, input-output data, and the flows of commercial and financial payments and receipts between areas.

The above discussion throws up an ecological framework for the study of city growth rather than suggests a theory of urban growth itself. It is not difficult to chart the broad lines on which such a theory would be constructed. The growth of cities would be comprehended as the result of basic economic, social and cultural forces that shape human life in a complex advanced (and urbanised) society. The spatial internal structure of the city will alter as individuals and groups readjust their locations in response to changing needs and changing economic conditions and circumstances. Economic growth will manifest itself in the city-region in an extension of the central city's boundaries and/or in the emergence of new and often highly specialised sub-dominant centres. At the same time, growth in the national economy will have repercussions on the structure and growth of cities via its impact on the supra-regional functions of business firms located in metropolitan city centres. If the human ecologists see the fundamental problem of human beings as how to organise themselves in their natural and material environment in such a way as to achieve a better satisfaction of their wants,

---

[21] Pappenfort, D. M. (1959) The Ecological Field and the Metropolitan Community: Manufacturing and Management. *American Journal of Sociology*, **65**

[22] Duncan, O. D. and associates (1960) *Metropolis and Region*

then their primary concern is with an economic problem, though one with considerable social consequences. In the context of urban growth, this means that cities will grow broadly for the same reasons as the aggregate economy grows, but because the city is most easily recognised as a social organism its expansion cannot be understood solely, perhaps not even primarily, in economic terms. Ecological and sociological interpretations of city growth are vitally important to an appreciation of how cities are structured, how they function and how they expand.

5 The communications theory of urban growth

One example of a sociological, even an interdisciplinary, theory of urban growth is that suggested by Meier.[23] He conceptualises the city in terms of human interaction. Transportation and communications are the main media for interaction. Cities originally developed and expanded because of opportunities for face-to-face transactions. But the direction of technical change and congested traffic systems are inducing a substitution of communications activity for transportation. The prevailing major agglomeration advantage of a city is now the benefits it offers of living close to centres of information exchange and to places where transactions are easier to complete. Urban growth manifests itself in an increase in the communications rate. Meier holds that the communications system is a reasonable base for building a theory of urban growth: as he puts it: 'The communications framework is most suitable for appraising the culture of cities. Much of that culture is expressed in the workplace, more in the market, a large share of it in the schools, and a great deal in leisure time activities.'[24] This statement makes it clear that it is public not private and personal communications which form the basis for urban expansion, because private communications are irrelevant to the study of the city's cultural processes that shape growth. Although Meier failed to elaborate how his theory could be made operational as a predictive approach, his concept of the **urban time budget,** i.e. the proportion of a day's time that a person would spend in various forms of public communication, is clearly intended as a device for making projections.

Much more work needs to be done on the role of communications in stimulating increased urban activity. Meier did not succeed in

[23] Meier, R.L. (1962) *A Communications Theory of Urban Growth*
[24] *Ibid.*, 7–8

establishing that an increase in communications activity was a necessary condition for urban growth, and failed to reveal a measurable relationship between a given change in the rate of communications activity and the associated change in urban growth. His insights are valuable in their emphasis on the behavioural aspects of city development, but at the same time it is difficult to accept that the communications framework is the single overriding element in urban growth. Webber's distinction between **urban places** (i.e. local areas of influence) and **non-place urban realms** (i.e. outward-looking spheres of influence at the global, national and regional levels) helps to build flesh on to the bare skeleton of communications theory.[25] Cities having a greater degree of contact with urban realms and a higher proportion of communications activity with such realms will tend to grow faster than cities the bulk of whose communications transactions occurs within the city itself.

6 City size and urban growth
A prevalent view amongst urban analysts is that size is a significant variable affecting urban growth. Their interpretation of the relationship between size and urban growth takes many forms. Some conceive of the city primarily as a location for industry. They argue that with industrialisation the city became necessary for economic reasons, since industry required access to a large labour pool and range of skills. Secondary factors then operated to expand the functions and increase the size of urban communities, since large population concentrations required increased services to maintain them – housing, social services, distributive facilities and (at a later date) leisure facilities. At the same time, economic and political centres of gravity tended to shift towards the city; urban attitudes and urban aspirations filtered through society, a process speeded up by improved transport and communications. If the city is predominantly a location for industry, its optimal and actual size responds to technological changes affecting industry and the requirements of an industrial labour force. Thus, it may be argued that more and more industries are clustering into mutually supporting complexes, based on input-output linkages and access to shared ancillary services, and that larger industrial complexes imply larger manufacturing centres. Moreover, many urban amenities require a

[25] See the brief references to Webber's ideas in Chapter 12 below

large population threshold for efficient operation. It needs a large city to maintain an airport, provide modern hospital services or support a computer complex. Small urban communities dependent on one industry may suffer in a world of rapid technical change from excessive instability and obsolescence.

An extension of the view that technical changes in industry favour large urban areas and handicap small ones is the **urban size ratchet** hypothesis. This states that only small urban communities are subject to decline, and that there is a critical size for a city beyond which absolute contraction will not normally occur. The argument is that 'at a certain range of urban scale, set by the degree of isolation of the urban place, the nature of its hinterland, the level of industrial development in the country, and various cultural factors, some growth mechanism, similar to a ratchet, comes into being, locking in past growth and preventing contraction'.[26] Possible explanations of this include: diversification of industry and of other economic functions in large cities insure against decline; large communities may gain more from central government financial assistance because they can be a more vocal, stronger pressure group, while the government for its part will be reluctant to abandon the large capital stock embodied in a city; with the expansion of consumer-oriented industries the large potential market of a city population assures growth, while on the supply side the presence in large cities of innovators, top managers and key personnel tends to make these cities the primary sources from which new industries develop.

Even if the urban size ratchet hypothesis is valid, so that cities above a certain minimum size rarely decline, it does not follow that cities above this minimum will continue to expand indefinitely. City growth rates will vary for many reasons other than size. The rate of urban growth may be a function of location in that cities in young, recently settled areas may grow faster than others. Cities with a more favourable employment and industry mix will also tend to grow rapidly, while a city's share in expanding growth industries will be dependent upon its success in interurban competition – and this in turn reflects relative agglomeration economies, availability of services, industrial sites and skilled labour, the efficiency of its transport network, and its tax structure and how this affects industry.[27] Moreover,

[26] Thompson, W.R., *op. cit.*, 22
[27] Chinitz, B. (1964) *City and Suburb: The Economics of Metropolitan Growth.*
3–22

when we consider the relevance of size, the largest cities, with a few exceptions, tend to grow more slowly than smaller ones. There may be a balance of opposing forces controlling the rate of city growth, represented by agglomeration advantages on the one hand and congestion costs and diseconomies of scale in public services on the other.

This possibility suggests that there may be something in the concept of an optimum city size. Economic, social and cultural criteria may be adopted to try to determine this optimum, but since the weighting of different criteria is bound to be subjective the choice of an optimum city size will be impressionistic. The main difficulty is how to balance economic efficiency criteria and non-measurable benefits such as the desire for **community participation potential**[28] and the congeniality of urban areas of different sizes. Furthermore, it is clear that the optimum will vary from society to society according to the institutional environment, levels of economic development and the definition of tolerable living standards. Finally, in a dynamic setting the optimum size will itself vary, and therefore does not provide a fixed reference norm against which urban growth patterns can be assessed. Factors changing the optimum level include improvements in transportation, communications and buildings technology and the application of management techniques in local government.

Criteria which might be employed to throw light on the usefulness of the optimality concept include: health factors (e.g. infant mortality may vary inversely with city size); public safety considerations (smaller cities have relatively less crime, and fewer car accidents and fire losses); municipal efficiency; educational facilities (large cities may spend more and have more complex buildings and equipment, but teacher/pupil ratios may be lower); better parks and public recreational facilities may be found in medium-sized cities than in very large or very small ones; large cities have an advantage in the variety of shops and personal services they provide, though not in standard shopping lines; the intangible benefits of smaller communities from the point of view of closer knit family life, housing facilities and providing a congenial atmosphere for life; not to mention strictly economic criteria such as the most efficient scale of urban unit for providing a representative 'mix' of urban services

[28] W.Isard's term, see Chapter 8.4

and facilities.[29] However, the problems of defining the optimum need not concern us here. If an optimal city size exists (even if it varies between societies and over time), and if the pressures of conditions above the optimum induce reactions from households and firms, this would explain a tendency for cities above the optimal size to grow more slowly.

An alternative explanation of why city growth rates may vary with changes in scale is the threshold concept.[30] This is based on the fact that as an urban area expands it comes up against barriers – due to topography, the public utilities network and existing land uses – which we may call thresholds of urban development. These barriers are not insurmountable but they can be overcome only at a high cost in capital investment. Confronted with a threshold, a town tends to keep within its limits for some time and expansion is consequently slowed down. Thresholds can take many forms: physical thresholds where expansion involves movement to high cost land; quantitative thresholds expressing the limited capacity of existing public utility works; and structural thresholds where internal urban structures restrict further expansion (e.g. population growth may require a large increase in the central shopping area which will be very expensive). The notion of threshold costs can be formalised by dividing the *per capita* investment costs necessary to locate a new inhabitant in a city into two components – normal costs and development costs. Normal costs are those not associated with a given location of investments necessary to accommodate new inhabitants; these remain constant or are a linear function of city size. Development costs (or threshold costs) are the fixed costs required to overcome the thresholds limiting development; they rise sharply with the onset of the threshold but decline once the threshold has been passed. Thus, the thresholds can be represented by peaks on the cost curve. The weaknesses of threshold theory are that it stresses development costs to the neglect of operating costs and that it fails to take account of the benefits of alternative patterns of urban

[29] See Duncan, O.D., The Optimum Size of Cities in Spengler, J.J. and Duncan, O.D. (1956) *Demographic Analysis.* 372–86

[30] Threshold analysis was developed in Poland by B. Malisz in 1963. See Hughes, J.T. and Kozlowski, J. (1967) Urban Threshold Theory and Analysis. *Journal of the Town Planning Institute,* **53** and Threshold Analysis – An Economic Tool for Town and Regional Planning. *Urban Studies,* **5** (1968); B. Malisz (1969) Implications of Threshold Theory for Urban and Regional Planning. *Journal of the Town Planning Institute,* **55**

expansion. Its importance in this context is that it offers an explanation of why cities and towns are unlikely to experience steady growth.

The urban growth process, however, may show considerable flexibility. If the capacity for attracting and expanding industry is a primary determinant of urban growth, a city may continue to grow fast by readjusting its spatial structure in a manner which enables it to absorb new industry efficiently. Suburbanisation of industry, transference of some of the functions of the central commercial core to suburban centres, redevelopment of central blight areas, extension of city boundaries and increased housing and commuting facilities are some of the more obvious readjustments of this kind.

At a more detailed level, there will be certain basic forces influencing the spatial distribution of industry relative to the agglomerative force of the urban market. The stronger the interlinkages of production, the more likely will firms in such industries seek an urban location; consumer goods industries tend to locate in accordance with population distribution, except that expensive luxury goods of occasional consumption will tend to be distributed, and where possible produced, in major cities. At the core of the city, high land prices rule out industrial plants with large space demands. Manufacturers locating at the core are there because of demand for centrality (such as printing) or because of interlinkages (e.g. garment-making). At distances further out, the dominant locating factor becomes access to residential areas for workers and access to transport routes. An industrial-residential zone may develop, the limits of which are set by the commuting limit. Wage costs tend to be high, but site costs and taxes lower than at the centre. At still greater distances, wage levels fall. The type and size of plant in such areas are determined by the supply and range of skills of available labour. Finally, at even greater distances from the urban core, population densities decline, labour is scarce, and wage costs may increase because of a need to import labour. Industries found in such areas tend to be capital intensive and are often located away from major urban centres for special reasons, such as access to raw materials or to confine their nuisance value. The inference to be drawn from these considerations is that, to the extent that urban growth depends upon industrial expansion, a city is more likely to grow fast if it can easily extend its boundaries outwards, thereby permitting the locational adjustments necessary for effective expansion to take place.

This emphasis on the city as a location for industry can lead to a one-sided view of urban growth, especially when it is argued that those cities grow fastest which have a more favourable industrial mix. The latter argument stresses the demand aspect of urban growth. Supply factors are also important. It might be argued that the growth potential of a city depends upon its ability to create and *attract* productive resources as well as to produce goods and services demanded in regional and national markets. The capacity of a city to expand its stock of resources internally is limited by the rate of natural increase in population, the capital accumulation of local firms and the propensity of local managers and innovators to raise productivity. For cities to experience high growth rates they must attract productive factors from outside; they must act as a magnet for migrants, outside capital, non-local managerial talent and innovations. Large cities are better placed than smaller urban units for this task. Their bigger labour markets and wider job opportunities attract more migrants, especially long distance migrants; large cities are more attractive centres for outside investors particularly with regard to consumer goods industries and services where access to a large potential market cuts down risks; larger communities often have the variety of amenities, cultural and leisure facilities necessary to attract executives from other cities and regions; finally, as pointed out in Chapter 12, large metropolitan cities tend to be primary centres of innovation. The upshot of this analysis is that growth in large cities will be self-generating, because large cities have a much greater potential for obtaining growth inputs.

Apart from the influence of size as a determining factor in the growth of the individual city, size is also relevant to an explanation of the pattern of city growth in the economy as a whole. The zone of influence (as measured by service areas, commuting zones, etc.) around a city tends to be directly correlated with city size. Urban communities both within that zone of influence and outside, but near its boundary, will be viable only if they do not attempt to compete with the metropolitan city itself. They will, therefore, be smaller in size and specialise in different economic functions. Generally speaking, the larger two given cities are the greater will be the distance between them. But all towns and cities in an economy will form part of a system in the sense that there is sufficient interdependence between urban centres for a change in one city to bring about changes in others. The system will have a vertical dimension which appears in ranking urban areas according to population size, types of function performed and size of service areas. The ranked order forms an urban hierarchy. This hierarchy will have a spatial aspect and a size aspect; here we are concerned with the latter.[31]

The crucial questions are: If there is an urban size hierarchy, is there any regularity in its ordering? Assuming a regular ranking exists, is it general enough to apply to all societies, or is it relevant only to societies that have reached certain levels of economic development? Most important of all, does the urban size hierarchy remain stable over time and if any law or theory can be established to describe the hierarchy, is it capable of predicting the broad course of urban growth in the system as a whole? Of attempts to answer these questions the most well known is the **Rank Size Rule,** associated with the work of H.W. Singer and G.K. Zipf.[32] In its simplest form, this rule states that the population of a given city tends to be equal to the population of the largest city divided by the rank of city-size into which the given city falls. This basic formula is in practice often modified by a constant to obtain a better fit to the distribution. In this modified form it may be written:

$$R^n P_R = M$$

where M and n = constants, and n must be positive.
P_R = population of Rth city.
R = size rank of Rth city in the system.

When $R = 1$, the equation requires, regardless of the value of n, that $P = M$. Hence the constant M equals the size of the largest city in the system. If there are X cities each of a size not less than the lower limit P_X, the size of city of rank X being P_X, the equation requires that:

$$X^n P_X = M = P_1$$

where the size of the largest city is P_1 or M.

This rule depicts a harmonic progression of cities within the

---

[31] The spatial aspect has, in fact, been considered in Section 2 above. There has been some controversy about the compatibility between the spatial perspective, as represented in the central place hierarchy, and the size perspective, reflected in the rank size rule. For an opinion suggesting that they are contradictory, see Dacey, M.F. (1966) Population of Places in a Central Place Hierarchy. *Journal of Regional Science*, **6** 27–33

[32] See Singer, H.W. (1936) The 'Courbes des Populations', A Parallel to Pareto's Law. *Economic Journal*, **46** 254–63, and Zipf, G.K. (1949) *Human Behaviour and the Principle of Least Effort*, 374

urban hierarchy. There are obvious difficulties in testing the hypothesis.[33] For instance, national boundaries may be the most convenient way of drawing the geographical limits of the system, but not the most appropriate. In some cases, such as a large county with a highly developed industrialised zone in one corner surrounded by a very large sparsely populated infertile region on three sides, the appropriate boundary of the system may be subnational; in other cases, the optimal system may be international. The equation does not hold for the United Kingdom, but shows a reasonable fit for cities in Western Europe as a whole. Another problem is the size of urban unit to be considered. How far should the rule be tested down the urban hierarchy? Does it apply only to large regional cities or to all urban communities? There will be some lower limit below which the rule will cease to be relevant, and in a comparative study this lower limit will vary according to the size and characteristics of different countries.

Another drawback of the hypothesis is that it *may* apply only to societies having certain characteristics which are not universal. It is possible that in country *A* the largest city may be several times the size of the second city, while in country *B* the first two cities may be of similar size, and no doubt examples could be found corresponding to these two cases. Most of the tests have been applied to the United States, and the rule may hold more when the system of cities to be tested is contained in a large national land mass, economically developed neither too densely nor too sparsely populated, and most of the cities in the hierarchy perform substantial regional or subregional functions. But there are marked international variations in urbanisation patterns, some of which reflect an imbalance in urban development which would certainly contradict the rank size rule. Indeed, there is evidence that developing countries are less likely to support the hypothesis than more advanced countries. As the United Kingdom's urban size hierarchy suggests, the hypothesis may not hold in small high population density countries, especially when the largest city is disproportionately big relative to total population. However, it is quite easy to construct an index of overall deviation from the rank size rule, by estimating the percentage of the population which would have to move from one city to another

[33] Browning, H.L. and Gibbs, J.P. Some Measures of Demographic and Spatial Relationships among Cities in Gibbs, J.P. (edit) (1961) *Urban Research Methods*, 436–59

to result in complete conformity to the rule. A major cause of divergence from the rank-size rule is the tendency for the primary city in a system to grow to disproportionate size. The hypothesis may receive wider support if applied only to societies which have passed a primacy test. An index of primacy may be estimated by dividing the population of the largest city by that of the second largest (or by the sum of the populations of any chosen number of cities next in rank in the hierarchy). If the index exceeds a certain prescribed value, the system may either be exempted from the test or else the weight of the largest city may be reduced.

The deviation index may be estimated for different periods of time, and whether or not this index changes in value will throw light on the instability or stability of the urban size hierarchy. If the rank size rule is confirmed, or if the deviation from it is small and does not alter over time, this suggests that there are some basic forces at work making for equilibrium among competing cities and resulting in steady urban growth throughout the system. But it is possible that individual cities will move up or down the urban hierarchy. Instability of ranking may indicate uneven rates of economic growth in different regions of the country. On the other hand, changes in the ranking of cities might reflect fast growth or relative decline in functionally specialised cities that cater more for national than regional needs. If the deviation index alters in random fashion in either direction, then the rank size rule will have no predictive power. Obviously, much more work needs to be done to assess the dynamic potential of the hypothesis. One possibility would be to compare changes in the deviation index with changes in the aggregate economy's rate of growth to illuminate whether or not, and if so how, the pattern of urban growth responds to changes in economic expansion in the economy as a whole.

There may also be some relationship between the rank size rule and the proportion of urban population. Some analysts have suggested that the urban fraction (i.e. the proportion of total population living in urban communities above a prescribed size) can be related to the total number of communities above that size in the following way:

$$U = a\sqrt{N}$$

where U = the urban fraction.
N = total number of communities.
a = a constant (or possibly a parametric variable).

If this relationship held it might indicate an equilibrium between the competing attractions of urban and rural life.

Rudimentary hypotheses of this type are only a starting point for an analysis of urban growth. Their usefulness is that they highlight the possible existence of regular orderly relationships between city sizes and urban growth, and provide a framework for further empirical studies and for a more systematic attempt to construct a theory of urban growth. Such a theory is still a long way off. One difficulty is that a purely economic theory of urban growth will be only a partial explanation, masking significant features of the urban growth process. An interdisciplinary approach is not merely desirable, it may be essential to a deeper understanding of urban growth.[34]

---

[34] Thompson has argued that a synthesis of a large number of case studies may be the best method of increasing our understanding. As he puts it: 'the economic historian may have fully as much to contribute to urban growth theory as either the economic theorist or the econometrician' (Thompson, *op. cit.*, 60)

Chapter 8

The urban public economy

1 Economic trends and urban government activity

Public finance at the urban government level is an important topic for consideration, primarily because trends associated with continued economic growth and rising living standards result in stability at least, and most probably some increase, in the share of GNP taken by urban government services. In the United Kingdom, for example, the share of total local authority expenditure in GNP rose from 12·3% in 1950–1 to 15·4% in 1967–8.[1] With increased urbanisation we might expect a relative increase in urban public services; as people congregate together externalities and scale economies are created in services that are in many cases more conveniently supplied by the public than the private sector. However, this trend is not inevitable. A high proportion of goods and services can be supplied by either public or private agencies, and whether they are produced as public goods or as private goods depends on consumer preferences – preferences that include non-economic as well as economic variables. Thus, a community or even a nation may opt for private supply despite the fact that public supply may be more efficient.

An obvious example at the urban level is in the field of urban transport. In metropolitan centres and other large cities, efficiency criteria are likely to suggest a shift from private cars to public transport. Yet the inhabitants of such cities may be unwilling to accept the consequences, and may still continue to use their cars, possibly to an even greater extent. Convenience, prestige and desire for privacy may have higher priorities in their preference functions than community efficiency. As one prominent urban economist has put it: 'the strategy and tactics of cost minimisation are often not

[1] From data given in the *Annual Abstract of Statistics, Financial Statistics* and *Monthly Digest of Statistics*. Since, however, the share of local authority expenditure in GNP stood at 15·1% in 1938–9, it might be dangerous to argue the case for a secular rise in this share from the figures given above

appropriate in our affluent society.... It is very hard to believe that the consumer-taxpayer will opt for utilitarian public goods to substitute for or complement his high-style private goods.'[2] But choosing private cars rather than public transport may give rise to substantial urban expenditures on roads, street systems, car parks and traffic control. It is conceivable that the total absorption of resources necessary to accommodate the private car may be so huge that urban expenditure in support may be greater than the capital investment required to build the alternative public transport system.

This last point illustrates the generalisation that much of the need for increased urban government activity has developed as a by-product of economic trends in the private sector. Rising real incomes have resulted in demands for higher quality in the supply of urban services – more efficient refuse disposal, better schools and demands for raising the school-leaving age, improved roads, etc. The general increase in urban population and particularly the concentration of more and more urban inhabitants in single large centres have necessitated new urban government functions. Diseconomies of scale have forced urban governments to take action in certain fields: measures to deal with traffic congestion and controls and inspection to prevent overcrowding are merely two examples. The wider diffusion of external economies in large communities may also require a greater degree of intervention by the public sector to ensure adequate provision for social wants that are satisfied by services available to all, but from which individuals derive unequal benefits. Technological changes in the economy as a whole also influence the role of the urban government sector. Again, some of the consequences of technical change are caught in the net of externalities, particularly in the transport field. Thus, the point where increasing use of the motor car justifies investment in elaborate and expensive traffic control systems and the distance from the city centre at which an airport should be built are decisions that may fall to urban governments. Technological change may set difficult fiscal problems for the urban government. Again using the private motor car as an example, its extended use may place public transport systems under severe cumulative financial pressure – the 'fewer passengers – higher fares – poorer services' syndrome.

Of the general economic forces affecting urban government

[2] Thompson, W.R. (1965) *A Preface to Urban Economics.* 269

activity, none has had a larger impact than the changing population and residential structure of the city itself. The movement of people, predominantly high income families, to the suburbs has had its origins in many factors (rising urban populations, changing tastes in housing, transport improvements) that do not concern us here. What is clear is that suburban growth has had tremendous repercussions on urban public finance. The most important is that average income levels have been reduced in city centres (accentuated by decentralisation of industry and commerce), so that the taxable capacity of central districts is lowered. At the same time, the concentration of low income families in such districts (associated with a higher proportion of larger families, higher delinquency rates and a higher incidence of health and welfare problems created by overcrowding) calls for increased urban social and welfare expenditures. This divergent movement in taxable capacity and expenditure requirements is probably the most pressing fiscal problem facing the government of a large city. Furthermore, suburban development facilitates, and perhaps by force of example makes necessary, expenditures on physical rehabilitation and redevelopment in areas around the core of the city. Finally, suburban growth itself demands heavy investment in arterial roads, public utilities and social overhead capital to link the central city with its suburbs and to accommodate and cater for rapid expansion in the suburban areas.

2 Local government and the triple budget function

We have suggested above some major reasons why the scale of urban government expenditures is substantial. We may begin our discussion of public finance in an urban context,[3] with an assessment of the relevance of the three functions of the budget to urban communities.[4] As is well known, the operation of the public sector cannot be

---

[3] In this chapter we deal exclusively with the tax and expenditure functions performed by *urban* governments. Much of the argument could equally be applied, though with slight differences in emphasis and treatment, to other subnational levels of government – from regional governments down to small local authorities operating in rural areas

[4] Musgrave, R.A. (1959) *The Theory of Public Finance*. Ch. 1, A Multiple Theory of the Public Household. 3–27, and Ch. 8, 179–183. See also Hirsch, W.Z. Urban Government Services and Their Financing in Hirsch, W.Z. (edit) (1963) *Urban Life and Form*. 129–66 and Brazer, H.E. Fiscal Implications of Metropolitanism. 127–50 in Chinitz, B. (edit) (1964) *City and Suburb: The Economics of Metropolitan Growth*

explained in terms of a single group of principles. The public sector concerns itself with several separate, though interrelated, functions that have to be dealt with, to a large extent, in isolation. These functions can be related to three broad objectives: (1) to supplement the mechanisms of the private sector in adjusting the allocation of economic resources (the Allocation Branch); (2) to bring about desired changes in the distribution of income and wealth (the Distribution Branch); and (3) to achieve stabilisation of economic activity or, more generally, to attempt to reconcile the goals of price stability, full employment and fast growth (the Stabilisation Branch). The control of each of these branches must be undertaken on the assumption that the other two branches operate effectively. For example, diverting resources to satisfy public wants is planned in the Allocation Branch as if resources are fully employed and the 'desirable' income distribution achieved. Although the tax and expenditure measures required in each individual branch may ultimately be consolidated in an overall view of the public sector and its activities, the basic aim must be efficient budget planning at the individual branch level. For our purposes, this requires an assessment of the role to be played by local (urban) governments in the performance of each of the three broad functions.

It is argued here that urban governments should be mainly concerned with the Allocation Branch. Their task is to provide public goods and services, and to participate in raising the revenue to finance these services, in conditions where the central government is assumed to have achieved its objectives regarding income distribution and economic stability. This viewpoint depends upon the proposition that local governments are ill-fitted to achieve redistributional and stabilisation goals.

In a multi-level fiscal system, there is a strong case for distributional adjustments to be made by the central government. If the national government has adopted an explicit income distribution goal, this goal will not be attainable if local governments adopt overt redistributional measures, since these will either offset or reinforce national policies. Moreover, if local authorities are given distributional functions, their actions may be neutralised by out-migration of people and, more seriously, of firms. The results may interfere with locational efficiency.

On the other hand, it is obvious that actions taken by urban governments will have effects on the distribution of income, especially when decisions are being made about the level of particular services to be supplied and how to raise the necessary revenue, and when urban government 'takeovers' of privately supplied services are under consideration. The redistributional consequences will tend to be greater the larger the size of the urban government unit. This is because as the size of unit increases, intra-area *per capita* income differentials tend to widen, welfare expenditures with redistributional effects are more extensive, and the potential power of the lower income groups tends to be stronger. Nevertheless, urban governments should not formulate explicit redistributional goals. If their allocative measures have side-effects on income distribution and if intervention on distributional grounds is considered desirable and necessary, then these side-effects should be taken into account by the central government in operating the Distribution Branch.

Similar arguments can be applied in determining overall responsibility for stabilisation measures. In this case, too, urban government activities will have repercussions on the stability, or otherwise, of economic activity. These repercussions are probably becoming stronger as the size of the capital budgets operated by local governments increases. Moreover, the lag of expenditure behind the voting of funds and the long gestation period of many urban capital projects may result in the capital formation activities of urban governments having an inherent stabilising character, though the extent to which this is true depends on the periodicity and timing of the business cycle. But although some co-ordination may be permitted between central and local governments, responsibility for compensatory finance has ultimately to be taken at the national level. Apart from this, there are several reasons why urban governments are not appropriate agencies for applying stabilisation measures. Firstly, local needs for public goods and services are inflexible in the short run, they are mainly geared to population changes and there must be continuity for effective satisfaction of public wants. Secondly, with locally applied measures there may be sizable geographical leakages over the boundaries of the government area resulting in inter-community equity problems. Thirdly, the absence of monetary powers and, in many cases, control through stringent debt limits are major constraints on local action. Finally, and perhaps most important of all, stabilisation policies pursued by some localities may have destabilising effects on economic activity in others. The results may be harmful to locational efficiency, especially since locally initiated employment policies may impair inter-area mobility of labour.

The most useful role that urban governments can play in public finance is, therefore, to assist in the allocation of resources. The public sector has an allocating function to perform because the market mechanism fails to achieve an optimal allocation of resources. Some causes of inefficient allocation relate to private wants – the influence of monopoly and the presence of external economies and diseconomies are two examples – and these may require corrective intervention, though in some cases (e.g. anti-monopoly legislation) no questions of budget policy are involved. However, many of these divergences from optimality are minor so that the satisfaction of private wants can normally be left to market forces.

Where the public sector is necessary is to satisfy public wants, since here the market mechanism fails completely. The primary category of public wants is **social wants.** These are wants that are met by services that are consumed by all, though utilisation may differ among individuals. Since people cannot be excluded from the benefits of such services, some of them will not voluntarily pay for the services, and therefore social wants cannot be satisfied by the market. They must be satisfied by the public sector, if at all. Among services satisfying social wants we may include national defence, street cleaning and lighting, flood control and other services improving the welfare of the community as a whole. Another group of public wants, **merit wants,** consists of needs that could be met by the market but which are not because consumers choose to spend their incomes on other goods and services. Here budget policy interferes with consumer sovereignty and aims to correct individual choice. In other words, society feels that the market supplies too much or too little of particular goods and services, and therefore the government interferes with its operation via taxes and subsidies. Sometimes, action will be taken to cut down on consumption of certain goods and services such as imposing purchase taxes on cigarettes. More usually, the budget will aim to provide more of a service than the market economy by subsidising education, medical treatment and housebuilding. The distinction between social wants and merit wants is not always clear-cut, however. The benefits of a free education service accrue to the individuals receiving them (i.e. school pupils and students), but there are external economies flowing from having a better educated society and this is a gain to everyone.

If the budget function of the Allocation Branch is to provide the goods and services that satisfy public wants, and to command the resources for this provision through tax revenue, the crucial question here is how this concerns urban governments. There is the vital problem of the level of government that should be made responsible for satisfying particular public wants. The benefits of some services accrue to everyone in the whole country (defence is the obvious case), while other services may benefit the citizens of one or more regions, or the inhabitants of a single community. The appropriate fiscal unit will be determined partly by this factor, but also by the optimum administrative area, the extent of scale economies in the supply of certain services, and by the degree of areal spillovers of benefits and costs. We may discover that some services are most efficiently handled by the central government, others by urban authorities and still others by regional (or state) governments.

Another quite independent question is, once the public services to be provided by urban governments are determined, whether we should aim at uniformity of services among communities or whether it is desirable that the quantity and quality 'mix' should vary in response to differences in community preferences. A related point in regard to taxation is whether 'equal tax treatment of equals' is a desirable principle to follow in determining the total tax bill (central and local) paid by individuals. One advantage of having many urban governments providing a variety of patterns of public services financed by differential tax burdens is, as will be argued later, that it introduces an element of consumer choice relating public want satisfaction to individual preferences, since people are free to move from the jurisdiction of one urban authority to that of another.

We must also pay attention to the methods of raising revenue to finance public services, and this factor too may help determine the division of responsibility between central and local governments. Generally speaking, if optimal allocation is to be achieved without side-effects on income redistribution, methods must be sought that ensure that public service benefits are paid for by those enjoying the benefits. This means increased reliance on user charges and taxes relying on the benefit principle. This is not an easy task: collective consumption means some benefits cannot be assigned to individuals, understating of preferences by consumer-voters may reduce tax liability for public services, and the benefits of services provided by one urban government may be enjoyed by residents in others (especially by commuters).

3 Urban fiscal problems

A *Fiscal implications of spatial dispersion*

It will be useful to illustrate some of the above points with a brief review of some of the main fiscal problems facing urban governments, followed by a more detailed treatment of (1) economies of scale in urban government services and whether or not there is an optimal size of administrative unit; (2) inter-community mobility as a method of bringing satisfaction of public wants into line with consumer preferences; and (3) alternative methods of financing local government services.

Given that there are strong forces making for an increase in the demand for urban government services, one of the most vexing questions facing urban, especially metropolitan, governments is how to obtain more funds than are available from existing revenue systems without harming the activities of the private sector. This task may require improvements in fiscal machinery, the assumption of wider fiscal powers and organisational and managerial innovations at the local government level. Although the obstacles in the way of this include deficiencies in revenue-producing machinery, such as over-reliance on general taxes (that inhibit obtaining a mandate for higher levels of spending) even where user charges are feasible, difficulties also arise because of the inevitable dispersion of economic activity over space. Thus, the fact that many economic activities cross political boundary lines makes it very difficult to relate benefits and taxes at the urban government level. In particular, the separation of the political jurisdictions in which individuals are taxed and in which they receive benefits from services handicaps the rational determination of how much of a community's income should be allocated to the supply of government services. Moreover, this separation is not a rarity but is quite common. The separation of workplaces from residences may create disparities between taxable capacities and service requirements; the need to provide services for commuters creates pressure for taxation without representation. Thus, commuters demand services, such as traffic improvements on lines in and out of the city, that resident consumer-voters are not willing to supply.

Although the ideal theoretical solution to these problems is to give greater play to market forces in determining the quantities and quality of government services to be supplied, it is by no means easy to do this. The main reason for this, as we shall see below, is the restricted scope in practice for the introduction of user charges. These problems are not evaded if we abstract from inter-community movements for work, shopping and leisure. The benefits and costs of many urban government services spill over from one area to the next even without commuting activities.[5] Those who lose as a result may object to local tax increases unless the leakages are closed or offset by fiscal adjustments between separate units.

The task facing urban governments is also often complicated by discrepancies in the taxable capacity of communities relative to their needs for essential services. Examples include the community of low income workers lacking industry or commerce because the labour force commutes to workplaces in neighbouring areas, and wealthy communities that successfully keep out low income residents by not having subsidised housing while land values and house prices remain prohibitively high. The most troublesome case, however, arises within metropolitan centres, when high income families migrate to the suburbs leaving central core areas with a heavy concentration of low income families and massive demands for welfare and social expenditures. In addition, these core areas require essential infrastructure expenditures to support the flow of commuters for work, shopping and leisure in the central city (though these may be financed out of metropolitan and/or national revenues). The most dangerous feature of the urban blight problem is that the discrepancy between taxable capacity and expenditure requirements will tend to become cumulative unless offsetting action is taken by the urban authorities.[6]

B *Urban budget decisions*
The fiscal problems facing urban governments involve policymakers in three types of decision, each a separate link in the chain of the decision-making process. Firstly, it has to be decided which services should be provided by which level of government and just how area-wide the basis for provision should be. This involves questions of economies of scale, administrative convenience, desire for com-

---

[5] For a classification of the spatial consequences of public service benefits see Tiebout, C.M. (1961) Economic Theory of Fiscal Decentralisation, in Universities-N.B.E.R. *Public Finances: Needs, Sources and Utilisation.* 79–96

[6] See Baumol, W.J. Interactions of Public and Private Decisions. 1–18 in Schaller, H.G. (1963) *Public Expenditure Decisions in the Urban Community*

munity participation, the extent of area spillovers in costs and benefits, and inter-regional and inter-community equity considerations. The business is complicated by the fact that the demands for public wants that are satisfied by different levels of government are not independent. Central government expenditure programmes may have adverse effects on urban government services. An instance is where subsidised roadbuilding promotes use of the private car, leading to intensified traffic congestion within cities and reduced incentives to improve the public transport system.

Secondly, once the responsibility for supplying services has been settled, policymakers must decide whether these services should be financed by taxes or by specific charges. The scope for charges will be investigated below, but since their feasibility depends upon the divisibility of the service and the absence, or very limited nature, of external economies, it is clear that many services must be financed through taxes. If this is so, governments are faced with the difficulty of how to make consumers reveal their preferences. The ordering of community preferences through ballot-box and other political methods provides only a very imperfect solution. Although it is argued in Section 5 below that freedom to move to areas supplying a public service 'mix' that accords with individual preferences introduces a quasi-market mechanism obviating this particular difficulty, institutional rigidities probably mean that inter-area mobility is too restricted to achieve this end.

Furthermore, if taxes are required to finance public services provided by urban governments as well as taxes for central government purposes, equity problems arise, particularly the implications of multi-level finance for the 'equal treatment of equals' principle. Consider a situation where urban governments are autonomous and differ from the central government only with respect to area covered. Let us assume that all services are of a kind that benefit either individuals over the whole country or individuals in one locality only. If this is the case, the central government will supply services of the former category, while urban governments provide the services that benefit only the individuals within their boundaries. It may be argued that the principle of equal treatment of equals applies to central taxation on a nationwide basis, and that the same principle applies to local taxes among equals within any one urban area but *not* over urban areas considered as a whole. Thus the total tax burden on individuals (central plus local taxes) is not consistent with the principle. This is not undesirable. A fundamental purpose of having different levels of government is to allow individuals living in different areas to express different preferences for public wants. This must lead to differences in the level of taxation and public services. Although the consequent differentiation in tax levels may have adverse effects on resource allocation and the optimal location of industry, this is a cost that society may wish to bear. Moreover, **horizontal equity** (the principle that people in equal situations should pay the same *total* tax bill wherever they live) may result in fiscal irresponsibility, since individuals in a locality may vote additional public services while bearing only a fraction of the increased cost, since they have the assurance that the increase in local taxes will be offset by a reduction in central taxes.

A better rule is that people with equal incomes should experience the same **fiscal residue** or net benefit derived from fiscal operations. Citizens of different urban governments will then be able to enjoy varying levels of local government services at their cost. If these services are financed by taxes determined by benefits, the fiscal residue enjoyed by different tax-payers will be unaffected. The practical difficulty of imputing benefits from public services to individuals in order to measure fiscal residue remains. Moreover, the analysis becomes much more complicated if we recognise that the benefits of public services do not easily split up into those affecting everybody in the nation and those affecting people in one locality only. The answer to this problem might be different combinations of areal political groupings, each combination bearing some relation to the areal spread of the benefits accruing from a particular service.

The third level of decision in the urban budget-making process is, having decided on whether services are to be financed by taxes or charges, to choose the type and rates of tax or charge to be imposed. This is primarily a technical problem, though not without theoretical undertones. Some of the more general considerations and principles required to solve the problems of raising revenue for particular services are discussed briefly in Section 6 below.

4 Scale economies and efficient urban government units

The search for a definite unambiguous optimal size for an urban government area is utopian. Scale economies and diseconomies in the supply of public services may vary widely from service to service.

The composition of the pattern of public services required may be quite different even among communities of the same size. Even if we could conceive of a 'standardised' city and a representative bundle of public services of given quality, and could obtain a weighted optimum that maximises net economies of scale for the municipal functions considered, a reasonable solution would still be far away. The city size that maximises scale economies may not be appropriate for either administering public service functions or for raising revenue. Moreover, there are subjective factors that are difficult to quantify. Citizens may want to retain control over the public services that are supplied, and may wish to participate personally in the decision-making processes. As minimum standards in the quality of public services supplied are more easily attained with rising urban incomes, this desire for direct participation and involvement may increase. In other words, the demand for political participation may be highly income-elastic.

The objective here is much more modest than attempting to find an optimal urban government size. It is to obtain some approximations to an assessment of the factors that might be considered when judging whether or not a given administrative authority was an efficient unit for doing its job. This aim requires discussion of: economies of scale in urban government services, how to balance subjective notions about self-government and participation with the objective technical economies of scale, the appropriate level of government for provision of different categories of public service, and the advantages and disadvantages of large local government units. The generalisations offered below are not intended as a substitute for detailed empirical investigations into the efficiency of urban government units in a specific institutional setting.

The question of whether or not there are significant economies of scale in the provision of public services cannot really be divorced from applied studies. An extended discussion of these is beyond our scope, and the investigations that have been undertaken yield ambiguous results. Generally, they tend to suggest that there are no significant scale economies in public services, though the validity of this generalisation varies from service to service and from economy to economy (depending on differences in the level of technology, spatial population patterns, and international as well as intercommunity variations in patterns of group behaviour and social organisation).[7] There are certain public services where scale economies exist: water supply, local government administration, municipal housebuilding especially where industrialised building techniques are adopted, sewage plants and other main engineering services are cases in point. But if we assume that separate structures of administrative areas are not feasible for each individual function, it is doubtful whether we can ascertain an optimal service unit since it is probable that there are no marked economies of scale in the most important categories (as measured by share of total urban

---

[7] The more general U.S. studies are Hirsch, W.Z. (1959) Expenditure Implications of Metropolitan Growth and Consolidation, *Review of Economics and Statistics*, **41**; Brazer, H.E. (1962) Some Fiscal Implications of Metropolitanism, in *Metropolitan Issues: Social, Governmental, Fiscal,* and *City Expenditures in the United States.* (N.B.E.R., 1959). Hirsch found evidence of economies of scale only in water supply and sewage services which account for only a small proportion of total expenditures. His conclusion was that medium-sized communities within the 50,000–100,000 population range might be the most efficient. Brazer found no significant relationship between population size and *per capita* expenditures on different municipal functions, except for police protection and even in this case other independent variables were more important. However, he found some evidence of a relationship between *per capita* expenditures and population density (except for roads and recreation), and within metropolitan regions capital expenditure tended to be higher in cities with a relatively high proportion of its population living in suburbs. However, a main problem is that the quality of a public service may change with the size of unit supplying it, so that scale economies in larger communities might not be revealed because they are offset by improved services rendered. Brazer recognised this to be a serious possibility, while Hirsch assumed the difficulty away. For the United Kingdom, an early study by Lomax, K.S. (1943) Expenditure per Head and Size of Population. *Journal of the Royal Statistical Society*, **106** found that authorities of up to 100,000–150,000 in population size scale economies kept *per capita* expenditures down, while above that level diseconomies asserted themselves and expenditure per head increased with population size. More recently, a limited inquiry into Scottish burghs for Police, Health and Welfare, and Cleansing (burghs were chosen rather than cities because disparities in population density would be smaller, and the three services examined were chosen because of rough uniformity in the quality of services supplied) revealed no significant relationship between population size and *per capita* expenditures, Hughes, J.T. (1967) Economic Aspects of Local Government Reform. *Scottish Journal of Political Economy*, **14** 123–4. To be more effective, future studies will have to abandon reliance on expenditures per head as an indicator, and concentrate on measuring the influence of scale on costs per unit of (homogeneous) output. First steps in this direction are presented by Gupta, S.P. and Hutton, J.P. (1968) Economies of Scale in Local Government Services. *Royal Commission on Local Government in England*, Research Studies No. 3

expenditures), and hence in the supply of public services as a whole. Moreover, at some level of population diseconomies will emerge for particular services, and diseconomies may be evident for some functions before economies are maximised in others. Furthermore, the extent of scale economies is not constant over time. Improvements in urban technology and variations in the rate of application of management techniques and in the supply of local authority managerial talent may result in marked intertemporal differences in scale economies realised. Despite these complications, the fact that scale economies exist in the supply of some public services but not in others is of some significance. One inference to be drawn from it is that a multilevel fiscal system may provide public services more cheaply than a single unit system. The higher units in the fiscal hierarchy can concentrate on the functions where scale economies are marked, while the lower level authorities can provide those services for which the optimum population size is small. But, as suggested above, there are obvious limits to divisibility into hierarchy ranks.

The most interesting theoretical point is whether, if we construct **net economy curves**[8] (i.e. economies less diseconomies) for each public service showing how net economies vary with city size, these curves can be aggregated to yield a total net economy curve for all public services so as to pinpoint the size of urban government unit most consistent with economic efficiency. If we make certain restrictive assumptions (full knowledge of how costs vary with output; no excess capacity; no variations in level of individual demand with changing city size; and that quantification of external economies and diseconomies is possible), then we may plot the net economy curves for each public service. The trouble starts when we attempt aggregation. Different communities will require different quantities of individual public services. The solution to this heterogeneity is to hypothesise a 'standardised' city with a given distribution of public service requirements. The drawback is that no actual urban area may remotely resemble this standardised city. Moreover, there is a weighting problem; the strategic importance of a public service may be far greater than its quantitative share in total urban expenditure. For instance, in a city with an unfavourable topographical situation it is arguable that the net economy curve in public transport should be

---

[8] Isard, W. (1956) *Location and Space Economy*. 182–8

given a weight in excess of that warranted by the anticipated levels of expenditure on it. The justification for this is that if the areal unit chosen is inefficient from the point of view of providing a public transport system this might have a harmful effect on economic activity in the city. The provision of public services in the city cannot be treated in isolation from economic conditions in the private sector, and a particular public service may be strategically important because of its potential repercussions on total urban income.

A third objection to aggregation is that it assumes that the net economy curves are independent of each other. In many cases this assumption is invalid. Scale economies in different public services may be interdependent. For example, if a city runs an electric train service economies in public transport may be directly related to economies in electricity generation. For these reasons, it would be a chimera to seek an ideal size of urban area for urban government services as a whole. It is less ambitious but more practical to use scale economy estimates for each urban function separately as a guide to ensure that a population concentration which is grossly inefficient for supplying major public services is not chosen as the administrative unit.

Even if we limit the analysis to *separate* public services, it does not follow that the size of urban unit to provide an individual service will be determined by economic efficiency criteria alone. In many urban government services, consumer-voters may prefer small administrative units that are not of least-cost size on the grounds that small units enable them to retain a degree of control and to participate in influencing decisions. The preferred size of area for administering a particular service will be the result of a balance between this subjective factor (what Isard calls **community participation potential**)[9] and the objective relationship between scale and unit costs. A difficulty is that we lack a method for comparing the subjective gain in CPP with losses in economic efficiency. On the other hand, CPP as a a psychic income element must have an equivalent monetary value and some quasi-scientific method may be employed to measure it. If this were possible, it might aid the allocation of different categories of municipal functions to different levels of government. Two extreme cases may be mentioned, on *ceteris paribus* assumptions.

[9] Isard, W. (1960) *Methods of Regional Analysis.* 527–33

Local governments should be allocated those functions with a high CPP level when the administrative area is small but which falls off sharply as average size increases, with negligible scale economies and no other cogent reasons against local administration. On the other hand, the central government could take charge of those public service functions where CPP is low at all administrative area sizes, where major scale economies are attainable in the national economy, and where other factors favour central control.

Economies and diseconomies of scale and desire for personal participation do not exhaust the considerations that influence the appropriate size of governmental unit for administering specific public service functions. Other factors may be mentioned briefly in a general assessment of the advantages and disadvantages of large units. Other than scale economies, large units have two main advantages. Firstly, they minimise areal spillovers in costs and benefits that distort budget decisions on the level of urban government services to be supplied. With small units, these spillovers and the accrual of benefits to outsiders may have serious adverse effects on resource allocation. But if governmental units are large, and their boundaries are drawn up in the light of information about the areal spread of benefits – requiring the use of concepts such as labour market areas, the complementary regions of central places, the drawing power radius of cities with respect to shops and other services – spillover distortions may be drastically reduced.

Secondly, a large government area tends to have superior revenue raising powers. This is because large units dampen the intensity of inter-community competition for industry, and discourage out-migration of firms to less heavily taxed communities (tax havens).[10] Moreover, increasing the size of an urban government area may have the political convenience of apparent, but not real, equalisation of the tax bases and public service requirements between the sub-areas contained within it. In this way, the need for open cross-community subsidies is eliminated though gross inequalities between benefits received and taxes paid by groups of individuals will remain, though hidden under the surface. It might be argued, however, that where requirements and service costs are very uneven between communities especially in the large metropolitan area that the most

---

[10] Of course, since this restricts the freedom of firms and individuals to assert their preferences, it is a doubtful advantage

effective solution is not so much a single large administrative area, but transfer of ultimate responsibility to the central government. Functions for which such a transfer might be appropriate include certain spheres of welfare, urban renewal, and metropolitan transportation. Thirdly, a few public services have special characteristics which mean that they must be provided on an integrated area-wide basis or not at all. An obvious example is air pollution, since measures to control this must be administered over a large area if control is to be effective.

As for disadvantages of large administrative areas, we have already mentioned the possibility of scale diseconomies and the loss of personal contacts and control where services are supplied by large units. Another relevant factor is where there are spatial differences in benefits received from a given service. For instance, the benefits of a recreational park built at a certain location will taper off with increasing distance from the park. Attempts to relate taxes to benefits will break down if such a service is financed over a large area. As a generalisation, the greater the spatial differentiation in benefit levels from a given service, the more appropriate it is for the service to be supplied by small local government units. Another disadvantage of large urban government units is that it restricts the choice facing mobile consumer-voters when they look for a community that provides a services/taxes combination that matches their preferences. The fewer the areas, the smaller the choice and the less effective is this quasi-market mechanism. The importance of inter-community migration as a factor leading to a closer compatibility between the level of public services and individual preferences is discussed in the next section.

In conclusion, it is clear from the above argument that there is no single size of urban government unit that is optimal for the satisfaction of all public wants. Some functions are best performed by large units, others by much smaller units. For this reason, a multi-level system of government will be much more efficient than a single unit system. An ideal theoretical solution might be to have a different structuring of urban government boundaries for the provision of each public service, but in practice the cumbersomeness of overlapping units, the interdependence of investment decisions in different public services and administrative inconvenience would lead to inefficiencies. Moreover, the level of urban government that is optimal for performing a given set of municipal functions may not be of optimal size for financing these services. Even if we could delimit the urban government area that best supplies a public service from the point of view of economic efficiency, this may not be the preferred size when subjective factors such as community participation potential and local identity considerations are allowed for. The reconciliation of these often conflicting forces and a solution to these problems must be attempted on a pragmatic basis.

5 Consumer preferences and spatial mobility between urban communities

According to the analyses associated with Musgrave and Samuelson,[11] there is no equivalent of a market solution to determine the level of expenditure on public goods. If all consumer-voters could be made to reveal their true preferences for public goods, the quantity of such goods to be produced and the appropriate taxes (if decided by the benefit approach) could be determined. But there is no market mechanism (in the form of market bids) to ensure that consumer-voters state their true preferences. Indeed, consumers might rationally understate their preferences in order to consume public goods while avoiding, or at least reducing, their tax liability. The solution to this difficulty is an imperfect one, achieved through a political mechanism. Some kind of voting process or group decision is determined that offers the best approximation to a true preference solution, and individuals are then compelled to adhere to the group decision.

Although this kind of analysis applies to central government expenditures, it does not deal satisfactorily with local expenditures. Let us accept that the supply of local public goods should be determined by the preferences of the beneficiaries. Given that individual preferences differ and that social goods are paid for by members of a group, it is in the interests of individuals to associate with those who have similar preferences for social goods. It pays people with strong preferences for public services to join together in one community, while those with low preferences for public goods and services may associate with each other in another. Those who are dissatisfied with the pattern of local expenditures relative to tax levels in the urban areas where they live may register their consumer

[11] Musgrave, R.A. (1959) *The Theory of Public Finance*. 9–13, and Samuelson, P.A. (1954) The Pure Theory of Public Expenditures. *Review of Economics and Statistics*. 36 387–9

preferences by moving to a more fiscally congenial urban unit. To the extent that co-association and inter-urban moves are possible, there is a quasi-market mechanism working to provide social wants.

This argument stems from a theory suggested by C.M.Tiebout.[12] If we consider a city resident about to move there will be many variables influencing his locational decision, economic and non-economic. 'Value for money' in public services and the quality and quantity of such services relative to his preferences will have considerable priority among these variables – the quality of education, the availability and cost of parks, police protection, etc. To the extent that these factors are considered, he will probably base his location decision on the prevailing level of government services and taxes provided by different communities; since future changes in the level of these services are hard to forecast they will be given only minor consideration. The larger the number of communities and the greater their differences the more likely that the consumer-voter will satisfy his total preference function.

Tiebout illustrates these generalisations with a specific model. He assumes: consumer-voters are fully mobile so that they will freely move to a community where their preferences are best satisfied; full knowledge of inter-community differences in revenue and expenditure patterns; a large number of communities; no restrictions on mobility because of the availability of employment opportunities at some places but not at others (for instance, everybody might be assumed to be living on dividends); and no external economies or diseconomies between communities. Given these assumptions, in the limiting case where constant unit costs in supplying public goods prevail and if there is an infinite number of communities, then the consumer-voter will move to the community that exactly satisfies his preferences. This is true, because this limiting case allows for a one person community. The demand for public goods will be determined in exactly the same way as it would be by market forces.

This case is rather unrealistic. It is made more plausible if we assume that there are limits to optimum community size, i.e. there are limits to economies of scale. This assumption guarantees a determinate number of communities. We may further assume that centres below the optimum try to attract new residents in order to

[12] Tiebout, C.M. (1956) A Pure Theory of Local Expenditures. *Journal of Political Economy.* **64** 416–24

reduce their average costs of supplying services, while those above the optimum size will seek to lose population, or more plausibly will take no action to prevent out-migration to suburbs or to other cities. Except in a state of equilibrium, some consumer voters will be dissatisfied with the expenditure patterns of their community. Because our latest assumptions yield a finite number of communities, they will choose the next best substitute if no community exists that precisely reflects their preferences. This choice will exist because of product differentiation among local governments. This product differentiation will reflect preferences for private over public sources of supply, or vice versa, differences in tastes for public services, and variations in the desire for close control over local government processes. Dissatisfied consumer-voters will move except in the rare case where a local authority wields monopoly power, in the sense that there is no other community with a preference pattern close enough to be a substitute for it. Although inter-urban migration will be multi-directional, a net movement will take place out of communities larger than the optimum to communities smaller than the optimum.

Thus 'moving or failing to move replace the usual market test of willingness to buy a good and reveals the consumer-voter's demand for public goods ... each locality has a revenue and expenditure pattern that reflects the desires of its residents'.[13] It is an important feature of the model that towns and cities do not have to face the problem of adapting their policies to the preferences of their inhabitants. The difficulties are solved by market forces since the local governments attracting the optimum number of residents are shown to be those with the most preferable revenue and expenditure patterns. At the same time, the allocative mechanism works far from perfectly, especially when the assumptions in conflict with reality are dropped. To the extent that consumer-voters choose a second best community because none exists that exactly meets their preferences, there is a departure from optimality. Moreover, unless we hold to the assumption of constant unit costs, a change in a city's population will alter the costs of some of its public services, and this fact will cause the quantity produced to change which may induce dissatisfaction among other consumer-voters. Once again, the allocative mechanism will be disturbed. It is also necessary to

[13] *Ibid.*, 420

accept that it costs money to move from one city to another. The mobility cost is the cost necessary to register preferences; the higher the level of such costs the greater the discrepancy between actual and optimal resource allocation.[14] Finally, where the provision of public services leads to external economies, the case for integration of urban units becomes quite cogent. The emergence of large fiscal units results in greater incompatibility between individual preferences and prevailing public service and local tax structures. The advantages of external economies may be achieved only by thwarting individual preferences.

Returning to the earlier assumption of zero transportation costs in locational choices, we can illustrate how this market-type mechanism may work by considering some specific cases. First, assume that people have the same incomes but different preference patterns for public goods. Then it will be advantageous for individuals to join a community the citizens of which have similar preferences to their own. Generalising, with reference to social wants people gain from having preference patterns similar to others; but with private wants the opposite tends to hold true (for example, the necessity of paying higher tariffs for peak-season holidays). Secondly, consider the case where people have similar preference patterns for public goods but vary in income. It pays wealthy people to associate with other high income receivers, while attempting to exclude those having low incomes. The latter, however, if rational, should try to enter a community with the highest average income possible; this holds true when taxes are proportional, even more so with a progressive tax system. By such a move, poor citizens have an opportunity to enjoy the benefits of public services that they desire greatly in excess of the cost of these services to them. A third case where people differ in both incomes and preferences is much more difficult to determine. Broadly speaking, the wealthier individuals will choose the community that best accords with their preference pattern for public services, provided that the tax structure of that community does not require them to finance these public services in excess of the benefits they receive from them. Low income individuals will tend to choose

---

[14] This problem is not confined to satisfaction of social wants, however. Satisfying private wants can, if goods are available at locations other than the consumer's own location, also mean less than optimal efficiency in resource allocation. As Tiebout puts it 'Spatial mobility provides the local public goods counterpart to the private market's shopping trip' (*loc. cit.*, 422)

communities that offer them the *highest* ratios of benefits to costs of a bundle of public goods that they desire to consume.

To sum up, the hypothesis is that the possibility of moving from one community to another creates a form of market mechanism in local finance. The problems involved in the determination of social wants within a single community remain, but choosing between communities becomes a market decision. As a result of mobility from less to more desirable fiscal areas a more homogeneous set of preferences will tend to be found within any one community, and the task of determining the level and distribution of expenditures on public goods is simplified. In particular, the problems posed by failure to reveal preferences are solved. If we accept this argument, then a number of policy implications flows from it. Since many small political areas increase choice, municipal integration can be justified only if more of at least one service is supplied at the same total cost without reductions in the quantity or quality of any other service. Secondly, policies to promote residential mobility and increase information available to the consumer-voter will improve the allocation of local government expenditures. Thirdly, to facilitate individuals obtaining the necessary knowledge on which to make choices, it is desirable that communities should have, as far as is possible, fairly stable revenue/expenditure patterns.

The value of Tiebout's model as a practical solution to the question of how to allocate resources among local public goods is open to objection. The restrictive assumptions of the model rule out many of the factors that create urban fiscal problems – bars to mobility, cross-community movements resulting in a situation where commuters enjoy benefits that they may not pay for, the constraints on free choice imposed by differential employment opportunities, the costs of moving, substantial external economies in the provision of public services, etc. In particular, the costs associated with moving from one community to another may be so large that fiscal considerations will have only a minor effect, and in most cases will have insufficient influence to induce consumer-voters to move on this account alone. There may be a pattern of intra-city movement, for instance people moving from city centres into the suburbs, but though public expenditure and tax criteria may be a factor in these moves (for instance, differences in the quality of education provided in various communities within a metropolitan region) non-economic variables may assume greater importance. Moreover, with centrifugal movements to the suburbs, as one problem is solved (the determination of social wants) another is created – the incompatibility between heavy demands for public (including welfare) expenditures in central communities and the low taxable capacity of low income residents there.

The restrictions due to the availability or lack of employment opportunities are also serious. A high proportion of inter-city and inter-regional migration is explained by people moving to better jobs. The increased job opportunities are the main motivation for such migrants, not the possibility of finding a fiscal pattern more suited to their preferences. Admittedly, when people move to new jobs they will be able to choose their place of residence from a number of adjacent communities, and if these communities differ substantially in their public expenditure and tax levels the decision to obtain a home in one rather than in another may be based on such considerations. Of course, other factors will also influence choice, particularly the availability of accommodation and its cost.[15] In moves of this nature the fact that migrants are primarily moving to better jobs is not of much consequence. The improvement in allocation takes place just the same. Yet, to the extent that greater compatibility between the fiscal structures of urban areas and individual preferences is achieved as a by-product of migration for improved employment opportunities, the mechanism operates effectively only if migration is high relative to total population. Although geographical migration to better jobs may be high when considered in absolute terms, it is usually small relative to the large mass of immobile population. Thus, the market mechanism for adjusting community preference problems to community fiscal structures works, but it works very imperfectly.

6 Methods of financing urban government expenditures

The basic problems involved in raising revenue for urban government services are: Under what conditions should the central government intervene? Should central intervention involve tax-subsidy transfers either for redistributional purposes or satisfaction of merit wants and/or should it take the form of central government grants? If the latter, what circumstances favour general cash (i.e.

---

[15] This factor is, of course, not completely independent of public expenditure decisions, especially in communities where public housing accounts for a high proportion of the total housing stock

block) grants, equalisation grants, specific grants or matching grants? Should urban governments raise their revenue by specific user charges or by general purpose taxes? In cases where general taxes are necessary, should these be property or non-property taxes? Space forbids a detailed discussion of these factors. In addition, nothing will be said here about the role that local authority borrowing might play in financing services involving capital investment or about tax-sharing schemes with the central government. We shall concentrate on the issues arising from the problem of whether to rely on specific user charges or on taxes, to be followed by an outline of the general conditions under which central government grants may be justified.

The case for user charges as a method of financing urban public services, where such charges are feasible, is very strong. User charges are the most obvious means of trying to bring payments for services more closely into line with benefits. That beneficiaries of public services should support these services by making direct voluntary payments in proportion to benefits received is a preferable course on equity grounds to compulsory levies raised according to ability to pay or some other principle. The efficiency case for user charges is even stronger. They help to bring demand and supply into balance in situations where excess demand leads to heavy social costs – the demand for car parking facilities, for example. They mitigate the misallocation of resources that results from service benefits being appropriated by individuals from outside the area where the services are supplied. If financed by taxes levied on an area's residents a situation of this kind can result in underinvestment in public services vital to growth – such as transport facilities. At the other extreme, they may prevent too many resources being allocated to satisfying a particular social want. We may conceive of circumstances in which citizens enjoying equal incomes share the cost of a service equally, yet in which no one person is able to reduce his share in the cost by economising or limiting his demands; the result may be gross excess supply of that particular service.

The advantages of user charges are therefore considerable. Their drawback is that they may not be feasible. User charges should encourage the economic use of resources (for example, metered charges may induce consumers to conserve electricity). Conversely, a charge is not justified if it results in underutilisation or waste of resources, such as when a rise in bus fares results in a marked drop in passenger traffic in non-rush hours. For charges to be effective, the immediate benefits of a service should be enjoyed mainly by the person paying for it. This means that when an individual chooses to abstain from using a service because of the charge the rest of the community does not suffer. In other words, the external economies of a service should be minimal for charges to work best.[16]

Moreover, if user charges are being considered as a substitute for general taxes in financing a particular service already in existence, the chances of introducing them depend on the distributional impact of the charge relative to the general tax displaced. Financing education by user charges might have adverse effects on income distribution. Those who favour such a step would argue that it would markedly increase the efficiency of resource allocation, and that redistributional considerations could be handled through the central tax system (possibly involving income tax rebates to low income families). But sound economic theory does not always make for practical politics.

The main difficulty in the way of adopting specific charges is how to relate the charge to benefits received. The service must be divisible into units the use of which by individuals can be measured. There is the question of whether or not charges can be related to benefits in a manner compatible with equity. This, in turn, gives rise to how benefit should be measured. Should it refer to the cost of providing the service to the individual or is benefit proportional to the amount an individual is willing to pay rather than do without the service? Most important of all is the relationship between the feasibility of user charges and allocation efficiency. This requires investigation of how far the marginal cost pricing concept can be extended into urban government services. If charges could be assessed on marginal cost principles, the exercise of free choice by individuals would be conducive to fiscal harmony. But the relative social costs incurred by alternative combinations of individual choices are difficult, if not impossible, to measure. Moreover, even where user charges are adopted, pressure of urban authorities for funds may demand general purpose taxes as well with adverse effects on resource allocation. If specific charges are levied, they should be set at a level which adds to revenue in excess of the revenue flow from marginal cost pricing.

[16] Elementary education and sanitation are two services with pronounced external economies. See the classification in Brownlee, O.H. User Prices vs. Taxes. Universities – N.B.E.R., *Public Finances, op. cit.*, 424

When user charges are not practicable,[17] general taxes will be employed if revenue is to be raised locally for urban government services. For services rendered to commuters (i.e. services arising from separation of residences from places of work, shopping and leisure), non-property taxes, e.g. local sales taxes, are to be preferred. Apart from the possibility of introducing urban income taxes, property taxes (real estate tax, rates, etc.) are in all other cases the most favoured general purpose method of financing local government services. The main argument used in justification of this type of tax is that since the revenue raised is used to finance beneficial services benefits accrue to property in consequence. At the same time, such a tax captures very imperfectly a proportion of the unearned increment in land values associated with increased urbanisation. But property taxes probably divert an excess allocation of resources into services satisfying public wants. This is most clearly seen with a rating system. If, as seems likely, industry and commerce bring a net fiscal gain to the community (i.e. receive less in services than they pay in taxes), residents may enjoy a higher public service/tax cost ratio than otherwise. Under a rating system individuals may vote a higher tax rate. This yields an increase in receipts for financing services for individuals higher than the tax increment, since some of the increase in rates falls on industry. The result is that too many resources are allocated to the urban government sector because expenditure benefits are underpriced to the individual consumer-voter. In addition, the locational efficiency of industry may be disturbed. At the more attractive locations (e.g. those locations characterised by strong agglomeration economies) where industry is already established, the cost on industry of public service requirements may be much higher than elsewhere,[18] diverting new firms to less profitable locations.

There is a tendency in most countries for local expenditures to rise faster than local revenue. This reflects forces making for increased government activity and the obstacles in the way of new kinds of local taxes. Gaps between local expenditure and revenue emerge,

---

[17] For a discussion of the practicability of user charges in relation to specific services see Vickrey, W.S. General and Specific Financing of Urban Services, in Schaller, H.G., *op. cit.*, 62–90

[18] Offsetting this, there is a tendency for low rates to prevail in industrial suburbs. This might reflect successful political pressure by industry, but a more likely explanation is a large tax base relative to expenditure requirements

and these have to be filled by grants from the central government. There are also other reasons why central grants may be justified. Aid from the central government may be useful for subsidising poorer urban areas with below average taxable capacity but high expenditure requirements.[19]

Grants may also be an effective means of stimulating expenditures on specific services. The obvious examples are where the government assures to citizens in all localities that certain levels of social wants are provided for. This applies particularly to social wants that benefit the nation as a whole as well as the locality, such as education, or wants that are accepted as social wants at the local level but recognised as merit wants nationally.

Financial assistance from the central government may be very appropriate in situations where the provision of public services locally confers substantial external economies on non-residents or on the economy as a whole. Again, this would justify government aid for education; a less obvious instance would be to subsidise the cost of services provided for outsiders thus helping local decision-making to be more consistent with efficient resource allocation. Another argument is that where the costs of supplying a particular service are very uneven between communities the central government may step in, especially if a nationally set minimum standard is imposed on the service in question. Finally, local methods of raising revenue may be administratively inefficient. Small authorities may not be able to handle complicated revenue raising systems, so that if there are marked variations in size between urban government units central grants may be administratively convenient. Moreover, there is a case for revenue to be raised by the central rather than urban government if tax rates differ widely between authorities. Very wide variations in local tax rates may result in resource misallocation, as individuals and firms migrate to evade heavy taxation.

There are several possible methods of central government aid. These include tax-sharing schemes which can work effectively despite political and equity difficulties, and loans on favourable terms to urban governments. The most widely used device, however, will be central government grants, though these take many forms:

[19] See Musgrave, R.A. Approaches to a Fiscal Theory of Political Federation. Universities – N.B.E.R., *op. cit.*, 97–133

1 *General cash grants*

General block grants may be given to local governments without restriction as to their use. Lump-sum grants of this kind are particularly appropriate for aiding poorer authorities. They are intended primarily as a redistributional measure and are aimed at ensuring that even the poorest urban government can provide a minimum level of social wants in general (the Rate Deficiency Grants in the United Kingdom are of this general type). Although, at first sight, income-equalising assistance of this kind would appear to interfere with allocative efficiency, this is not necessarily the case. If block grants enable poor authorities to raise the quality of public services they supply, such grants may be corrective in their allocative effect by reducing the influence of differences in public service provision on migration decisions.

2 *Unconditional specific grants*

These refer to grants given for a specific purpose, but without any stipulations on quality of service required. Grants of this kind are inferior to lump sum grants from the point of view of the receiving government. The reason is that they restrict community choice in public services. As a result of grants of this kind, a given amount of urban government expenditures can be had at different costs to local taxpayers depending on the composition of public services selected. Some public services will now require 100% local funds; others might require no local funds whatsoever. Since grants enable the total supply of public services to be increased, it is possible that provision of non-grant-aided services may expand. Nevertheless, specific rather than block grants will distort community choice to favour, relatively, the grant-aided services.

This point can be illustrated with the aid of a simple diagrammatical model, analogous to that comparing the effects of direct and indirect taxes on the allocation of resources. In figure 8.1 we assume that the urban government supplies only two services, one of which is grant-aided by the central government. The grant is a straightforward proportional grant, varying according to the number of units of the grant-aided service supplied. At the risk of oversimplifying, we assume that the revenue raised from local sources remains unchanged after the grant is made.[20] With no grant, *AB*

[20] The consequences of relaxing this assumption are outlined by Williams, A. (1963) *Public Finance and Budgetary Policy*, 174–6

REGIONAL ECONOMICS

in figure 8.1 is the possibility line showing the possible levels of services that could be provided out of local resources; the chosen combination is where this line is tangential to the highest indifference curve, i.e. at I. Now we suppose that a specific proportional grant is

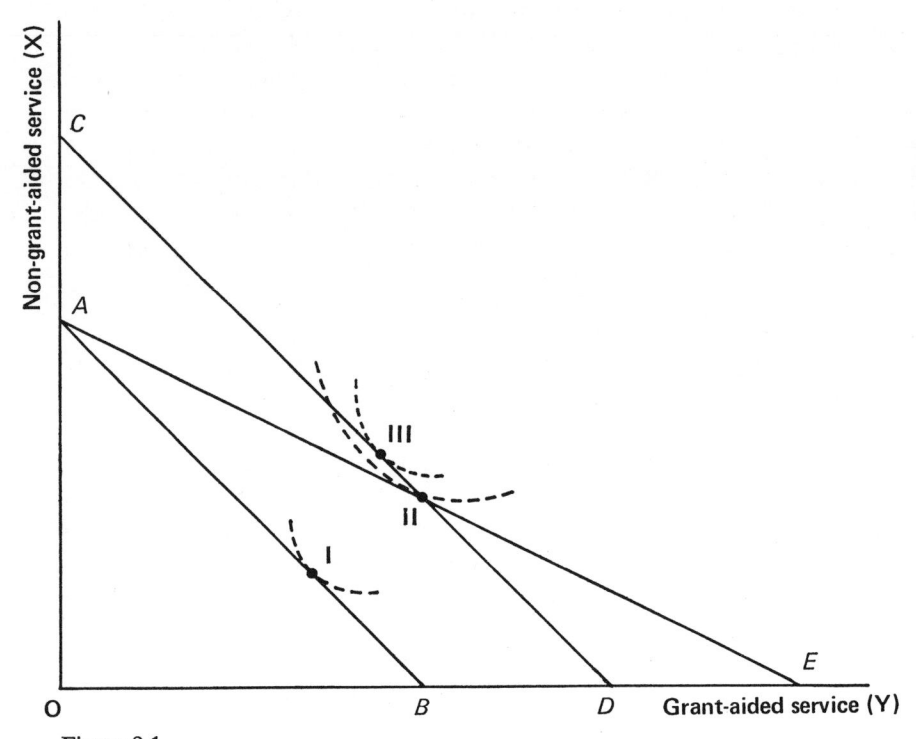

Figure 8.1

made to the service Y; the line AE indicates how provision possibilities are increased. The selected combination of services shifts from I to II, a case where the supply of both services is increased despite the grant being payable only to one service. However, if a general block grant of the same amount had been made, the possibility line would have been given by CD. With the block grant, resource allocation would have been improved and the urban government better off. Since CD runs through II, the combination of X and Y represented by II could be achieved with the block grant just as with the specific grant. However, with the block grant the government can move from II to III on CD, increasing the supply of service X relative to service Y but moving on to a higher indifference curve. It follows that the urban government authority will prefer a lump-sum grant to a specific grant of the same amount. This conclusion remains unaffected if we allow variations in local revenue and take account of multiplicity of services.

3 Conditional specific grants

Where specific grants are adopted, conditions in addition to limiting the grant to a particular service may be imposed. For example, the grant may only be forthcoming if matched by a given proportion of local revenue. It may be stipulated that urban governments finance, say, 60% of a particular service and the central government will supply the remaining 40%. Although there is some interference with local budgetary freedom, the results are not grossly harmful unless the central government provides a very high percentage of the total cost. This reduces the incentive of urban governments to economise and results in excessive discrimination by local decision-makers in favour of aided services with very low local 'matching'. The restricting conditions may take other forms: detailed control over actual spending of the grant; restrictions on the type, level and quality of service to be provided; or possibly control over local spending on the service. The most common condition attached to a specific grant is where some predetermined minimum standard of service is laid down. This arises particularly in cases where the central government is concerned with social or merit wants that confer substantial external economies on society as a whole.

The effect of a conditional grant is shown in figure 8.2. A grant is given to assist the financing of service Y which shifts the possibility line from AB to AC. A minimum standard requirement is imposed so that in order to receive the grant the urban authority must supply at least OM_1 units of Y. Again, we ignore any possible effects that a grant might have on the employment of local resources. Before grants are awarded the government chooses position I on AB. If a simple proportional grant were given, the optimal free choice combination would be represented by position II on AC. However, the minimum standard requirement (M_1) precludes this, and the best position is therefore III. The freely chosen position II is preferable to the best position III attainable by satisfying the conditions of the grant (being on a higher indifference curve), but position III is in turn better than the selected position I in the absence of a grant. On

REGIONAL ECONOMICS

the other hand, if the minimum standard was set at a higher level (M_2) the best position attainable IV is not only inferior to position II but also to position I (on a lower indifference curve). The preferences of the community are such that in this latter situation the grant will be rejected.

It may also be seen from figure 8.2 that if the rate of grant were

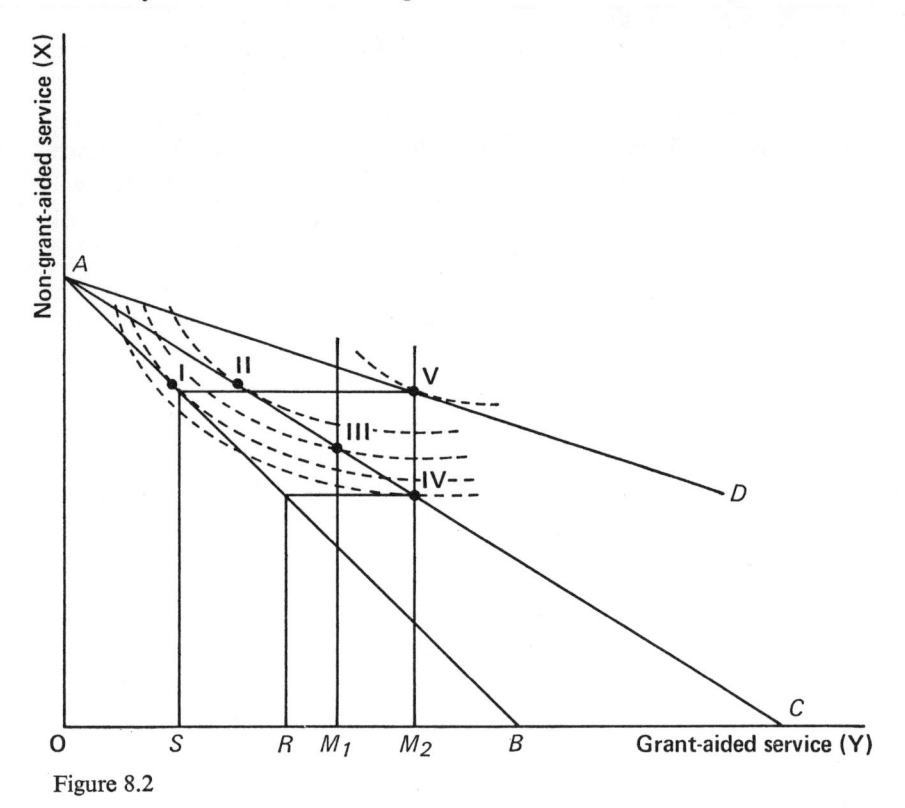

Figure 8.2

increased, by swinging the possibility line AC upwards on its pivot, but the minimum level of provision requirement OM_2 still retained, there would at first be no increased supply of the grant-aided service. What happens is that the increased earmarked grant is used to free local resources for expanding the supply of the service which receives no grant. The supply of the grant-aided service will not increase until the grant is raised to such a level that the possibility line becomes AD. Only then is OM_2 units of the grant-aided service supplied as the level of provision that would be freely chosen by the local government (at V) if the grant were unconditional. This means, of course, if the central government wishes to impose a minimum provision level of OM_2, it is much more expensive to achieve with an unconditional grant than with a conditional one. This is because an unconditional grant to guarantee OM_2 units of service Y requires the equivalent of SM_2 in grant aid, while the conditional grant involves not less than RM_2.

As a generalisation, convenience favours block grants where distributional factors require subsidies to poorer authorities while specific grants could be used when the central government wishes to stimulate particular types of expenditure. Normally, the central government will insist on attaching strict conditions to specific grants since this will facilitate imposition of minimum service requirements on laggard urban authorities and will prove less expensive than unconditional specific grants. Of course, some sacrifice will have to be made in terms of resource efficiency. However, there is no inherent reason why the two objectives of central government assistance, those relating to income redistribution and those relating to provision for the satisfaction of merit wants, should be kept separate. Redistributional elements may be incorporated in specific grants by explicitly discriminating in the award of such grants between rich and poor urban areas.

7 Summary

There are basic economic forces at work making for a rise in urban government expenditures, a rise that in most economies is running ahead of increases in GNP. A case exists for a division of budget functions between the central government and local governments. So far as is possible, urban governments should concentrate on allocating resources for the satisfaction of social wants and merit wants leaving fiscal measures to stabilise income and to ensure its proper distribution in the hands of national policymakers. The central government will also have some responsibility for satisfying public wants, but many public services will be supplied and financed by lower level governments while others will be administered at the community level but supported by central government grants. Urban budget decisions are complicated by several problems: the difficulties of raising sufficient revenue to meet the increased demand for urban expenditures; the fact that the organisation of economic activities crosses over local political boundaries; areal spillovers of benefits and costs from public services; incompatibility between the taxable capacities of some urban areas and their public service requirements; urban blight in large cities associated with migration of high income groups to the suburbs; the possible contradiction between scale economies suggesting large urban units and the desirability of promoting local initiative and community interest favouring small ones; the extent to which conformity should be fostered in the patterns of urban government services; the choice between alternative methods of raising revenue.

Although economies of scale probably are significant for certain public services if not for many others, it is impossible to determine *a priori* the optimal government area from an economic efficiency point of view. The individual weights in a total net economies of scale index vary according to individual community preferences and according to economic conditions within each city or urban area. Moreover, the preferred size of urban government unit will probably also depend on non-economic variables such as the desire for individual participation and local political control. On balance, however, large units will be preferred to smaller ones, partly because spillovers are thereby minimised, partly for administrative convenience and partly because larger authorities tend to have superior revenue-raising powers.

One of the main purposes of having different levels of fiscal authority is to permit public wants to be satisfied at the sub-national level according to the different preference patterns of different communities. A large choice of fiscal communities with a great variety of combinations of public service provision and tax structures has the advantage that it introduces a market element into a problem that otherwise has to be solved by political means. If restrictions on inter-area mobility are few, minorities do not have to be compelled by political decisions on budget questions since individuals can always move to a community that provides a public service/tax rate pattern that, more or less, satisfies their personal preferences. Theoretically, inter-community migration obviates one of the main obstacles facing fiscal authorities, how to get consumer-voters to reveal their true preferences for public goods.

As for the methods of financing urban public services, allocative efficiency criteria favour user charges rather than general taxes. User charges help to align marginal costs and marginal benefits and to keep supply and demand in balance. In many cases, however, the indivisibility of a service, the existence of marked external economies and diseconomies, and the inadequate public revenues that result from attempts to rely on marginal-cost pricing methods make user charges impracticable. Whether user charges and/or general taxes are employed, the exigencies of urban government funds are likely to demand financial assistance from the central government. This can be given in many ways, but block grants and grants-in-aid of specific services tend to be the main devices adopted. Block grants interfere less with the efficiency of resource allocation and are particularly appropriate to attempts to achieve redistributional objectives. But the central government may also want to intervene to guarantee citizens minimum public service standards and to influence the satisfaction of certain merit wants. This kind of policy normally requires specific grants. It will be much more economical to national budgets if the government stipulates conditions attached to these grants, though the stricter the conditions the greater the distortions of free community choice.

Part C
Regional economics

Chapter 9

The regional framework

1 The region as a concept

Consideration of what constitutes a region and of how the national economy may be sub-divided into a system of regions would appear to be an essential prerequisite for the analysis of regional economic phenomena. But the problem is a knotty one, plagued with ambiguities, and it is sometimes possible for the regional economist to avoid facing it at all. He may, for instance, accept a *fait accompli* and work with the administrative regions adopted by government departments. Indeed, if his interest is in empirical research he may have no other choice since data may only be available for official regions. Alternatively, especially if concerned with theory or conceptual analysis, he may adopt a Walrasian general equilibrium approach, treat the nation as a one-point economy, and arbitrarily divide it into as many regions as he desires independent of the space factor. Much of regional macroeconomics, in fact, follows this approach, though it is argued later that future developments in regional economic theory need to incorporate distance variables in general equilibrium analysis. Finally, if the researcher is mainly interested in the analysis of the spatial dimension as it affects economic activities rather than in regional policy decisions, he may be able to ignore the concept of 'region' altogether and refer only to the much more neutral concept, space. The problems of definition may consequently be less critical than they appear at first sight. Nevertheless, it would be a serious omission to neglect altogether how the concept 'region' might be defined.

One major ambiguity arises from the fact that the size of a region might vary from a small population centre and its environs to a massive sub-region within a continent, depending on the range and type of questions under study. Both extremes of scale might be permissible under different sets of circumstances. Indeed, it can be argued that any major land mass (probably a national economy but conceivably a continental land mass crossing national boundaries) can be organised into a hierarchical system of regions of different sizes, in which each region of a given rank embraces a number of smaller regions (or sub-regions) of the rank below. Whether one chooses a rank as a base for analysis which contains, say, ten regions or a rank which contains one hundred would depend on the aim of the inquiry. All the analysis that follows will assume that the system of regions considered as a whole is a national economy bound by the same legal system, institutional framework and subject to a high degree of economic integration. However, how the national economy should be sub-divided into regions is not self-evident. The number of regions to be considered is a constraint on the choice and definition of a region, and this number would depend on the form and nature of the analysis. The approximate number of regions called for has to be predetermined before regional delimitation can be attempted. Broadly speaking, when regional analysis is comprehended as an adjunct to national planning a system of less than ten regions may be the appropriate degree of subdivision. Physical planners, on the other hand, will probably wish to work on the basis of a much larger set of regions.

Contiguity provides a second constraint. In dividing the national economy into regions all of the area of the country must be absorbed within one region or another. If this condition is not met, the interrelationships between the aggregate economy and the individual parts that comprise it will be distorted. This limitation on regional boundaries also applies to space within regions as well as between regions.

Subject to these constraints, there are a number of different approaches to the definition of regions. Virtually all these fall within three main categories: uniform or homogeneous regions; nodal regions; and programming or planning regions. The view of a region as a natural homogeneous area is based on the idea that separate spatial units can be linked together on the grounds that they exhibit certain uniform characteristics. Such characteristics might include similar production structures, homogeneous patterns of consumption and like occupational distributions of the labour force; they might reflect geographical factors such as the ubiquity of a dominant natural resource, or a similar topography or climate; or again, they might include non-economic variables such as uniform social attitudes, a 'regional' identity or a similar political outlook. A major problem in attempting to delimit homogeneous regions is that some areas will in some respects seem to be similar to one region but in other respects will show features suggesting a closer link with a neighbouring region. Boundaries are, therefore, likely to be blurred and arbitrary. Bogue and Beale attempted to draw up homogeneous regions on the basis of broad geographic areas of specialisation in a massive empirical analysis of the United States, but their task was simplified, and their results rendered deficient, by conceiving homogeneity primarily in terms of agriculture.[1]

A possible criterion for defining homogeneous regions is on the basis of similarity in *per capita* income levels. This criterion may be particularly valuable if applied dynamically rather than statically, stressing the 'interdependence among individual incomes in the process of development'.[2] According to this view, a region grows and declines as an entity, rather than having its total income change as the outcome of separate, sometimes offsetting, influences on individual activities located at particular centres within the region. This hypothesis that similar average income levels provide a standard for grouping spatial units into an integrated region has been implicit in the discussions of other regional economists. D.C.North, for example, has suggested that the unifying cohesive force behind a region is the dominance of its economy by an export base.[3] The changes in the level of activity of the export base may convey impulses to income levels throughout the region so that there is a uniform direction of movement in incomes over the region as a whole. On the other hand, if the export base is concentrated at a central location within the region dynamic changes may manifest themselves more in changing rates of interaction between the peripheral borders of the region and its centre of agglomeration. This process would be more consistent with the concept of a polarised region as outlined below.

R. Vining, too, recognised that a region might be organised around its export sector, with this sector acting as the source of flows injected into the region by the national interdependent economy and also providing the channel through which external

[1] Bogue, D.J. and Beale, C.L. (1961) *Economic Areas of the United States*
[2] Balassa, B. (1962) *The Theory of Economic Integration*
[3] North, D.C. (1955) Location Theory and Regional Economic Growth. *Journal of Political Economy*, **63**

disturbances entered the region. These arguments imply that it is inter-regional exchange of goods and services rather than intra-regional exchange which counts. Vining's analysis went further, however, by suggesting that areas might be combined into a region if they shared a similar cyclical experience. He particularly drew attention to highly unstable regions with low average but high marginal propensities to consume home products (reflecting extreme specialisation and heavy dependence on inter-regional trade and low income elasticities of demand for imports respectively), while demand for their export products was highly elastic.[4]

This emphasis on the region as a business cycle concept is rather narrow, but it can be widened to encompass regional macroeconomic analysis as a whole – that is, the theories of regional income determination and regional growth as well as regional business cycles. Regional macroeconomic analysis implies homogeneity in a sense because it aims at predicting short-run and long-run variations in regional economic activity in terms of the behaviour of certain parametric variables, such as the marginal propensity to consume and to import, the marginal capital-output ratio and the average savings-income ratio. In order to have predictive power it is necessary to assume that these variables are of similar constant values over the region as a whole, or else that they change in a regular, foreseeable manner. This would be impossible if the overall regional parameters were the average of very wide variations within different parts of the region. In this latter situation, there might be a case for greater areal subdivision. In other words, in extending the tools and concepts of macroeconomic theory to regional analysis, we ignore the problems arising from intra-regional differentiation and, consequently, treat regions as uniform, homogeneous, and in the final analysis as spaceless, entities.

Intra-regional differences are, in fact, quite obvious in many economic phenomena, and in some cases may override features of uniformity. For example, most regions will contain both rural and urban areas and, therefore, it may be quite inaccurate to speak of similar income levels or consumer tastes. Population distribution is almost certain to be uneven over a wide area, and the existence of high density clusters and sparsely populated areas next to each other

[4] Vining, R. (1949) The Region as an Economic Entity and Certain Variations to be observed in the Study of Systems of Regions. *American Economic Review*, Papers 39 89–104

may have tremendous economic significance. Reasons of this kind have led many regional analysts to abandon the idea of uniform homogeneous regions. 'Complete homogeneity is unworkable, theoretically undesirable, and in fact unobtainable except in reference to a large homogeneous region.' This is especially so when a region contains important cities since 'large urban centres always introduce heterogeneity'.[5]

Nodal, or polarised, regions emphasise the interdependence of different components within the region rather than inter-regional relationships between homogeneous regions. Since the functional links between spatial units are limited by space, nodal regions usually take explicit account of the distance factor as revealed, for example, in gravity potential models. To this extent, they are more realistic, and some analysts, especially geographers, have argued that 'nodal regions are the real regions of the earth' to be contrasted with the 'more stereotyped subjective maps of homogeneous regions'.[6] Nodal regions are composed of heterogeneous units, but these are closely interrelated with each other functionally. These functional interconnections are most clearly visible as flow phenomena – flows of population, goods and services, communications and traffic. These flows do not occur randomly over a region at even rates. Rather, the heaviest flows tend to polarise towards and from one or two dominant centres, which are usually large cities. In this sense, the nodal region focuses attention on the controlling centre of the region rather than on drawing the boundaries. It is the high degree of interdependence between the nucleus and the elements around it which determine the structure and character of the region not the spatial area of the region as a whole. Those who favour the nodal approach to defining regions stress particular kinds of spatial organisation within the region, such as urban place hierarchies, the city or metropolitan region, and areas of 'metropolitan dominance'.

Emphasis on the 'nodes' or 'poles' inevitably diverts attention from the delimitation of regional boundaries to the centre of the region. Consequently, the boundaries of a nodal region are not easily defined. But the nodal approach clearly demonstrates not only the functional interdependence between a region's internal components but also between its nodes and the nodes of other

[5] Gajda, R.T. (1964) in *Geographia Polonica*, **4** 185, Methods of Economic Regionalization
[6] Ullman, E. quoted in *ibid.*, 16

regions. The latter may be revealed in transportation networks, power grids, communications networks, water supply channels, inter-regional migration flows and flows of raw materials and manufactured commodities, all connecting nodal regions themselves in a wider spatial framework. The functional linkages within regions, however, are better derived from service connections than from production links, since while the production connections of plants may be spread across the national economy service functions are more likely to be performed at the regional and sub-regional levels.

Polarisation flows, their rate and their orientation, can be shown in many ways: the distribution area of retail and wholesale goods and the relative traffic of such goods over different parts of the trade area; freight and passenger movements, such as intra-regional commodity flows, commuting patterns and migration flows; telephone communication densities and newspaper circulation areas; financial ties; domiciliary origin of students at educational institutions; the area supplied by centrally located social services and leisure facilities; labour catchment areas and journey to work patterns. Flow densities can be used to identify the dominant nodes, since the density of most types of flow will be higher between the dominant node and any given population centre within the region than between the latter and any other centre. Moreover, although the problems of determining boundaries are difficult, where the flows fall below certain arbitrarily defined densities will give some guide to delimitation. Of course, the boundaries of service areas for separate items of retail trade (and for particular cultural and leisure facilities or other service functions) will vary, and will also be different from the market areas of manufacturing firms supplying regional markets and from the outer limits of the labour catchment areas of the dominant employment centres in the region. Nevertheless, from an overlapping group of different service areas and zones of influence it should be possible to elicit a realistic, if rather imprecisely defined, regional boundary. Of course, if there is a hierarchy of service functions service areas will be of different size relating to services of a given rank; obviously, only the trade areas of the highest ranking services should be used for delimiting regional boundaries.

The city region (or metropolitan region) is a major type of nodal region. Such a region has one or more control centres, characterised by a densely populated urban area surrounded by outer rings in which population density and the degree of interaction fall with increasing distance from the centre, and with distance from transport routes radiating from the centre. At greater distances will be located satellite communities functionally linked through residence-workplace interconnections and commuter flows. Such a region may also include an intensive agricultural sector chiefly concerned with supplying the region's population. As economic growth advances, functional links between the different units of the region are strengthened, and flows of population movement, goods and communications increase; intra-regional interdependence increases. One consequence of the city region concept is that the condition of contiguity may not be satisfied. When interaction declines below a threshold level, the outer limits of the city region give way to rural areas that are not integrated with any metropolitan centre. Thus, between city regions may be located rural borderland areas that are not linked with any nodal region as defined.

A third concept of the region is that of the planning region, or programming region. This is defined in terms of the coherence and unity of economic decision-making. Implementation of a regional policy demands a capacity for action, and this rests with governments in most cases. It might be argued, therefore, that regions need to be defined as political jurisdictions of various sizes and levels, though a programming system might be flexible enough to deal with overlapping jurisdictions. In socialist economies, in particular, economic regionalisation means the division of a country for planning purposes into several parts which both fulfil specific tasks in the national economy and provide the basis for the organisation of economic administration bodies at the regional level. However, planning regions may be either well-designed or badly designed. If there are in reality concrete regions in the sense of natural areal units formed under the influence of economic forces, then it may be suggested that planning regions should be adjusted until they conform with the boundaries of natural regions. If planning regions are defined indiscriminately without regard to functional linkages between separate spatial units so that areas are included in the planning region which have a higher degree of interdependence with nodes external to the region, then planning decisions may be ineffective. But policy formulation also requires information and statistical data, and if these are collected only on a regional basis rather than by sub-regional building blocks, then there is no serious alternative for planning purposes to administrative regions.

There is a widespread view that the nodal region in general, and the metropolitan region in particular, is the optimal planning unit. To the extent that this is true, then planning regions and nodal regions may coincide. Similarly, there is no inherent contradiction between the concepts of nodality and homogeneity. Even if regions were defined on the basis of combining units showing uniform homogeneous characteristics, there would still be polarisation flows between centres within such a region. Whether the analyst directs his attention to the homogeneous features of the region or to its nodal characteristics will depend on the nature of his inquiry. If his interest is in the inter-regional relations (for example, the transference of cyclical impulses from one region to another) it may be appropriate to treat regions as uniform, while if his primary concern is with the planning problems of the single region it will almost certainly be necessary to concentrate on the polarisation aspects and the inter-dependence between separate sub-regional units.

Moreover, emphasis on one type of region rather than another may depend on the structure of the regional system considered as a whole. If the national economy divides easily into a number of regions of similar size with well-defined unambiguous internal structures, then such an economy may reasonably be described in terms of uniform regions. But if the regional system is unbalanced, with, for example, one or two very large highly developed regions and several much smaller ones, or is composed of regions with economic structures that do not conform to the notion of clearly marked geographic areas of specialisation, then the analysis of such a system may be possible only in terms of polarisation flows stressing the functional inter-relationships not only within but between regions. The choice of an ideal type of region is, therefore, constrained by the purpose for which delimitation of a set of regions is required, and by the overall structure and degree of integration of the system as a whole.

The next preliminary step is to outline the nature and objectives of a regional accounting framework which provides the base on which the superstructure of regional income analysis and growth theory is based. Such a framework assumes regions that are either homogeneous or planning regions. Although inter-regional accounting systems recognise the spatial distinction between the region as an income and consumer unit and the region as a production unit, distance variables and intra-regional functional linkages over space (as opposed to the interindustry interrelationships characteristic of input-output accounts) are ignored.[7]

2 Regional accounts

A *Introduction*

Regional accounts fulfil a similar function to national accounts; that is, they provide a useful foundation for regional economic analysis in the same way as national accounting lays a base for the study of macroeconomic theory. There is, however, a major difference between the uses to which regional and national accounts are put. Whilst the latter are used primarily to analyse questions of short-run cyclical stability, regional accounts are more frequently employed in the analysis of long-run secular trends or structural changes between and within regions. Cyclical interrelationships and problems of short-run regional interaction are not, as Chapter 11 demonstrates, excluded from the regional analyst's range of interests, but he is likely to be more concerned with formulating theories of regional growth and explaining how individual regions adapt to long-run processes of growth in inputs, technical progress and structural change.

The sets of regional accounts required to deal with these problems are much more complex than the simple rudiments outlined here.[8] But the characteristics and functions of accounting systems are broadly the same, regardless of the complexity or simplicity of their structure. Although regional accounting and regional economics deal mainly with the same variables, the accounting relationships are somewhat different from theoretical relationships. The former express identities, typically balance-sheet identities, which are true by definition. Theoretical relationships, on the other hand, are derived for explanatory and predictive purposes; they are less precise, and are intended only as approximate generalisations. Because of their greater precision, accounts can fulfil a valuable service for theory, since they compel theorists to define their concepts clearly and also to fit their theories into a framework which is consistent with the collection of statistical data and other information.

[7] However, nodality becomes a necessary element in the construction of urban accounting systems or other forms of **intra**-regional accounts

[8] For attempts to handle such problems with regional accounting concepts see the Committee on Regional Accounts volumes, Hochwald, W. (edit) (1961) *Design of Regional Accounts*; Hirsch, W.Z. (edit) (1964) *Elements of Regional Accounts*; Hirsch, W.Z. (edit) (1966) *Regional Accounts for Policy Decisions*

In other words, regional accounting systems can aid the development of regional economic theory by providing a consistency-checking device and by inducing the formulation of theoretical hypotheses that have operational value.

The value of regional accounts goes beyond assisting the evolution of theory. They can provide an extremely fruitful framework for the regional policymaker. Firstly, they may provide a base of information for decision-making by public and private agencies at the sub-national level. Secondly, they may facilitate 'impact-evaluation' – that is, tracing the repercussions through the regional system of national policies or changes in the aggregate level of economic activity. This last function of regional accounts highlights a significant difference between the regional and national accounting frameworks. It is permissible to construct a national accounting framework, which, in effect, assumes a closed system. Imports and exports may be allowed for in order to equalise both sides of an account, but may not be given a determining influence. With regional accounts, such a procedure would render regional analysis meaningless. A region must be treated as an open economy, and accounts constructed in a way that facilitates tracing the impact of external forces on local production flows. The accounts structure must be able to accommodate both endogenous and exogenous elements, and to show the interactions between national, regional and inter-regional activities. In other words, a well designed regional accounting framework needs to have a general equilibrium character, able to show the interplay between the public and private sectors, the individual region and the 'rest of the world', etc. This does not prohibit, of course, the construction of subsidiary accounts for partial analysis and formulation of a policy to deal with a limited local problem.

A meaningful set of regional accounts must make provision for the relationships between the individual region and all other regions and the rest of the world and for the activities of the central government. Quantitative estimates need to be assigned to regional imports and exports because individual regions may vary widely in the values of their marginal propensities to import. Moreover, the difference between regional residential income (i.e. income received) and regional geographical income (i.e. regional domestic product) may be large because places of work and residence may be found on opposite sides of a regional boundary and because a high proportion of a region's capital may be owned by non-residents. This distinction gives rise to serious difficulties. Within a national economy many inter-regional transactions are not subject to administrative controls and are, consequently, not recorded. Yet for the policymaker an estimate of regional income received may be vital for an assessment of the size of the regional market. The upshot is that inter-regional trade flows and the balance of payments between regions, which are consolidated out of national accounts, are essential components of a regional accounts framework. The justification for making explicit allowance for the central government in regional accounts is even more obvious. Economic conditions in particular regions may be influenced to a considerable extent by the budget activities of the central government, as a result of the differential impact of government investment in promoting regional development and because the relative contributions of individual regions to total tax revenue will vary, often widely.

These two considerations make it clear that the conventional structure of national accounts may not be appropriate for a regional accounting system: 'the major regional problems are different from those posed at the national level, and it does not necessarily follow that they require a complete set of national income and product accounts as their basic framework of economic information'.[9] For example, in impact-evaluation studies the industrial breakdown of a region may be more useful than division into such items as savings and investment. In view of income spillovers that are difficult to trace, there are greater possibilities of building a system of regional accounts based on a geographical breakdown of national inter-industry sales and purchases estimates than on a disaggregation of national income flows. Data may be more easily obtainable on an industry basis, and can often be identified by region.

Finally, preoccupation with regional accounts at the conceptual level must not obscure the fact that a set of such accounts is an empirical framework. Regional accounts are a link between statistical data and theoretical constructs. To perform this function effectively the information from which accounts can be constructed must be available or, at least, not too difficult to collect. In some countries, especially those without State or regional administrations within a federal system such as the United Kingdom, sufficient

---

[9] Ruggles, R. and Ruggles, N.D. Regional Breakdowns of National Economic Accounts. 132, in Hochwald, *op. cit.*

information for construction of operationally useful accounts does not exist.[10] Much of the data is very expensive to obtain, and a substantial proportion is impossible to measure without new data-recording agencies. Estimates of income received may be needed for policy purposes, but where transactions between regions and the rest of the country are not submitted to administrative controls it will be almost impossible to trace them. Multi-plant firms operating in several regions may give rise to serious statistical problems. Some plants may produce intermediate goods in a region which are used as raw materials in finishing plants sited in other regions, and the value of production may be difficult to record. Data on profits by region may not be provided for in the accounting systems of such firms. Allocation of indirect taxes to different regions may also be impossible, especially when raw materials or intermediate goods are taxed at the port of entry before being forwarded to their ultimate destination. Similar problems result where home-produced goods are taxed at the factory before distribution to consuming industries elsewhere in the country. These points are raised as a reminder that a conceptual framework for regional accounts is only the beginning of handling the problem, not its complete solution.

B *Regional income and product accounts: an example*
As an example of income and product accounts applied to a regional system, we may refer to the set suggested by Richard Stone and his associates at the Cambridge Department of Applied Economics.[11] This model adopts a traditional functional division of activity into three main types: production, consumption and investment. In an open economy it is necessary to accommodate transactions with the rest of the world. The easiest way to do this is to combine all other regions in the system and the rest of the world outside the system into a single account, thereby reducing inter-regional informa-

---

[10] This is not to say that it is impossible to construct a set of regional accounts for a country such as Britain. See the set for 1948 by Phyllis Deane reproduced in Isard, W. and Cumberland, J.H. *Regional Economic Planning: Techniques of Analysis for Less Developed Areas.* (O.E.C.D., 1961), 295

[11] Stone, J.R. Social Accounts at the Regional Level: A Survey in Isard and Cumberland, *op. cit.*, 263–95 and comments by Geronymakis, S. *ibid.*, 297–303. For similar examples see Leven, C.L. Regional Income and Product Accounts: Construction and Applications, 148–95 in *Design of Regional Accounts, op. cit.*, and Peacock, A.T. (1965) Towards a Theory of Interregional Fiscal Policy. *Public Finance.* **20**

tion requirements to a minimum. The complete set of accounts relating to inter-regional flows are made to balance by introducing appropriate transfers. A set of accounts is also included for the activities of the central government. Although nominally located in the capital, the central government has branches and departments in many regions. Many of the transactions carried out by these departments have no regional significance, but if they were assigned to the region in which the capital was located they might distort inter-regional comparisons severely. Thus, there are great dangers in assigning central government activity to regions at all. Stone's framework consequently takes central government consumption and investment out of the regions and accounts for them separately; on the other hand, the producing activities of the government are included with all other forms of production in the regions.

The complete set of accounts is presented in matrix form in Table 2. The subscript j refers to one of the regions, g to the central government and r to all regions and the rest of the world. In Table 2 the first three rows and columns represent the set of three accounts for a region. All imports are routed through production and the incomings into the production account of a region are shown in the first row; these are matched by outgoings shown in the first column. The income and outlay account of region j is presented in the second row and column. The third row and column give the incomings and matching outgoings of the capital transactions account of region j. These three accounts include 14 entries for each region. The totals of the three accounts yield: for the production account gross regional domestic product at market prices; for the income account gross regional income plus net current transfers; and for the capital account the gross addition to regional wealth in the form either of investment in stocks and fixed assets or of a net increase in claims on others.

The central government accounts are shown in rows 4–6 and columns 4–6 of Table 2. Since central government productive activity is taken account of in the regional production accounts, there are only zeros in row and column 4.[12] Row and column 5 show the incomings and outgoings of the central government income and

[12] In Stone's original formulation, which was used as a basis for actual statistical estimates, the central government's internal account was used to find a place for the income of the armed forces and to accommodate the residual error found in official national income estimates. These have been excluded here

REGIONAL ECONOMICS

Table 2

Regional accounts system with government in an open economy: matrix form

from \ to	region 1 P	region 2 Y	region 3 K	central government 4 P	central government 5 Y	central government 6 K	all regions and rest of world 7 P	all regions and rest of world 8 Y	all regions and rest of world 9 K
region									
1 production	O	C_{jj}	V_{jj}	O	C_{jg}	O	X_{jr}	O	O
2 income	Y_{dj}	O	O	O	G_{jg}	O	Y_{jr}	G_{jr}	O
3 capital	O	S_{jj}	O	O	O	T_{jg}	O	O	O
central government									
4 P	O	O	O	O	O	O	O	O	O
5 Y	I_{gj}	D_{gj}	O	O	O	$-S_{gg}$	Y_{gr}	O	O
6 K	O	O	B_{gj}	O	O	O	$-V_{gr}$	O	B_{gr}
all regions and rest of world									
7 P	O	O	O	O	C_{rg}	O	O	O	O
8 Y	O	O	O	O	G_{rg}	O	M_{rr}	O	O
9 K	O	O	B_{rj}	O	O	T_{rg}	O	N_{rr}	O

Key to table 2

Y_{dj} = gross domestic product at factor cost of region j (also includes stock appreciation)

I_{gj} = indirect taxes less subsidies paid by region j

C_{jj} = consumption by residents and local authorities of region j

V_{jj} = gross investment in region j in fixed assets and stocks including stock appreciation. (Investment of central government is excluded and shown separately)

C_{jg} = sales by region j to central government for consumption purposes

X_{jr} = net exports by region j to all other regions and the rest of world

S_{jj} = gross saving of region j

D_{gj} = direct taxes on income paid by region j to central government

G_{jg} = current transfers, gifts and grants received by region j from central government

Y_{jr} = net receipts of factor income by region j from all other regions and rest of world

G_{jr} = current transfers received by region j from all other regions and rest of world

T_{jg} = net capital transfers received by region j from central government

B_{gj} = net borrowing by central government from region j

B_{rj} = net borrowing by all other regions and rest of world from region j

C_{rg} = government current expenditure abroad on goods and services outlay account, i.e. the central government's current account. Row and column 6 represent the central government's capital account. It can be seen from these that government saving and investment have here been displaced from their expected position. The reason for this is clear from the incoming entries into the government capital account (row 6). These entries are government borrowing and government disinvestment, or in total the negative of the gross addition to the wealth of the central government. In other words, they correspond to the negative of the outgoing entries in the regional capital accounts (column 3). Finally, rows and columns 7–9 represent the production, income and outlay and capital accounts respectively for all regions and the rest of the world.

These accounts lend themselves to aggregation to yield the standard domestic and national totals. For example, gross domestic product at factor cost plus stock appreciation $= \sum_j Ydj$, that is, the sum of the domestic products of the regions in the economy. Similarly, total consumption $= \sum_j C_{jj} + \sum_j C_{jg} + C_{rg}$.[13]

C *Regional input–output accounts: an illustration*
An industrial breakdown at the regional level may be very useful for tracing the effects of exogenous changes on the regional economy. For such a purpose input–output accounts probably have greater value than income and product accounts. For this reason, although the data requirements for making an inter-regional input–output model are heavy, some conceptual discussion of input–output accounts is not out of place. Such accounts should be regarded as

---

[13] It is easy to translate the matrix of Table 2 into traditional accounting form, as shown by S. Geronymakis in Isard and Cumberland, *op. cit.*

G_{rg} = government current transfers abroad net
$-S_{gg}$ = dissaving of central government
Y_{gr} = net factor income payments received by central government from all regions and rest of world
T_{rg} = net capital transfers paid to rest of world by central government
$-V_{gr}$ = gross disinvestment in fixed assets and stocks by central government
B_{gr} = net borrowing by central government from rest of world
M_{rr} = balancing transfers to income and outlay account, i.e. net receipts from the country from the sale of goods and services and in the form of factor income
N_{rr} = balancing transfer to capital transactions account, i.e. rest of the world's balance on current account with the country

an extension and modification of income and product accounts rather a contradiction of them. If each of the regional production accounts is subdivided by industry, we obtain a set of inter-industry accounts which trace the flow of goods and services from one production sector to another. The regional accounts relating to consumption and investment are consolidated and removed to a non-production account relating to final demand. In regional applications, the familiar input–output matrix is extended to reflect locational as well as industrial aspects of production. Just as interindustry analysis breaks down total production and consumption by commodity, so inter-regional analysis decomposes these aggregates by region. Formally, there is no inherent difficulty in combining the two types of disaggregation. Empirical problems are, however, multiplied, since the types of data required need to be broken down by region and by commodity. The double disaggregation means that the model describes inter-regional trade as well as regional production.

Regional input–output models incorporate the basic assumptions of general Leontief models. Each commodity is supplied by a single industry or sector of production; only one method is used for producing each commodity and each sector has only one primary output. There are, therefore, no joint products. Inputs purchased by each sector are a function only of the level of output of that sector. This usually takes a stronger form: that input functions are linear – in other words, constant input coefficients are assumed. Thus, no substitution is possible between inputs in the production of any commodity, and there are constant returns to scale. The additivity assumption is also made, that is, that the total effect of carrying on several types of production is the sum of the separate effects. This rules out external economies and diseconomies. Finally, problems of capital and capacity are ignored; current flows of inputs and outputs are considered the significant variables.

Extending the analysis to an inter-regional setting, it is convenient, and sometimes necessary to make additional assumptions.[14] Firstly, we assume that the system is closed; there are no

---

[14] For discussions of regional input–output analysis and its problems see Chenery, H.B. and Clark, P.G. (1959) *Interindustry Economics*, especially Chs. 2, 3 and 12; Leontief, W.W. (1951) *The Structure of the American Economy, 1919–39*; Leontief, W.W. et al. (1953) *Studies in the Structure of the American Economy*, Chs. 4 and 5; Leontief, W.W. (1966) *Input–Output Economics*, Ch. 11;

imports from or exports to the outside world, and exports from one region constitute imports into another. This unrealistic assumption is not absolutely necessary; an easy solution is to treat the rest of the world with which all external trade is conducted as if it were a single region. However, we shall retain the closed national economy assumption for convenience. If a region's exports are another region's imports, we do not have to treat exports as autonomous but can explain their levels within the system, in that the exports of a commodity can be described solely in terms of the demand for imports in other regions of the system.

In order to be able to do this satisfactorily, we have to assume a certain stability in the geographical distribution of production. A regional inter-industry analysis must not only assume stable production coefficients but also stable trading coefficients, so that the repercussions of an autonomous change are not distorted by geographical differences in the location of final demand or in sources of supply. H.B. Chenery and L.N. Moses in their respective studies of the Italian and American economies assumed that imports were a fixed fraction of total supply of each commodity. All sectors in a region were assumed to take the same percentage of its needs from a given sector in another region. Stated explicitly, this means that 'all the consuming industries absorb the domestic output of any given type of commodity combined in a fixed proportion with a certain type of its competitive imports, the proportion itself being determined by the ratio of the total imports of the particular type of goods to their total supply'.[15] In other words, not only were trading patterns by type of input assumed constant at the aggregate regional level, but they were also constant and identical for each receiving industry in a region.

This assumption freezes the spatial structure of each region (just

---

Isard, W. (1960) *Methods of Regional Analysis*, Ch. 8; N.B.E.R., Studies in Research in Income and Wealth, Vol. 18, *Input–Output Analysis: An Appraisal* (1955); Isard, W. (1951) Interregional and Regional Input–Output Analysis. *Review of Economics and Statistics*, **33**; Moses, L.N. (1955) The Stability of Interregional Trading Patterns and Input–Output Analysis. *American Economic Review*, **45**; Leven, C.L. *loc. cit.*; Stone, J.R. *loc. cit.*; Cao-Pinna, V. Problems of Establishing and Using Regional Input–Output Accounting, and de Torres Martinez, M. and Lasuen Sancho, J.R. Discussion Paper. 305–38 and 339–58 in Isard and Cumberland, *op. cit.*; Kuenne, R.E. (1963) *The Theory of General Economic Equilibrium*. 395–435

[15] Leontief, *op. cit.* (1951), 164–5

as the input coefficient restrictions freeze the technological structure of the economy), and implies fixed regional supply areas for each and every consuming industry using a particular input. This assumption is very restrictive since, in reality, the supply patterns of individual industries for a given input may vary widely because of vertical integration, different locations within a given region or institutional ties. Here, since we are concerned with conceptual analysis rather than the data needs for an operational model, we can afford some flexibility by allowing the import proportion of a given input to vary *between* consuming sectors, though the import coefficient remains constant for any given sector. However, the relative contribution of different regions to the imported input requirements of a given sector in another region remains constant so that constant geographical patterns of supply are still required. This implies comparative stability in relative prices between regions (since changes in relative prices would induce some change in the pattern of flows) and no changes in inter-regional competitiveness in the supply of a particular commodity. These assumptions are still somewhat restrictive, since, in reality, there is probably even less justification for expecting stability in import coefficients than in input coefficients.

Finally, we assume that imports enter a region only through the inter-industry transactions matrix. Imports of a commodity are, therefore, considered as inputs and are fed directly into the producing sectors. They enter final demand only indirectly, as part of a regional industry's domestic output. This requires that each commodity is treated both as an intermediate and as a final good, unless we can assume that final demand for commodities which have complete rows of zero cells in the inter-industry account can be satisfied internally. It may be unrealistic in some cases to assume that imports enter only the producing sectors as inputs and never go directly to final consumption; for example, if a large consuming centre is located near the supplying region's boundary while the production plants of a sector are sited at the maximum distance from that boundary we would expect to find supplies of finished goods being sent direct to the point of consumption rather than the commodity being exported as an input to the distant plants, converted into final output and returned to the consumption centre. This latter possibility obviously involves inefficient cross-hauling. In this case, it is the concept of distance which gives rise to the problem, and Kuenne has argued that inter-regional input–output models are implicitly spaceless. We further assume that no primary inputs (such as labour and capital) are imported.

In allowing the constant import coefficients to vary from one purchasing sector to another rather than assuming that imports remain a fixed identical proportion of total supply in each sector à la Chenery, we are following a suggestion of Miss Cao-Pinna.[16] For operational possibilities all imports need to be separately tabulated by sector of origin and by sector of destination, and this means adding an inter-regional trade matrix to the local one. The input–output matrix will, therefore, have more rows than columns. The rows are broken down into two sets of accounts, one assigned to the regional production sectors and the other to inter-regional sectors, while the columns are assigned only to regional sectors. Two separate sets of technical coefficients are involved: one for the domestic input–output ratios, the other expressing the ratios between imported inputs and domestic outputs.

A hypothetical set of inter-regional input–output accounts is presented in Table 3. In an operational model, a compromise has to be made between the number of regions and the number of commodities included to reduce the computational tasks. For expositional purposes, we shall limit the analysis to two regions (A and B) and three commodities (1, 2 and 3) only. The inter-industry accounts are shown in the upper left hand quadrant of the table. Production activities are grouped together into a number of sectors, in this case three. Each sector appears in the accounting system twice, as a producer of output and as a user of inputs. The elements in each row show the disposition of the output of that sector in each region, and by source (whether domestic or imported), and the aggregation of these elements gives the total intermediate use by region (W_i).[17] The remaining uses, such as consumption, investment, government absorption and exports, that figure so prominently in income and product accounts, are here consolidated into the item 'final use' (Y_i). In the table, we disaggregate this into two items, final domestic use and exports, shown in the top right hand quadrant of the table as ($D_i^A + X_i^{AB}$).

[16] Cao-Pinna, *loc. cit.*, 308–11

[17] In the explanation that follows, we generalise by using the subscript i to indicate commodities, and j to indicate purchasing sectors. Since each of our three commodities is also a sector, i may be equal to j

Table 3

Inter-regional input–output accounts: 2 regions and 3 commodities (sectors)

from	to	purchasing sectors 1	2	3	total intermediate use	final domestic use	final use exports	total final demand	total demand = total supply	supply imports	domestic production
production sectors	1	X_{11}^{AA} X_{11}^{BA} X_{11}^{BB} X_{11}^{AB}	X_{12}^{AA} X_{12}^{BA} X_{12}^{BB} X_{12}^{AB}	X_{13}^{AA} X_{13}^{BA} X_{13}^{BB} X_{13}^{AB}	W_1^A W_1^B	D_1^A D_1^B	X_1^{AB} X_1^{BA}	Y_1^A Y_1^B	Z_1^A Z_1^B	X_1^{BA} X_1^{AB}	X_1^{AA} X_1^{BB}
	2	X_{21}^{AA} X_{21}^{BA} X_{21}^{BB} X_{21}^{AB}	X_{22}^{AA} X_{22}^{BA} X_{22}^{BB} X_{22}^{AB}	X_{23}^{AA} X_{23}^{BA} X_{23}^{BB} X_{23}^{AB}	W_2^A W_2^B	D_2^A D_2^B	X_2^{AB} X_2^{BA}	Y_2^A Y_2^B	Z_2^A Z_2^B	X_2^{BA} X_2^{AB}	X_2^{AA} X_2^{BB}
	3	X_{31}^{AA} X_{31}^{BA} X_{31}^{BB} X_{31}^{AB}	X_{32}^{AA} X_{32}^{BA} X_{32}^{BB} X_{32}^{AB}	X_{33}^{AA} X_{33}^{BA} X_{33}^{BB} X_{33}^{AB}	W_3^A W_3^B	D_3^A D_3^B	X_3^{AB} X_3^{BA}	Y_3^A Y_3^B	Z_3^A Z_3^B	X_3^{BA} X_3^{AB}	X_3^{AA} X_3^{BB}
total purchases (i.e. produced inputs)		U_1^A U_1^B	U_2^A U_2^B	U_3^A U_3^B							
value added (primary inputs)		V_1^A V_1^B	V_2^A V_2^B	V_3^A V_3^B		V_D^A V_D^B	V_X^{AB} V_X^{BA}	V_Y^A V_Y^B	V^A V^B		
total production + imported inputs		$X_1^A + M_1^A$ $X_1^B + M_1^B$	$X_2^A + M_2^A$ $X_2^B + M_2^B$	$X_3^A + M_3^A$ $X_3^B + M_3^B$		D^A D^B	X^{AB} X^{BA}	Y^A Y^B	Z^A Z^B	X^{BA} X^{AB}	X^{AA} X^{BB}

Key to table 3

Subscripts A and B = Region A and Region B
Subscripts 1, 2 and 3 = commodities (sectors) 1, 2 and 3
Z_1^A = total supply of commodity 1 in Region A
X_1^A = total production of commodity 1 in Region A
X_1^{BA} = total imports of commodity 1 in Region A from Region B by Region A
X_1^{AB} = total exports of commodity 1 of Region A to Region B
X_{12}^{AA} = amount of commodity 1 domestically produced used in sector 2 in Region A
X_{12}^{BA} = amount of commodity 1 imported from Region B for use in sector 2 in Region A

Y_1^A = final demand for commodity 1 in Region A
D_1^A = final domestic use of commodity 1 in Region A
W_1^A = total intermediate use of commodity 1 in Region A
U_2^A = total use by sector 2 in Region A of inputs purchased from other industries
V_2^A = total use of primary inputs (value added) in sector 2 in Region A
X_1^{AA} = domestic production of commodity 1 in Region A
M_2^A = total use by sector 2 in Region A of imported inputs purchased from industries in Region B

The columns of the top left hand quadrant of the table show the role of sectors as a purchaser of inputs, inputs for a sector in a given region being taken from all other production sectors at home and outside the region (except in cases where there are zero cells). The aggregation of these purchases gives total purchases of produced inputs (U_j). To obtain total production plus imported inputs for use in sector j ($X_j + M_j$) primary inputs are added to total purchases. By primary inputs, we mean direct payments for primary factors (land, labour and capital) which comprise the value added in the sector, shown in the bottom left hand quadrant as V_j. Finally, in the bottom right hand quadrant is found the direct input of primary factors to final use, the most conspicuous examples of which are government employment and domestic service. Although such transactions do not normally enter inter-industry models, their inclusion helps to make the total consistent with regional (and national) aggregates.

The design of the input–output accounts is based upon a division of uses into two categories – intermediate and final – and a corresponding division of inputs into 'produced' and 'primary'. The first distinction is logically similar to that in income determination analysis between 'induced' and 'autonomous' components. One of the main functions of input–output accounts is to enable analysts to be able to work out the effects of an autonomous disturbance, i.e. a change in final demand, on inter-industry transactions, and hence on total production in each sector of the economy.

In Table 3, the symbol Z_i^A represents total supply of commodity i in region A, and this is broken down into two components, imports (X_i^{BA}) and domestic production (X_i^{AA}). Through the balance equation, which states that for each commodity total supply is equal to total demand, Z_i^A can also be equated with total demand in Region A, that is, with total final demand minus exports, or total intermediate use plus final domestic use ($W_i^A + D_i^A$).

In order to be able to explain the magnitudes of the inter-industry flows in terms of the levels of production in each sector, some comment is necessary on the individual cells of the inter-industry matrix. The demand (X_{ij}^{AA}) of each industry (j^A) for each commodity produced domestically (i) can be expressed as a function of its own output level. Assuming zero fixed cost elements, the input function becomes:

$$X_{ij}^{AA} = m_{ij}^{AA} . a_{ij}^A X_j^A \qquad (1)$$

where a_{ij} = marginal input coefficient, and $m_{ij}{}^{AA}$ = proportion of commodity input i supplied domestically in Region A.

Similarly, the demand of industry (j^A) for imports of commodity (i) can be expressed as the function:

$$X_{ij}{}^{BA} = m_{ij}{}^{BA} \cdot a_{ij}{}^{A} X_{j}{}^{A} \tag{2}$$

where $m_{ij}{}^{BA}$ is closely related to the marginal propensity of industry j in Region A to import commodity i from Region B. In fact, $m_{ij}{}^{BA}$ equals

$$\left[\frac{X_{ij}{}^{BA}}{X_{ij}{}^{AA} + X_{ij}{}^{BA}} \right]$$

Obviously, $m_{ij}{}^{AA} + m_{ij}{}^{BA} = 1$. By use of these constant coefficients, which are both the strength and the weakness of the input–output model, we can estimate the quantitative effects of changes in the demand for outputs on the demand for inputs, both intra-regional and inter-regional, through the inter-industry matrix.

The relationships of the inter-regional input–output accounts can be expressed in the form of a number of identities. We set some of the main examples below.

$$Z_i{}^A \;\; = W_i{}^A + D_i{}^A \;\; = X_i{}^{AA} + X_i{}^{BA} \tag{3}$$

$\phantom{Z_i{}^A \;\;=}$ Total demand $\;\;$ Supply in
$\phantom{Z_i{}^A \;\;=}$ in Region A Region A

This is the important balance equation, with exports deducted from total final demand and also from production.

$$W_i{}^A = \sum m_{ij}{}^{AA} a_{ij}{}^{A} X_j{}^{A} + \sum m_{ij}{}^{BA} a_{ij}{}^{A} X_j{}^{A} \tag{4}$$

 Total intermediate demand
 for commodity i in Region A

Also

$$X_i{}^{BA} \;\; = \sum_j m_{ij}{}^{BA} a_{ij}{}^{A} X_j{}^{A} \tag{5}$$

 Imports of
 Commodity i
 by Region A

Substituting (4) and (5) into (3), we obtain:

$$X_i{}^{AA} \;\; = \sum_j m_{ij}{}^{AA} a_{ij}{}^{A} X_j{}^{A} + D_i{}^{A} \tag{6}$$

 Domestic produc-
 tion of i in Region
 A minus
 import content

THE REGIONAL FRAMEWORK

Total production in Region A is equal to total intermediate use plus total final demand minus imports:

$$X_i^A = W_i^A + Y_i^A - X_i^{BA} \qquad (7)$$

so that

$$X_i^A = X_i^{AA} + X_i^{AB} \qquad (8)$$

This can be rewritten as:

$$X_i^A = \sum_j m_{ij}^{AA} a_{ij}^A X_j^A + D_i^A + \sum_j m_{ij}^{AB} a_{ij}^B X_j^B \qquad (9)$$

From the columns of the accounts, we can derive total production in terms of the aggregation of domestic inputs. Thus,

$$X_j^A = U_j^A + V_j^A - M_j^A \qquad (10)$$

and since

$$U_j^A = \sum_i m_{ij}^{AA} a_{ij}^A X_j^A + \sum_i m_{ij}^{BA} a_{ij}^A X_j^A \qquad (11)$$

and

$$M_j^A = \sum_i m_{ij}^{BA} a_{ij}^A X_j^A \qquad (12)$$

then

$$X_j^A = \sum_i m_{ij}^{AA} a_{ij}^A X_j^A + V_j^A \qquad (13)$$

Since $\sum_i X_i^A = \sum_j X_j^A$,[18] equations (9) and (13) can be aggregated for each region, and are then equal to each other. This yields:

$$\sum_i \sum_j m_{ij}^{AA} a_{ij}^A X_j^A + \sum_i D_i^A + \sum_i \sum_j m_{ij}^{AB} a_{ij}^B X_j^B =$$
$$\sum_j \sum_j m_{ij}^{AA} a_{ij}^A X_j^A + \sum_i V_j^A \qquad (14)$$

Eliminating all inter-industry transactions (which according to our assumptions eliminate imports as well), this leaves the national income identity $\sum_i Y_i = \sum_j V_j$. In other words, final demand is equal to total factor payments, which corresponds to the identity of gross national product and gross national income.

Finally, the external balance of Region A can be expressed in the form

$$B^A = \sum_i X_i^{AB} - \sum_i X_i^{BA} \qquad (15)$$

[18] The equality is not affected by the import position, since $\sum_i X_i^{BA} = \sum_j M_j^A$

or
$$B^A = \sum_i \sum_j m_{ij}{}^{AB} a_{ij}{}^B X_j{}^B - \sum_i \sum_j m_{ij}{}^{BA} a_{ij}{}^A X_j{}^A \qquad (16)$$

In a two-region model, one region's exports equal the other's imports, therefore the negative of B^A represents the external balance of Region B.

Inter-regional input–output accounts have been described in some detail. They can be made consistent with income and product accounts, but their emphasis is different. Income and product accounts concentrate on the components of final demand, while input–output accounts are concerned with the inter-industry transactions that lie behind changes in final demand. Much of the analysis which follows in later chapters will be framed in terms of income theory rather than inter-industry analysis.

This approach is not intended to denigrate the value of input–output techniques for regional analysis. Rather it is chosen in the belief that the tools of comparative statics income analysis and dynamic growth theory are more appropriate to an explanation of regional business cycles and regional growth, especially when our interests are theoretical rather than empirical. As an operational technique for empirical research, inter-regional input–output analysis has much to commend it, despite the weakness of its constant coefficient assumptions for long range predictions and its huge data requirements. There are methods which can be adopted to limit the information required to construct an operational model, and constant coefficients can be dropped provided changes in the parameters are predictable. Despite this, it remains true that with such models 'we buy the possibility of answering complicated questions at the price of building in certain rigidities'.[19]

[19] Stone, *loc. cit.*, 289

Chapter 10
Inter-regional income theory

1 The regional economic base

The idea behind the theory of the regional economic base is that the sole (or at least the primary) factor determining the overall level of activity in a region is the level of activity in those sectors, or fractions of sectors, which are sustained by demand outside the region. Base theory is, in fact, an offshoot of the theory of regional income determination, and the base multiplier is a crude form of regional income multiplier that neglects the repercussionary effects of an expansionary process on imports and indirect exports.

The elements of base theory can be illustrated with the aid of a simple model. Let Y represent a region's disposable income, D equal domestic net absorption (i.e. non-basic income), and X be total exports (including not only commodity exports and tourist earnings but net wage payments and property income received by the region's residents from outside as well as net transfer payments from outside). X therefore represents the economic base. We may write:

$$Y = D + X \qquad (1)$$

If we call the region's current account balance B and regional imports M, then

$$B = X - M \qquad (2)$$

The region's output can be allocated in three ways: consumed at home (D); exchanged for imports (M); or lent outside the region (B).

$$\therefore\ Y = D + M + B$$

or
$$\frac{D + M + B}{Y} = 1 \qquad (3)$$

If the base ratio is represented by non-basic income/economic base, then it equals D/X.

247

Substituting from equation (2) we obtain:

$$\frac{D}{X} = \frac{D}{M+B} \tag{4}$$

Since from equation (3) we know that $(D+M+B)/Y=1$, then D and $(M+B)$ must move in opposite directions.

These equations are, of course, little more than identities. For a meaningful analysis we must assume that D, M and B are each a function of regional income Y, and that exports (X) are autonomous, determined by external forces and independent of Y. To investigate the effects of change in the regional economic base, we need to know the relevant marginal propensities. Let d, m and b represent the marginal propensities to spend on home products $(\Delta D/\Delta Y)$, to import $(\Delta M/\Delta Y)$, and to lend abroad $(\Delta B/\Delta Y)$. If the base increases by an amount ΔX and d is constant, the equilibrium level of regional income will rise by

$$\Delta X \cdot \frac{1}{m+b}[1]$$

Consequently, the increase in domestic activity ΔD associated with the increase in the base ΔX is given by:

$$\Delta D = d\Delta Y = \frac{d}{m+b} \cdot \Delta X \tag{5}$$

The influences of changes in activity on the base ratio depend upon the relationship between the marginal and average propensities to spend domestically, provided that we make the simplifying assumption that $(M+B)/Y = m+b$.

Since from (4) above we know that:

$$D = \frac{D}{M+B} \cdot X \tag{6}$$

then dividing equation (5) by (6) yields:

$$\frac{\Delta D}{D} = \frac{d}{m+b} \cdot \frac{M+B}{D} \cdot \frac{\Delta X}{X} \tag{7}$$

---

[1] Here we make the simplifying assumption that changes in income outside the region induced by changes in income in the region are negligible. Our analysis is adapted from Sirkin, G. (1959) The Theory of the Regional Economic Base. *Review of Economics and Statistics*, **41** 426–9.

INTER-REGIONAL INCOME THEORY

We have assumed that $m+b=(M+B)/Y$. Consequently, if $d=D/Y$, then:

$$\frac{\Delta D}{D} = \frac{\Delta X}{X} \qquad (8)$$

Thus, non-basic and basic income increase by the same proportion, the base ratio is unchanged and the export base theory is justified. But if $d > D/Y$ the base ratio will rise over time, while if $d < D/Y$ the base ratio will fall.

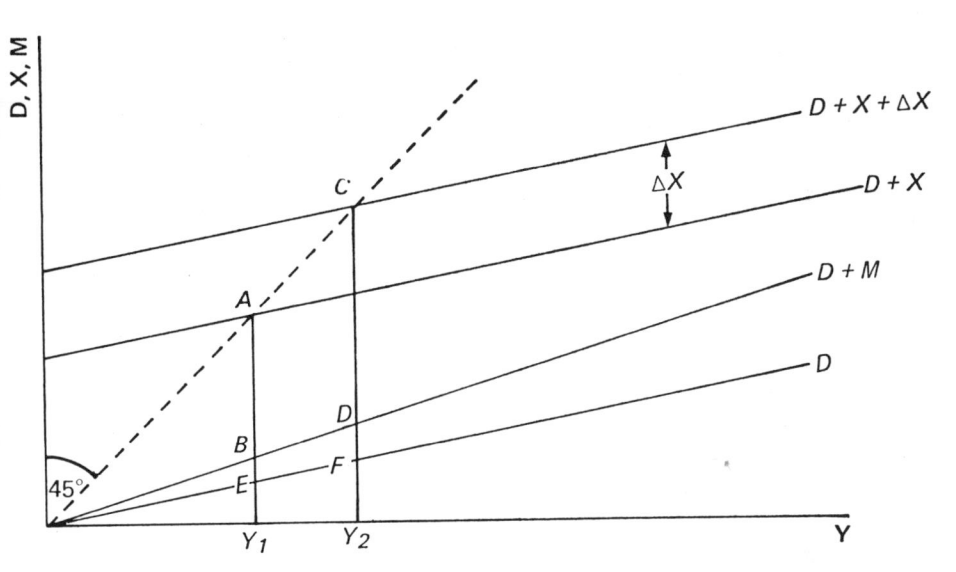

Figure 10.1

These relationships may be illustrated diagrammatically with the aid of a 'Keynesian cross' diagram. In figure 10.1 expenditure on home produced goods (D) and imports (M) are linear functions of income (Y). The export base (X) is constant. Thus, the equilibrium level of income Y_1 is given by the intersection of $(D+X)$ with the 45° line, where total effective demand equals total output. Now let us suppose that the export base increases by ΔX. This raises the equilibrium level of income to Y_2. Because the D function is linear through the origin, then $d = D/Y$ and the base ratio remains unchanged, i.e. $FY_2/CF = EY_1/AE$.

This increase in the export base leads to an increase in the region's current account balance (B) from AB to CD, by an amount equal to

$b\Delta Y$. Y_2 will persist as the new equilibrium level of regional income if the region increases its lending outside the region by $b\Delta Y$. Alternatively, the import function may shift upwards (via an increase in m) sufficiently to close the balance of payments gap. If neither of these forces operates then the export base will fall so as to equilibrate the balance of payments by a reversion to the original income level Y_1.

This theory is oversimplified. The assumption that the size of the export base is the single determinant of the level of regional income is heroic. A significant proportion of regional investment is determined autonomously, and changes in consumption, private investment or government expenditure could stimulate regional income quite as easily as export expansion. The theory dismisses residentiary (i.e. non-basic) sectors as passive elements in regional income change. Improvements in efficiency in residentiary activities may reduce factor costs of possible regional exports, so that the causal sequence runs both ways. Similarly, since a region must make the best use of its resources between export and residentiary sectors, a decline in export activity may be associated with rising regional income if a transfer of factors to local activity approximates more closely to the optimal allocation of resources. More important, residentiary sectors may expand independently of changes in the export base and raise regional income. For example, migration into the region induced by non-economic factors may lead to more residentiary activity (increased investment in social capital, for instance) without any expansion of the export base.

A more general case is where regional income rises as a consequence of increased residentiary activity in import-replacement industries.[2] This is illustrated in figure 10.2. The export base (X) remains unchanged, and total expenditure on home produced goods and imports $(D+M)$ is given. Initially, the function D_1 represents regional output absorbed domestically at each level of income. The equilibrium level of income is determined by $D_1 + X$ at Y_1. However, we assume that an upward shift occurs in the D function, raising it from D_1 to D_2. This is not because there has been a rise in total spending, but simply a transfer of expenditure from imports to domestic goods. This import replacement expansion raises the equilibrium level of income from Y_1 to Y_2, where the new function

[2] The above points are discussed in Tiebout, C.M. Exports and Regional Growth and North, D.C. (1956) Exports and Regional Growth: A Reply. *Journal of Political Economy*, **64**

INTER-REGIONAL INCOME THEORY

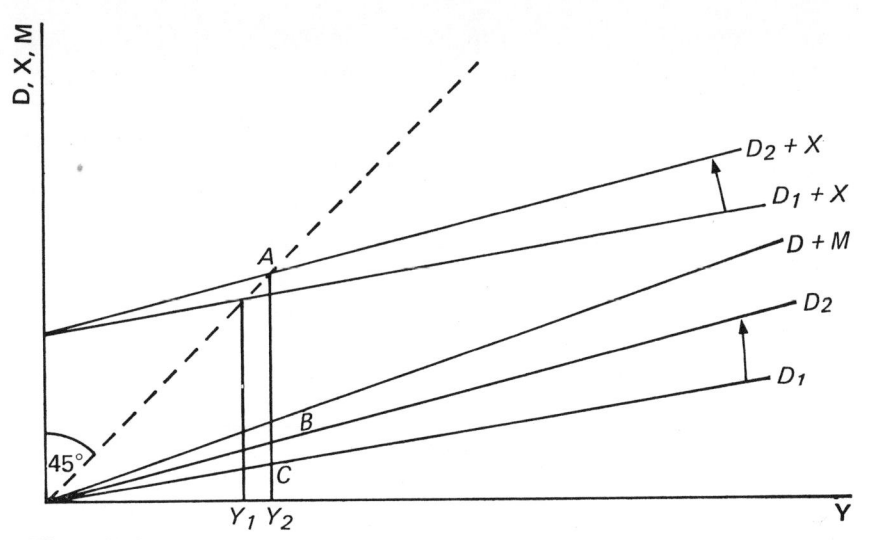

Figure 10.2

$(D_2 + X)$ intersects the 45° line. This involves a rise in the base ratio from CY_2/AC to BY_2/AB.

A major drawback of the export base theory is that it is inappropriate for an analysis of a multiple region system. In the first place, it reduces to a two-region model, the region under consideration and the rest of the world. This would not be a serious simplification if the marginal propensities to import from all other regions were equal. The multiplier effects on regional income of an increase in the export base will depend on the drain into imports and external lending. If marginal propensities to import vary from region to region, the overall multiplier effect (and therefore whether or not the base ratio changes) will be determined by which regions are affected by the increased import demand, and by the values of the marginal propensity of the expanding region to import from each of them. Thus, base theory with its heavy concentration on the causal role of exports neglects imports and consideration of the influences acting upon the propensity to import.

Secondly, in a system of many regions the realistic multiplier to explore is not the crude export base multiplier but the general interregional multiplier which takes full account of feedback effects.[3] In a

[3] Such a multiplier is outlined in the next section. See also Isard, W. *et al.* (1960) *Methods of Regional Analysis* 205–13

multi-regional world a rise in imports in Region A will stimulate expansion in other regions, their incomes will increase leading to higher imports from A with further income-raising effects, and so on. Thus, Region A's exports are a function of incomes in all other regions, and their incomes are influenced by imports of Region A, which in turn are a function of its own income. In other words, if we wish to elaborate base theory analysis into inter-regional multiplier terms it is necessary to drop the original assumption that the exports of a region are independently and autonomously determined. It is also essential to explore the repercussionary effects on inter-regional trade of an increase in the export base far beyond the initial import or external lending leakages associated with the rise in the income of the region under consideration. This involves abandoning another of the earlier assumptions, that is, that changes in income elsewhere in the region induced by changes in income in the region are negligible. In this way we would stress the mutual interdependence between regions in a multiple region system and avoid the unidirectional causation and the lumping together of all regions into the 'rest of the world' inherent in the export base theory. On the other hand, it would be idle to pretend that the much greater theoretical precision of the inter-regional multiplier formulation could be achieved without some sacrifice in terms of operational value.

The value of the base ratio as an explanatory variable will depend on the size, character and structure of the region under consideration, and as the structure changes so may the size of the base ratio. Other things being equal, exports for large regions will tend to be less important as a component of aggregate demand, and a higher proportion of investment will be determined autonomously internal to the region. This partly explains why most empirical studies of the export base have been applied to small areas, such as an urban community. On the other hand, large regions tend to have a more diversified industrial structure relative to the composition of demand. Small regions, especially cities, may be highly specialised and the satisfaction of consumer wants may depend on imports. Accordingly, the base ratio, $D/(M+B)$, will be low due to a high M/Y. Of course, this does not rule out the predictive power of the theory unless the marginal propensity to import (m) has a high degree of instability. A high propensity to lend abroad (B/Y) will also decrease the base ratio, though again the question of stability arises. Even though it can be argued that balance of payments equilibrating mechanisms operate more effectively inter-regionally than internationally, there may nevertheless be considerable short run instability (variations in b).[4] Finally, 'feedback' effects of income expansion on the rest of the world may be considerable in the case of large regions. Despite the tendency of such regions to have lower marginal propensities to import, if the region is large and income levels high the absolute magnitude of import leakages boosting income elsewhere in the system may be very great indeed. The neglect of the indirect repercussionary effects on inter-regional trade and income inherent in the export base approach will in such circumstances be very serious.

The stage of development of a region may also be a critical factor in determining the usefulness of the export base theory. The demand for the products of a less developed region will tend to be income inelastic, and the marginal propensity of the rest of the system to import from such a region will be less than that region's marginal propensity to import from the rest of the world. Moreover, the supply of investment goods in less developed regions will tend to be inelastic, and the theory requires modification in such cases to take account of the import of investment goods.[5] If an addition to the export base requires more investment, the income-raising stimulus will be weakened if additions to capacity have to be met by importing capital goods from outside the region (though this is more of a long-term than a short-run problem). The combination of these two factors means that for an underdeveloped region a rise in income in the rest of the world will lead only to a very modest increase in its export base, while the effects of this base increase on regional income will be quite small due to huge import leakages.

Finally, the application of base theory assumes that unemployed resources are available.[6] If the regional economy is fully employed the short-run effect of an increase in the export base will be not an expansion in regional income but a fall in internal absorption (i.e. a fall in D/Y), and therefore a fall in the base ratio. The factor can be taken account of in the diagrams given above by adding a vertical line at the appropriate point to represent the full employment frontier. If a rise in the export base makes the $(D + X)$ function intersect the 45° line beyond full employment, then the rise in exports can

---

[4] See Section 5 below

[5] Krutilla, J.V. (1955) Criteria for Evaluating Regional Development Programmes. *American Economic Review*, **45**

[6] Balassa, B. (1962) *The Theory of Economic Integration*. 208

only be made effective at the expense of domestic production. However, even if the regional economy is below full employment we cannot ignore the possibility that the value of the base multiplier may be reduced by bottlenecks in certain sectors and/or by increased import leakages associated with inelasticities in the domestic supply of capital goods.

To sum up, the limitations of the export base theory stem largely from its implied assumption that the coefficients involved are stable, and that the marginal and average propensities are equal (that $d = D/Y$, $m = M/Y$, and $b = B/Y$). This assumption is vital for prediction from the theory because of the difficulty of measuring the marginal propensities directly. Thus, in order to find d the procedure adopted is very often to measure D/Y, and to assume that $d = D/Y$. But the coefficient may well be unstable in the short run, while in the long run changes in the structure of the regional economy (variations in the degree of specialisation, development of import substitutes, etc.) are likely to alter the base ratio (via changes in the value of the average propensities). Moreover, the neglect of inter-regional interdependence and the repercussionary indirect effects of an expansion in a region's export base on incomes and trade elsewhere in the system suggests that for theoretical purposes the export base theory should give way to an inter-regional multiplier approach. But the theoretical inferiority of regional economic base theory does not necessarily imply that the concept is worthless as a planning and forecasting tool, provided its limitations are kept in mind.

2 A model of income determination in a multiple region system[7]

One of the main weaknesses of export base theory is, as we have seen, its assumption that exports are determined autonomously and its consequent neglect of feedback effects. For a more sophisticated analysis we need to develop an inter-regional multiplier by introducing interdependence into a system of many regions. This can be obtained via construction of a simplified model of income determination in a closed system of n regions. The technique involved is essentially the same as that used for adopting comparative static national income models to take account of international trade.

The net income of a region, as of a nation, consists of consumption

---

[7] This model is adapted from Metzler, L.A. (1950) A Multiple Region Theory of Income and Trade. *Econometrica*, **18** 329–54.

INTER-REGIONAL INCOME THEORY

expenditure *plus* net investment *plus* exports *minus* imports. The following assumptions are made: that consumption, net investment and imports are all dependent upon the domestic income level; that exports are a function of income in the $n-1$ regions;[8] that prices and costs are constant; that the system is initially in equilibrium, that a disturbance takes place in Region 1 the effects of which are traced through the *n*-region system. If, for example, domestic investment rises in Region 1,[9] the demand for goods and services will rise throughout the system, and if the system is stable a new equilibrium will eventually be established in all regions. Before the effects of a disturbance can be traced, however, we need a system of equations for the *n* regions.

Let $M_1(y_1)$ be an import function showing how total imports of Region 1 from all other regions are related to the net income (y_1) of the importing region. Then if $M_{n1}(y_1)$ represents imports of Region 1 from Region *n*, we may write:

$$M_1(y_1) = M_{21}(y_1) + M_{31}(y_1) + \ldots + M_{n1}(y_1)$$

Since the system as a whole is closed, one region's imports are another's exports. A specific export function is unnecessary, since all inter-regional trade can be expressed in terms of import functions. Thus, for example, Region 1's exports can be described in terms of imports by Regions 2, 3, ... *n* from Region 1.

Furthermore, since both consumption and investment have been assumed functions of income, the equations can be simplified by combining both consumption and investment in a total expenditure function rather than using separate functions for each component. Let us refer to this total expenditure function for Region 1 as $E_1(y_1)$ showing how expenditure on consumption and net investment is related to Region 1's income. $E_1(y_1)$ covers all expenditures of Region 1 including imports. Total imports, $M_1(y_1)$, must be subtracted from $E_1(y_1)$ to show how expenditure by the region affects its net income.

From the fact that a region's income = total expenditure − imports + exports, we can draw up *n* equations for a general economic system of *n* regions as follows:

---

[8] This requires the ancillary assumption that the import content of a region's exports is the same as the import content of domestic goods

[9] It is relatively easy to handle more complex disturbances, since these can usually be translated into expenditure changes in one or more regions

255

$$\begin{aligned}
y_1 &= E_1(y_1) - M_1(y_1) + M_{12}(y_2) + M_{13}(y_3) + \ldots + M_{1n}(y_n) \\
y_2 &= E_2(y_2) - M_2(y_2) + M_{21}(y_1) + M_{23}(y_3) + \ldots + M_{2n}(y_n) \\
y_3 &= E_3(y_3) - M_3(y_3) + M_{31}(y_1) + M_{32}(y_2) + \ldots + M_{3n}(y_n) \\
&\qquad\qquad\qquad\qquad\qquad\qquad\qquad\qquad\qquad\qquad\qquad (1) \\
y_n &= E_n(y_n) - M_n(y_n) + M_{n1}(y_1) + M_{n2}(y_2) + \ldots + M_{n,n-1}(y_{n-1})
\end{aligned}$$

With n regions, assuming constant prices, n equations are sufficient to determine the level of income in each region.

A crucial question is whether the system is a stable one. It can be demonstrated mathematically[10] that if the marginal propensities to spend ($e_1, e_2, e_3, \ldots e_n$) in every region are less than unity then the system is stable. Conversely, if the marginal propensities to spend in every region exceed unity then the system is unstable. This conclusion is scarcely surprising since it is merely a generalisation of the conditions of income stability in a single closed economic system. In intermediate situations, some regions will have marginal propensities to spend <1 while in others the marginal propensity to spend will be >1. The system will then be stable if the weighted average of the e's for all regions in the system is less than unity (i.e. if the regions with low propensities dominate), while it will be unstable if regions with marginal propensities to spend greater than unity predominate.

3 The inter-regional multiplier

Let us assume that the system described above is stable, in other words that regions with $e<1$ predominate. In this case if an increase in investment is sustained for long enough, a new equilibrium corresponding to the higher rate of investment will eventually be established throughout the system.

Let A_1 represent autonomous investment in Region 1 which imparts a disturbance to the equilibrium of the system. Then the first equation of the static system (1) above becomes

$$y_1 = E_1(y_1) - M_1(y_1) + M_{12}(y_2) + M_{13}(y_3) + \ldots + M_{1n}(y_n) + A_1$$

The remaining $n-1$ equations in (1) remain unchanged.

The degree of income expansion in Region 1 resulting from the stimulus A_1 will depend on the inter-regional multiplier, K_1. The rise in income depends on the increase in expenditure following from the stimulus, the extent of leakages through imports, and the secondary rise in Region 1's exports due to the fact that import leakages

---

[10] For the mathematical proof see Metzler, *loc. cit.*, 336–43

INTER-REGIONAL INCOME THEORY

from this region boost income, and hence import demand, in other regions.

If the marginal propensity to spend of Region $1 = e_1$

the marginal propensity of Region 2, 3, ... n to import from Region $1 = m_{12}, m_{13}, \ldots m_{1n}$

the marginal propensity of Region 1 to import from Regions 2, 3, ... $n = m_{21}, m_{31}, \ldots m_{n1}$

the inter-regional multipliers for Regions 2, 3 ... $n = K_2, K_3 \ldots K_n$,

we may write

$$\frac{dy_1}{dA_1} \text{ (i.e. } K_1) = \frac{1}{1 - e_1 + m_1 - (dM_{12} + dM_{13} + \ldots + dM_{1n})/dy_1}$$

$$= \frac{1}{1 - e_1 + m_1 - (m_{12}.dy_2/dy_1 + m_{13}.dy_3/dy_1 + \ldots + m_{1n}.dy_n/dy_1)}$$

$$= \frac{1}{1 - e_1 + m_1 - (m_{12}.m_{21}.K_2 + m_{13}.m_{31}.K_3 + \ldots + m_{1n}.m_{n1}.K_n)} \quad (2a)$$

This is the value of the inter-regional multiplier for Region 1.

Since the increase in Region 1's income is equal to A_1 multiplied by the value of the multiplier, import leakages will total $m_1.A_1.K_1$. These leakages will be distributed through the system according to the disaggregated marginal propensities of Region 1 to import from each of the $n-1$ regions.

Thus, exports of Region 2 (3, ... n) will rise by

$$m_{21}(m_{31}, \ldots m_{n1}).A_1.K_1$$

An increase in exports of each region will have a multiplier effect on the income of that region in the same way as a rise in domestic investment. Thus, the increase in income of $n-1$ regions consequent upon a rise in autonomous investment A_1 in Region 1 can be stated in the following equations:

$$dy_2/dA_1 = m_{21}.A_1.K_1.K_2$$
$$dy_3/dA_1 = m_{31}.A_1.K_1.K_3$$
$$\ldots\ldots\ldots\ldots\ldots\ldots\ldots\ldots\ldots\ldots\ldots\ldots \quad (2b)$$
$$dy_n/dA_1 = m_{n1}.A_1.K_1.K_n$$

where

$$K_2 = \frac{1}{1 - e_2 + m_2 - (m_{21}.m_{12}.K_1 + m_{23}.m_{32}.K_3 + \ldots + m_{2n}.m_{n2}.K_n)}, \text{ etc.}$$

The multiplier (K_1),

$$\frac{1}{1 - e_1 + m_1 - (m_{12}.m_{21}.K_2 + m_{13}.m_{31}.K_3 + \ldots + m_{1n}.m_{n1}.K_n)}$$

illustrates how income in Region 1 is affected by an increase in autonomous investment in that region, while equations (2b) describe the repercussionary multiplier effects on all the remaining $n-1$ regions.

An interesting question is how the value of this inter-regional multiplier for Region 1 compares with:

(i) the Keynesian investment multiplier for a closed regional economy with no external trade leakages (i.e. $1/(1-e_1)$);
(ii) the regional trade multiplier which takes account of external trade leakages through imports but ignores the secondary repercussions on exports resulting from income expansion in other regions (i.e. $1/(1-e_1+m_1)$).

In the normal case, where all the marginal propensities to spend are less than unity then:

$$\frac{1}{1-e_1+m_1} < \frac{dy_1}{dA_1}$$

$$\text{or } \left(\frac{1}{1-e_1+m_1-(m_{12}.m_{21}.K_2+m_{13}.m_{31}.K_3+\ldots+m_{1n}.m_{n1}.K_n)}\right)$$

$$< \frac{1}{1-e_1} \qquad (3)$$

If all regions have marginal propensities to spend <1, the value of the inter-regional multiplier (K_1) lies between the upper limit of the closed economy multiplier and the lower limit of the normal regional (foreign) trade multiplier. But if one or more regions have marginal propensities to spend >1, the upper limit may not hold and in certain cases dy_1/dA_1 (K_1) may exceed the value of the closed economy multiplier ($1/(1-e_1)$).

The rationale for these conclusions is quite obvious:

A The basic regional trade multiplier is the smallest of the three multipliers because though it permits leakages of spending through imports it assumes that a region's exports are given and independent of its imports. In other words, it excludes the probability that as imports rise the level of income in other regions will also rise thereby boosting, to some extent, the demand for a particular region's exports.

B The multiplier outlined here (K_1) takes account of this secondary expansion in a region's exports. Since the sum of ($m_{12}.m_{21}.K_2 + m_{13}.m_{31}.K_3 + \ldots + m_{1n}.m_{n1}.K_n$) is positive, this inter-regional multiplier is greater than the simple regional trade multiplier.

C The Keynesian closed economy investment multiplier makes no allowances for leakages of increases in spending through imports or for the return of some of these leakages through increased exports. Since the secondary rise in exports is normally smaller than the increase in imports, the closed economy multiplier ($1/(1-e_1)$) will normally be greater than the inter-regional multiplier K_1.

Inter-regional trade spreads the benefits of a rise in investment in one region over the whole system, thereby diluting the stimulus to income in the region where the disturbance originated. For the inter-regional multiplier (K_1) to exceed the value of the closed economy multiplier, the secondary rise in exports must be larger than the import leakages associated with the rise in investment in Region 1. A necessary but not sufficient condition for this to happen is that the marginal propensity to spend in some regions of the system must >1.

4 Balance of payments implications

A process of income expansion through the system of regions will result in changes in their current account balance of payments. In the new equilibrium some regions will have improved balances while others will have balances less favourable than before the old equilibrium was disturbed.

Let us consider the relations between two regions, Region 1 and Region n, comparing a position of equilibrium in terms of income and current account balance of payments with a position after an investment stimulus in Region 1 has worked itself out. The effects of income expansion in Region 1 on the balance of payments of the two regions can be summarised into two components:

(i) **primary effects** Income expands in Region 1, imports from Region n to Region 1 rise, and this gives Region n a temporary surplus and Region 1 a deficit in their balance of payments.

(ii) **secondary effects** The rise in income in Region n associated with expanding exports will boost its demand for imports, resulting in a rise in imports from Region 1 to Region n.

The secondary effects, therefore, tend to offset the primary changes, and the net effect on the balance of payments of each region will depend on whether the secondary changes are greater or smaller than the primary changes.

The problem is to investigate the determinants of the magnitude of these changes. The simplest approach is to formulate the balance of trade of a region in terms of its own income. This can be done in the following way despite the fact that the balance of payments of a given region depends upon the incomes of all regions on the system. An excess of a region's exports over its imports is equivalent to an excess of its total income over its total expenditure on consumption and net investment. Thus, if the current account balance of payments of a region, say Region n, is denoted by b_n, we may write:

$$b_n = y_n - E_n(y_n) \qquad (4)$$

and

$$\frac{db_n}{dA_1} = (1 - e_n)\frac{dy_n}{dA_1} \qquad (5)$$

Since $dy_n/dA_1 > 0$, the direction of change in Region n's balance of payments depends upon that region's marginal propensity to spend. If $e_n < 1$, $db_n/dA_1 > 0$ and the balance of payments of Region n will be improved by expansion in Region 1, even after allowance has been made for the secondary rise in imports into Region n. Conversely, if $e_n > 1$, $db_n/dA_1 < 0$ and Region n's balance of payments will deteriorate, because the secondary rise in Region n's imports will more than outweigh the initial rise in its exports.

To generalise, if $e_{(2, 3, \ldots n)}$ are all < 1, the expansion of income in Region 1 improves the balance of payments of all other regions in the system. Consequently, Region 1's balance of payments will deteriorate. Thus, an expansion of income in one region normally moves the balance of trade against that region and in favour of all other regions, so long as all the marginal propensities to spend are below unity, and this result does not depend on the relative values of regional import propensities. On the other hand, if $e_{(2, 3, \ldots n)}$ are all > 1, then Region 1 will have a more favourable balance as a result of an expansion in its own income. In this case, measures to increase employment in this region such as a government investment programme will not create a balance of payments deficit. In intermediate situations, where some marginal propensities to spend exceed unity while others fall below unity, the effect on Region 1's

INTER-REGIONAL INCOME THEORY

balance of payments will depend on the balance of influence between the stable and unstable regions, in other words on a weighted average of the marginal propensities to spend of Regions 2, 3, ... n, where the weights are related to all the relevant marginal propensities to import.

Let us look at the balance of payments of Region 1 directly. We may write:

$$b_1 = y_1 - E_1(y_1) - A_1 \qquad (6)$$

since we include in Region 1's total expenditures on goods and services the autonomous expenditures, A_1. As before, Region 1's current account balance is the difference between its income (y_1) and *total* expenditure ($E_1(y_1) + A_1$).

Differentiating b_1 with respect to A_1 we obtain

$$\frac{db_1}{dA_1} = (1 - e_1)\frac{dy_1}{dA_1} - 1 \qquad (7)$$

In normal cases, where all marginal propensities to spend are less than unity, then $dy_1/dA_1 < 1/(1 - e_1)$ (from equation (3) above), and applying this fact to equation (7) we can derive the following limits for the movement in Region 1's balance of payments:

$$0 > \frac{db_1}{dA_1} > -1 \qquad (8)$$

Thus, where the marginal propensities to spend are all less than unity, income expansion in Region 1 will move the balance of payments against it. However, the magnitude of the deterioration in the balance will be less than the increase in autonomous investment (A_1).

On the other hand, if $e_1 > 1$ the limits of (8) do not apply. From equation (7) it is clear that db_1/dA_1 is less, algebraically, than -1. The deterioration in the balance of payments will therefore exceed the autonomous investment stimulus (A_1). A region with such a high propensity to spend will be very unstable, and likely to be involved in severe balance of payments problems.

However, if the rest of the system is more unstable than Region 1, i.e. if a large number of regions have marginal propensities to spend >1 while $e_1 < 1$, then equation (7) shows that Region 1 may experience a favourable movement in its balance of payments following an expansionary income process originating in Region 1. The reason for this is that in this situation dy_1/dA_1 (or $K_1) > 1/(1 - e_1)$; in other words, the secondary rise in exports from Region 1 exceeds the rise in imports associated with its increase in income. This result, however, requires an unlikely coincidence of propensities to spend greater than unity in several other regions of the system.

5 Regional balance of payments: mechanisms of adjustment[11]

If equilibrium in the regional system is disturbed by, say, an investment injection in one or more regions we have seen that the likely result is balance of payments surpluses in some regions and current account deficits in others. Will such balance of payments disequilibria be rectified, and if so how?

Although some of the equilibrating forces operating in both the international economy and a system of regions are similar, there are substantial differences in the adjustment processes. Many of these stem from differences in the respective institutional frameworks. Countries can use exchange rate, tariff, monetary and fiscal policies in attempts to remedy balance of payments disequilibria, though these attempts may be constrained by the pursuit of other goals such as full employment and price stability. In a regional system, on the other hand, the exchange rate is fixed because of a common currency, the money supply and fiscal weapons are largely outside the control of regional authorities, and tariffs and other traditional instruments of commercial policy are not normally available to regions. On the other hand, broadly speaking, factors are more mobile regionally than internationally,[12] and factor movements may rein-

[11] Reading on this topic includes Balassa, B. (1961) *Theory of Economic Integration*. 252–73; de Scitovsky, T. (1958) *Economic Theory and Western European Integration*. 80–95; Hartland, P. (1949) Interregional Payments Compared with International Payments. *Quarterly Journal of Economics*, **63**; Ingram, J.C. (1959) State and Regional Payments Mechanisms. *Quarterly Journal of Economics*, **73** and comment by Pfister, R.L. and reply by Ingram (1960) *Quarterly Journal of Economics*, **74**; Bowsher, N.N., Daane, J.D. and Einzig, R. (1957) The Flow of Funds between Regions of the United States. *Papers and Proceedings of Regional Science Association*, **3**; Emmer, R.E. (1957) Influences on Regional Credit Expansion. *Proceedings of Regional Science Association*, **3**; Von N. Whitman, M. (1967) *International and Interregional Payments Adjustment: A Synthetic View*. Princeton Studies in International Finance No. 19; *Record of the Federal Reserve System Conference on the Interregional Flow of Funds* (1955)

[12] This statement applies more to labour than capital. If the bulk of new investment is undertaken by large international companies capital may flow overseas more easily than to lagging regions within the country where the company is based

force price and income effects as means of balance of payments adjustment.

In what follows, we shall retain the assumption of a closed system of regions. In an open system, however, the balance of payments of each region does not necessarily have to be in equilibrium, provided that a region's balance of payments with other regions and foreign countries considered together is in equilibrium. If this condition holds for all regions, then balance of payments equilibrium is also achieved in the national economy. In addition, it has long been known that in a Keynesian model income and employment equilibrium in an open economy (region) does not in fact require balance of payments equilibrium.[13] Instead, the condition of equilibrium is that:

$$\text{Investment} - \text{Savings} = \text{Imports} - \text{Exports}.$$

Thus, an import surplus can be maintained if an excess of imports over exports is coupled with an excess of domestic investment over domestic savings. Overall regional equilibrium can be maintained in a region with a current account deficit provided the import surplus is financed by an inflow of savings from outside the region.

Temporary disequilibria in regional balance of payments may often be rectified by movements of short-term funds. But if a region's balance of payments problem is more than transitory, additional equilibrating forces may be required: the price effects characteristic of a classical adjustment mechanism; the income effects emphasised in Keynesian models; government transfers and, perhaps even more important, financial assistance by the central government to depressed regions experiencing current account deficits; inter-regional mobility of both capital and labour. The relative contribution of these factors to equilibrium will vary according to the economic characteristics and the institutional framework of the system of regions, and will certainly differ in weight from the forces conducive to international balance of payments equilibrium.

We must first consider the argument that equilibrating capital movements are sufficient in themselves to correct tendencies to balance of payments disequilibria in inter-regional trade.[14] Often, it

---

[13] Bronfenbrenner, M. (1939–40) The Keynesian Equations and the Balance of Payments. *Review of Economic Studies*, **7** 180–4

[14] For instance, Ingram, *loc. cit.* and Scitovsky, *op. cit.*

is maintained that the necessary readjustments can be achieved by transfers from banks in one region to banks in another, or by the flows of funds accompanying the purchase of securities by banks in surplus regions and their sale by banks in deficit regions. These alternatives imply two different regional banking structures. The first case refers to a fully integrated national economy where there is a small number of banks with countrywide branch banks in all regions. The outpayments from a region consequent upon a balance of payments deficit will create no difficulties because total reserves and deposits remain unaffected, and the transactions are effected simply by transfers from some branches to others. The results will be different in the second case, where we have a country with regional banks (either where there are single branch banks or where at least some banks operate in one region only). Outpayments by banks in a deficit region will reduce the level of reserves and deposits there but raise them in current account surplus regions. Under a fractional reserve system, losses (gains) in reserves would tend to result in multiple deposit contraction (expansion). However, this need not happen. If banks hold easily marketable claims such as government securities, changes in money supply and credit conditions within regions can be avoided. Banks in deficit regions could then make up their reserves by selling short-term securities, while banks in surplus regions holding excess reserves may be willing to buy the securities offered. Flows of this kind can deal with temporary disequilibria but not with chronic balance of payments deficits due, say, to a decline in a region's major export sector. In such situations, regional banks will be forced to meet the loss in reserves by contracting loans. This would lead to a fall in investment and income in the region, reducing import demand and thereby tending to correct the deficit. On the other hand, where the cause of a deficit is a fall in export demand or some other factor reflecting structural disequilibrium in the region, capital flows may be destabilising rather than equilibrating. Investors may attempt to transfer funds to other regions where investment opportunities are greater, and this will tend to accentuate the decline in reserves.

Scitovsky believes that capital flows will have an equilibrating role for different reasons, and that capital movements can deal with less transitory disequilibria than those considered above. Starting from the condition of regional balance of payments equilibrium (that $I - S = M - X$), he considers the case of an open region with excess investment and an import surplus. Security yields and interest rates will rise gradually but cumulatively in such a region, matched by falls in security yields and interest rates in other regions with excess saving and an export surplus. These changes in yields and interest rates will tend to restore balance of payments equilibrium. In an integrated capital market a difference in yields between regions will induce capital movements to the high yield region, while interest rate differentials may exert an equilibrating influence by inducing an equilibrating flow of funds and by causing investment and income to change in an equilibrating fashion. Scitovsky considers that the presence of equilibrating capital flows between regions is the main explanation of the absence of balance of payments difficulties in inter-regional relations. Through them investment in each region is equated with the region's saving ± net flow of funds.

The institutional framework facilitates this via a well integrated capital market and by (where it exists) branch banking on a national scale, since these will ensure that both short-term and long-term funds have a high mobility. The process is lubricated by automatic changes in the national distribution of money supply. Funds flow to regions where investment exceeds savings for a number of reasons: because the public's demand for holding money rises and falls with incomes inducing a movement of funds towards prosperous areas; because immigration into prosperous regions will normally be accompanied by an inflow of migrants' liquid assets; and because the demand of the business community for holding money varies directly with the level of activity. The demand of a region for additional loanable funds is greater than its real investment by its working capital requirements. This requires no real saving but can be accommodated by elasticity in the credit system. Nevertheless, if the rate of expansion in the demand for money varies between regions, funds will almost certainly have to be transferred from slow to fast expanding regions.

This analysis is open to a number of objections. The capital market may discriminate between borrowers for several reasons, some of which may be correlated with regional location. Security yields and interest rates are unlikely to vary much from the national level especially for securities which are sold in national financial markets. If there are no differentials, then capital will not flow in the required direction. Most serious of all, it assumes that a current account deficit will always be caused by a process of income expansion and that it will be the prosperous regions that have import surpluses. This implies that the framework of the analysis is a comparative static general equilibrium model in which equilibrium in a system of regions is disturbed by a rise in investment in one region which results in a balance of payments deficit there. With persistent balance of payments problems due to structural disequilibria such as a permanent fall in export demand, on the other hand, depressed regions will be the import surplus regions and capital will tend to flow out rather than in. Thus, whether inter-regional flows of funds are equilibrating or not depends on the source and extent of the balance of payments disturbance, and on the economic characteristics of the regions affected.

For regions experiencing chronic balance of payments problems movements of equilibrating capital funds are most unlikely to provide an effective remedy. In the long run other adjustments will be necessary. The assumptions necessary for adjustment via price effects, i.e. a close relationship between money supply and the price level and price flexibility, are no more likely to hold in a regional system than in the international economy. Even if balance of payments disequilibria give rise to changes in money supply within regions (a result which may be avoided for some time with a highly developed banking system and stocks of liquid assets marketable over the whole system of regions) price adjustments will be very small. Wages will be very sticky between regions; regional earnings may vary but wage rates may be agreed nationally and applied over the country as a whole making money wages less flexible than might otherwise be the case. Commodity price adjustments will be too limited for similar reasons, namely the fact that most producers will cater for national and world rather than regional markets and will set prices which tend to prevail in all regions. Where the tendency to uniform prices is not backed up by legalised restrictions on competition (such as resale price maintenance), increased competition in deficit regions may bring about some downward adjustment in prices, but this will tend to be confined to goods sold locally not exported and can be regarded primarily as a response to falling incomes within the region.

Income effects will probably be stronger than the price effects but nevertheless are insufficient in themselves to restore equilibrium. If a region develops a balance of payments deficit because of a fall in its exports (or because imports increase at the expense of domestic production) regional income will fall and, to the extent that imports are a function of income, the deficit will be reduced. At the same time, the income in expansion surplus regions will boost imports reducing their balance of payments surplus. This is the effect of the inter-regional multiplier. The equilibrating influence will depend on the value of the marginal propensity to import in each region relative to the export base multiplier. Since regional marginal import propensities tend to be larger than those of national economies, income effects may be more equilibrating in inter-regional balance of payments adjustments than in the international economy.

The fiscal operations of the central government may play a role in inter-regional balance of payments adjustments. No similar mechanism exists in the international economy. Under this heading we should consider taxes, transfer payments and government expenditures; inter-regional transfers of existing government securities must be ignored as these are likely to reflect short-term flows of funds as banks in surplus and deficit regions make adjustments to their reserves. The activities of the central government may have an equilibrating effect either as a result of built-in stabilisers or because it intervenes directly to boost activity in depressed regions.[15] Tax receipts and transfer payments, such as unemployment benefit and general social security payments, may act automatically as built-in stabilisers in the balance of inter-regional payments. Taxes represent a regional outflow of funds that rises and falls with regional incomes and activity and the greater the progressiveness of the tax structure the greater the stabilising effect. Transfer payments can be regarded as a regional inflow of funds negatively correlated with regional income levels.

The government may also attempt to deal with the problems of unemployment, lower than average incomes and other symptoms of depressed regions by direct financial assistance. Since these regions characteristically suffer from balance of payments deficits the inflow of government expenditure will have an equilibrating effect. The inflow of government funds may accommodate the import surplus without calling for a reduction in the region's imports. If the stability condition $m+e<1$ (where $m=$ marginal propensity to import and $e=$ marginal propensity to spend domestically) is fulfilled,

---

[15] The problems of regional stabilisation policy are dealt with more rigorously and in much more detail in Chapter 14 below

the stabilisation policy will tend to reduce the balance of payments deficit.[16]

It would be misleading, however, to assume that government fiscal activities are always equilibrating. In certain circumstances tax receipts and transfer payments will have a disequilibrating effect. This will happen where a region's import surplus is the result of income expansion rather than a fall in exports. Moreover, government expenditures can sometimes throw the regional balance of payments further away from equilibrium. Obvious examples are the granting of government defence contracts to firms in surplus regions and debt service payments to holders of the National Debt who may be disproportionately concentrated in prosperous (probably surplus) regions. Despite these qualifications if the government takes steps to support depressed regions running balance of payments deficits, especially those suffering from falling export demand, its measures will normally lead to a net inflow of government funds into such regions with an equilibrating effect on their balance of payments.

Finally, long-run migration and capital flows are an important adjustment mechanism for dealing with persistent imbalances in regional payments, and again this is an equilibrating force not often at work in the international economy. The causes of factor movements are very complex and diverse,[17] and the explanation given here is somewhat over-simplified. With an integrated capital market, capital will flow to regions offering the higher yields and in this way a geographical redistribution of the system's savings is achieved so that the supply of savings available in each region may be greater or less than the amounts of savings generated internally. The flow of funds can take many forms: the migration of equity capital, direct lending to subsidiaries located in other regions, the floating of new securities in other regions. Such flows will be equilibrating, of course, only if the long-term yields are higher in regions with balance of payments deficits. Where the balance of payments deficit of a region originates in a process of income expansion, the excess of investment over savings in that region will generate higher yields than elsewhere and induce an equilibrating flow of long-term capital. On the other

---

[16] This is because the inflow of government expenditure (ΔG) will raise the region's imports by more than in the policy's absence by an amount given by $\Delta M = m.\Delta G/(1-e)$. If $m+e<1$ then $\Delta M < \Delta G$ and the policy makes a net contribution to eliminating the balance of payments deficit

[17] See the analysis in Chapter 12

hand, when the balance of payments deficit is associated with a chronic decline in export demand, investment opportunities will be reduced in such a region and long-term yields (as opposed to short-term interest rates which may rise as a result of the monetary consequences of losses in reserves) will tend to fall rather than rise. Capital will in this case flow out rather than in, aggravating the imbalance.

The converse position holds with regard to labour migration. Where the deficit is the result of rising incomes, labour if it moves at all will flow in the wrong direction. Where the balance of payments deficit reflects structural disequilibrium in the regional economy, labour will move in the required direction from the depressed to prosperous regions. The earnings of the immigrants into the latter will constitute a further addition to regional income and a rise in import demand. The consequent increase in imports will tend to eliminate the balance of payments surplus of such regions, and the net effect is therefore equilibrating. An offsetting factor is that migrants may take capital with them; the associated capital flows will therefore be disequilibrating if the deficit results from chronic depression in a region though equilibrating if the deficit follows from a process of income expansion.

Although regions normally have no access to the controls and policy instruments available to nations, they have the benefit of other potential equilibrating variables which operate very weakly, if at all, in the international economy. Transitory imbalances in regional payments may be rectified by flows of short-term funds, but persistent and chronic imbalances will require other influences in addition to price and income effects. These are long-term inter-regional movements of capital and labour and regional variations in contributions to government receipts and in benefits from government expenditure. As we have seen, these variables may under certain conditions disequilibrate rather than equilibrate. It depends very much on the source and character of the balance of payments disturbance. If the deficits occur temporarily in prosperous regions as a result of an increase in income, movements in short-term funds will correct them. If chronic deficits arise mainly in depressed regions, possibly due to declining export industries, then income effects and relative price changes probably associated with shifts in resources to more efficient uses, outward migration and government fiscal activities may operate in the long run to restore equilibrium. An outward flow of private capital may be an offsetting influence. But it is possible to conceive of a situation where a prosperous region incurs more than temporary balance of payments deficits because of a persistent tendency for its income to rise faster than other regions (though since such a tendency will probably be associated with rapidly expanding exports the situation may be rare); in this case, the net effect of these long-term forces could be disequilibrating though this probably depends on the rate at which private long-term capital flows into the region.

The apparent smoothness of the adjustment mechanism in inter-regional payments as compared with the severe imbalances sometimes found in the international economy should not be taken to imply that the equilibrating forces in inter-regional relations are always effective. Statistics of the national balance of payments are much more readily available, national imbalances are heavily publicised and many national policy objectives impinge strongly on the balance of payments. The adjustment process in inter-regional payments is much less visible, whether a surplus or deficit exists is very often unknown, and regional policies aim at goals other than remedying the regional balance of payments (though higher than average levels of unemployment or an outdated industrial structure may be correlated with a balance of payments deficit). Because little is heard of chronic regional balance of payments deficits, it would be wrong to assume that they never exist. We may simply not know how to recognise their symptoms, or we may diagnose, not necessarily wrongly, another disease. For example, high regional unemployment levels and a persistently high rate of outward migration may reflect, among other things, difficulties in adjusting to a balance of payments deficit.

6 The gravity concept and regional macroeconomics

The principle behind gravity models is that the influence of an economic force at any point in space is directly related to the size of the force and inversely related to the distance between its source and the point in question. We might expect such models to be at the heart of spatial economics as a theoretical and empirically fruitful approach treating the distance factor explicitly. Regional economics, on the other hand, in concentrating on the pattern of interrelationships between a system of regions, has tended to ignore spatial elements by assuming, in effect, that a regional system is a set of spaceless points. This line of thinking is fostered by the theoretical lineage of much of regional economics from a macroeconomic framework applied to open systems and from sets of regional accounts in the national income-social accounting tradition.

A strong advantage of regional macroeconomics of this type is that it is easily adaptable to a study of dynamic factors over time, thereby helping to explain intertemporal differences in regional growth. But illuminating as this kind of analysis is, it suffers from the serious defect that it cannot satisfactorily explain why growth in some regions persistently lags behind growth in others. The answer in many cases is that certain regions are peripheral, being located at great distances from the centres of growth, and do not benefit to any great extent from areal spillovers. Moreover, regional macroeconomic systems neglect in their implicit assumption of spacelessness the significance of spatial differentiation within a region, the fact that some sub-regional locations benefit from agglomeration economies. Understanding of inter-regional relationships and the pattern of growth *within* regions often demands recognition of the significance of the distances that separate regions and of the spatial unevenness of economic activity within a region. One method of achieving this is to graft the gravity concept on to a regional macroeconomics framework.

We do not intend to present a systematic fusion of these two approaches here. We shall ignore, for instance, the problems arising from spatial differences within regions. To permit this, let us assume that regions are circular areas where all economic activity (production and intra-regional consumption) is clustered at the centre of the circle reflecting strong agglomeration economies. We may then concentrate on suggesting how distance and size variables can be taken into account in determining the extent of inter-regional trade within a simple Keynesian regional income model. The simplest method is to show how distance and size may influence the value of the parameters of the model.[18] We shall illustrate the basic idea in a crude and oversimplified manner, but it is clear that the procedure is capable of much greater refinement.

Assume three circular regions (Regions 1, 2 and 3) arranged as

---

[18] Another possibility is to use the concept **income potential** (see Chapter 6.2, 127–8). But income potential is an artificially constructed index in which the identity of real income levels in individual regions is completely lost. Sacrifice of the macroeconomic content of regional income analysis seems an unnecessarily high price to pay when the method suggested in the text is feasible

shown in figure 10.3. Let the radius of each region be 100, 300 and 500 miles respectively. If economic activity in each region is concentrated at its centre, and distance is represented by d, then d_{12} and $d_{21} = 400$ miles; d_{23} and $d_{32} = 800$ miles; and d_{13} and $d_{31} = 1,200$ miles.

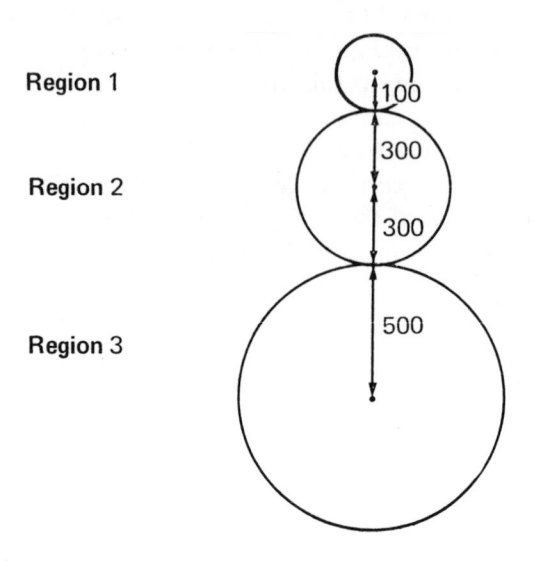

Figure 10.3

We may further assume that the marginal propensity to import of each region is an inverse function of the level of regional income and that income is correlated with a region's size. This reflects the generalisation that the larger the region the less will it tend to rely on imports. If we make the simplifying assumption that the level of imports in each region is the same, we may write:

$$m_n = \frac{K}{Y_n} \qquad (1)$$

where K is a constant, and M_1, M_2 and $M_3 = K$ (m = marginal propensity to import, M = imports and Y = income). Assuming that each pair of regions engages in trade, the marginal propensity to import of, say, Region 1 (m_1) may be subdivided into m_{21} and m_{31}. The relative marginal propensities of Region 1 to import from Region 2 and Region 3 are inversely related to their distances, d_{21} and d_{31}. This may be shown as

$$\frac{m_{31}}{m_{21}} = \frac{d_{21}}{d_{31}} \qquad (2)$$

Ceteris paribus, the propensity of one region to import from another is reduced as the distance lengthens between them. This is the most obvious way of introducing the distance element into an inter-regional income model.

A simple regional income model may be described by the generalised system:

$$Y_n = e_n Y_n - m_n Y_n + m_{n1} Y_1 + m_{n2} Y_2 + \ldots + m_{n,n-1} Y_{n-1} \quad (3)$$

where e = marginal propensity to spend. The model simply states that income equals domestic expenditure minus imports plus exports. The system is in equilibrium if we assign values to the parameters as given in Table 4. The set of equations described by (3) is satisfied, and

Table 4

A simple regional income model: equilibrium condition

Assumptions
(i) K (i.e. M_1, M_2 and M_3) = £150 million.
(ii) d_{12} and d_{21} = 400 miles; d_{23}, d_{32} = 800 miles; d_{13}, d_{31} = 1,200 miles.

Parameters of the system
$e_1 = 0.967$; $m_1 = 0.5$; (from assumption 2) $m_{31} = 0.125$ and $m_{21} = 0.375$.
$e_2 = 0.895$; $m_2 = 0.3$; $m_{32} = 0.1$; $m_{12} = 0.2$.
$e_3 = 1.0625$; $m_3 = 0.15$; $m_{13} = 0.06$; $m_{23} = 0.09$.

Equilibrium results
$Y_1 = £300m$; B_1 (i.e. $X_1 - M_1$) = £10m.
$Y_2 = £500m$; $B_2 = £52.5m$.
$Y_3 = £1000m$; $B_3 = -£62.5m$.

total net exports equal total net imports. Departures from equilibrium could be explored as in the similar, but spaceless, model of Section 2, but there is no need to consider such complications here. Oversimplified as this example is, it includes two basic elements that bring the concept of space into a regional income framework: first, that large regions tend to have lower marginal propensities to import than small areas; secondly, that distance reduces the propensity of one region to import from another. The economic justification for these propositions is obvious: first, that large regions have more diversified economic structures and tend to have less need of imports to satisfy essential demands, especially for capital goods; secondly, that transport costs and lack of contact between markets and suppliers reduce trade. If empirical tests of these propositions show them to be misleading, a much more sophisticated analysis may be required. But, however it is achieved, some consideration of the spatial factor makes regional income determination and trading models more realistic and meaningful.

Chapter 11
Regional business cycles

1 Approaches to cyclical analysis

There are several methodological approaches to the study of regional fluctuations. These are by no means mutually exclusive. A comprehensive discussion of regional business fluctuations probably demands not only a macroeconomic-type model describing the process of income generation and the inter-regional transmission of disequilibrating impulses but also a microeconomic view stressing a region's industry mix and its cyclical sensitivity, the role of factor movements, and the influence of specific external factors such as innovations, transport improvements and urbanisation.

One form of investigation is to explore the hypothesis that the cyclical sensitivity of different regions can be explained by the industrial composition variable. The business cycle in this view is regarded as a national-industrial phenomenon, and regional cycles are merely the local manifestations of cyclical changes in national industries. Thus, the method imputes to each regional industry the national average cyclical change in activity in that industry. Any regional cyclical experience not explained by its industry mix can be regarded as a residual. The value of the industry-mix technique depends, of course, on the relative size of this residual, and this is a problem to be resolved empirically.

There are strong theoretical objections to this approach. In the first place, the hypothesis assumes that industries are homogeneous regionally, that the characteristics of a particular industry in Region *A*, or *B*, or *C* are carbon copies of its characteristics in the national economy. In fact, there will tend to be marked differences in structure within the same industry between regions. For instance, there will be variations in the age and size distribution of firms. Where old-established high-cost plants predominate in a region slumps may be deeper, especially in industries characterised by multiplant firms.[1] Regions with large firms may experience stronger upswings since investment by small firms may be held back by financial constraints. The type of market an industry serves is also important. The cyclical performance of industries serving local markets will be affected by the individual characteristics of the region (tastes, income levels, demographic composition). At the other extreme some regional industries will serve world markets, and their cyclical experience will be different assuming that world demand fluctuates dissimilarly to national demand. Another point is that in an advanced economy inter-industry relations spill over regional boundaries. For example, a firm producing a given range of intermediate goods in Region A may draw all its inputs from firms outside the region but sell its output to firms inside, while a similar firm in Region B might buy within the region but sell outside. It is improbable that these two firms would fluctuate precisely like their national industry.

A variant of the industrial mix methodology is that which assumes that cyclical stability is a function of the degree of regional diversification. But there are difficulties in defining 'diversification': it might mean a balance between non-durable (stable) and durable (unstable) industries, or an industrial structure corresponding closely to that of the national economy, or the nearest approximation to equal weighting in all industries. Even if diversified regions (however defined) were cyclically stable, they have drawbacks. They sacrifice the benefits of specialisation and scale economies. Since their marginal propensity to import tends to be low they will find it difficult to pass on internally generated contractions to others by reducing imports. On the other hand, regionally oriented stabilisation measures may be more effective because of restricted spillovers.

It is obvious that such facts as the percentage of a region's activities in durable industries, the diversity and balance of its industrial structure, the cyclical sensitivity of each of its industries and their rates of growth are very relevant to understanding regional cycles. But if the industry mix technique is to be more than a supplementary tool it must explain and predict regional cycles to a large extent. If its predictions were reasonably accurate, then its value would be clear regardless of theoretical objections levied against it. Thus, the

[1] This is because the parent organisation may close down altogether its least efficient plants in a recession, and in a dispersed industry such plants may be the only ones in that industry in certain regions

hypothesis stands or falls on its compatibility with empirical evidence. Although results have varied, the overwhelming consensus of evidence is that the residual is large, and regional cycles cannot be primarily explained by industrial composition.[2]

The trend-cycle relationship may be explored with the aid of industrial composition analysis by asking whether or not a predominance of fast-growing industries in a region influences its cyclical pattern. Borts discovered that rapidly expanding regions experienced cycles of smaller amplitude than their industry mix would lead us to expect, while fluctuations in stagnating regions were more severe. Alternatively, we could study the relationship between regional fluctuations and growth with the aid of the type of inter-regional business cycle model developed later by introducing a growth trend into the autonomous variables in the model.

We shall confine ourselves here to a few broad statements. There is a fairly strong *a priori* case, supported by some empirical evidence, for believing that regional growth differentials play a major role in accounting for the diversity of cyclical patterns between regions. Fast growing regions tend to have stronger booms and weaker slumps, while stagnating regions suffer from weaker upswings and deeper slumps. Possible reasons for this include: the geographical distribution of innovations and technical progress may be heavily skewed in favour of certain regions; investment opportunities, rates of return and hence speed and strength of recoveries may differ widely among regions; fast growing regions have a higher proportion of the more efficient low-cost firms, and these are more able to maintain output in recessions; probably even more important, booms in fast-growing regions are stimulated by inward migration, and at the same time house-building and other expenditures catering for an expanding population may have a marked stabilising function even in slumps. But a proper appreciation of the interconnections between regional cycles and regional growth require, in addition to a more precise theoretical analysis, full scale empirical studies.

The economic base concept is sometimes used as a tool of regional cycle analysis. The base (i.e. the export sectors serving national and

---

[2] For example, see Garbarino, J.W. (1954) Some Implications of Regional and Industrial Differences in Unemployment. *Proceedings of Western Economic Association*; Neff, P. (1949) Interregional Cyclical Differentials. *American Economic Review*, Papers 39; Borts, G.H. *Regional Cycles of Manufacturing Employment in the United States, 1914–53* (N.B.E.R., 1961)

international markets) imports outside disturbances and transmits them to the region. These result in fluctuations in regional income payments which affect retail sales and other local service industries. There is obviously something in favour of concentrating on exports as a disturbance of regional equilibrium. As we move down the scale of economy size exports tend to increase in importance. If national cycles are primarily regarded as investment cycles, there is a case for treating local cycles as export cycles. But emphasis on exports does not inevitably lead to acceptance of the export base approach, but instead merely draws attention to the need to allow for inter-regional trade coefficients in a regional cyclical model.

The base concept has, in fact, only a very limited usefulness as a technique for the study of regional fluctuations. There is no inherent reason why the base multiplier should remain stable. The multiplier repercussions on local activity will vary in magnitude, according to the particular export sector where the generating impulse is located. Also serious is the base method's neglect of inter-regional trade and factor mobility, its failure to recognise that a region is located within a national economic system composed of differentiated regions, and its artificial division of the world economy into a single region and the rest of the world. Since an important aspect of regional business cycles is inter-regional transmission of cyclical impulses, the base concept approach is very inadequate.

Finally, there is a serious illogicality in the methodology since while it concentrates on exports to the neglect of other autonomous impulses it virtually ignores imports, or at best gives them no role of influence in the system. Local induced investment expenditures, of course, will have no income generating effect if they are spent on imported capital goods, and the marginal propensity to import as well as the composition of imports between capital and consumption goods may be crucial variables. In the absence of autonomous disturbances an equilibrium level of regional income will be maintained if the injection through exports is equal to the drain through imports. Other things being equal, for cyclical stability a region needs a higher marginal propensity to import in slumps than in booms.

Even if we reject the export base approach we must not neglect exports as an element in regional cycles. If the export sector is heavily loaded with capital goods while local industries are disproportionately weighted with consumer goods and services, then the export sector may be the primary source of instability even though its size may be small. An important question is therefore whether or not export sectors are made up of the most unstable industrial groups. Although this is primarily an empirical question, there are some *a priori* arguments that support the 'export = unstable; local = stable' hypothesis. Inventory investment and industrial plant investment are probably the most unstable investment categories; the latter exhibits relatively concentrated locational patterns suggesting that it figures prominently in inter-regional trade. Construction, on the other hand, which shows a certain degree of stability, at least in recessions, is predominantly a local sector. Similarly, in consumption the more unstable categories (consumer durables) are produced under conditions of large-scale economies, leading again to concentrated production spatially and to a high degree of inter-regional trade. Consumer durable industries are normally export sectors, whereas many consumer non-durables and (especially) service trades will be both stable and highly localised. If these propositions are valid, then the export sector may be the primary disturber of regional equilibrium.

The deficiencies of the export base approach suggest that inter-regional trade multiplier models may be more useful for cyclical analysis. In these models regional exports are no longer regarded as autonomous, but are a function of the incomes of other regions in the system. The result is that the multiplier effects of a shift in a region's expenditure function will be determined not only by its own consumption and import functions but also, via induced changes in its own exports, by the consumption and import functions of other regions. This approach is much more sophisticated than the base concept. It is concerned with such factors as the cyclical sensitivity of different types of export and import composition, the effect of fluctuations in imports and exports on the amplitude, periodicity and the timing of turning points in different regions, and the transmission of the disequilibrating impulses through a system of regions. Although by stressing the role played by inter-regional trade in regional fluctuations it suggests a need for detailed empirical analysis of the structure of such trade, for example the study of 'carrier' industries and the spilling-over of inter-industry relationships from one region to another, it has led to very little empirical research of this kind. Instead, the main work in this field has been in terms of theoretical formulations of macroeconomic inter-regional multipliers. From the theoretical viewpoint, this technique is capable of considerable precision; at the empirical level, problems arise because even if data are available usually only average multipliers can be estimated, though marginal multipliers are required.

A rather serious defect of inter-regional multiplier models is that they overemphasise inter-regional trade as the determinant of regional business fluctuations to the exclusion of autonomous impulses, particularly forces generated from within a region. In their purest form, such models merely provide a transmission mechanism. They show how a disturbance once it occurs, will be propagated from one region to another, but they fail to explain how fluctuations in income are generated in the first place.[3] In other words, they do not offer us a fully fledged theory of regional business cycles.

Keynesian macroeconomic analysis is not the only alternative to industry mix techniques in the study of regional cycles. There is another quite different range of techniques that can be employed. These include multi-regional studies, primarily empirical; identification of particular impulses that can influence cyclical experience, such as technical change, transport developments, urbanisation, migration etc.; exploration of the interconnections between national cycles and regional cycles. For instance, it is possible to explain the behaviour of the aggregate economy in terms of fluctuations in the component regions. This is feasible since the cyclical pattern of the national economy is no more than a weighted average of the cycles in each region.

The value of analyses of this kind is that they are able to take account of the more dynamic elements in regional fluctuations (such as changes, intertemporally and spatially, in the rate of innovation) that cannot be fully integrated into short-run income generation models, and can also evaluate the strategic influence of specific stochastic disturbances that can only be treated in a general way in more formal models. Such analyses very often include detailed historical studies, for instance, tracing the impact of a particular transport innovation on cyclical patterns geographically and over time. Isard refers to 'the rich and relatively untapped potential for significant regional analysis oriented to the broad sweeping historical process'.[4] Studies of this kind are a very useful complement to the

---

[3] See for example Polak, J.J. The Post-War International Cycle, especially 249–52 in Lundberg, E. (1955) (edit for I.E.A.), *The Business Cycle in the Post-War World*

[4] Isard, W. *Methods of Regional Analysis, op. cit.*, 221

more precise formalisations of inter-regional business cycle models. However, they generally have a strong empirical bias, while the inter-regional business cycle models represent a more theoretical approach. Because of the scope of this book, we choose to develop the latter. But had our aim been to investigate into the nature of regional fluctuations in depth we should have required statistical analysis on a multi-regional basis and techniques for assessing the impact of strategic variables, especially exogenous variables, in regional cycles. We mention empirical approaches here to make it clear that inter-regional business cycle theory is insufficient for a comprehensive analysis of regional fluctuations.

2 An inter-regional multiplier-accelerator model

The construction of inter-regional business cycle models is not a difficult task. The requirements of such a model are basically two: (1) a mechanism for transmitting fluctuations in activity from one region to another; and (2) a mechanism for producing the cycle itself. To meet these requirements we need to combine international trade and business cycle theory. Business cycle theory alone yields models showing how an exogenous increase in exports will boost domestic activity, and under certain conditions will give rise to continuous fluctuations, but it fails to take account of inter-regional trade, the existence of which propagates cycles from one region to another. On the other hand, international trade theory with the aid of a foreign trade multiplier mechanism can illustrate the transmission of fluctuations between regions but does not clearly show how the cycle is produced in the first place. Amalgamating the two lines of thought, however, gets rid of the major deficiencies of the partial approaches.[5]

There is considerable variety in the type of cyclical model which can be constructed, but here we shall concentrate on a simple multiplier-accelerator theory. In addition to the necessary closed economy business cycle assumptions (in this model pre-eminently

---

[5] Pioneers in this field include Metzler, L.A., Chipman, J.S., Polak, J.J., and Isard, W. Useful references are Simpson, P.B. (1953) *Regional Aspects of Business Cycles and Special Studies of the Pacific Northwest.* (University of Oregon) and Engerman, S. Regional Aspects of Stabilisation Policy in Musgrave, R.A. (edit) (1965) *Essays in Fiscal Federalism.* The most comprehensive and most illuminating piece of work, however, is Airov, J. (1963) The Construction of Interregional Business Cycle Models. *Journal of Regional Science,* 5 1–20

the simplified linear, proportional consumption function and the fixed capital-output ratio), there are certain other assumptions that are specific to regional business cycle analysis. Because business cycle analysis is short-run, we assume a given distribution of economic activity; thus, the regional incidence of induced consumption and induced investment has a fixed geographical pattern. We further assume that the services of factors of production are mobile between regions and that the capital market is so perfect and the supply of credit so elastic that all firms can obtain all the capital they require at constant interest rates. Finally, we assume that funds move between regions as income expands,[6] and that balance of payments changes are confined to the current account.

We start with a standard income generation model. For region I:

$$Y_i = C_i + I_i + X_i - M_i \qquad (1)$$

and

$$E_i = C_i + I_i \qquad (2)$$

where Y = national income, C = consumption, I = investment, X = exports, M = imports, E = expenditure, and assuming that there is no government activity.

It is clear that expenditure (E_i) equals income (Y_i) only if $X_i = M_i$. If income is greater than expenditure, the excess income comprises the net foreign balance, while if expenditure exceeds income the gap is filled by an import surplus. For the system of regions as a whole, however, total exports and total imports are equal. Consequently, the sum of all regional incomes (ΣY_i) has to equal the sum of all regional expenditures (ΣE_i).

We let total investment I_i be composed of an induced investment element I_{d_i} and an autonomous element A_i. We allow each region to import both consumption goods (C_{M_i}) and induced investment goods $I_{d_{M_i}}$, and similarly exports may consist of both consumption and investment goods. Since total imports of a region comprise consumption and induced investment goods, so that $M_i = C_{M_i} + I_{d_{M_i}}$, and if we let net regional expenditure on domestic production for consumption purposes be written C_{H_i} and for induced investment be $I_{d_{H_i}}$, we may rewrite equation (1) as follows:

$$Y_i = C_{H_i} + I_{d_{H_i}} + A_i + X_i \qquad (3)$$

[6] In international trade theory the equivalent assumption is that countries are prepared to finance without limitation deficits in their balance of payments

or $$Y_i = E_{H_i} + X_i$$

where E_{H_i} represents domestic expenditure, i.e.

$$(C_{H_i} + Id_{H_i} + A_i)$$

Assuming the simplest form of consumption function, that is a linear and proportional[7] function, and an income-consumption spending lag of one period we may write:

$$C_{H_{i_t}} = m_{ii} Y_{i_{t-1}}$$

where m_{ii} is the domestic marginal propensity to consume.

Exports of consumption goods from Region i to each other Region in the system may be shown by

$$C_{ij_t} = m_{ij} Y_{j_{t-1}} \quad (i \neq j)$$

where m_{ij} is the propensity of Region j to import from i. Both the marginal propensities to consume and to import are assumed constant, therefore equal to average propensities.

If K_i = actual, and $\bar{K}_i$ = desired stock of capital in Region i, and b_i = the total capital coefficient of Region i, then the capital-output relation lagged one period is given by:

$$K_{i_t} = b_i Y_{i_{t-1}}$$

Since, by definition, $I_t = K_t - K_{t-1}$, and assuming that the desired capital-output relation is always achieved ($K_i = \bar{K}_i$) then we obtain:

$$I_{i_t} = \bar{K}_{i_t} - \bar{K}_{i_{t-1}}$$
or
$$I_{i_t} = b_i [Y_{i_{t-1}} - Y_{i_{t-2}}]$$

Allowing for inter-regional trade, the capital goods produced for induced investment purposes by Region i will consist of domestic capital goods induced by changes in the level of Y_i, and exported capital goods induced by changes in the income level of other regions.

Thus $$Id_{H_t} = b_{ii}[Y_{i_{t-1}} - Y_{i_{t-2}}]$$

and $$Id_{ij_t} = b_{ij}[Y_{j_{t-1}} - Y_{j_{t-2}}]$$

---

[7] For those who dislike the strict proportionality assumption, the constant term in the consumption function may be taken account of in the autonomous expenditure component, A_i

Having derived the consumption function and the induced investment function, we are now able to rewrite equation (3) which gives us the inter-regional multiplier-accelerator model[8] we require:

$$Y_i = m_{ii} Y_{i_{t-1}} + b_{ii}(Y_{i_{t-1}} - Y_{i_{t-2}}) + A_i + \sum_{j=1} m_{ij} Y_{j_{t-1}} + \sum_{j=1} b_{ij}(Y_{j_{t-1}} - Y_{j_{t-2}}) \qquad (4)$$

If there are n regions, then we obtain n equations.

The nature of the mathematical solution to these equations depends upon the character of the inter-regional system. There are three different possibilities:

(1) the system is **indecomposable** if each region trades directly or indirectly with every other region;

(2) it is decomposable if some regions are isolated or if there are blocs which trade only with each other;

(3) the **completely decomposable** case is where each region is isolated, and there is no inter-regional trade.

In case 1 we find the solution by solving one simultaneous system; the solution of case 2 requires both simultaneous and single systems; in case 3 the solution demands, of course, solving only single equations. In an advanced highly developed economy, case 1 is likely to be the appropriate one. In a system of simultaneous difference equations, the same roots appear in the solution of the time path of income for every region. Thus, in an indecomposable system the time paths of every region have a common qualitative character, this being determined by the common dominant root (that is, the largest root in absolute value). The cycles in each region will share a common periodicity; moreover, if one time path is explosive the others will also be explosive, and similarly, if one cycle is either damped or

---

[8] The direct derivation of equation (4) from equation (1) for a simple two-region model can be shown as follows:

$Y_1 = C_1 + I_1 + X_1 - M_1$
$= C_{H_1} + C_{M_1} + I_{d_{H_1}} + I_{d_{M_1}} + X_1 - M_1 + A_1$
$= (m_{11} + m_{21}) Y_{1_{t-1}} + (b_{11} + b_{21})[Y_{1_{t-1}} - Y_{1_{t-2}}] + m_{12} Y_{2_{t-1}} + b_{12}(Y_{2_{t-1}} - Y_{2_{t-2}})$
$\qquad - m_{21} Y_{1_{t-1}} - b_{21}(Y_{1_{t-1}} - Y_{1_{t-2}}) + A_1$

Cancelling out, this yields:

$Y_1 = m_{11} Y_{1_{t-1}} + b_{11}(Y_{1_{t-1}} - Y_{1_{t-2}}) + m_{12} Y_{2_{t-1}} + b_{12}(Y_{2_{t-1}} - Y_{2_{t-2}}) + A_1$

Similarly,

$Y_2 = m_{22} Y_{2_{t-1}} + b_{22}(Y_{2_{t-1}} - Y_{2_{t-2}}) + m_{21} Y_{1_{t-1}} + b_{21}(Y_{1_{t-1}} - Y_{1_{t-2}}) + A_2$

regular the others will be likewise. However, the cycles in every region are not identical, but will exhibit differences in amplitude. Where these differences are not attributable to stochastic disturbances, they are the result of different values being assigned to the structural coefficients. Thus, the amplitude of the cycle traced by income in any region depends upon the values of all the m's and the b's in the simultaneous difference equation which determines the time path of its income. In particular, the amplitude of any regional cycle will depend upon (a) its internal structure of output – that is, the division between production for consumption and for investment, and (b) the extent of its trading relationships with other regions, and on the stability or instability of these regions. But though the amplitude of regional cycles will normally vary, the general character of the cycles in all regions and in the overall system (i.e. the nation) will be the same.

In the Samuelson multiplier-accelerator model for the national economy it is possible to determine in advance the nature of the time path from knowledge of the structural coefficients, and the character of the cycle can easily be discovered by reference to Samuelson's parametric map. A similar device is not possible for simultaneous systems for there are too many coefficients even in the simplest two-region model. We have to resort to approximate solutions, for instance by partial experiments. Thus, we could hold constant all the structural coefficients except two, then see what effect altering the values of these two variable coefficients had on the time path of regional income.

Damped or constant amplitude fluctuations occur only when the parameters in the equations have unrealistically low values. If we assign realistic values to them we almost inevitably obtain explosive growth patterns. The addition of inter-regional trade coefficients makes the multiplier-accelerator model even less satisfactory as a stylised version of real world cycles than when the model is applied to the national economy. This does not necessarily mean that the model has to be written off in the study of inter-regional business fluctuations. But if we are to give the structural coefficients values that have a measure of realism, then we can only get regular or damped fluctuations by introducing buffers into the model. Full employment of labour, regional productive capacity constraints, or regional bottlenecks in the supply of investment funds are examples of the buffers that might be brought into the system. Alternatively, a more comprehensive multipler-accelerator model could be deployed allowing for activities by the central government. In such a model it would be easy to explain the halting of regional income expansions by deflationary measures dictated by national economic considerations. A third alternative is to substitute some other kind of business cycle model altogether. The model outlined here is only an example; inter-regional business cycle models can easily be constructed for all the major theories of fluctuations by adapting multi-sector models of income determination. This is because an inter-regional business cycle theory does not need to include geographical or spatial determinants. Regions for this purpose can be treated in the same way as other kinds of sector within the national economy.[9]

[9] For example, see the work of Chipman, John S. (1950) The Multi-Sector Multiplier. *Econometrica*, **18** 355–74, and *The Theory of Inter-Sectoral Money Flows and Income Formation* (1950)

Chapter 12

Factor mobility

1 Factor mobility and general equilibrium

The conditions of general equilibrium have been touched upon in earlier discussions of spatial price theory and the general theory of location. We must now return to examining these conditions with specific reference to factor mobility. This requires adapting theorems developed in international trade theory to an inter-regional context. Mundell showed that in a situation where factor mobility was perfect but commodity mobility was not, and given inequality in factor prices between countries, then factors would move in such a way as to equalise factor prices, eliminating factor movement and equalising commodity prices.[1] The model necessitated certain restrictive assumptions, but once these were clearly stated gave rise to a commodity price-equalisation theorem. As is well known, this is the reciprocal of the familiar Heckscher–Ohlin factor price-equalisation theorem. Samuelson showed that in the case of two goods and two factors, factor price-equalisation would result from trade in the absence of factor movements by establishing a unique relationship between relative factor and commodity prices. He assumed: identical, linear, homogeneous production functions for each good between countries; diminishing returns along isoquants for each good; irreversible factor intensities at all possible factor price ratios; and perfect competition, so that factor returns are valued according to their marginal revenue products. These assumptions give, if we further rule out complete specialisation, a unique relationship between commodity and factor prices in all countries. A final assumption of zero transport costs ensures commodity price equalisation between countries under free trade. Commodity price

---

[1] Mundell, R.A. (1957) International Trade and Factor Mobility. *American Economic Review*, **47**

equalisation results, under the above assumptions, in factor price equalisation.[2] The cases where goods and factors each exceed two in number and where the number of goods does not equal the number of factors cause more trouble, but the difficulties can be solved with reasonable ease except when the number of factors exceeds the number of commodities.

The factor-price equalisation analysis assumes free trade in goods but factor immobility, while the Mundell analysis was conducted in terms of perfect factor mobility but no free trade. Within the theorem's assumptions, we obtain the same results from either free trade or factor mobility since they both eliminate price differentials in product and factor markets. But this does not necessarily mean that free trade and factor mobility are perfect substitutes for each other. A recent article has argued that the fact that both free trade and factor mobility completely equalise prices does not guarantee that they are equalised at the same levels. Moreover, capital is difficult to transfer without commodity movements, while in situations characterised by multiple equilibrium possibilities, there is no guarantee that free trade would result in the same equilibrium as factor movements. In an inter-regional system, however, this problem can be neglected, since it would be unrealistic to assume perfect mobility of goods and immobile factors or vice versa. Instead, we find a higher degree of, but imperfect, mobility of factors than between countries and a close approximation to free trade. If all other necessary assumptions held, there would be a more rapid movement towards equilibrium than in the international economy. There is no need, therefore, for us to assume no trade in commodities. Such an assumption would be inconsistent with empirical observation, and commodity flows may compensate for the imperfections in factor mobility. On the other hand, concentration on factor mobility enables us to discuss comparative advantage in terms of production location rather than regional trade, which is advantageous from a theoretical point of view, as is noted below.

In perfect competition, the optimal regional allocation of resources maximises national output, and represents a Pareto optimum where it is impossible to increase the value of any output in one region without decreasing the value of some output in another region. A

[2] Samuelson, P.A. (1948) International Trade and Equalisation of Factor Prices. *Economic Journal*, **58**, and (1949) International Factor Price Equalisation Once Again. *Economic Journal*, **59**

static equilibrium in the regional allocation of resources will tend to be maintained, once established, unless underlying parameters, such as the level of technology or demand functions, shift. There are three conditions for equilibrium: (a) equal factor prices between regions; (b) equal marginal physical products of each factor in the production of each good in every region; and (c) with zero transport costs equal prices of identical goods in all regions. Competition ensures that the price of each factor is equated with its marginal revenue product, and conditions (b) and (c) make the marginal revenue product of each factor equal in each region. Assuming i different factors (a, b, c ... i) and n different regions (x, y, z ... n), if $P=$ price and $M=$ marginal revenue product, we may write the equilibrium conditions:

$$P_a = M_{ax} = M_{ay} = M_{az} = \ldots = M_{an}$$
$$P_b = M_{bx} = M_{by} = M_{bz} = \ldots = M_{bn}$$
$$P_c = M_{cx} = M_{cy} = M_{cz} = \ldots = M_{cn}$$
$$\ldots\ldots\ldots\ldots\ldots\ldots\ldots\ldots\ldots\ldots\ldots\ldots\ldots\ldots\ldots\ldots\ldots\ldots\ldots\ldots\ldots$$
$$P_i = M_{ix} = M_{iy} = M_{iz} = \ldots = M_{in}$$

These equilibrium conditions are guaranteed by the assumptions of the factor price equalisation model. There are two basic questions to be raised. Is the model more, or less, applicable to an inter-regional system than to an international economy? Is there any tendency towards such an equilibrium within a national economy, and what limits or prevents its attainment? Although these questions overlap, an attempt will be made to answer them in turn.

There are several reasons why the model is more relevant to a regional than an international system, in addition to the obvious facts that commodity trade is freer and factors more mobile. In the first place, regional production functions within a country are probably more similar than international production functions. The hypothesis of inter-regionally linear homogeneous production functions has not been rejected by studies of United States manufacturing industries.[3] Secondly, the danger of reversals in factor intensity is less likely in regional than in international production

---

[3] For example, Minasian, J.R. (1961) Elasticities of Substitution and Constant Output Demand Curves for Labour. *Journal of Political Economy*. Evidence supporting international differences in production functions was presented by Arrow, K.J., Chenery, H.B., Minhas, B.S. and Solow, R.M. (1961) Capital-Labour Substitution and Economic Efficiency. *Review of Economics and Statistics*, **43** 242–3

analysis. If the relevant production functions were of the C.E.S. (constant elasticity of substitution) variety with different elasticities of substitution between industries, then relative capital/labour intensities could reverse for any given two commodities as factor prices change. But the variation in relative factor prices is much smaller between regions than between countries. One empirical test found that for manufacturing in the United States regional rankings of capital/labour ratios were very similar for a large group of industries.[4] This supported the 'strong factor intensity' hypothesis which is a necessary but not sufficient condition for factor-price equalisation.

Thirdly, demand functions for traded commodities are more alike between regions than internationally. If demand functions are different between two trading areas so that one demands more goods the production of which uses intensively its relatively abundant factor, then the area's physically abundant factor may be economically scarce. A regional analysis concentrating on factor mobility and regional specialisation in production can avoid this difficulty which arises in international tests that emphasise commodity trade. It was the possibility of dissimilar demand functions that prompted Valavanis-Vail to argue that the Heckscher–Ohlin proposition that a country would specialise in *exporting* goods using relatively more of its abundant factor should be amended to read 'producing' rather than 'exporting.[5] Finally, the Heckscher–Ohlin model assumed that units of factors were homogeneous both within and between countries. Superficial observation suggests that the quality of inputs may be more directly comparable inter-regionally than internationally.

But acceptance of the view that the assumptions of the factor-price equalisation model bear a closer approximation to the realities of a regional than an international system does not imply that price equalisation will in fact occur.

A regional test of the Heckscher–Ohlin theory of comparative advantage was carried out on regions in the United States by

---

[4] Moroney, J.R. (1967) The Strong Factor-Intensity Hypothesis: A Multisectoral Test. *Journal of Political Economy*, **75** 241–9

[5] Valavanis-Vail, S. (1954) Leontief's Scarce Factor Paradox. *Journal of Political Economy*, **62** 523–8. Price equalisation results if regional variation in demands just compensates for different regional resource endowments so that, relative to consumer demand, resources are equally scarce among regions

Moroney and Walker.[6] The basis of the test was that the Southern regions of the United States are relatively labour abundant, while the non-South is relatively capital abundant, a view supported by lower wages (in the South which are not explicable in terms of relatively lower demand schedules for labour) and by the tendency for the relative cost of capital to be higher rather than lower in the South. The theory predicts that the regions of the South will specialise in production of goods requiring relatively more labour because these goods can be produced more cheaply in the South. This would result in the South specialising in industries producing goods with a relatively low capital-labour ratio. Two hypotheses were tested: that there is an inverse rank order between capital-labour ratios and location quotients; and that there is an inverse rank ordering between capital-labour ratios and percentage changes in location quotients. The first hypothesis failed to predict the types of manufacturing activity where the South's comparative advantage is to be found, but the tests performed on the second hypothesis suggested that the South tended to attract more strongly the relatively labour-intensive industries during the period 1949–57, in line with the Heckscher–Ohlin theorem. The authors' explanation of the failure of the first hypothesis to pass the test was that natural resources as well as capital and labour endowments are an important determinant of comparative advantage, so that certain industries (such as tobacco, paper, petroleum and chemicals) occurred in the South because the essential natural resources were available.[7] The model tested included only labour and capital as productive factors, a much narrower definition than suggested by Heckscher and Ohlin. The results obtained from testing both hypotheses are not necessarily, as appears at first sight, inconsistent. Initial natural resource endowment may be a primary determinant of the initial structure of comparative advantage, but in the course of subsequent development relative capital/labour endowments may be important as an influence on the pattern of industrial growth. Thus, the Heckscher–Ohlin hypothesis may have some value in predicting regional patterns of

---

[6] Moroney, J.R. and Walker, J.M. (1966) A Regional Test of the Heckscher–Ohlin Hypothesis. *Journal of Political Economy*, **74** 573–86

[7] Elsewhere (*Journal of Political Economy*, **75** (1967), *loc. cit.*) Moroney suggested that the influence of different natural resource endowments on labour-productivity differentials might explain favourable statistical results from international tests of the classical comparative-cost theory

industrial growth and specialisation, though there are many steps from this conclusion to the concept of an equilibrium characterised by factor price equalisation.

There are two broad categories of reasons why factor- and commodity-price equalisation will not occur, so that, at best, we find only a tendency towards equilibrium. The first group refers to the lack of realism in the assumptions. Although unreal assumptions are not in themselves sufficient grounds for rejecting a model, they are more difficult to justify if the theory's results are completely at variance with the facts of the real world. A second group of factors responsible for the failure of equilibrium to be attained stems, at bottom, from the model being framed in static terms while factors and goods move within a regional framework that is inevitably dynamic.

The assumption of zero transport costs is not very satisfactory for the regional economist with his interest in distance variables. Models with uniform goods prices between regions are 'essentially spaceless', and the existence of transport costs for factors, especially labour if not capital, will impose constraints on how factors move in response to regional differences in factor prices. The regional economist will want to include the production and consumption of transportation services in his general equilibrium analysis.

Consumption of transportation is related to the level of interregional trade, and the production of transportation services requires the same factors as the production of other goods. It can then be shown that factor prices will differ between regions because of the cost of transportation. Lefeber demonstrated that in perfectly competitive equilibrium not only do factor prices equal their marginal products but factor prices differ between regions by the marginal cost of transporting one unit of the factor from one region to another. Moreover, factors employed in transportation have to receive the same price as in local production.[8] As for goods, their prices too will not be uniform between regions but will differ in equilibrium by unit transport costs; that is, commodity prices are equalised after the deduction of transport costs.[9]

The factor-price equalisation theorem depends upon constant returns to scale, hence the assumption of linear homogeneous

---

[8] Lefeber, L. (1958) *Allocation in Space*; see also Chapter 5.4
[9] This was demonstrated above, Chapter 2.1

production functions. If scale economies dominated regional industrial complexes factor movements might widen rather than narrow regional factor-price differentials. International trade theorists admit the existence of scale economies and diseconomies but do not give them much attention. Regional economists cannot afford to do this, since their analyses give considerable attention to the problem of why economic activities agglomerate at certain locations rather than others, a tendency that is not easily explained without reference to economies of scale. For example, economies of production in the city may permit producers to pay higher wages, part of the increment of which compensates for the higher cost of living there (i.e. agglomeration diseconomies in consumption). Regional differences in factor rewards might therefore reflect regional variations in the degree of urbanisation, because factors may be induced to move to large cities where social overhead capital and other agglomeration economies contribute to higher factor returns.

Inter-regional factor mobility is less than perfect. Distance may limit the movement of labour, and workers (and managerial personnel) may be immobile because of preferences for living in one region rather than another, ignorance of income-earning opportunities, migration costs and non-economic considerations. Capital may not flow freely because of imperfect knowledge on the part of investors, rigidities in the capital market and variations in regional tax structures. Natural resources are normally immobile and regional endowments may differ widely in quantity and quality. Given the existence of constraints on free mobility of factors, the question then becomes whether or not relatively free inter-regional trade will equalise factor prices. In a static setting perhaps trade will have this effect, but the result is much less clear-cut when we recognise that the appropriate setting is, in fact, dynamic. A truer picture is that factors will continue to flow in a way that tends towards, but never reaches, long-run equilibrium. Resources are depleted and new ones are discovered, technical advances are introduced, demand and tastes change, capital accumulates and labour supply increases at different rates. In moving from comparative statics to dynamics, factor flows and regional growth rates interact upon each other in a complex manner that does not inevitably lead to equilibrium. For instance, if the savings-income ratio was higher in one region than another as a consequence of a previously higher growth rate or a higher than average concentration of property owners, this could be an important determinant of capital flows other than those connected with an equilibrium allocation of resources.[10]

In a dynamic economy the Heckscher–Ohlin assumption of identical production functions loses much of its justification. Regional diffusion of innovation rates vary because of the time element in the diffusion process and because innovations are normally accepted in some regions (especially those containing metropolitan cities) much earlier than in others. Moreover, technological change normally accrues disproportionately to different industries and hence to different regions, possibly upsetting equilibrating tendencies and imparting new disturbances in the form of factor movements. There is some evidence that technical change has increased the demand for skills and resources in rich more than in poor regions, and also for the hypothesis that the rate of technical change is an increasing function of research and development expenditure which is also higher in wealthy regions.[11] Managerial efficiency may also differ considerably from one region to another, possibly as a result of the influence of sociological factors on business behaviour.

Even if we accepted that market forces would equalise factor prices, this does not necessarily imply equal *per capita* incomes in all regions. Firstly, property income may be unequally distributed among regions. If factor owners receive the same rates of return in all regions so that factors are optimally allocated, but if residents of some regions own a larger *per capita* volume of factors than residents elsewhere, then regional incomes per head will vary. Secondly, regional variations in labour force participation rates will lead to differences in regional *per capita* income. Finally, we have to take account of differentials in labour skills that can best be regarded as regional differences in the stock of human capital. This does not conflict with the price equalisation of *homogeneous* factors but will result in regional income differences.

The above arguments explain why full factor-price equalisation and convergence of incomes do not occur between regions. It is possible, on Heckscher–Ohlin lines, to construct a static model which does result in equilibrium, but the assumptions necessary to achieve this end assume away many of the variables that arouse the

[10] See Chapter 13
[11] Olsen, E. (1965) Regional Income Differences within a Common Market. *Papers and Proceedings of the Regional Science Association*, **14** 35–41

interest of the regional analyst. Since factors move normally in response to long-term forces it might be argued that a dynamic analysis is essential, and with growth and development we cannot, if we accept the views of economists such as Myrdal,[12] be sure that change will be equilibrating rather than disequilibrating. The search for the conditions of dynamic long-run equilibrium in response to factor movements is irrelevant if the inter-regional growth process is characterised by discontinuities, intermittent disturbances and marked instability.

2 Labour migration

A *Internal migration and its role*

Neoclassical general equilibrium theory predicts that in a situation characterised by inter-regional differentials in real wages, labour will migrate from the low-wage to the high-wage regions until real wages are equalised. This conclusion rests upon several critical assumptions: a comparative statics framework; homogeneous labour; constant returns to scale; zero migration costs; perfectly competitive labour markets; workers move in response to wage differentials and for no other reason. But migration is a dynamic process, and migration will be associated with other changes in economic conditions in both emigrant and receiving regions. We cannot be sure that migration will be equilibrating in its effects, since in certain circumstances it may accelerate growth in regions of destination while slowing it down in regions of origin. Differences in the quality and type of labour will complicate the picture and distort the predicted results. For example, out-migrants may be unemployed and their leaving may have negligible effects on prevailing wage levels in the region. Another possibility is that the arrival of unskilled in-migrants into a region may free more highly-skilled workers for jobs in which their productivity and wages are higher, thereby tending to raise the region's average wage level rather than to lower it. Heterogeneity of labour provides another reason additional to institutional rigidities and unionisation why labour markets are not perfectly competitive. The assumption of zero migration costs is patently unrealistic. Apart from travel costs for the migrant and his family,

---

[12] For another sceptical view see Haavelmo, T. (1954) *A Study in the Theory of Economic Evolution.* 84–104

there are resettlement costs involved particularly in finding and paying for new accommodation, and more intangible 'social distance costs' which can be assigned a monetary value in many cases since there will often be some earnings differential which will bribe the migrant to give up his home environment. Because the highest net migration flows are found from low wage to high wage regions, there is a danger of assuming that the wage differential motivated the flow. This need not necessarily be the case. Distance travelled and relative job opportunities may be significant variables in explaining inter-regional mobility of labour. Moreover, if migrants are unemployed or, in the case of rural–urban migration, if they have been expelled from the land, no wage differential may be required as an inducement to move. Some migrants may move for non-economic reasons: search for a good climate, following relatives or friends, or simply desire for a change. These complications, among others, mean that neither uniform generalisation nor precise prediction are possible.

Even if economic conditions favour migration from one region to another and individuals are not unwilling to move, it does not automatically follow that migration will take place. Lack of knowledge about employment opportunities and uncertainty about their availability, differences in the occupational structure of potential sending and receiving regions, problems connected with the absorption of a high inflow of migrants (especially the provision of housing and social services), are the kind of factors which can interfere with inter-regional mobility predicted from analysis of wage, income, employment and growth differentials. Moreover, most people have some locational inertia because of socio-cultural ties to the region in which they live, and even if they have a fairly high propensity to move it may take more than a marginal adjustment in earnings and opportunities to induce them to migrate. The efficiency of wage differentials as a device for securing geographical mobility obviously depends on institutional assumptions, not only mobility-conscious and financially motivated workers but also a flexible competitive economy, particularly in regard to geographical labour markets. Institutional factors may be the main forces impeding labour mobility in less advanced economies. On the other hand, institutional restrictions on mobility are probably fewer between regions than between countries. It is easy to account for inter-regional wage differentials especially when comparing rural with urban regions: high capital-labour ratios, scale economies and high income elasticities of demand for manufactures explain high wages in the latter, while displacement of labour through mechanisation in agriculture combined with high rates of natural increase account for low wages in the former. It is much more difficult to determine the conditions under which these wage differentials, once they have arisen, will result in equilibrating labour movements.

The ability of the destination region to absorb in-migrants may limit future inflows. The provision of housing, schools, public utilities and social services may require co-ordination of an inflow of capital with the migrants. The necessary capital may be obtained in many ways: the migrants may bring it with them; social capital expenditure may be financed by income receivers in other regions, through taxes or subscription to local authority issues; or capital may be made available from higher savings in the receiving region. But if the finance required fails to materialise, or if there is a long time-lag of social service provision behind population increase through in-migration, the resulting congestion may choke off the future flow of migrants into the region. Furthermore, the capacity of individuals to migrate depends on the availability of finance to cover the costs of migration. If this accrues from current private savings migration will tend to take place in periods of expanding economic activity and income growth. State assistance can also play an important role in helping individuals who wish to move to do so by loans or grants.

Although the direction of migration is normally from low to high wage regions, it is by no means clear that regional wage differentials induce the movement of labour. It is equally, if not more, plausible that both migration and wage differentials may reflect the same underlying forces, particularly inter-regional differences in the rate of economic growth and in population movements. Employment opportunities and greater stability, security and continuity of employment in industrial regions may be more important than higher earnings in inducing migration. Empirical investigations suggest that the rate of rural–urban migration is primarily determined by the level of activity in high-income non-agricultural regions, and that the rate of exodus from agricultural employment shows a significant negative correlation with the *overall* unemployment rate. However, in a highly industrialised economy successful in maintaining a relatively high level of employment throughout the economy, wage differentials (and expectations of future employment opportunities) may be more important in determining migration flows.

B *Theoretical hypotheses*

The classification of hypotheses of migration falls into two broad categories: *deterministic models* in which the rate of migration is determined by objective economic conditions, and individuals are treated as rational economic beings; *probabilistic models* that make allowance for attachment to a region, inertia and exercise of free choice by individuals. The former are easier to handle, but the latter are more realistic since locational inertia is a real obstacle to labour mobility. Three major controlling variables are common to both groups of hypotheses: distance travelled between the point of origin and possible destinations; the differential attractiveness of areas, reflected in such factors as variations in economic opportunity and wage differences; the availability of information to potential migrants.

The classical theory of migration depended upon the optimum population concept and marginal productivity theory. The optimum distribution of population is that which maximises real income per head in each region; in perfect competition this will also maximise national income per head. With a constant capital stock, a given level of natural resources and assuming no technical progress, the level of income per head depends upon the opposing forces of scale economies and diminishing returns and there will be a single maximum on the curve relating regional income per head to population size in each region. Maximisation of national income per head will only be achieved if the variable input, labour, moves from one region to another until, under conditions of perfect competition, the marginal product of labour is equated to the wage level in and between regions.[13] An optimum geographical distribution of population is then achieved since no worker can gain by changing his location. The analysis is subject to serious objections. Its dependence on marginal productivity theory involves perfect competition assumptions, and it can be argued that in the space economy imperfections in competition cannot be ignored. Even more vulnerable is the static framework within which the analysis is conducted, for only within such a framework has the optimum population concept any meaning. Once we permit a rise in population to be associated with capital accumulation and technical progress, then *per capita* income curves

---

[13] A summary of the classical position can be found in Isaac, J. (1947) *Economics of Migration.* 70–102

may have several maxima at varying population sizes. Moreover, population continuously changes in size and structure, and the rate of change in population may have substantial economic effects which cannot be encompassed in a continuous function that simply compares income per head with population *levels*.

A simple hypothesis is to relate the level of migration to the distance variable, by using a gravity potential model on lines suggested by J.Q. Stewart and G.K. Zipf.[14] In its simplest form, the hypothesis states that the number of migrants to a given centre (m) will vary in proportion to the population of centres sending the migrants divided by distance to the attracting centre. If there are n centres (1, 2, 3 ... n) then the total number of migrants to m is proportional to

$$\left(\frac{P_1}{d_{1m}} + \frac{P_2}{d_{2m}} + \frac{P_3}{d_{3m}} + \ldots + \frac{P_n}{d_{nm}} \right)$$

where P = population and d = distance.

A similar theory that also attempts to generalise the expression of the relationship between migration and distance was put forward by Stouffer. However, he argued that the relationship between mobility and distance depended on an auxiliary relationship expressing cumulated intervening opportunities as a function of distance. His hypothesis attempted, therefore, to unify the distance variable and the influence of differentials in opportunities (such as job opportunities) within a single functional relationship. This may be expressed as:

$$M_{nm} = a \frac{X_m}{X_{nm}}$$

where M_{nm} = number of migrants from origin n to destination m.
a = constant.
X_m = number of opportunities at m.
X_{nm} = number of intervening opportunities between n and m.

One test of the hypothesis using Swedish data was quite favourable, considering the limitations of the data used and the difficulties involved in defining 'opportunities'.[15]

[14] Zipf, G.K. (New ed., 1965) *Human Behaviour and the Principle of Least Effort*. Ch. 9 347–415
[15] Isbell, E.C. (1944) Internal Migration in Sweden and Intervening Opportunities. *American Sociological Review*, **9**

A quite different set of models, though still within the deterministic group, can be constructed when attention is diverted from the influence of the distance factor to the role played by differences in the relative attractiveness of the source and destination regions. If migrants tend to move from slow-growing to rapidly expanding regions an elementary model may state that:

$$M_{ij} = f(g_j - g_i)$$

Thus migration from region i to region j is a function of the differential in the growth rates of output (g) between the two regions concerned. A similar expression would be to make migration a function of the gap in unemployment rates, the difference in ratios of unemployed to unfilled vacancies, or relative income levels in the two regions.

A refinement of this type of hypothesis is to allow for both 'push' and 'pull' forces. Thus, it might be argued that out-migration from region i (M_i) is independently determined, in the sense of being governed by characteristics *within* the region, such as the average income level, incidence of poverty, high unemployment or declining job opportunities. However, the *distribution* of this given level of out-migration from region i between other regions in the system (1, 2, 3 ... j) may then be determined by relative growth rates ($g_1 - g_i, g_2 - g_i, g_3 - g_i ... g_j - g_i$) or relative income levels. The region with the highest growth rate will take the largest share of region i's migrants, the region with the next highest growth the second largest share, and so on. But this model ignores the role of distance completely, and neglects the possibility that inter-regional migration trends may reflect historically developed customary migration patterns.

In contrast with the above deterministic models where if economic conditions (such as earnings differentials) are favourable labour migrates, probabilistic models can be constructed where the decision to migrate rests upon the individual. Although substantial earnings differentials will induce some migration, non-economic criteria have also to be taken into account and for some individuals reluctance to move can be a factor potent enough to offset large income gains. There are great dangers, therefore, involved in equating capacity or incentive to move with actual migration. A primary reason why mobility must be defined as propensity to move rather than as movement is that migration often involves risk and uncertainty. Only a small proportion of spatial moves are cases where a worker moves from one job to another, the availability and terms of which are known with complete certainty. It is necessary to distinguish between mobility to a certain more attractive job, mobility when a worker leaves a job to move to another area without a specific new job in view, and the mobility of the unemployed in order to secure employment. The second of these three types of mobility is probably the most common and involves the greatest risks, while even migration of the unemployed is not free from uncertainty. In conditions of uncertainty it is not possible to predict the rate of migration with confidence because time preferences will vary from individual to individual, and many may be reluctant to sacrifice certain present income for a larger but uncertain future income. Other elements influencing the situation include: attachment to a region; the extent of family or personal links with other localities; the marital status and family responsibilities of the potential migrant; the quality of knowledge and information about job opportunities outside one's home locality; regional differentials in the supply of accommodation; the presence or absence of borrowing facilities to finance migration costs; inter-regional comparisons in the supply and cost of social services; and, of course, distance which governs the level of travel and removal costs.

The decision to move will depend upon three main factors: the earnings gain from moving, the direct costs of movement and the disutility of moving (or what Balassa calls the 'intangible costs of migration'[16]). The supply curve for migrants, relating the number of migrants on the horizontal axis and potential income gains on the vertical, will slope upwards from left to right in the same way as any other normal supply curve. Thus, the volume of migration from one region to another varies directly with the income differential between the two regions. This supply curve will intersect the vertical axis rather than pass through the origin because a prerequisite of moving is that the direct costs of movement can be covered by the income gain. These direct costs include transport costs, removal expenses, legal fees on house sale and purchase, readjustment and resettlement costs incurred in finding suitable accommodation, etc. The earnings gain required to induce migration will vary from individual to individual partly because of variations in the direct costs of

[16] Balassa, B. (1962) *The Theory of Economic Integration.* 86

movement (due to family size, type and quality of present and desired accommodation, distance of intended move, etc.) but primarily because the disutility of moving is much greater for some people than for others. Individuals with no roots or family ties in a particular locality may be willing to move if income gains just exceed migration costs. But since potential migrants of this kind are atypical, increasingly larger gains will be necessary to stimulate higher and higher levels of migration.

There are several conceivable ways of showing how the migration decision depends upon income gains, migration costs and the disutility of moving. One obvious possibility is to argue that an individual will move if the total direct costs of migration plus the indirect costs, calculated by imputing a monetary value to the preference for not migrating, is less than the discounted stream of the earnings differential gained as a result of moving. This formulation gives rise to certain difficulties. The natural method for the individual to express his reluctance to move is not by imputing a monetary cost to it but rather by rationalising his preference for staying where he is by underestimating the monetary gains from migration. Secondly, discounting the stream of income gains involves conceptual problems. Is the discount rate chosen the 'social discount rate' or should it reflect the time horizon of the individual when he estimates the gains from moving? One might argue that differences in time horizons and time preference ought automatically to have been taken into account in arrival at the social discount rate, yet it is clear that in considering employment at another location some individuals might look, say, five years ahead while others might look ten years ahead. For example, the rate at which individuals discount the future will vary widely between the old and the young.

These difficulties can be obviated if we employ a different formulation. Firstly, we assume that migrants borrow the capital cost of migration. This corresponds with reality in many cases, and is also relevant to policy discussions since loans to mobile workers may be an important arm in a regional strategy. Migration costs may be expressed as a constant annual sum representing repayment of the capital over the borrowing period plus average annual interest charges. The rate of interest charged will then be the market rate, while the borrowing period will be determined by the individual's time horizon (i.e. the number of years of income gains taken into account when considering whether to move or not) or in the case of

State-aided migration the period will be arbitrarily fixed by the State. Secondly, this annual repayment on migration costs can now be compared directly with the annual earnings differential obtained as a result of moving. If potential migrants were all 'economic men' they would move if the annual income gain exceeded the annual interest and repayment charge on migration costs. But we know that most individuals will have a preference, often a very strong preference, for staying where they are. They will tend to rationalise a decision not to move by reducing the annual income gain until it falls below migration costs; this reduction factor, representing inertia, might be called a migration propensity coefficient. This coefficient will fall between the values of unity and zero. In the limiting case where it equals unity, an individual will move if his annual income gain exceeds the annual cost of migration no matter how small the excess. In the other limiting case where the coefficient is zero an individual will not move irrespective of how large the income gain. Thus, an individual will move if $R < m.\Delta Y$, where R = annual interest and repayment charge on migration costs, m = the migration propensity coefficient ($1 \geq m \geq 0$), and ΔY = the increment to annual income obtained as a result of moving. The value of R depends upon total migration costs, the rate of interest and the borrowing period (which will be related to the migrant's time horizon).

This is clearly not a deterministic hypothesis. Not only will migration costs and income gains differ between individuals, but also the reluctance to move. In fact, the migration propensity coefficient may alter drastically in value over time for any given individual. It may have a zero value when an individual refuses to look at job opportunities elsewhere because, for instance, he may be well satisfied with his present job and location. It may also vary as marital status and family responsibilities increase and according to the degree of attachment of an individual to an area (which may be related to his past location pattern). However, just because the hypothesis describes migration in terms of individual response, it does not inevitably follow that it has neither generality nor operational value. If inter-regional earnings differentials are wider for skilled than for unskilled workers, it helps to explain why skilled workers may in an industrial economy be disproportionately concentrated among migrants (higher income gains). Rising transport costs and changes in the availability and cost of housing will reduce migration by raising the annual migration cost, R. Tight credit conditions and insecurity in a below full employment situation will both raise R, the former via its effect on interest rates and the supply of loan finance, the latter by reducing the migrant's time horizon and hence the borrowing period. Even the migration propensity coefficient may show some degree of regularity according to groups rather than varying at random from individual to individual. For instance, single persons will have a higher coefficient than those who are married, and the young will have higher coefficients than the old. Similarly, inhabitants of a given region may tend to have uniformly high or low propensities to move, depending on sociological and historical conditions. Thus, in a situation where *objective* conditions suggest it would be profitable for migrants to move from one region to another, it may be possible to predict the actual level of migration from an analysis of the age, sex and occupational distribution of the population, the socio-economic characteristics of the sending and receiving regions and other factors influencing the model's variables, particularly the migration propensity coefficient.

3 Mobility of capital

In a perfect market, assuming that the costs of transporting capital flows are zero and no uncertainty, capital will flow towards areas offering a higher return and away from those areas offering the lowest return, tending towards an equilibrium in which rates of returns are equalised. Although there may be considerable regional variations in the savings–income ratio and in gross regional savings, there is no reason why these savings should be absorbed in the region in which they are created. With a highly developed capital market (a necessary but not sufficient condition for the assumptions of zero transport costs and perfect knowledge) the supply of capital will be offered to all parts of a country by predominantly national financial institutions and markets, the total supply being equal to gross national saving. The demand for capital will be determined by the relative investment opportunities in each region in a dynamic setting, or by the divergence between actual and equilibrium regional capital stocks in a comparative statics setting. If regional demands are very volatile this could result in disequilibrium.

Apart from the latter possibility, there are several reasons why the inter-regional market for capital is less than perfect. Unlike labour (where both the existing labour force and new entrants are potentially mobile), most of the existing capital stock is 'sunk' into equipment, machinery and infrastructure and is therefore tied to a given location. Physical capital can be shifted only gradually and indirectly by a diversion of replacement investment. Capital funds for new investment accruing from current and past savings, on the other hand, may be highly mobile. But even with regard to new funds, there are restrictions on mobility. Some investment projects may be very large, so that indivisibilities require capital to flow in very large lumps if at all. This may prevent marginal adjustments in response to slight regional differences in rates of return. Moreover, especially when the direction of the capital flow is from rich to poor regions, the capital may be required for infrastructure projects many of which will reap external economies. In the absence of subsidies or capital supplied by the state, capital flows will only tend to equate private rates of return rather than social returns. The assumption of perfect knowledge is more difficult to maintain than, say, in the labour market; knowledge of wage differentials (even in real terms) is obviously more accessible and more definite than knowledge of differentials in rates of return on regional investment projects, which are subject to miscalculations with regard to profit expectations.

The major interference with capital mobility arises, however, from uncertainty and risk differentials. Mobility requires that all firms in the regional system should have access to credit on equal terms in addition to capital moving to areas offering higher returns. Risks may be considered greater in regions which have experienced lower *average* returns on capital in the past even though the current *marginal* rate of return may be higher than in other regions. Uncertainties may arise because of regional variations in tax structures and local policies affecting investment decisions, and because of expectations as to how such policies may change in the future. Although allowances for uncertainty may be made by reducing the value of expected rates of return, uncertainty and risk components normally show themselves as an increase in the cost of obtaining capital. It is rarely justifiable in regional analysis to assume a single national interest rate obtaining in all regions. Indeed, interest rates (or more accurately, the costs of obtaining capital and its terms of supply) may exhibit a tendency to vary directly with distance from major financial centres, a tendency which could be formalised with the aid of a gravity model.

A condition of equilibrium is that the cost of capital should be

REGIONAL ECONOMICS

equal to its marginal product in all regions. But rates of return will be equalised only if the cost (or price) of capital in one region is the same as in every other. We have seen that with commodities the price of a good may differ between regions by unit transport costs. With capital, although it is permissible to assume zero transport costs, we have to take account of uncertainty and risk elements which result in regional variations in the price of capital. Thus, although equilibrium requires equalisation of capital costs and returns *within a region* it does not necessarily demand equalisation of capital costs *between regions*. Equilibrating capital flows do not, therefore, inevitably lead to equalisation of regional rates of return on capital.

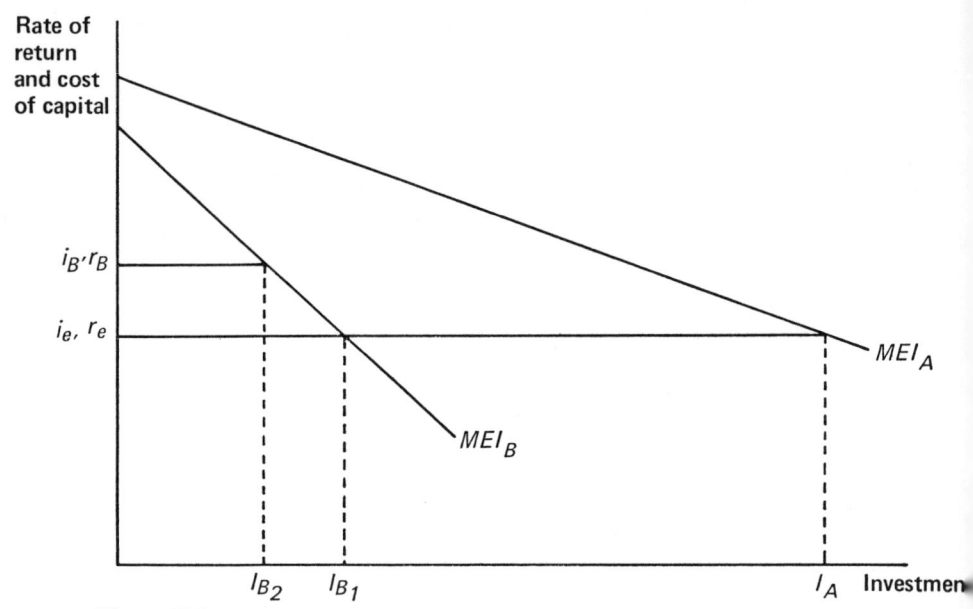

Figure 12.1

This can be illustrated with a simple model. Figure 12.1 shows the marginal efficiency of investment schedules of two regions A and B. These schedules are constructed to represent the current investment opportunities in each region by summation of particular investment projects and the expected rates of return on them in descending order, so that the schedules slope downwards from left to right. The level and shape of each schedule depends on: (1) the demand curves for the region's products; (2) the size of the region's capital stock and its age distribution; (3) the prices of current inputs; (4) the rate of technical progress and its character (i.e. whether or not it has a factor bias); and (5) the prices of new fixed capital goods. The schedule for Region B, MEI_B, lies below MEI_A throughout its length, reflecting the fact that the average rate of return on investment in Region B is less than in Region A. This is not inconsistent with the marginal rate of return at any point in time being higher in B than in A.

We assume that although savings will be generated internally in each region the total flow of savings can be tapped by a national capital market so that funds will move from one region to another according to the relative rates of return in each region. If we permit both regions to have equal access to capital, we can assume a national interest rate, i_e, which represents the cost of capital in each region. Business firms in each region will desire to invest up to that point where the expected net return from the last unit of investment covers the cost of obtaining the funds required. Capital will flow between regions until the marginal return of investment in each region is equal to the interest rate, i_e. The level of investment in Regions A and B equals I_A and I_B respectively. Market forces have then resulted in an equalisation of rates of return to capital at the level r_e.

The assumption of equal access to funds may be unrealistic. An alternative assumption would be that the cost of available funds is higher in B than in A, on the grounds that B is the less profitable region on average because of lower average rates of return. This fact makes suppliers of capital less confident that prospective rates of return will cover costs. They consequently add a risk and uncertainty premium to the unit cost of capital for investment in Region B, raising it to i_B. Capital still flows from one region to another, rates of return are equated to capital costs, but investment in Region B will be lower, I_{B_2}, and rates of return are not equalised between the two regions. The equilibrium rates of return are now r_e in Region A and r_B in Region B.

This model is still greatly oversimplified. It assumes that the costs of obtaining investible funds are invariant to changes in the level of investment. This presumption of a horizontal cost of funds schedule lacks realism. Instead, there is much to be said for regarding the cost of funds schedule as having two sections, a horizontal section relating to the funds made available by the retained profits of

REGIONAL ECONOMICS

existing firms in each region and a rising section indicating that increasing capital sums can only be obtained at a rising cost once internal funds have been exhausted.[17] This alters one of the assumptions made above. Before, we assumed that savings internally generated within each region could flow anywhere according to relative rates of return between areas. This is now modified to state that private savings have this property but corporate savings are reinvested in the region where they arise. This is in reality not inevitable, since a region's corporate savings could be reinvested anywhere especially if the firms concerned are national rather than regional organisations, but it has considerable analytical convenience.

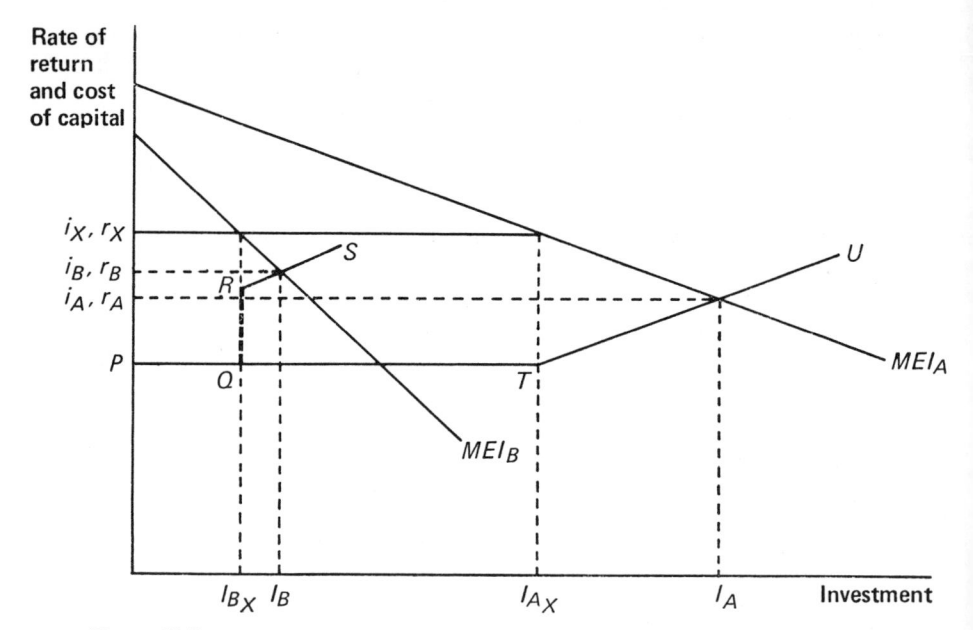

Figure 12.2

We obtain two marginal cost of funds schedules, one for each region, as shown in figure 12.2, *PQRS* for Region B and *PTU* for Region A. Each schedule has a horizontal section representing the internal funds available for investment in each region which consist

[17] Duesenberry, J.S. (1958) *Business Cycles and Economic Growth.* Chs. 4 and 5; Gordon, R.A. (1961) *Business Fluctuations.* Ch. 6

308

of accruals from current and past retained profits of firms located in the regions. The horizontal section (*PQ*) is shorter for Region B than for Region A (*PT*), because the lower average profitability of investment in Region B results in smaller internal funds available for investment. The cost of internal funds, however, is the same in both regions. The cost of internal funds is the opportunity cost, as measured by the returns available from placing them in securities if not used for investment. Since firms in both regions have the same access to investing in securities through the nation (assuming zero transfer costs), the opportunity cost of internal funds will be the same in both regions. Both cost of funds schedules start to rise when internal funds are exhausted, the rising sections of each schedule indicating the cost of outside funds to firms in each region. In Region B the schedule will start to rise at a higher level than in Region A (at *R*, so that there is a discontinuous gap *QR*) and will also have a steeper slope. Lower average returns in Region B affect the capital market's expectations, so that funds will flow into Region B only if a higher price is paid for them. In other words, the higher average returns obtained in Region A induce investors to expect that the prospective marginal rates of return have a greater likelihood of being achieved than in Region B.

The equilibrium level of investment, after capital flows, and the equilibrium rates of return are determined by the intersections of the respective marginal cost of funds and marginal efficiency of investment schedules. Thus, investment in Region A will be at the level I_A, where the marginal rate of return and the marginal cost of financing are r_A and i_A, while for Region B the equilibrium values are I_B, r_B and i_B. Once again, the mobility of capital fails to equalise regional rates of return. In this model, however, there is a special case in which rates of return are equalised. This occurs when the rate of interest on securities rises so that investment in both regions can be financed solely out of internal funds, that is, to i_X where investment equals I_{A_X} and I_{B_X}. Thus, investment in both regions and hence capital flows depend not only on the levels and slopes of the *MEI* schedules but also on the location and shape of the respective *MCF* schedules. Unless interest rates are prohibitively high for external financing in which case there will be no inter-regional capital flows, it is unlikely that capital flows will equalise rates of return between regions though they will tend to equilibrate the costs of and returns to capital within regions.

This analysis falls within the realm of comparative statics. In a dynamic framework *MEI* schedules will tend to shift much more than *MCF* schedules (though the horizontal sections of these schedules may vary markedly in length because of fluctuations in profits). The marginal efficiency of investment schedules may shift for many reasons: technological change resulting in new products and/or new production processes; changes in demand for output, affecting the demand for investment via the capital-output relation; changes in expectations; variations in relative factor prices; variations in replacement demand. Moreover, there is no reason to expect these shifts to occur to the same extent, or even in the same direction, in all regions. There may be marked differences between regions in the rate of growth in demand and in the rate of productivity growth, and these differences will affect the *MEI* schedules. The consequent shifts will have much more impact on capital flows and equilibrium rates of return than changes in the availability of funds. In addition, in a dynamic economy the factors behind the *MEI* schedule will be continuously changing, so that an equilibrium between the cost of capital and its rate of return within each region will never be reached, though capital flows may nevertheless have an equilibrating tendency. On the other hand, as is argued later,[18] capital flows in a dynamic system of *multi-sector* regions may widen rather than narrow regional rates of return.

4 Spatial diffusion of innovation and technical progress

A closed region may grow not only because of a fast rate of expansion in its stock of inputs, labour and capital, but also because it deploys its existing inputs more productively. Similarly, just as an open region may increase its growth rate by importing capital and labour from elsewhere it can achieve the same result by importing a more advanced technology (or even improved methods of industrial management). In a limiting case, a region with a constant capital stock and labour supply, no internal technical advances, no capital imports and no immigration of labour, may still grow (assuming perfect malleability of capital and inter-sectoral mobility of labour) if it benefits from an inflow of technological or other productivity-raising advances from elsewhere. In other words, the spatial transmission of technical progress is an essential element in an analysis of

---

[18] See the analysis in Chapter 13, Section 7

factor mobility and has some influence on the conditions of optimality in resource allocation.

The validity of this point depends on the assumptions that technical progress does not take place at an equal constant rate over space, neither does it occur at random over space. There are quite obvious arguments to support these assumptions. For instance, to the extent that there is substance in the 'learning by doing' thesis, then technical progress will be concentrated at locations where the *past* rate of growth in investment (or output) has been high. In such a case, agglomeration economies will be reinforced. However, these reinforcing tendencies of technical progress may be minimised if technical advances can be transmitted rapidly through space. In an advanced economy, the marginal costs of transferring technical knowledge are probably low since it is fairly cheap to transmit information about technical advances through existing communications channels, subject to the qualification that the destinations for this information lie along the routes that these channels take. In an underdeveloped economy, on the other hand, the costs of transmission may be prohibitive because of high overheads required to build up the communications network. However, even in an advanced economy the ubiquity of the communications network does not mean that transmission of technical advances gives rise to few problems.

Major problems emerge because availability of technical knowledge at a given location does not guarantee its application. If technical progress is 'embodied', for example, then its wide scale application requires a high current rate of investment. If conditions permit only a slow accumulation of capital in an area, that area may not be able to gain the full advantage from new technical knowledge. The 'embodied' character of much technical progress also means that a given advance will be of value only to one industry, or at best a few industries in the economy. The scope for application of technical advances at a specified location depends on the presence there of certain industrial sectors. But each industry is not distributed evenly over space; indeed, the reverse is often found. If there are substantial economies to be gained from regional specialisation, many industries will be found heavily concentrated in some parts of the economy but totally absent from others. Moreover, even if we assume low transmission costs and a high proportion of disembodied technical progress, the ability of an area to absorb its benefits will depend on the response and reactions of entrepreneurs and investors within the area itself. The socio-economic determinants of the level of 'growth-mindedness' in a particular area may severely limit or enlarge its absorption rate of outside technical improvements. Finally, whatever the level of communication costs involved in transmitting new technical knowledge, monopolistic elements may slow down the spatial mobility of technical progress. Secrecy, patent agreements and discrimination by financial institutions supplying long-term capital are obvious examples of market imperfections that can result in a much slower spatial transmission of new technical knowledge than would otherwise occur. On the other hand, the essential features of the space economy, in particular the fact that both transport and communication costs are non-zero, result in some immobilities in the migration of technology.

These few *a priori* generalisations will have to serve instead of a deductive theory. Research into the spatial diffusion of innovations has tended to be mainly empirical, and if it has thrown up a theory it is an inductive one. Moreover, this work has been done by geographers and sociologists rather than economists, and in fact, a theory of spatial diffusion of technology cannot be purely economic in character.[19] Generalising from the experience of diffusion of the motor car and radio, Hägerstrand argues that the well-known idea of a time path sequence in innovation has a parallel in space. Although innovations are of many different kinds, their spread tends to conform to an S-shaped time distribution, when the number of adopters (individuals, firms, cities, etc.) is measured over time. The curve shows a slow take-off curve of varying length, an intermediate stage of very rapid development and a final stage of retardation in which diffusion asymptotically approaches a saturation ceiling. There are, of course, different speeds of diffusion and irregularities

---

[19] Important examples include Hägerstrand, T. (1952) The Propagation of Innovation Waves. *Lund Studies in Geography*, Series B. Human Geography, No. 4 and Aspects of the Spatial Structure of Social Communication and the Diffusion of Information. *Papers and Proceedings of the Regional Science Association*, **16** (1966) 27–42; Ullman, E.L. (1958) Regional Development and the Geography of Concentration. *Papers and Proceedings of the Regional Science Association*, **4**; Thompson, W.R. (1961) Locational Differences in Inventive Effort and Their Determinants, in N.B.E.R., *The Rate and Direction of Inventive Activity*; Redlich, F. (1953) Ideas, Their Migration in Space and Transmittal over Time. *Kyklos*, **6**. For a recent theoretical discussion see Morrill, R.L. (1968) Waves of Spatial Diffusion. *Journal of Regional Science*, **8**

in this pattern from one innovation to another. This innovation time pattern has been represented as typical for many decades.[20]

The more recent contribution is to suggest that each phase of this growth curve has a spatial counterpart. In the *primary stage* adopters are concentrated at the innovation centre and possibly in clusters at other large centres. The urban hierarchy canalises the course of diffusion: the innovation centre is very often the primary city or some other metropolitan centre, then the centres next in rank follow.[21] However, with the passing of the initial time phase the percolation down the central hierarchy scale is broken up. Instead, expansion occurs at a rapid rate in the vicinity of the original innovation centres rather than at a great distance away from them. The friction of space puts outlying large centres out of the immediate range of the diffusion influence, and the neighbourhood effects predominate. This accounts for the fact that though most innovations are adopted at a higher rate than the economy's mean rate in cities and large towns (obvious exceptions are innovations in the agricultural sector, such as new agricultural machines), certain rural districts surrounding the innovation centre may also apply the innovation at a rate above the mean.

In the third stage as saturation is approached, there may be some levelling in regional disparities. Saturation may be reached around the innovation centre while the rate of diffusion is still low in distant areas. The overall deceleration in the diffusion pattern may hide a catching up process in which the innovation is still spreading through distant areas though adoption at the centre is halted. The time taken in moving from the primary to the tertiary stage will vary among innovations; both the motor car and radio reached temporary saturation levels quite quickly; innovations that start in an untypical manner, i.e. not in the large metropolis but in outlying areas, may move through the different phases quite slowly.

It is most unlikely that this spatial diffusion pattern could be explained primarily by economic variables, such as area differentials in the level and distribution of income. If economic influences alone were responsible, they would result not so much in long time lags between adoption in different areas as in all areas closely following the innovation centre but reaching saturation at different levels, the

[20] See, for example, Merton, R.K. (1934–5) Fluctuations in the Rate of Industrial Invention. *Quarterly Journal of Economics*, **49**

[21] For analysis of central place hierarchies and their significance see Chapter 7.2

level attained being governed by the impact of economic forces. This would, of course, require evenly distributed information about the innovation at the outset. But as the movement through hierarchically arranged centres and in the neighbourhoods of the innovating centre suggest, information is not evenly distributed. Information flows along the main communications routes, and in fact innovations starting from the same centre but at different points of time tend to propagate along similar routes and, therefore, according to the same spatial pattern. This pattern remains stable even though the individuals and firms adopting innovations may change. If the communications network is complex and highly developed, information about innovations may travel long distances. On the other hand, the importance of neighbourhood effects suggests that information extends only to restricted distances around the centres of innovation. The explanation of this would seem to be the degree of social contact among individuals; evidence in the United States, for example, gave strong indications that the spread of new drugs among doctors took place along a social network. Since social contact networks are much weaker between countries than within countries, this would help to explain why international diffusion almost always occurs via the metropolises and leading centres while intra-national diffusion shows itself in neighbourhood effects as well as through the urban hierarchy.

The efficiency of the communications network between cities and other large centres depends not only on its physical character but on the receptivity of those individuals and institutions that receive information, i.e. on **communication nodes**. In general terms, this may be determined by how outward looking are cities lower in the hierarchy than the metropolis. Webber's concept of non-place urban realms is very relevant here. Webber classifies different kinds of organisation into a hierarchy of levels, from the individual and family group, through neighbourhood- and community-oriented organisations, to city, region, nation, and ultimately world-serving activities. If we estimate the distribution of time spent by a city's inhabitants in each level of service, we can obtain profiles with the aid of which one city can be compared with another. Regional, national and world-oriented activities account for much more time in a highly urbanised city. Thus a high degree of urbanisation develops when citizens are receptive to international and cosmopolitan values, more nationalistic than average, tolerate provincialism but repress parochialism. Generalising, Webber views urban communities in two perspectives – one where interaction takes place in a particular metropolitan community, the other representing a wider perspective embracing the nation and the world. Improvements in transportation and communications mean that individuals, firms and organisations more and more conduct transactions and maintain links on a wider basis. These links extend to a variety of non-place communities, called 'urban realms'.[22] It is important, therefore, to look at interaction systems which extend into larger urban realms, some global, some national and some multi-regional, as well as within the urban region itself. Those centres whose dominant activities are oriented to supra-regional functions rather than to regional or purely urban functions are likely to absorb innovations emanating from an outside centre much more rapidly than cities lacking this orientation.

At a more specific level, spatial transmission of technical progress affecting an area's growth performance will refer more to industrial innovations or new managerial techniques than to new consumer products (motor cars, radio, etc.). The propensity of a peripheral area to receive information on industrial innovations will depend on special factors in addition to a developed communications network. Such factors will include the presence of trained scientists and technologists, highly qualified managerial personnel and centres of decision-making (e.g. large independent industrial firms). Available evidence suggests that dispersion of individuals and firms of this type is not common; instead heavy concentration tends to be the rule. In the United States, more than 90% (measured by value of output) of industrial corporations are located in the industrial belt States and in California. The location of leading scientists and technologists, the size and distribution of university libraries, the geographical distribution of research institutes and of patent activity all point to massive localisation based on internal and external economies of scale in these two major areas.[23] Concentration of innovation and decision-making in these core areas reinforce their other locational advantages – access to markets and scale economies. At the same time, peripheral areas are unlikely to compensate for these disadvantages by rapid application of innovations introduced elsewhere, since marked localisation of innovating

[22] Webber, M.M. The Urban Place and the Nonplace Urban Realm in Webber, M.M. (edit) (1964) *Explorations in Urban Structure*
[23] Ullman, *loc. cit.*

activity attracts to the innovation centres most of the individuals and firms that have a high propensity to adopt new ideas and technical improvements.

To sum up, the traditional theory of spatial diffusion of innovations suggests that where there is a highly developed communications network then new innovations will spread, though sometimes with a considerable time lag, to major centres in peripheral areas as well as in the vicinity of the innovation centre. But this theory is an inductive theory, developed from particular cases that are not representative of the many different types of innovation. In particular, case studies have been based on new types of consumer goods rather than on industrial innovations and new production techniques. Yet when we are considering the impact of the spatial transmission of technical progress on growth in fringe areas, it is these latter innnovation categories that we have in mind. For wide diffusion of these innovations, a sophisticated communications network and the existence of outward-looking leading cities in peripheral regions are necessary but not sufficient conditions. We also require the presence in these areas of the kind of individual and organisation that can rapidly assess the potentialities of new innovations and are willing to take risks in applying them. But if agglomeration economies in growth industries are substantial, these industries and their best qualified personnel will be heavily localised in the core areas. The fringe areas will lack both the adopters and the economic activities offering the scope for applying new innovations. An important factor in the receptivity of an area will be branch plants of nationally-based industrial organisations. But branch plants are unlikely to flourish in industries where scale economies are sizeable. If economic conditions favour a fast growth in factor inputs at core areas, these same conditions are likely to result in these core areas being the main innovation centres in the economy and to militate against a rapid, wide diffusion of technical progress to outlying regions.

5 The mobility of managerial talent

In discussions of factor mobility, the entrepreneurial function is often neglected. The main reasons for this neglect would seem to be: (1) the fact that static general equilibrium theory assigns no role to entrepreneurs other than to combine other productive factors, and (2) the impossibility, on grounds suggested below, of incorporating the entrepreneurial factor in a determinate theory. But the role of managers and entrepreneurs can be crucial in a dynamic economy. As suggested above the efficiency of managers can be the primary determinant of whether or not new innovations are accepted in a region. The quality of decision-making in conditions of uncertainty may have a vital influence on regional growth rates.

The need for managerial resources varies from region to region according to their relative levels of economic development. Managers are important to the continued expansion of highly developed regions and high quality personnel are demanded there in larger numbers. On the other hand, the shortage is most severely felt in less developed regions, especially in areas attempting to promote industrialisation. The need for mobility depends on the relative strengths of supply and demand within each region. The internal supply and demand functions are probably very inelastic in the short run and may not intersect, so that structural disequilibrium is possible in the absence of migration of managers to excess demand regions. On the other hand, the necessity for inter-regional managerial transfers may be reduced through the operation of natural forces tending to equilibrate intra-regional supply and demand functions, despite their inelasticity. It might be argued that the supply of managerial talent in a region in period t is a function of the structure of the region's economic system in periods $t-1, t-2, \ldots t-n$. Regionalism might then be a significant consideration in that the economic, social and cultural development of regions varies in respect to variables affecting the supply of entrepreneurship. Such variables include, in addition to salary levels varying directly with past growth rates, the degree of social acceptance of business as a profession, attitudes towards risk-taking, the past structure of industries in the region which mould the type of manager created, the availability of business education and training, etc. The demand for managerial resources in a region will also tend to reflect its past experience, particularly its recent growth rate (on the reasonable assumption that expectations of future growth will reflect current and past performance). Thus, supply and demand for entrepreneurs can both be regarded as functions of the region's past. Moreover, factors favourable to a high entrepreneurial birth rate tend to be found in regions with a high growth rate, whereas regions with an environment not conducive to the creation of managers are likely to have a poor growth record. Thus, a favourable socio-economic structure and cultural environment (which determine the internal supply curve for entrepreneurs) tend to be positively correlated with a region's growth rate (the main influence behind its demand curve for entrepreneurs). This interdependence between growth rates and social climate reduces the need for inter-regional managerial mobility.

Despite this important qualification, efficient allocation of resources will still normally require the migration of managers from some regions to others. This is particularly the case when there are discontinuities in regional growth rates, especially when less developed regions with a poor growth experience are attempting to shift their growth rates upward. But there is no guarantee that entrepreneurs will migrate to such regions in response to the increased demand for them. An obvious point is that a high differential in salary (or in the case of owners of capital in the rate of return) is often needed to induce managers to move. There are many reasons for this in addition to a monetary incentive to move, but most of them can be reduced to a strong locational preference for living in a certain place. In many cases there is a psychic income element attached to an accustomed environment, and this means that entrepreneurial locations have to be stated in terms of maximising satisfaction rather than in terms of maximising salary or profits.[24] Since satisfaction cannot easily be measured if at all, any model based on it is indeterminate. A profit or salary maximising theory would be more operational, but it would lose generality. The fact is that though it is often permissible to assume rational economic man in a spaceless world, nostalgia for home roots or for a familiar environment cannot be ignored in the space economy because of its influence on the location of economic activity and of managerial personnel. Moreover, a migrating entrepreneur may face considerable risks associated with the problems of adapting to a new location, and if he fails to settle there may be difficulties in readjusting if he decides to return to his original home. Thus, monetary differentials are not the sole explanation of whether managers migrate or not.

There is a strong tendency for managerial talent to be highly concentrated at centres of innovating activity and in large cities where agglomeration economies exist. This primarily reflects the demand for executives in such centres, but managers often have a predilection for living and working in large cities because they offer

---

[24] One solution to this difficulty is to assign a pecuniary value to psychic income, but this may be impossible to accomplish

the social, leisure and cultural facilities that professional classes require. Managers may consequently be more willing to move to regions containing large cities, particularly those having a cosmopolitan non-parochial outlook (i.e. in Webber's terminology, with national-oriented 'urban realms'[25]). The industrialised region with a complex of sizeable cities or the partly developed region dominated by a regional metropolis is likely to attract managers more easily than the rural region with few large population centres. For reasons of this kind concentration on inter-regional migration flows of entrepreneurs may obscure the essential inter-urban character of managerial mobility. The rate of in-migration tends to fall off as we move down the urban hierarchy from the primary city and other metropolitan centres. A rough testable generalisation is that the higher the economy's overall growth rate (unless expansion is confined to one or two regions) the further down the urban hierarchy managers are willing to move, and the higher the returns offered in each size-class of cities.

A final factor influencing the rate of migration of entrepreneurs and executives is the availability of routes from one region to another.[26] Transfers within a company are a main channel of movement. If nationally-based corporations have branch plants in several regions mobility is easily achieved without requiring salary differentials. In other circumstances the social network of personal contacts may be important in the transfer of managerial personnel as in the diffusion of innovations, though the area over which the network operates may be relatively small thereby limiting the distances moved. More important may be the circulation of information media dealing with job advertisements, since, unlike labour, executives almost always move to particular jobs. As for the migration of entrepreneurs as opposed to executives in general, these rarely migrate if in control of existing firms, though they may move with greater freedom when setting up new establishments. Small entrepreneurs may move with their capital especially in an institutional environment where policies differentiate in favour of certain regions with investment incentives. Reverting to the case of national companies, technical changes may be reducing the necessity of actual physical migration by senior executives. Increased communications,

[25] See Section 4 above

[26] For a discussion of the function of such routes in an international setting see Fforde, J.S. (1956) *An International Trade in Managerial Skills*

introduction of electronic data processing methods and new management techniques are making it possible for more and more managerial functions relating to branch plants located in other regions to be exercised from metropolitan head offices.

When we confine discussion of factor mobility to a consideration of two homogeneous factors, labour and capital, in a comparative statics framework it is relatively easy to construct a model where factors move in response to differentials in regional factor prices and where equilibrating tendencies assert themselves. When variations in regional natural resource endowments, the diffusion process of innovations and the mobility of managers and entrepreneurs are taken into account within a dynamic economy, the picture becomes much more complicated. A region's stock of natural resources is immobile but nevertheless constantly changing with the depletion of old resources and the discovery of new ones; the diffusion of innovations and new ideas spreads along what is almost a predetermined route; while the propensity of managers and executives to move from one region to another is influenced by many factors other than salary differentials. For these reasons the attempt to outline the conditions of inter-regional general equilibrium in a two-factor model gives only a very imperfect impression of the role of the mobility of productive resources in regional development. Structural rigidities, strong agglomerating tendencies and sporadic disequilibrating forces make the assumption of automatically self-correcting factor flows misleading.

Chapter 13
Regional growth

1 Introduction

A possible approach to the theory of regional growth is to adapt models originally developed for national economies to a regional context. The deficiencies of these models are at least as serious for regions as for nations. For instance, the preoccupation with equilibrium growth may be particularly misleading in regional analysis because the transmission of impulses across regional boundaries is likely to result in disequilibrating forces in some regions if not in others, if only because regions lack the instruments for corrective action against external disturbances. On the other hand, unlike some theories of regional growth which concentrate on how expansion takes place within a single region these models are flexible enough to simulate inter-regional growth. As far as any single region is concerned, the conditions for equilibrium growth are less restrictive than in the national case for factor movements may play an equilibrating role in both Harrod–Domar type and neoclassical models if the internal rate of population growth and/or the internal savings-income ratio (or in the neoclassical structure the internal rate of capital accumulation) are of the wrong magnitude for maintaining equilibrium. Yet steady state growth in the whole system and in each region is very difficult to obtain since it requires that the determinants operate in such a way as to keep the system and each region in it growing at the *same* constant rate.

The objective of 'balanced growth' has been given some stress by regional analysts. This term is open to two main interpretations. The first requires that poorer regions grow faster than rich ones so that income levels tend to equality; in this context 'balance' means 'convergence'. The second interpretation, the one considered here, demands only that the rate of growth in the poor regions keep pace with that in the prosperous regions. In this case, the whole system and the constituent regions grow at the same rate, but in consequence the absolute income differentials between rich and poor areas widen. It is important to note that it is insufficient for dynamic equilibrium that each region grow steadily if the rates of growth are unequal. In a two region system, for instance, if the two regions grow at constant but different rates the aggregate growth rate rises.[1] Dynamic equilibrium is in fact a possibility in two situations. Firstly, the growth rate of each region may alter in each time period in such a way that the aggregate growth rate remains constant. In the absence of a strong equilibrating mechanism this is most unlikely, and no reasonably based model can be constructed to fit this case. The second case is where the growth rate of each region is not only constant but equal. If all regions grow at the same constant rate then the aggregate must also grow at this constant rate. Thus in a two region system, if the growth rates of Regions 1 and 2 are g_1 and g_2 respectively, the condition of dynamic equilibrium is that $g_1 = g_2 =$ a constant.

Our view is that although growth in a regional system may not be characterised by a steady constant growth rate in each region, nevertheless equilibrium growth models are a useful starting point and pedagogic device for analysis of regional growth. A recent article by Hartman and Seckler[2] has taken a more extreme view, and suggested that it is misleading for a regional growth model to yield a solution to an equilibrium growth path. This is not only because of income

---

[1] As pointed out by Phelps Brown, E.H. and Ozga, S.A. (1955) Economic Growth and the Price Level. *Economic Journal*, **65**

[2] Hartman, L.M. and Seckler, D. (1967) Toward the Application of Dynamic Growth Theory to Regions. *Journal of Regional Science* **7** 166–73. They themselves put forward a multiplier-accelerator growth model in which exports are treated as an autonomous variable and investment is induced by changes in domestic consumption and changes in exports. They assume that the consumption function is linear, that the average and marginal propensities to consume are equal, and that consumption lags one period behind income. They also treat imports of consumer goods as a constant fraction of consumption, while capital goods imports are assumed to be a constant fraction of investment. They analyse whether or not endogenous growth is likely in a single region, and do not consider inter-regional repercussions. They show that the growth path of regional income can be described by the second-order difference equation:

$$Y_t = X_t + (1 - m_K)b(X_t - X_{t-1}) + c(1 - m_C)[1 + (1 - m_K)b]Y_{t-1}$$
$$- [c(1 - m_C)(1 - m_K)b]Y_{t-2}$$

where $Y =$ income, $X =$ exports net of imports used in producing exports, $c =$ marginal propensity to consume, $m_C =$ fraction of consumption imported, $m_K =$ fraction of investment imported, and $b =$ the accelerator leakages into other regions, but primarily because the supply of savings in a region is endogenous, whereas the equilibrium growth paths for closed economies are set by an exogenously determined supply of savings. Savings flow into and out of regions quite freely in response to investment opportunities. Regions can therefore become net debtors or creditors for long periods of time, so that, it is argued, there is no clearly defined equilibrium growth rate for a region. This position differs from our own only in degree of emphasis and judgment. The free movement of capital (and labour) may have an equilibrating role and thereby makes the narrow conditions for equilibrium in a steady growth model less restrictive. On the other hand, if the initial values of the parameters were such that the region was growing steadily the openness of the region might permit factors to flow in or out and thereby disturb the steady growth path. In other words, in an open economy *both* the opportunities for dynamic equilibrium *and* the risks that an initial equilibrium will be disturbed are increased. Whether steady growth is more likely or less likely depends upon whether or not factor movements are equilibrating.

2 Harrod–Domar models

If aggregate growth theories are applicable to regional analysis, the Harrod–Domar group of models is a well qualified candidate for two reasons. Firstly, as a Keynesian demand-dominated theory it appears quite relevant to an explanation of growth in lagging regions, the problems of which are more likely due to lack of effective demand rather than to shortages of supply. Lagging regions normally suffer from unused productive factors, especially labour, and the assumption of continuous full employment associated with neoclassical models is less appropriate to regional development problems which often arise from resources being unemployed in some regions but not in others. Secondly, the Harrod–Domar formulation may if certain values are assumed for the main parameters result not in steady expansion but in cyclical growth. It is arguable that a model which can in some circumstances lead to steady growth but in others can lead to cycles is particularly suitable for regional analysis because of the tendency for inter-regional growth to display cyclical characteristics.[3]

---

[3] This tendency is explained as follows: if an autonomous stimulus disturbs equilibrium in one region the consequences of this on income expansion elsewhere

We start by making certain simplifying assumptions: a one good economy, and that the good can be used either for consumption or as an input; labour is the only other input and is homogeneous; constant returns to scale; no technical progress. The specific assumptions of the Harrod–Domar model are: (1) a constant propensity to save (S/Y or s); (2) fixed coefficients in production; (3) the labour force grows at a constant rate n, where n is the rate of population growth. The equilibrium conditions have to be satisfied from the point of view of both inputs. If we assume that the equilibrium rate of growth cannot be maintained with either growing excess capacity or increasing unemployment, then for steady growth the economy must grow at the rate which ensures both full capacity and full employment. In steady state growth, the capital stock must grow at the same rate as output, thus $g = I/K$ (where I is planned investment and K is the capital stock). But for equilibrium planned saving must continuously equal planned investment. Thus, we may write $g = I/K = S/K = S/Y \cdot Y/K = s/v$ (where v is the capital output ratio). To keep the labour force fully employed, output must, since labour requirements per unit of output are given, grow at the same rate as labour supply, therefore g must equal n. Thus steady growth requires that $g = n = s/v$.

If we adopt this for regions rather than the national economy, then the requirement for steady growth in the i-th region is simply:

$$g_i = n_i = s_i/v_i \qquad (1)$$

If the regions were closed economies then the equilibrium conditions are the same as in the national case. But the system as a whole will only grow steadily if the equilibrium growth rates in all regions are the same so that the overall rate of growth $G = g_i$. In this case, the rate of population growth must also be the same in all regions, as must the propensity to save and the capital-output ratio. Of course, if we allow regional capital output ratios to differ from each other, then a region may, for example, have a higher propensity to save offset by a higher capital-output ratio without damaging equilibrium. But this possibility does not free the restrictive conditions of equilibrium to any great extent. Any hope that the crucial constants will have the

in a multi-regional system are likely to be different in impact from region to region. This is because, even if marginal propensities to import remain constant, these constant propensities are likely to vary in magnitude (in at least some cases) among all possible pairs of regions same values in all regions will depend, in the first place, on how homogeneous the regions of the system are.

However, regions are open economies. If the requirements for equilibrium are not satisfied internally, then inflows and outflows of goods, labour and capital (savings) may take place in a manner which maintains equilibrium. From the viewpoint of one region, imports as well as savings can be counted as leakages from effective demand, exports as well as investment can help to fill the gap between domestic consumption and capacity output, and excess savings can be diverted to other regions by running an export surplus. Furthermore, if population grows too fast to be absorbed into employment at the current growth rate of output net migration may keep the rate of growth of labour supply in balance with output.

In an open economy, the static equilibrium condition is

$$S + M = I + X \qquad (2)$$
$$\text{Savings \quad Imports \quad Investment \quad Exports}$$

This may be rewritten

$$(s+m)Y = I + X$$

where m = marginal propensity to import (assumed constant).

or $$I/Y = s + m - (X/Y)$$

The condition of equilibrium $g_i = s_i/v_i$ consequently becomes

$$g_i = \frac{s_i + m_i - (X_i/Y_i)}{v_i} \qquad (3)$$

Any tendency for savings to exceed investment does not necessarily result in disequilibrium provided the gap between savings and investment is exactly closed by running an export surplus equal to the gap.

Similarly, excess labour may be eliminated by out-migration or a deficiency in labour supply can be met by in-migration from other regions in the system. Thus, the requirement for equilibrium with regard to labour becomes

$$g_i = n_i \pm r_i \qquad (4)$$

where r is the rate of migration, expressed as the number of migrants in each time period as a percentage of the regional population.

Discussion of the requirements of equilibrium growth in a single region is unsatisfactory. This is because it neglects the conditions of equilibrium growth in the rest of the system. Furthermore, it ignores the reverberations of changes in a region's imports on incomes in other regions, and through them on its own exports. The result is that a region, by growing so as to employ fully its own capacity, may at the same time alter the requirements of equilibrium in other regions and therefore for itself. In other words, it is inappropriate to study the regional economy in isolation for the conditions for equilibrium growth in the component regions of the system are interdependent.[4]

To explore briefly the implications of this, let us consider a closed system of two regions, Region 1 and Region 2. The equilibrium growth rates of the two regions are derived from equation (3) above, and are as follows:

$$g_1 = \frac{s_1 + m_1 - m_2 \cdot Y_2/Y_1}{v_1} \tag{5a}$$

and
$$g_2 = \frac{s_2 + m_2 - m_1 \cdot Y_1/Y_2}{v_2} \tag{5b}$$

This is because $X_1/Y_1 = M_2/Y_1$, and if we multiply the numerator and denominator by Y_2 we obtain $m_2 \cdot Y_2/Y_1$ where m_2 is the marginal propensity to import of Region 2 (M_2/Y_2).

Furthermore, let us assume that Region 2 has a higher rate of population growth than Region 1. For equilibrium to be possible, there must therefore be migration out of Region 2. The equilibrium rates of growth are therefore derived from equation (4):

$$g_1 = n_1 + r_1 \tag{6a}$$
and
$$g_2 = n_2 - r_2 \tag{6b}$$

r_1 is obviously R/P_1 and r_2 is R/P_2 where R represents the number of migrants and P_1, P_2 stand for the populations of Region 1 and 2. The migration flow itself must obviously balance in that the number of migrants from Region 2 must always equal the number of immigrants into Region 1.

Since dynamic equilibrium requires that both regions should grow at the same rate, then from equations (5) the rates of growth of the capital stock in both regions must be equal so that:

$$\frac{s_1 + m_1 - m_2 \cdot Y_2/Y_1}{v_1} = \frac{s_2 + m_2 - m_1 \cdot Y_1/Y_2}{v_2} \tag{7}$$

[4] For analysis in terms of an international economy see Johnson, H.G. (1958) *International Trade and Economic Growth*. Ch. 5

Retaining the assumption that capital–output ratios and propensities to save are equal in both regions, then the condition of steady growth is that the balance of payments of both regions remains continuously in equilibrium. If the initial income levels of both regions are equal this condition requires that their marginal propensities to import are also equal; if, on the other hand, initial income levels diverge (for example, $Y_{10} > Y_{20}$, where Y_{10}, Y_{20} represent the initial levels of regional income) then the poorer region must have a higher propensity to import for balance of payments, and hence overall, equilibrium to be possible. However, the typical case where initial income levels are unequal is probably not adequately represented by an assumption of equal propensities to save. Instead, it is more plausible to assume that the poorer region will have a lower propensity to save than the richer region. Now the attainment of equilibrium depends on a flow of savings (capital) from the region with the higher income (Region 1) to the low income region (Region 2). In other words, the region with the lower initial income must run an import surplus if dynamic equilibrium is to be possible.

If we let b_1 represent Region 1's export surplus as a fraction of its income, and b_2 be the import surplus/income ratio of Region 2 then equation (7) can be simplified to:

$$\frac{s_1 - b_1}{v_1} = \frac{s_2 + b_2}{v_2} \tag{8}$$

We still assume that $v_1 = v_2$.

Then $s_1 - b_1 = s_2 + b_2$ becomes

$$\frac{S_{1_t} - B_t}{Y_{1_t}} = \frac{S_{2_t} + B_t}{Y_{2_t}}$$

where B = the balance of payments surplus of Region 1 (deficit of Region 2) in time period t.

Or
$$B_t = \frac{S_{1_t} \cdot Y_{2_t} - S_{2_t} \cdot Y_{1_t}}{Y_{1_t} + Y_{2_t}}$$

and since Y (the overall income of the system) $= Y_1 + Y_2$

$$B_t = S_{1_t} \cdot \frac{Y_2}{Y} - S_{2_t} \cdot \frac{Y_1}{Y} \tag{9}$$

In other words, the balance of payment surplus (or outflow of

REGIONAL ECONOMICS

savings) of the higher income region must equal the difference in the internal savings of the two regions weighted respectively by the ratio of the income of the *other* region to the income of the system as a whole.

For equilibrium growth from the point of view of labour input, migrants must flow from the region with the faster rate of population growth (assumed to be Region 2) in a manner that equates the rate of growth of labour supply in the two regions. Thus, equilibrium requires that:

$$n_1 + r_1 = n_2 - r_2 \qquad (10)$$

or
$$\Delta P_1 + R/P_1 = \Delta P_2 - R/P_2$$

and this gives
$$R = \frac{\Delta P_2 . P_1 - \Delta P_1 . P_2}{P_1 + P_2}$$

Since $P = P_1 + P_2$, the overall rate of migration (i.e. the flow of migrants expressed as a percentage of the population of the system as a whole, R/P) becomes

$$\frac{R}{P} = \frac{\Delta P_2 . P_1 - \Delta P_1 . P_2}{P^2} \qquad (11)$$

Migration must continue at this rate for the regional economies to grow at the steady rate which will keep their labour forces fully employed.

This analysis assumes that activity rates (i.e. the proportions of the population at work) are the same throughout the whole system, so that the labour force $L = wP$, where w is a constant representing the activity rate. If this assumption is relaxed, the conditions for full employment equilibrium become more flexible. For instance, Region 1 may have a higher activity rate so that $g_1 > n_1$ and satisfaction of equation (10) is unnecessary. Also plausible is that the numbers of workers in the annual flow of migrants exceeds wR_t (where $t = 1$ year), reflecting the fact that the age structure of migrants is more likely to be skewed towards working age groups than the structure of immobile population. If this is the case, the migration rate will not need to be as high as demanded by equation (11). Thus, the rate of growth in the labour force in each region is governed by three variables – the rate of natural increase, the activity rate, and the rate of in- or out-migration. If the rates of natural increase are unequal between regions, equilibrium growth may still result from either migration out of regions with rapidly growing populations or by differentials in regional activity rates.

An important question is whether or not there are equilibrating tendencies in the system. Except in the special case where the rates of growth of labour supply and propensities to save happen to be equal in both regions, flows of labour and capital will be necessary to maintain steady state growth. The question is will these flows be equilibrating or not? In the model described above we assumed that the income of Region 1 was higher than Region 2, and that Region 1 had a higher propensity to save but a lower rate of population growth. In effect, therefore, we were making the further assumptions that savings are an increasing function of the level of income and that the rate of population growth is an inverse function of the level of economic development in a region (if we use regional income levels as an approximate indicator of the stage of economic development reached). There is probably a fair measure of empirical support for these assumptions. Given these assumptions, then equilibrium growth requires labour to migrate from low-income to high-income regions and capital to flow in the reverse direction. The need for labour migration may not be strictly necessary if the differential in the rate of population growth is small. In such a situation the rate of growth of labour supply may be equated in the two regions by higher activity rates in the high income region offsetting its slower population growth. If we assume equal activity rates, however, or if the population growth differential is large, labour will have to migrate from low to high income regions.

Whether, in fact, the flows of factors are equilibrating or not is really a matter for empirical substantiation since there is no clear theoretical indication. On *a priori* grounds, we should expect labour flows to be more likely to be equilibrating than capital flows. This is because labour will tend to move from low to high income regions because the latter will be able to offer higher money wages and, more important, greater employment opportunities. Whether the rate of migration will be at the required rate to equate regional rates of growth of labour supply is much less clear. This is because equal rates of growth in labour supply (and in the aggregate rate of growth) do not necessarily mean equal employment opportunities in the two regions. There is no strong case for believing that capital will flow in the right direction, that is, from high income to low income regions. As we shall see, in the neoclassical framework this might follow from the fact that the relative marginal productivities of capital and labour may change in favour of capital in the low income region, since the faster rate of expansion in labour supply than in the capital stock in this region should lower the marginal product of labour relative to capital. Apart from the point that it may be illegitimate to import neoclassical analysis into a demand-oriented model of this kind, this analysis is essentially static and stands on a strict *ceteris paribus* assumption. It is difficult to adapt it to a dynamic setting.

There are other arguments used to support the hypothesis of capital flows from high to low income regions but they are not strong. In fact, unless investment opportunities are abundant in low income regions (because of higher risks and the greater cost of investible funds, they need to be *more* abundant) and are near exhaustion in high income regions, then capital will not flow in the required direction. Indeed, it may tend to flow in the opposite direction since investment opportunities (certainly when viewed subjectively) may be greater in the high income region. In this case, capital flows will be disequilibrating, accelerating the rate of growth in the richer region and slowing it down in the poorer one. But, as stated above, whether capital flows are equilibrating or disequilibrating is a matter for empirical verification. If the assumptions of this analysis operate, market forces are likely to induce migration of labour in the right direction but may result in disequilibrating capital flows, unless current investment opportunities are disproportionately concentrated in low income regions. If capital flows are disequilibrating and if equilibrium growth is the objective, it will be necessary to intervene to make capital flow from high to low income regions.

The above discussion investigates the conditions of equilibrium growth. Equilibrium growth may be exceptional rather than the rule. Finally, therefore, we must consider the conditions that determine whether regional growth rates rise or fall over time. These influences are, in fact, implicit in the preceding equations. If we consider equations (5), and look at the case where the equilibrium growth rate of Region 1 is higher than that of Region 2, then it follows that g_1 must rise and g_2 must fall continuously over time. The reason for this is that if $g_1 > g_2$ then Y_2/Y_1 becomes smaller; thus in equation (5a) $m_2 \cdot Y_2/Y_1$ becomes smaller with the result that g_1 becomes larger. Then the growth rates of the two regions must diverge because if Region 2 were to grow at the same rate the exports of Region 1 would be a decreasing share of total output and therefore an increasing proportion of its output would have to be absorbed by investment and g_1 would rise. On the other hand, Region 2 could not continue to grow at the same rate, since its exports (i.e. the imports of Region 1) would be an increasing fraction of its total output; a declining fraction of its output would therefore be available for investment, and g_2 would fall.

The conclusions are obvious. With balance of payments equilibrium, regions should grow faster the higher their propensities to save and the lower their capital–output ratios. Surpluses and deficits in regional balances of payments take the form of capital outflows and inflows. Net capital imports are net additions to the aggregate savings of regions enabling them to increase their rate of growth. Thus, regions with net import surpluses (returning to equation (3) where $m_i - (X_i/Y_i) > 0$) should grow faster than other regions. Similarly, from the point of view of labour rather than capital inputs, regions experiencing net immigration, representing additions to internal labour supply, should tend to grow faster than regions affected by net emigration.

3 Equilibrium growth in a neoclassical model

Just as Harrod–Domar type models can be adapted to a system of regions, neoclassical models are capable of a similar reformulation. As is well known, the main difference between the two categories of theories is that while Harrod–Domar models are demand-oriented the neoclassical model concentrates on the supply side. The conditions for equilibrium growth are less restrictive than in the Harrod–Domar model, for the assumption of fixed coefficients is relaxed. Instead we assume a continuous function linking output to inputs of the two factors, capital and labour. The capital–output ratio now becomes a variable and flexibility in this ratio may permit steady growth. The rate of growth in income is determined by three elements: capital accumulation, an increase in labour supply, and what may be broadly called technical progress. We assume that the rate of technical progress is, within each region, a constant function of time. Given a production function for the i-th region of the following type:

$$Y_i = f_i(K, L, t) \qquad (1)$$

where Y = real regional income, K is the capital stock, L the supply of labour, and t represents time which brings technical progress with it, we can if we make certain simplifying assumptions derive an equation to describe the determinants of the rate of growth in each region. If we assume that the allocative mechanism works so that factors receive their marginal net products, either because of perfect competition or because the system behaves in the same way as under perfect competition, and we assume constant returns to scale, it is possible to derive from the above production function the equation:

$$y_i = a_i k_i + (1 - a_i) n_i + T_i \qquad (2)$$

where y = rate of growth of output (or income), k and n the rates of growth of capital and labour respectively, T the rate of technical progress (i.e. the annual rate of growth of output due to technical progress alone), a = capital's income share (or the marginal product of capital, $\Delta Y / \Delta K$, multiplied by K/Y), and because of constant returns $(1-a)$ = labour's income share (or $\Delta Y / \Delta L . L/Y$), all referring to region i.[5]

The neoclassical model requires that there is continuous full employment of the capital stock, a demand that calls for some mechanism to equate investment with full employment saving. The rate of interest may be an instrument for this purpose, since in a neoclassical world (and therefore ignoring Keynesian objections) there will be a level of the rate of interest (r) that will make investment equal to full employment savings. Abstracting from risk and uncertainty, the equilibrium rate of interest will equal the rate of profit, which in turn equals, on our assumptions, the marginal product of capital. Thus, we may state that a requirement of equilibrium is that:

$$MP_{K_i} = a_i \frac{Y_i}{K_i} = r \qquad (3)$$

In other words, the rate of capital accumulation in each region must be, for equilibrium growth, such that the marginal product of capital in each region is equal to the national interest rate, r. If the interest rate is given, this means that Y and K must grow at the same rate if a is to remain constant. An equilibrium condition is, therefore, that $y_i = k_i$.

The equilibrium growth rate of output and capital can now be obtained by substituting y_i for k_i in equation (2). Let us do this for a

[5] The derivation is straightforward and is well known. See, for example, Meade, J. (1961) *A Neo-Classical Theory of Economic Growth.* 8–12

two-region system where the subscripts 1 and 2 refer to regions 1 and 2. Then we get:

$$y_1 = k_1 = \frac{T_1}{1-a_1} + n_1 \qquad (4a)$$

and

$$y_2 = k_2 = \frac{T_2}{1-a_2} + n_2 \qquad (4b)$$

It has been noticed earlier that for equilibrium in the whole system the growth rates in the component regions must be constant and equal. Furthermore, for equilibrium growth in the neoclassical model output and capital accumulation must also expand at the same constant rate. Within each region they must both grow at the rate given in equations (4). Thus, an equilibrium condition for the system is that:

$$\frac{T_1}{1-a_1} + n_1 = \frac{T_2}{1-a_2} + n_2 \qquad (5)$$

Whether steady growth is possible, therefore, assuming that the prior condition that the marginal product of capital in each region equals the interest rate holds, depends on what happens to the three variables – the rate of growth of labour supply (n), the rate of technical progress (T), and the share of capital in income (a).[6] In the rather restrictive case where all these three variables are constant and equal in the two regions there will be equilibrium growth. If the rate of growth in the supply of labour varies between the two regions, steady growth may still result if, with capital's income share the same in both regions, the region having the most rapidly growing labour supply has the lower rate of technical progress. With different a's in the two regions there may be steady growth if the capital–output ratios are flexible enough. For instance, if the labour force of Region 1 grows faster than that of Region 2, provided that $n_1 \leq T_2/(1-a_2) + n_2$

---

[6] A test of this neoclassical growth model with United States data, correlating actual growth rates with $[T/(1-a)+n]$, yielded rank correlation coefficients of 0·953 when actual growth was measured in terms of regional income produced in the period 1929–53 and of 0·929 when growth was measured by personal income, 1929–59. Both these coefficients were statistically significant at the 1% level. The author concluded: 'Considering the numerous data deficiencies ... the neoclassical growth model in long-run equilibrium explains the pattern of regional investment expenditures and growth rates with considerable precision' (Romans, J.T. (1965) *Capital Exports and Growth among U.S. Regions*. 98)

holds and T is positive, then there will be some capital–output ratio that will maintain equilibrium in the system. Whether the required capital–output ratio falls within the feasible range of values that may be assigned to it, and whether this value is in fact obtained, is another matter. We may also consider the special case where $n_1 = n_2$; if the ratio of the labour force to the population remains constant then the rate of growth in output per head is given by $(y - n)$, and steady growth requires that this rate be equal to $T/(1 - a)$. If regions enjoy different rates of technical progress they will then, *ceteris paribus*, tend to grow at different rates. But again, equilibrium can be restored by different capital–output ratios. Thus, in our model, if $T_1 > T_2$ there may still be dynamic equilibrium if $a_2 > a_1$ (i.e. since $MP_{K_1} = MP_{K_2}$ if $K_2/Y_2 > K_1/Y_1$). In addition, of course, since the rate of technical progress has been assumed constant then the income share of capital within each region must also remain constant: this requires that technical progress is neutral in its effects on the two factors (i.e. does not alter the ratio of their marginal products) and that there is perfect substitutability between the two factors. Given these conditions, differences in the rates of technical progress may be offset by different capital–output ratios. This special case illustrates the key element in neoclassical models: that flexibility in the capital–output ratios may keep economies on an equilibrium growth path.

In equilibrium, total investment in the system of regions must equal total savings. But this does not necessarily mean that the savings generated within each region will be such as to ensure that rate of capital accumulation that satisfies the equilibrium condition $y = k$. Instead some regions may import capital from others. Capital imports into a region can be defined as imports minus exports $(M - X)$. The equilibrium condition for each region is that $M_i - X_i = I_i - S_i$ subject to the constraint that $\sum I_i = \sum S_i$. Thus the extent of capital imports can be determined by comparing the rate of investment with the rate of savings. If we assume that savings are proportional to income, then $S_i = s_i Y_i$; investment $I_i = k_i K_i$. Thus capital will be imported into a region if $k_i K_i > s_i Y_i$, or if the rate of growth of capital is greater than the ratio of domestic savings to capital:

$$k_i > \frac{s_i Y_i}{K_i} \tag{6}$$

Since equilibrium requires output to grow at the same rate as capital, and also requires the marginal product of capital in each region to be equal to the national interest rate ($MP_{Ki} = a_i Y_i/K_i = r$), then (6) may be rewritten as:

$$y_i > s_i \frac{r}{a_i} \qquad (7)$$

For capital imports to take place and to maintain equilibrium growth, this inequality must hold for at least some regions of the system. Reverting to our two region system again, if $y_1 = s_1 r/a_1$ and $y_2 = s_2 r/a_2$ steady growth will occur with the internal rates of capital accumulation equal to the internal generation of savings. If, on the other hand, $y_1 > s_1 r/a_1$ then for equilibrium $y_2 < s_2 r/a_2$. In steady growth $y_1 = y_2$, therefore $s_2 r/a_2 > s_1 r/a_1$. Capital must flow from Region 2 to Region 1 for steady growth in the whole system, and for this to be possible Region 2 must have a higher propensity to save and/or a lower share of income received by capital (meaning, since in equilibrium the marginal products of capital are equal in all regions, a lower capital–output ratio). Thus, the requirements of steady growth in the Harrod–Domar and the neoclassical applications to inter-regional growth are much the same, and both models lead to similar conclusions.

The main factor influencing capital imports when we depart from steady growth is clear from (7) above. The higher a region's rate of growth the more likely that it will import capital. If all regions have more or less the same propensities to save and the same income shares accruing to capital then the fastest growing regions will tend to import capital from the slow growing ones.

Finally, although we initially assumed that the national interest rate is given, it can be shown that this rate is fully determined by the model. The equilibrium rate of interest must be such as to equate the total investment of the system with total savings:

$$\Sigma I_i = \Sigma s_i Y_i = \Sigma r (s/a)_i K_i \qquad (8)$$

Thus the national interest rate r is given by:

$$r = \frac{\Sigma I_i}{\Sigma (s/a)_i K_i}$$

If s/a is the same in all regions, we may conclude that the national rate of interest is proportional to the national growth rate of capital, k:

$$r = \frac{a}{s} \cdot k \qquad (9)$$

The above model shows how a simplified neoclassical analysis can be adapted for describing steady growth in a system of regions. The equilibrium regional growth rates, capital flows and the national interest rate are fully determined by the model itself.

4 The export base theory of growth

The 'export base' theory of regional growth, despite its severe limitations as an explanatory or a predictive hypothesis, requires a brief examination. The theory obviously stems from foreign trade multiplier concepts in comparative statics analysis. In an earlier chapter we analysed the conditions under which a change in the 'economic base' of a region could explain short-run movements in regional income. Some regional analysts have used the base concept dynamically, and argued that there is a long run (and stable) relation between a region's exports and its overall growth. The theory states that the growth of a region depends upon the growth of its export industries, implying of course that expansion in demand external to the region is the crucial initiating determinant of growth within the region. Thus, an increase in the **export base**, a concept denoting collectively all the exportable goods and services of a region, sets off a multiplier process where the multiplier is equal to total regional output divided by total exports. The presumption is therefore that all economic activities not for exports, especially the region's trade and service activities, are induced by the expansion or decline of export industries.[7]

The export base theory has a number of important general features. In the first place, it is clearly Keynesian income theory applied to an open economy and adapted to long-run analysis – but with this difference. Exports alone are elevated to a key role as the sole exogenous influence on aggregate demand, and other possible autonomous influences (shifts in the consumption function, domestic investment, or changes in the level of government spending) are

[7] See, for example, North, D.C. (1955) Location Theory and Regional Economic Growth. *Journal of Political Economy*, **63**; Tiebout, C.M. (1956) Exports and Regional Economic Growth. *Journal of Political Economy*, **64**, Reply. by North, D.C. and Rejoinder. by Tiebout, C.M.; Perloff, H.S., Dunn, E.S. Jr., Lampard, E.E. and Muth, R.F. (1960) *Regions, Resources, and Economic Growth*. Ch. 4; Romans, J.T. (1965) *Capital Exports and Growth among U.S. Regions*; and Thomas, M.D. (1964) The Export Base and Development Stages Theories of Regional Economic Growth: An Appraisal. *Land Economics*, **11** 421–32

relegated into insignificance. The export base theory goes much further than regarding the income of export industries as a net addition to the income of a region; it also implies that without an export base non-export industries would not exist in its stead, and that resources employed in sectors producing exportable commodities would either be unemployed or would never have been attracted into the region at the outset.

Secondly, the theory regards the export base as homogeneous in the sense that it pays no attention to the source of an increase in export demand. Thus, the world economy is broken down into only two components – the 'region' and the 'rest of the world'. Whether an expansion in exports originates in a neighbouring region or at the other side of the world is treated as a matter of indifference. In some cases the source of expansion in the export base may be critical for understanding and predicting the course of the region's growth. At best, therefore, this highly simplified theory obscures the functional ties between regions, and consequently throws no light on the process of inter-regional growth. On the other hand, and this is the third characteristic to be stressed, the export base theory does allot a central position in the analysis of regional growth to changing patterns of national demand. It is suggestive to the extent that it emphasises that to understand the regional growth process a region cannot be studied in isolation. Whether a region grows fast or not is unlikely to be decided within its own borders. The main determinant of its growth rate is much more likely to be the rate of expansion in the national economy (in some cases, in the international economy).

The export base proponents recognise that residentiary, or locally originating, activities may in some circumstances have more than a passive role. High levels of expenditure within a region by the central government may stimulate regional expansion. Migration into the region induced by non-economic stimuli may expand residentiary activities there without any change in the export base. Growth in local activities of an import-replacing character may also stimulate regional development. Moreover, improved efficiency in local industries, such as those supplying inputs to export industries, may have significant repercussions on regional activity by improving the competitiveness of the export base itself. But those who believe in the value of the export base concept hold that these cases of initiatory local activity are exceptional. They argue that increased investment in residentiary activity is primarily induced investment as a result of expansion in income received from outside the region, and that expanded employment in the region's local industries and services is mainly the consequence of long-run changes in income received from the export base.

This theory of regional growth may be useful for presenting a simplified impression of certain important characteristics of the historical development of regions in certain countries, but it can hardly claim validity as a general theory of regional growth. Its limitations are, in fact, quite serious. A good theory ought to aid understanding. The export base theory with its simple dichotomy between the region and elsewhere obscures the possibly important function played by inter-regional relations in the growth process. Secondly, the theory has doubtful value as a predictor of the course of events. It is most improbable that we could estimate from an increase in the size of the export base the net effect this has on regional growth. For instance, just how much of the increase in income leaks outside the region again in the form of imports will depend on the precise source and form of the increase in exports.

Some of the major drawbacks of the export base theory are already implicit in the preceding discussion. The export base model is best known as an exceedingly simple form of multiplier in the general theory of short-run regional income determination. As such it is a concept more appropriate to comparative statics than to dynamics. Moreover, in a multi-commodity world the repercussions on residentiary activities will vary, often markedly, from export sector to export sector. Expansion in different components of the export base could have widely diverse results for regional growth. Secondly, the theory ignores the fact that internal growth impulses may be vital factors in regional growth. In the long run, the stress on exports is far too narrow. The level of other exogenous variables (injections by the government, technological progress within the region, shifts in the investment and/or the consumption function) also need consideration, and in some sets of circumstances may induce more growth than a change in the export base. Thirdly, this neglect is the more serious the larger the region studied. As the size of region analysed increases, the relative importance of exports declines and the possible significance of other growth stimuli increases commensurately. Moreover, for large areas the multiplier feedback may be of some importance, emphasising the need for an inter-regional approach. Fourthly, residentiary activities may in some cases be a key element in expanding regional income. For instance, resources may be allocated more efficiently to local than to export sectors (due for example to a higher rate of technical progress in the former); in such an event a decline in export activity might even be accompanied by a rise in regional income. Fifthly, a region could grow in the absence of an increase in the size of its export base if there was an improvement in the region's terms of trade. Finally, the value of the export base concept is depreciated when we are concerned with an advanced diversified regional economy with complex export sectors catering for markets varying from limited areas to the national economy or even for world markets.

Is the export base theory inconsistent with the Harrod–Domar type (and neoclassical) models discussed earlier? A major inference to be drawn from these latter theories is that regions running import surpluses should grow faster than export surplus regions. The export base theory suggests that an expansion in the export base of a region (i.e. its gross exports) will induce a higher growth rate. If the theories are not to contradict each other, therefore, the export base model must assume that any autonomous increase in exports will set off a chain reaction of multiplier and accelerator effects to increase the level of regional income but also to increase imports by more than the original increase in exports, bringing about an import surplus. The condition fulfilling this is that the marginal propensity to spend exceeds unity. If the marginal propensity to spend is less than unity, expanding exports may have a dampening effect on the equilibrium rate of growth. Unless the marginal propensity to spend is greater than unity, export base theory is applicable only to regions with excess capacity and unemployment. If regions do not have this spare capacity, attempts to expand the export base as a means of raising the rate of growth will be self-defeating, since they will come up against the full employment barrier. However, we may conclude that there is no *necessary* inconsistency between the fact that regions with import surpluses have relatively higher growth rates and the export base theory in which export expansion leads to a faster growth rate. This is because there is no full employment or full capacity equilibrium implicit in the export base model itself. Instead, it implies either disequilibrium or an unemployment equilibrium. But the conditions that permit consistency are fairly restrictive.

5 The sector approach

One theory of regional growth that we may dismiss briefly in its crudest form, though it may point the road to a useful eclectic approach, is the so-called 'sector' theory. This begins from the Clark–Fisher hypotheses that a rise in *per capita* incomes would be accompanied by a decline in the proportion of resources employed in agriculture, and a rise in manufacturing (secondary) and later in service (tertiary) industries. The rate at which these sector shifts occur is regarded as the main determinant of how fast the economy grows. The reasons for the shifts are found on both the demand and the supply side: on the demand side, the income elasticities of demand for the goods and services supplied by manufacturing and service industries are higher than those for primary products, so that rising incomes are inevitably accompanied by a relative transfer of resources to the former; on the supply side, the necessary transfers of labour and capital are achieved as a result of differential rates of productivity growth in these sectors. It is argued that the secondary and tertiary categories enjoy greater advances in productivity, because of an association between fast growing demand and productivity growth (the combination may be due, for example, to economies of scale); because of their higher productivity these sectors are able to offer higher returns both to labour and capital, and these higher returns are responsible for initiating the required resource shifts.

Although the propositions that low levels of income per head are associated with a high proportion of the labour force in primary occupations and that high income levels are associated with an occupational structure biased towards tertiary industries may be reasonable as rough, working hypotheses, there is no inherent necessity in this relationship. In particular, the rigid primary-secondary-tertiary sequence has long been considered inadequate, especially with regard to the switch from manufacturing to service industries as incomes continue to rise in advanced economies. Moreover, it is not at all clear that sector shifts through this sequence are from low to high productivity sectors. The rate of productivity growth depends upon innovation and technical advance as well as upon economies of scale, so that there is no compelling reason why high income elasticities of demand and high productivity growth should go together. If productivity is higher in industries the demand for the products of which is rapidly growing, this could be due to a 'high productivity–low prices–expanding demand' causation rather than to the reverse, where demand governs the pace of productivity advance. At any point of time we will tend to find industries within each of the three broad sector categories with high income elasticities of demand and with high rates of productivity growth as well as industries within each group with lower than average ratings. Thus, the high level of aggregation involved in the primary-secondary-tertiary trichotomy hides significant differences from the point of view of future growth among industries within the three broad groups.

As an explanatory theory of growth, the sector theory is inadequate in that because of its focus on income elasticity of demand it merely outlines a suggested process of growth from some sectors to others on the *assumption* of a rise in *per capita* incomes. It offers no insights into the causes of growth itself. In effect, therefore, this approach begs the question.

Finally, the sector theory concentrates exclusively on internal developments, and neglects external stimuli to growth. It follows that the theory is more useful the greater the degree of self-sufficiency in the economy. Even with nations the foreign trade sector is likely to distort the sector sequence, but this is much more likely to happen with regions which tend to be much more open than countries. The sector approach gives no attention to inter-regional relationships, and this is a fatal defect.

Despite these drawbacks, the sector theory is a starting point for a disaggregated analysis of regional growth. The sectoral aggregates used in the primary-secondary-tertiary division are much too large to be meaningful, but something can be salvaged with more disaggregation. With modifications, the economic sector approach with its emphasis on sector productivity and the pattern of demand highlights the relationship between a region's industrial structure and its growth and level of income. The rate of intra-regional reallocation of resources to high productivity sectors may be a crucial determinant of how fast a region grows. This fact shifts our interest from macroeconomic growth theories to a microeconomic approach stressing the links between regional growth and industrial structure.[8]

---

[8] See the argument in Perloff, H.S. (1957) Interrelations of State Income and Industrial Structure. *Review of Economics and Statistics*, **39** 162–71

6 Industrial structure and regional growth

The interpretation of a region's growth in terms of the dynamics of its industrial structure is urged most strongly in the massive empirical study of United States regions, *Regions, Resources and Economic Growth* (1960) by H.S. Perloff, E.S. Dunn, Jr., E.E. Lampard and R.F. Muth.[9] Their argument is that the 'regional growth – industrial location framework of analysis provides a relatively comprehensive and consistent context for understanding and evaluating subnational economic and physical development'.[10] The analysis stands on three assumptions: that overall regional growth (the *volume* of economic activity) is determined by a different constellation of forces than is *per capita* regional income (the welfare aspects of growth);[11] that economic growth is an evolutionary process where the seeds of future development are to be found in past and present activities and decisions; and, most important of all, that the critical factors in changing patterns of regional growth are the locational and output decisions of business firms in the light of the input and market requirements of major industries in the economy.[12] They further believe that the growth performance of an individual region can only be assessed against the background of developments in the national economy.

Given the diversity of regional growth patterns, and accepting that each region's development stems from a myriad of complex but interrelated causal forces, it is not possible to elicit from the PDLM approach a formal theory of regional growth. Their study is a piece of intensive applied research and their interests were not primarily theoretical. Nevertheless, their detailed research was built upon a framework of analysis that attempted to indicate the significant features that a disaggregated theory might be expected to contain. At the same time, it must be remembered that the conceptual analysis which follows was conceived with close reference to empirical studies so that the level of abstraction is considerably less than found in our

---

[9] Hereafter called PDLM for brevity. For a summary see Perloff, H.S. and Dodds, V.W. (1963) *How a Region Grows*. Also see Perloff, H.S. Relative Regional Economic Growth: An Approach to Regional Accounts and Delwart, L. and Sodenblum, S. Regional Account Projections in the Context of National Projections, in Hochwald, W. (edit) (1961) *Design of Regional Accounts* and Borts and Stein, *op. cit.*, 44–7, 65–100

[10] Perloff, Relative Regional Economic Growth. *loc. cit.*, 39

[11] Influences on the course of inter-regional *per capita* income differentials are discussed briefly in the next section

[12] PDLM, *op. cit.*, vi

earlier discussion of regional growth models. The industry-orientation of the approach in itself, of course, limits the degree of abstraction, since patterns of industrial growth are too complex and many-sided to be handled with the tools of formal theory.

An obvious starting point is to look at the industrial composition of a region. If we consider a region as a component of the national economy it seems natural to think of it as a weighted representation of a set of national industries. If we were to attribute nation-wide characteristics to these industries regardless of where they were located this would throw up the hypotheses that a region with a preponderance of industries that are growing rapidly in the national economy will itself grow fast while a region with a large proportion of lagging industries will grow slowly. However, tests in almost all cases fail to support the hypothesis that a region's growth is explicable by its industrial composition. Regional industries do not always, or even normally, expand at the same rate as their national counterparts. The assumptions of the industry-mix theory may be invalidated by dynamic elements. For example, a region with a high share of stagnant industries may grow quite rapidly as a consequence of locational adjustments: existing locational advantages may not have been exploited, and these may attract new industries in the future; new locational advantages may develop, such as greater elasticity in the supply of labour as the result of in-migration in response to non-economic variables, and these may improve the competitiveness of the region's industries; technological change may affect the current inter-regional balance of locational forces; regional policies may operate, boosting the region's growth rate.

Emphasis on the share of nationally fast-growing industries in a region is, therefore, only half the story. It is true that some regions may grow rapidly because the composition of their industrial structure is favourable in the sense that it contains an above average proportion of rapid-growth industries. But a region may grow in a distinctively different way, as a result of 'within-industry' changes. The locational pattern of an industry may shift in favour of Region A and against other regions so that employment in that industry increases faster in Region A than in all other regions. This will induce higher growth in Region A, irrespective of whether the industry in question is a growth industry or not. In summary, a region may grow *either* because it has industries that are growing fast nationally *or* because it is gaining an increasing proportion of a given industry or industries, regardless of whether these industries are growing or not. Can these two separate effects be formalised?

Share analysis provides the first stage in the problem. It is concerned with the proportion of national industry totals (or other indicators of growth such as population and income) found within each region. As such, it gives a snapshot picture of a region's structure *vis-à-vis* the national economy. However, share analysis supplies only a static viewpoint.[13] If the researcher's preoccupation is with regional growth he will wish to study regional structure dynamically. For this purpose, he may adopt **shift analysis.** This is concerned with regional changes in indicators of economic activity between two defined points of time, and in particular concentrates on whether the regional change is greater or less than the national average change (i.e. whether the shift is upwards or downwards). The total shift measures the difference between the actual regional change and the change that would have occurred had the region grown at the national average rates. It is composed of two components: the **proportionality shift** and the **differential shift.** The proportionality shift measures the industrial composition effect, which arises from the fact that, nationwide, some sectors grow more rapidly than others. Thus, a region specialising in slow-growth sectors will show a net downward proportionality shift while a region favoured by a high share of rapid-growth sectors will show an upward proportionality shift. Differential shifts arise from the fact that industries grow in some regions faster than in others. Regions characterised by net upward differential shifts are areas in which locational advantages for particular activities have improved relative to other regions. The sum of the proportionality and differential shifts is equal to the total shift.

If we measure the shift in terms of employment, then conceptually the shifts can be represented in the following manner. Let the initial time period be denoted by o and the terminal period by t; let j be the subscript for the region, and i be the subscript for the industry. Employment in the i-th sector in the j-th region is represented by E_{ij}, total regional employment $= E_j$ (or $\sum_i E_{ij}$), national employment in the i-th sector $= E_i$ (or $\sum_j E_{ij}$), and total national employment in all industries can be represented by E (or $\sum_i \sum_j E_{ij}$).

[13] Shares can, of course, be compared at two different periods of time. However, this falls short of a dynamic analysis since it tells nothing about the growth pattern in the intervening period.

We may write the total shift as:

$$S_A = E_{j_t} - \left(\frac{E_t}{E_o}\right) . E_{j_o} \qquad (1)$$

The differential shift represents the same procedure applied to each industry in turn. Thus,

$$S_D = \sum_i \left[E_{ij_t} - \left(\frac{E_{i_t}}{E_{i_o}}\right) . E_{ij_o} \right] \qquad (2)$$

The proportionality shift (S_P) is equal to ($S_A - S_D$), so we may write:

$$S_P = E_{j_t} - \left(\frac{E_t}{E_o}\right) . E_{j_o} - \sum_i \left[E_{ij_t} - \left(\frac{E_{i_t}}{E_{i_o}}\right) E_{ij_o} \right]$$

$$= \sum_i \left(\frac{E_{i_t}}{E_{i_o}}\right) E_{ij_o} - \left(\frac{E_t}{E_o}\right) \sum_i E_{ij_o}$$

$$= \sum_i \left[\left(\frac{E_{i_t}}{E_{i_o}}\right) - \left(\frac{E_t}{E_o}\right) \right] E_{ij_o} \qquad (3)$$

It is important to appreciate that proportionality and differential effects are quite distinct phenomena, and their investigation requires us to look at quite different forces. To understand the proportionality effect we need to focus on forces affecting the composition of output on the national scene. Dominant among these are productivity changes on the supply side initiating resource transfer from low to high productivity sectors and income elasticities of demand on the demand side. These reflect other influences such as technological change, the introduction of new products, changes in tastes, etc., all of which affect the overall composition of national output. It is then necessary to analyse the advantages of each region for the national fast-growing or slow-growing industries.

The differential effect is explained by the fact that some regions gain over time a relative advantage compared with other regions in their access to markets and/or to inputs in relation to specific industries. This necessitates detailed analysis of local factors. PDLM refer to the technique as **input-output access** which enables the analyst to make a broad assessment of the growth potential of each region. They argue that 'inter-regional differences in access to inputs and markets can be expected to bring about different patterns of regional growth behaviour', and conversely that 'the various growth patterns displayed can be explained by identifying the relative advantages and disadvantages of the regions with regard to input and output access for the major types of economic activities'.[14] Apart from shift analysis, input-output access is the major contribution of the PDLM team to the understanding of regional growth.

Location theory suggests that growth in regional output is directly related to two factors: its access at competitive costs to inputs of production and its access to markets for the output of this production. Input-output access represents a netting out of the relative advantages and disadvantages of each region for production in a given industry or of all industries combined. However, the input-output requirements[15] vary so much from industry to industry that the balance of locational advantages and disadvantages should preferably be drawn industry by industry or, at least, on the basis of a selected group of industries – such as an industrial complex. The variety of experience between industries renders any attempt to evaluate input-output access in terms of an aggregate index for each region almost meaningless. The value of the technique is maximised when we consider specific functions within specific regions.

The importance of input-output access analysis is that it demonstrates that a region's growth potential depends on forces other than its industrial composition. It also stresses the immense variety possible in regional growth experience, and explicitly recognises the constraints placed on growth in certain regions because of specific locational disadvantages, such as distance from main markets or severe resource limitations. Some regions may have favourable input-output access only in relation to home markets, while others with poor access to inputs and output at home may enjoy substantial growth as a result of having a nodal position in respect to external resources and markets. Although regions vary widely in development potential, favourable access to external national markets may be a necessary prerequisite for regional prosperity. On the other hand, a region with an unfavourable industry mix is not inevitably condemned to slow growth. Not all regions can grow rapidly, but every region may hope to enjoy a rising average income level (as long as national growth continues) if it is willing to put up

[14] PDLM, *op. cit.*, 93

[15] Input-output access must not, of course, be compared with the technical inter-industry relationships of the Leontief-type input-output models

with the readjustments associated with the reallocation of resources in response to changing relative locational advantages.

This approach to regional growth is quite different from that advanced earlier in this chapter – less abstract and formal with all statements subject to confirmation by empirical observation, much less precise about its predictions, but more adaptable and with greater operational value. Yet macroeconomic theories and the industry approach to regional growth are not contradictory. On the contrary, they are complementary to each other, each technique viewing the complexities of regional economic growth from a different perspective. The crucial variables of the macroeconomic models (such as the savings-income ratio, the rate of population growth and migration rates) are all taken account of in input-output access, at least in general terms. Moreover, the assumption of a one-sector economy characteristic of many growth models is a device adopted to simplify the problem, and making this assumption does not necessarily imply that resource transfer between sectors is unimportant in regional growth. Appreciation of the complex nature of regional economic growth and its diversity probably demands a multidimensional approach, encompassing both formal growth models and industry-oriented analysis.

7 Long-run convergence of *per capita* incomes

Is the regional growth process equilibrating or not? In earlier discussions the concept of equilibrium was applied in at least three senses: equilibrium growth in the sense of regions growing at the same rate; a spatial equilibrium in the sense of no incentive for factors to move from one region to another which requires, assuming zero transport and transfer costs, equalisation of *homogeneous* factor returns between regions; and an equilibrating tendency in the sense that the growth process in a regional system leads to the convergence of regional *per capita* incomes. These three phenomena are quite different from each other, except under extremely restrictive assumptions. Here, we are primarily concerned with the last of the three. Unless initial regional income levels are identical, equal growth rates are incompatible with convergence since absolute income differentials will widen while relative income differences will remain the same. Equalisation of factor returns does not necessarily imply equal *per capita* incomes in all regions unless additional assumptions are made.

Investigations in the United States by R.A. Easterlin, F. Hanna, H.S. Perloff and associates, G.H. Borts and J.L. Stein and J.T. Romans[16] all find some evidence for the convergence hypothesis, though the process seems to be neither steady nor even continuous. Moreover, theoretical analysis earlier in this book has, on the whole, highlighted the role of equilibrating forces, though it was explicitly recognised that tendencies towards an equilibrium were not automatic, and that disequilibrating factors operated, at least intermittently, in a dynamic economy. In view of this, a reasonable starting point might be to consider the thesis of the main critic of convergence, Gunnar Myrdal.[17] His argument is that 'the play of the forces in the market normally tends to increase, rather than to decrease, the inequalities between regions'.[18] These forces lead to activities yielding above average returns being clustered in certain localities and regions at the expense of other areas in the country. Such a build-up of activities may have started originally because the agglomerating regions had a competitive advantage or because of access to an exceptionally good facility (such as mineral resources or a port), but it has become self-sustaining because of ever-increasing internal and external economies in such regions. Backward regions in the country fail to attract new activities, because their limited advantages, say cheap labour, do not exert sufficient attractive force to outweigh these external economies found at centres of agglomeration.

For this reason, the lagging regions in the country fail to attract lines of development that generate autonomous growth. The main influence on their economic progress will be the *induced* effects of expansion in the prosperous regions. These effects are classified into two categories: **spread** and **backwash** effects. The spread effects refer to the favourable impact of growth in the thriving region. The region around a nodal centre of expansion tends to gain from increasing outlets for agricultural products and may feel the benefits of stimuli

---

[16] Easterlin, R.A. Regional Growth of Income: Long-Term Tendencies, in Kuznets, S., Miller, A.R. and Easterlin, R.A. *Population Redistribution and Economic Growth, United States, 1870–1950*, Vol. II, *Analyses of Economic Change* (1960); Hanna, F. (1959) *State Income Differentials, 1919–54*. PDLM, op. cit., especially Part V; Borts, G.H. and Stein, J.L. (1964) *Economic Growth in a Free Market*; and Romans, J.T. (1965) *Capital Exports and Growth among U.S. Regions*

[17] As argued in Myrdal, G. (1957) *Economic Theory and Under-Developed Regions*

[18] *Ibid.*, 26

to technical advance. Raw material suppliers in quite distant regions may also benefit, even to an extent permitting the growth of consumer goods industries in these areas. But Myrdal argues that beneficial effects will normally be outweighed by adverse backwash effects. Thus, movements of labour, capital, goods and services are regarded as being disequilibrating, favouring the rich regions at the expense of the poor. For instance, migration may have harmful repercussions on the age distribution of the population in the sending region; the capital market will deflect savings from poor regions where the effective demand for capital is low to the prosperous regions where returns on capital are high and less risky; free trade favours the highly developed industrial regions, and the trade patterns of poorer regions are distorted to benefit the rich and to prevent industrialisation. Perhaps even more important, economic backwardness results in non-economic influences harmful to growth – low levels of education, lack of aspiration and other social attitudes incompatible with high rates of economic development and deterioration in the social capital of such regions.

The existence of two countervailing sets of forces, spread and backwash, does not imply an equilibrium. There is a special case where the two effects balance each other, but even this is not a stable equilibrium since any change in forces will start a cumulative upward or downward movement. Indeed, Myrdal argues that the emphasis of many economists on the likelihood of convergence stems from treating the concept of stable equilibrium as if it had 'teleological significance' rather than 'as a very abstract, almost crude and usually unrealistic theoretical assumption'.[19] He also criticises economists who support what he calls the 'equality doctrine' for their artificial separation of economic and non-economic variables and for their abstraction from the latter. Not only may non-economic variables be important in explaining regional growth differences, but they also tend to operate in a disequilibrating manner. Myrdal's arguments highlight how particular forces affecting regional income differences may interact under certain circumstances, but he neglects the fact that factor movements may be equilibrating and that there are other influences at work tending to promote convergence. He fails to develop a comprehensive analysis and to establish a general case for growing regional income inequalities.

[19] *Ibid.*, 144

Inter-regional factor flows may lead to convergence. In a comparative statics model given certain restrictive assumptions, it can be shown that the marginal product of capital falls and the marginal product of labour rises with a rise in the capital/labour ratio.[20]

We assume that: (1) the total supply of labour is fixed for all regions; (2) one homogeneous commodity is produced in each region, and that the output of this good can be used as a capital good without incurring additional cost; (3) transport costs are zero with the result that the price of output is the same between and within regions; (4) the production function of each region is identical, takes the form $Y=f(K, L)$ and is subject to constant returns to scale; (5) pure competition exists in each region. The fourth assumption means that the marginal physical products of labour and capital (MP_L and MP_K) are functions of the capital/labour ratio (K/L).

As can be seen from figure 13.1 the marginal product of capital function is negatively sloped. As the K/L ratio increases, MP_K falls. The marginal product of labour function, on the other hand, is positively sloped, so that MP_L increases as the K/L ratio rises. Because of pure competition, the marginal product of labour equals the real wage (the wage being measured in units of physical output). Because each region produces a homogeneous output with identical production functions, the region with the higher K/L (Region 1) has the higher real wage (w_1) and the lower marginal product of capital (r_1). Conversely, Region 2 which has the lower K/L ratio (R_2) has the lower real wage (w_2) but the higher marginal product of capital (r_2). Thus, the essential characteristic of this highly simplified model is a negative correlation between the real wage and the marginal product of capital throughout the system of regions described.

This model predicts that capital will flow from high to low wage regions since the latter offer higher returns to capital, while labour will tend to flow in the opposite direction. Low wage, low income regions should, therefore, experience the higher growth rates of capital and the greater increases in wages. But if the assumptions of the model are relaxed and if dynamic influences in the economy are fully taken into account, it is much more difficult to justify automatic convergence.

For example, if low wage regions have higher rates of natural

[20] See Borts, G.H. (1960) The Equalisation of Returns and Regional Economic Growth. *American Economic Review*, **50**, and Borts, G.H. and Stein, J.L. (1964) *Economic Growth in a Free Market*. 48–64

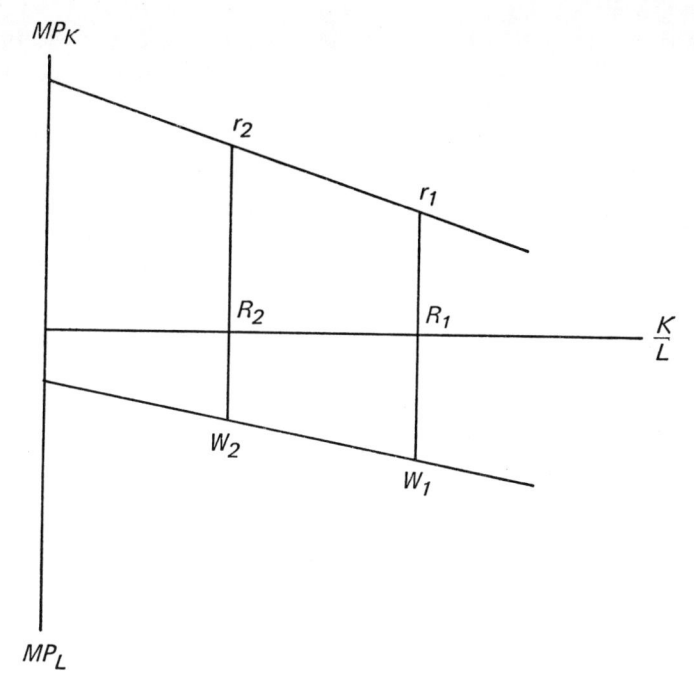

Figure 13.1

increase in population, out-migration may fail to raise wages. Moreover, employment opportunities may be a greater inducement to migrate than wage differentials, and there is no inherent necessity for high wages and new job opportunities to be closely correlated. Institutional factors, migration costs and locational preferences inhibit migration, so that inter-regional wage equalisation will not be attained. Labour may also migrate for non-economic reasons, and if this is the case the direction of movement may be disequilibrating rather than equilibrating. Finally, in the long-run migration may have other effects additional to its influence on wages, for instance on consumption levels, social capital utilisation and regional growth – and these may boost income growth in the high income regions by raising the demand for labour by more than the increment to labour supply.

Despite these qualifications, labour probably moves more easily than capital. The convergence hypothesis requires, firstly, that the marginal return to capital is higher in low income regions and, secondly, that capital is mobile enough to seek these higher returns.

There is no guarantee that either requirement will be met. In the simple model referred to above, low income regions offer the higher returns to capital because of the negative correlation between wages and the marginal efficiency of investment. In a dynamic framework, however, the marginal efficiency of investment schedules in each region may be continuously changing because of technical changes, inter-regional variations in demand, changes in expectations, and differences in replacement investment demand. These changes may work in favour of high income regions. For instance, it was shown in Chapter 12, Section 4 that innovations and technical progress are not spread evenly throughout a regional system but will tend to perpetuate the agglomeration advantages of currently prosperous regions. There are several reasons for this: to the extent that technical progress is 'embodied', such regions may have an industrial composition favourable to technological advance; the main innovational route may be down the urban hierarchy so that if the level of urbanisation is higher in these regions, they may have a greater capacity to accept technical change; the recipients of new techniques, i.e. high calibre managers, may be disproportionately concentrated in high income regions. Moreover, even if marginal returns to capital are higher in low income regions, the capital market may be too inefficient for capital to flow there. High income regions will generate more savings as a result of higher incomes and (possibly) higher propensities to save, but these savings may still be invested in the home region because of 'psychic income' factors and/or overestimation of agglomeration economies.

Even within the context of the comparative statics model discussed above, factor flows may cease to be equilibrating if we relax two assumptions of the model – a single commodity and regionally identical production functions. These relaxations provide additional reasons why high wage regions may grow faster than the low wage regions. Their production functions may be such as to yield higher marginal products of labour; higher capital-labour ratios mean higher output per worker, and therefore higher wages. Increasing capital intensity may more than offset any equalising effects of in-migration. More important, in a disaggregated model changes in the composition of national demand may favour the export products of a high income region, so that it grows faster because of an export boom and favourable terms of trade for its products sold in national markets. To consider the simplest case, assume a two-region economy consuming only two goods, and let each region specialise fully in the production of one of the goods. A progressive change over time in the composition of final output, reflecting perhaps a difference between the two goods in respect to income elasticity of demand, would tend, *ceteris paribus*, to alter the relative rates of growth of labour demand in the two regions and thereby increase the relative level of income per worker in the region specialising in the good favoured by the shift. Capital will also tend to accumulate at a faster rate in this region.

The generalisation thrown up by these arguments is that the introduction of dynamic elements, such as differential rates of population growth, technical changes, changes in consumption patterns, and so on, may abort the conclusions drawn from the static model that factor flows will equalise returns to factors between regions. Dynamic factors achieve this result in two ways: firstly, by giving rise to disequilibrating factor movements; secondly, and more commonly, by operating in such a way as to offset or outweigh equilibrating factor movements. The point is that though dynamic forces do not inevitably work in favour of divergence, at the same time they 'contain no inherent bias in the direction of convergence.[21] As a final illustration, we may mention the effects of locational shifts in industry. Suppose a progressive shift in the location of a given industry took place in favour of certain regions, because of relative input-output access advantages. This shift would tend to raise workers' wages in the gaining regions because of favourable changes in the rates of growth of labour demand. Intertemporal shifts in favour of high wage regions would offset any tendencies to convergence in regional levels of income per worker fostered by immigration into these regions.

Inter-regional factor mobility neither ensures full convergence of *per capita* incomes nor is it the only possible source of convergence. These two points may be considered in turn. Let us leave aside all the problems and difficulties discussed in the preceding paragraphs and assume that factor-price equalisation (for *homogeneous* factors) is achieved between all regions. Does this equalise regional *per capita* incomes? No, except under extreme assumptions. Even if returns to homogeneous factors are equalised, inter-regional wage differences

---

[21] Easterlin, R.A. (1958) Long Term Regional Income Changes: Some Suggested Factors. *Papers and Proceedings of Regional Science Association*, **4**

will persist because of the lack of homogeneity in labour. In a multi-sector economy, workers of different groups will receive different real wages even in long-run equilibrium. Inter-regional wage differences will reflect differences between regions in their occupational structures, in the ratio of skilled to total workers, and in their employment structures, because of other heterogeneity elements such as sex and colour. Behind these variations in the structure of the labour force lie differences in industrial composition and in the degree of urbanisation. Secondly, labour participation rates may vary between regions because of differences in unemployment and in the ratios of labour force to total population. In the United States, however, a reduction in inter-regional differences in labour force participation rates has been a factor promoting convergence in *per capita* incomes. Thirdly, even if all factors receive the same rate of return, *per capita* incomes may still differ if wealth owners are regionally concentrated – in other words, if the residents of some regions own a greater *per capita* volume of resources than residents in others. In so far as regional income differentials are a function of the location of the residences of property owners, convergence will not take place.

In addition to inter-regional factor mobility, another major source of convergence is the intra-regional reallocation of resources from low wage to high wage industries. In the aggregate theory, the growth of the real wage was associated with an increase in the regional capital-labour ratio; in a disaggregated model average real wages may increase as a result of a reallocation of the region's output in favour of capital-intensive sectors. In particular, much of the difference in incomes between regions may be traced to different proportions of resources employed in agriculture. As agriculture is a low income industry with a low capital-labour ratio in many regions, intra-regional resource movements out of agriculture into other industries can raise average income per head.[22] The scope for convergence through intra-regional reallocation is consequently much greater in agricultural regions, and this might explain a tendency for such regions to experience higher rates of growth of *per capita* income.

A final possible factor in *per capita* income convergence could arise from the phenomenon of economic maturity in high income regions. Thus, because of inherent retardation tendencies the growth rates of

[22] For a formal analysis see Borts and Stein, *op. cit.*, 25–34

certain regions might fall off after a lengthy period of development. For instance, it might be argued that there is a relationship between the age of manufacturing industry in a region and its growth rate. Income growth in an old-established manufacturing region may slow down or cease altogether because of a decline in entrepreneurial dynamism or a slowing down in the rate of growth of demand for old products combined with high transition costs inhibiting the development of new industries. The value of these arguments is unclear. The decline of entrepreneurship with an industry's age is more of a cliché than either a well-established fact or a theoretical prediction. Barriers to entry in new industries are not necessarily higher in mature than in other regions. Moreover, experience in production may bring about more technological change, and an assessment of retardation tendencies in mature regions depends on a relative evaluation of the early-start thesis compared with learning theory.

Another hypothesis is that old regions inevitably slow down as they exhaust their external economies and agglomeration effects. A major objection to this is that exhaustion of external economies does not mean that new firms are denied the use of existing social capital and the range of service facilities available in an area, it only means that costs cannot be reduced further as a result of scale expansion. Even weaker are the suggestions that high local taxes and heavy unionisation in mature regions will discourage new industry on which future growth depends. Old regions are not necessarily more heavily unionised than new, and even if they are, their unions may be less rather than more militant than those in new areas. Moreover, if local taxes are higher in mature regions (a proposition that needs to be established) private industry may nevertheless be attracted by high levels of social expenditures.

If there is substance in the maturity hypothesis, it is probably to be found in the forces making for convergence that have already been considered. Thus, growth in an old-established region may stagnate because the potentialities of sectoral shifts from low to high return industries have been exhausted. Moreover, labour supply in such regions may be highly inelastic because of limited scope for rural-urban migration in highly urbanised regions so that regional population growth is determined by lower urban net reproduction rates. This may be exacerbated by national immigration controls restricting an increase in labour supply from overseas sources. A marked retardation in the growth of labour supply may have a multiplier repercussionary effect on regional growth because it may be associated with slower technological change. These two factors could explain why industries in mature regions often grow much more slowly than their national counterparts.[23]

Our analysis has indicated several theoretical explanations for the possible convergence of regional *per capita* incomes, and has also suggested reasons why such a convergence process would, almost certainly, be incomplete. In conclusion, it is appropriate to refer to the broad results of empirical investigations into the long-run relative *per capita* income behaviour of United States regions.[24] These all point to a clear trend towards *per capita* income equalisation since 1880, though the rate of convergence was often unsteady and occasionally reversed itself, as in the 1920s. The convergence process exhibited certain characteristics: the 'pulling down' of high income regions towards the national average (mainly as a result of immigration) was more evident than the 'pulling up' of low income regions; equalisation was far from complete, and indeed the rank order of both States and multi-state regions according to *per capita* income changed very little over the period; the paths to rising incomes were varied, since in some states rapid population growth and economic expansion went together (the Far West, South-West, Florida, Virginia and the eastern Great Lakes states) while, at the other extreme, some states made substantial *per capita* income gains despite a declining population (Oklahoma, Arkansas and Mississippi).

As for the causes of convergence, inter-regional factor movements appeared less important than their emphasis in the theoretical literature might suggest. Easterlin's data showed little convergence in agricultural wages between regions in the period 1880–1950, and although non-agricultural wages converged the tendency was not strong. PDLM supported this, by showing a moderate fall in the relative variation of wage income *per capita* between 1920 and 1950 but a widening of absolute differentials. Immigration into fast-growing, high income regions, however, held their *per capita* income growth in check. More significant convergence forces were declining

---

[23] It should be clear from the analysis of the preceding section that we do not attach much significance to an unfavourable industrial composition as a major cause of maturity characteristics

[24] For more details the sources cited on p. 348 n. 16 should be consulted.

inter-regional differences in property income *per capita* and a marked steady convergence in regional non-agricultural/total employment ratios. Inter-regional differences in property income per head were large (for instance, in 1950 the level in Delaware was approximately nine times greater than in Mississippi), and convergence between 1880 and 1950 was strong. However, since property income accounted for only one-eighth of total personal income its impact on *per capita* income differentials was modest. The evidence suggested that the dominant factor behind differential changes in regional *per capita* income throughout the period 1880–1950 was changes in the relative importance of agricultural and manufacturing employment within each region. *Per capita* income increased most in states where the agricultural labour force share fell most, and the tendency to *per capita* income growth was even stronger in those states with the fastest growing manufacturing labour force shares. Some high income states grew more slowly because their scope for improving their internal allocation of resources was severely constrained. Inter-regional factor movements, the regional distribution of property income and the efficiency of intra-regional resource allocation all require analysis in any test of the convergence of *per capita* income hypothesis.

Chapter 14
Policy objectives and efficiency

In this chapter we deal with three separate topics. In Section 1 we show how a decision model may provide a convenient framework for regional policymaking. Such a model recognises the constraints and conditions of uncertainty within which the policymaker operates. We also briefly consider the scope and limitations of linear programming techniques in a regional policy.

In Section 2 we examine the problems arising from the formulation of policy goals, and illustrate the potential conflicts between regional and national interests, between the objectives of an individual region and other regions in a system, and between economic efficiency and equity goals.

Finally, in Section 3 we explore the relationship between different targets in a regional stabilisation policy and the types of expenditure programmes need to achieve them.

1 A framework for policy

A *Decision models*
The general analytical framework for the theory of regional policy is best represented by a decision model. Such a model recognises that there are limits to the control that policymakers can exercise, and consequently cannot predict precisely the results of policy measures; at best, it can only indicate a range of possible results. In other words, decision models deal with the problems of policymaking in conditions of uncertainty.

A simple form of decision model can be expressed as follows:

$$z = A(p, x, r)$$

where z = variables describing the set of *outcomes*.
p = set of *instrumental variables*.

x = set of *extraneous variables*.
r = set of *stochastic influences*.
A = set of rules describing the correspondence between the predetermined (independent) variables and the set of outcome (dependent) variables.

While z and p, x and r are vectors, A is the matrix of the economic structure of the region that links them.

Policymakers are concerned with p, the instrumental variables. These are the independent controllable variables (such as the amount of government investment in a region's infrastructure, the methods of taxation, the extent of government subsidies, etc.) that can be manipulated by the governments concerned to influence the rate and character of economic development in the region. The region's development can be quantified in terms of basic economic categories – production, consumption, investment, external trade. The aim of policy is to choose the appropriate instrumental variables and the proper values for them so as to achieve the most favourable outcome, a particular value for z. The instrumental variables do not have to be confined to the measures already in use. A decision model may act as a substitute for actual experiments by analysing the implications for regional economic activity of various possible instruments, e.g. different kinds of taxes or investment incentives.

Unfortunately for policy formulation, the set of outcomes is not the result of the instrumental variables alone as worked out through the structural matrix. Extraneous variables (x) and stochastic factors (r) also influence regional economic activity, and the policymaker has to attempt to take at least the first of these into account; the influence of r cannot because of the random nature of the variables be predicted. r represents the residual content of regional activity that cannot be explained by changes in the instrumental variables and in the extraneous variables that are specified. The value of the decision model for the regional planner depends, of course, on the assumption that the effect of changes in r is quite small. The extraneous variables, however, will be important elements in the model, and it is in estimating their value that the most serious predictive errors are likely to be found. The extraneous variables refer to changing economic conditions (and also relevant political and social factors) in the country as a whole and in the world – in other words, external to the region. The variables are described as 'extraneous' in the sense that the model does not take account of repercussions upon them from intra-regional changes. They include completely exogeneous elements such as the level of world demand for a particular commodity, but they could also include factors involving government decisions where these decisions are motivated by considerations that can make no allowance for regional implications – for example, the level of the central government's defence spending. Values for extraneous variables are not easily obtained, and sometimes the policymaker may have to make estimates that are little more than informed guesses.

The matrix A shows how the development of the region, as expressed in the set of outcomes, is linked to the instrumental and extraneous variables. It represents the structural relations that link the main elements in the regional system, and which have to be obtained from empirical research. Such links include the technical coefficients that quantify input-output connections, inter-regional trade propensities, the consumption function, the capital/output ratio, and so on.

If we have worked out the structural coefficients that are categorised in A, and if we have assigned values to the extraneous variables, x, then we can engage in regional planning by adjusting values for the instrumental variables in a manner which throws up a set of outcomes, z, which is consistent with our basic objectives. The different elements in the decision model will normally be expressed as a set of mathematical relationships. However, these relationships do not necessarily have to be formulated as equations. In certain circumstances the model will contain inequalities that enable us to set precise limits on the extent to which some of the variables, usually the dependent variables, can change in value. Another point is that it is difficult to place values on the instrumental variables unless the goals of policy are clearly defined. This raises the complex question of goal specification which is treated in more detail below.

Although a decision model is very often a programming model, this is not inevitable. In a programming model we commit ourselves to an optimising technique, where we maximise some index of welfare or growth or minimise the real costs of achieving a certain objective subject to certain specified constraints. The drawbacks of this type of model is that the goals it can attempt to achieve are often very narrow (i.e. they must be precisely measurable), and the fact that it cannot adequately deal with a complex set of multiple goals, since its basic technique is to optimise in line with the primary goal at the expense of relegating subsidiary goals to constraints.[1] But a decision model need not take this form. A simpler perhaps more realistic approach is to specify a number of quite separate goals, but to express these neither as maxima nor minima but simply as targets, i.e. levels of attainment. The policymaker's function is then simply to deploy and assign values to the required instrumental variables in a manner that ensures that these target goals are achieved. This is not too difficult provided the policymaker follows the golden rule that for each goal he requires a separate instrumental variable. If a region aims at seven different goals, then its policy formulators must draw upon seven instrumental variables, no more and certainly no less.

B *Linear programming*[2]

Resource scarcities make it inevitable that economic activity is built up at a limited number of more efficient locations, and it is this spatial imbalance that results in depressed regions. Linear programming is quite a suitable technique for dealing with problems of resource scarcity. It enables us to find out how to make the **best** use of the limited endowment of resources in either an inter-regional or in a regional setting, depending on the area under study. Linear programming is, therefore, an optimising technique. At the same time, and this is another reason why it is useful, it does not force us to plan on efficiency grounds alone. Policy objectives, even of a social and non-economic nature, can be incorporated into a programme by translating them into constraints on the programme. Thus, the programme optimises only within the limits set by these constraints. In this manner, linear programming facilitates a clearer and broader definition of basic goals than other analytical techniques.

Linear programming relates to problems where the objective is to maximise or minimise some linear function (called the *objective*

---

[1] However, a programming model can sometimes deal with the maximisation of multiple goals, where the number of goals is few and the goals are closely related. See Leven, C.L. (1964) Establishing Goals for Regional Economic Development. *Journal of the American Institute of Planners*, **30**

[2] The brief observations here do not include a technical treatment. For surveys of linear programming in general see Spivey, W. Allen (1963) *Linear Programming: An Introduction*; Dorfman, R., Samuelson, P.A. and Solow, R.M. (1958) *Linear Programming and Economic Analysis* and Garvin, W.W. (1960) *Introduction to Linear Programming*. For a technical discussion of linear programming in a regional context see Isard, *Methods ..., op. cit.*, 413–92

function), subject to certain linear inequalities (the *constraints*). Although in regional economics, maximising the sum of regional incomes is perhaps the most common objective of a programme, this is only one of many possibilities. Other examples of objectives include: maximising the growth rate of one or more regions, maximising *per capita* incomes in a region or in the nation as a whole, maximising new employment opportunities; minimising transport costs in inter-regional trade, minimising labour input or minimising total production (including transport) costs. Moreover, it is analytically practicable to draw up a programme comprising several different development goals. Although the objective function will then be rather more complex than the functions needed for simple objectives like those outlined above, it is feasible if the objectives can be stated in a linear function and if the problem of how to allocate weights to each objective is solved.

The constraints on the objective function may take various forms. The most obvious are, of course, resource constraints due to natural resource limitations or to restricted supplies of labour or intermediate goods. Such constraints emphasise the relevance of input–output analysis to linear programming. Also important are minimum standard constraints such as minimum levels of consumption,[3] or minimum acceptable levels of, or rates of decrease in, unemployment. The planners may attach some importance to reducing severe cyclical swings, and for this reason a stability constraint (for example, limiting the proportion of durable production in total output) may be added. Other possibilities include locational efficiency and 'mass behaviour-attitude' constraints. The first involves ensuring that fulfilment of a programme is subject to some specified efficiency criteria. The second refers to a much more intangible category of constraints, relating to factors such as a region's resistance to industrialisation, unwillingness to tolerate substantial rates of out-migration, traditional behaviour by a region's entrepreneurs. Constraints of this kind may be very important in reality, but they are not easily quantified and it is difficult to give them operational content. If a large number of these different kinds of constraint is imposed, they may be so restrictive that a programme proves insoluble. If this happens, the goals of the programme will have to be

[3] Alternatively, where the objective of the programme is to maximise consumption a net investment constraint may be imposed to maintain a specified minimum rate of growth

reformulated making them less ambitious. Ultimately a feasible programme can be established, that is, one that can realise the goals specified.

Although linear programming techniques are much more versatile than many other planning tools, they have quite serious limitations. The reliance on linear relationships is an obvious weakness. The assumption of linear production functions will be unsatisfactory especially where regional economies are dominated by decreasing-cost industries. Indeed, since linear theory is not normally capable of dealing with indivisibilities, varying returns to scale or with external economies and diseconomies, it is in some respects inappropriate for dealing with locational problems since returns to scale and externalities are often crucial in explaining why some areas rather than others expand. Another, but related, point is that linear programming often requires us to take existing regional patterns and structures as given. It does not guide us as to where new regional concentrations should be built up or where new social overhead capital should be constructed, yet these questions may be crucial in regional planning. Moreover, to the extent that economic growth is connected with increasing returns to scale, linear programming techniques cannot adequately handle long-term growth situations. Of course, the drawbacks associated with linearity assumptions would not arise if non-linear programming models were adopted. But the gain in conceptual precision would be more than outweighed by the loss in operational value. Moreover, the empirical difficulties that crop up in attempts to estimate external economies and diseconomies remain even if alternative planning techniques are employed.

Linear programming cannot easily handle relationships that are not quantifiable. Thus, the mass behaviour-attitude constraints referred to above can only be imposed if they can be translated into quantifiable terms. Similarly, a programming model cannot adequately take account of the effects of price changes and changes in the distribution of income, since this would require some kind of general welfare model involving comparison of personal preferences and utility schedules. But then it would be utopian to expect any operational planning model to consider all factors relevant to economic welfare. A more serious point is that it is difficult for linear programming to take account of household behaviour by introducing consumption activities explicitly into the model. For instance, most linear programming models assume demand to be price-inelastic.

This kind of assumption is partly consequent upon linearity (if consumer demand is a non-linear variable it cannot be handled by these models). But it is also explained by the need to specify a set of final product prices in advance in order to be able to carry out the computations of the programme, especially where many regions and many commodities are involved.

This need for advance specification of prices is another limitation of linear programming techniques. We require a set of finished product prices to solve a programme, yet if the technique is truly general initially hypothesising a set of final-product prices seriously narrows the scope for determining an optimal programme. Isard argues[4] that this problem is not intractable. Since planners will have considerable background information about likely consumption levels, they will not set final product prices inconsistent with their expectations of these levels. In addition, they may introduce further constraints (called *availability constraints*) that guarantee that the amount of each finished product available for consumption by households will achieve a certain level. From use of such constraints the planners may derive a set of subsidy prices which when added to the pre-assigned final product prices yield a set of adjusted final product prices. Once these adjusted prices are obtained, the model can be run without the availability constraints but with these new adjusted prices substituted for the original pre-assigned set. If it is still found that the resulting regional distribution of finished products available for household consumption is inconsistent with the levels of disposable income between regions, then the procedure may be repeated with new availability constraints. The planners in this way work towards a final set of prices that is consistent with their other research hypotheses and findings.

Apart from these, primarily conceptual, difficulties, the value of linear programming models depends on the extent to which they can be made operational. The most important task for planners is to scale models down to size so that numerical results can be achieved without, at the same time, neglecting basic interrelationships. If too many activities are involved models can easily become non-operational. The easiest way to avoid this danger is to supplement linear programming with other techniques (such as input–output analysis and comparative cost studies) in order to rule out activities that are

---

[4] Isard, *op. cit.*, 460–6

not feasible. Goals may have to be narrowed more than would be considered desirable in a theoretical approach in order to draw up a programme capable of solution. Finally, reliance on the **dual** may sometimes aid solution. Every linear programme expressed as a minimising function has a dual problem expressed in maximising terms, and *vice versa*. As a generalisation, planners would choose to solve the linear programme (the **primal**) or its dual, depending on which has the fewer constraints.

2 The consistency of policy goals

A *The national interest and regional objectives*

A rational regional policy should perform two broad functions. Firstly, it should help to promote growth in the national economy. Attempts to stimulate growth in a planned economy can scarcely avoid having a regional aspect. Desire for fast growth makes it necessary to compare the effects of expanding economic activity at alternative locations. It is impossible to decide how much to invest in certain sectors, pre-eminently transport and communications, without taking into account the present and expected future regional distribution of population and economic activity. Moreover, public investment decisions have often to be taken before private investment decisions. Assuming that social investment is relevant to growth, and if some of the obstacles to national growth are regional, a programme of social investment that discriminates between regions may increase the aggregate growth rate.

The second necessary function of a soundly based regional policy is to handle inequities resulting from large inter-regional disparities in indices of growth and welfare. This is obviously the concern of policymakers in lagging regions, but even a national preference function will include an equity as well as a growth component. The weight of the equity objective depends on economic conditions and the value system. For example, where regional differences in income per head are slight a national goal such as maximising *per capita* national income may be quite appropriate, but where these differences are wide the goal of narrowing them may receive higher priority. However, sensible application of equity goals in regional policies is difficult, even if (and these are big 'ifs') we assume that a region is a meaningful group of individuals for welfare purposes and that interpersonal comparisons are possible. For instance, acceptance of an income distribution goal does not necessarily provide blanket justification for subsidies to low income regions. A case in point is where private entrepreneurs in lagging areas are subsidised out of regressive taxes. Paradoxically, the result of policies adopted to raise incomes in depressed areas may be to benefit the rich in the poor regions at the expense of the poor living in rich ones.

Despite the relevance of equity criteria, the difficulties of quantifying precisely what is understood by 'national welfare' are so great that we may, as an approximation, have to equate the 'national interest' with efficiency. It can then be shown that there is no necessary consistency between regional and national objectives and that the two broad functions of a regional policy may conflict with each other. In particular, there may be antagonism between the objective of maximising real *per capita* national income and the aim of equalising (or at least bringing closer together) regional standards of living.

The trouble arises because the sum of maximised income per head in each region does not equal maximised national income per head, except in a world of perfect competition. Regional planners may implement measures to maximise regional income within a given region considered in isolation, but this may involve committing resources to uses that are inefficient from the national point of view. It is sometimes argued that a regional project is justified if the difference between national output with and without the project exceeds the costs of undertaking it. Apart from the difficulties of measurement, a criterion of this kind does not guarantee the most efficient use of resources. It would be more rational to compare the increment in output resulting from the project to the output increment resulting from all possible alternative uses of resources (including projects in other regions). Thus, in evaluating regional investment projects in terms of their costs and future benefits, we must consider the **opportunity cost** of an investment, as measured by returns to factors in alternative uses.

The potential conflicts can be illustrated with a simple example. Consider two industries A and B, and two regions 1 and 2. Industry B is more efficient in Region 1, while industry A is more efficient in Region 2. A is the more efficient industry nationally. Region 2 is the prosperous region, while Region 1 is stagnant. How does the planner make the optimal sectoral and regional investment decisions? If he chooses the industry first, he decides on A. Then he chooses the region, probably Region 1 on equity or social policy grounds. But this is inefficient. Suppose he decided on the priorities the other way around. First, he decides on the region – Region 1. Then he chooses the industry; obviously he chooses industry B which is more efficient in this region. In both cases, the opportunity cost, as measured by the return to investment in industry A in Region 2, is high. The planner's choices cannot be justified on efficiency grounds. This is despite the fact that national and regional planners are acting in accordance with a common criterion, i.e. to invest resources in the most efficient industries. But when, as here, the key industries in a region are not the key industries in the national economy, inconsistency between regional and national goals is inevitable.

If efficient resource allocation resulted in an approximate regional balance in economic activity and growth rates, the conflicts that emerged would be negligible enough to be overlooked. But the nature of the growth process itself rules this out. Regional growth is almost inevitably unbalanced: some regions are better endowed with resources than others; investment is lumpy, and many projects have to be undertaken on a large scale at a very limited number of locations (due to demand constraints) to be economic; external economies provide a strong motive for agglomerating industrial investment at selected locations; markets are not distributed evenly, and this results in inter-regional imbalance in transport developments and market-oriented industries. Thus, economic forces are likely to lead to growth being concentrated on a limited number of leading regions. Admittedly, the poorer regions may benefit from 'trickling down' effects (expanding exports of primary and intermediate goods, external finance of industries complementary to those in the rich regions, cheaper imports and job opportunities for their unemployed migrants), but the share of at least *some* regions in the benefits will be small.

The pursuit of unbridled efficiency irrespective of its regional consequences will have much less appeal to the regional than to the national planner. The former's concern will be primarily with the goals expressed in the regional community's preference function, and if the region lags behind the national economy in terms of economic growth the measures that he recommends are likely to be harmful to other regions; for example, devices to restrict migration may offset the development aims of other regions. Regions may lobby the central government for preferential treatment in government contracts, subsidies and public investment projects. Possible consequences are that public investment projects are allocated according to the degree of political heat created rather than on efficiency criteria or that they are dispersed among many regions at some cost in terms of scale economies foregone. The real possibility of antagonistic regional policies is so strong that severe limits must be placed on the decentralisation of regional planning. The responsibility must largely be placed in the hands of the national policymaker who must, in effect, act as an arbiter between regions.

Even if the ultimate responsibility of the central government is accepted by all, difficulties remain. The economic objectives pursued by regions will normally contain several variables, and the weighting of each variable may differ from region to region. With multidimensional goals, the differences in the preference functions of each region may make it most unlikely that these differences will automatically be resolved in a consistent ordering of these goals at the national level. For example, suppose three regions (A, B and C) agree on the priority of three objectives (X, Y and Z), but they give them different weights so that for Region A; $X>Y>Z$, for Region B; $Y>Z>X$ and for Region C; $Z>X>Y$. As it stands, no common ordering of goals can be obtained. Since Regions A and B say $X>Y$ and Regions B and C says $Z>X$, transitivity yields $Z>Y$. But Regions A and B say $Y>Z$, thus we have a fundamental contradiction. As Boudeville shows, however, the dilemma can be resolved. If the State intervenes as an arbiter and if a fourth objective is introduced without changing the ordering of the other three in any way, a solution is possible. Provided we give direct and indirect preferences the same weight, if three regions fail to agree on the ranking of objectives the State can intervene with a weight equal to the others and a different opinion, and make them agree.[5] The State may also act as a referee in solving other related problems. For example, suppose the regions of the system agree on a ranking of objectives, but need to be able to measure cardinally the different objectives in common terms so that an optimal programme can be drawn up for the regions as a whole. The State's function in this case will be to put forward a small number of alternative weightings of

[5] Boudeville, J. (1966) *Problems of Regional Economic Planning.* 131–5. The contradiction that may arise from multiple decision centres and multiple criteria is known as the *Condorcet paradox*. Domination matrices are the technique used to resolve this paradox. Boudeville gives a clear and simple demonstration

these objectives to the representatives of each region. In discussing these alternative proposals with a view to stating a preference for one, the regional policymakers will crystallise their opinions and normally be able to reach a decision.

The assumption of responsibility by the central government and its intervention as an arbiter may alleviate the danger of antagonistic regional policies, but it does not guarantee the consistency of optimal regional development with optimal national development. For instance, even in a straightforward case where all regions agree that maximising the growth of national income is the sole goal and where regions are prepared to put up with out-migration to achieve this goal, there are still problems. The population redistribution that results from regional differences in growth rates is not brought about without costs. Even if these costs are outweighed by social benefits through higher efficiency and output, the question remains how relocation costs are to be allocated between regions. The trouble is that each region's share in relocation costs does not necessarily equal its share in the gains, and those regions with an excess of costs over benefits are likely to take offsetting action. For example, a region faced with a large outflow of migrants, especially skilled and highly trained migrants, may find that expenditures incurred directly by the region on education and training these migrants who now make no direct contribution to raising regional output greatly outweigh any benefits gained. In this situation, the region might follow two courses of action both harmful to efficiency and to the agreed objective of maximising growth: steps may be taken to restrict out-migration with adverse effects on short-run growth, or the region might under-invest in human capital with deleterious consequences for long-run growth. This particular obstacle is not insuperable, for an obvious solution is for the central government to finance *all* educational, training and re-training expenditures. Nevertheless, the illustration is indicative of the general proposition that the sharing of the same economic goals by nation and regions does not ensure that what is best for the nation is also the best for each region.

It is clear, therefore, that there is no easy escape from the dilemma. If the maximum output for the sum of all regions (i.e. the nation) equals the sum of maximum outputs for each region only in perfect competition, one solution is to attempt to re-create, so far as is possible, the conditions of perfect competition in the real world. If we can assume that decision-making units (governments, firms, households and individuals) behave rationally in pursuit of a given objective (say, maximum income or maximum satisfaction) then the goal of overall efficiency is automatically maintained in a situation of general equilibrium among all the decision-making units, in which no single unit has any incentive to change. Whether the necessary readjustments to changing conditions and spontaneous return to equilibrium take place in a dynamic situation is another matter. But, on this kind of argument, the search for maximum efficiency in spatial allocation simply becomes a problem of simulating conditions under which general equilibrium continuously prevails.

This solution does not leave the government without a role, quite the reverse. It suggests that policymakers should reimpose the operation of market forces by using the price mechanism as a norm to channel resources into uses which maximise real income. Lefeber suggests the following three basic pricing rules: that the prices of goods must reflect real costs; that the prices of homogeneous goods should be the same at a given location and differ from place to place by the marginal cost of transportation; that the present discounted value of an investment at the optimal location should exceed, or be equal to, the present discounted value of the same project at any other location (a rule which takes some account of the important opportunity cost factor).[6]

The soundness of this thesis is not beyond dispute. It assumes that a stable dynamic general equilibrium is possible, and it further assumes that the price mechanism is an efficient spatial allocator. Indivisibilities (mainly in the form of economies of scale) throw doubt on the second assumption. Because of their existence, the marginal adjustments necessary to maintain the efficiency of the price mechanism as an allocator may not take place. By way of comment on the first assumption, it has to be recognised that interaction occurs between functionally linked but locationally separate economic activities. This means that the 'profit' (or 'utility') of any activity at any location depends on the way in which *all other* activities in the system are located. Thus, any slight change in conditions at one location not only affects profitability at that site but alters costs and revenues at every conceivable location. If we make the realistic assumption of spatial interaction between

[6] Lefeber, L. (1958) *Allocation in Space* and Regional Allocation of Resources in India. 18–29, in Rosenstein-Rodan, P.N. (edit) (1964) *Pricing and Fiscal Policies: A Study in Method*

different activities, then we cannot find a price system that will sustain equilibrium and preserve an optimal locational pattern.[7] This particular difficulty may be obviated by allowing for inertia in locational patterns, and explicitly introducing the fact that it costs money and time for firms and households to move from one location to another. But the recognition that fixed capital facilities may be immovable and that there are resistances to migration involves a major breach of the conditions that simultaneously optimise national and regional development.

Apart from these theoretical objections, there is the practical difficulty that enthronement of the price mechanism is unlikely to be accepted by those concerned with the welfare of chronically stagnant regions. The preference for the price mechanism as the spatial resource allocator stems, in fact, from one of two value judgments: either that the welfare of the group of individuals known as the region should be sacrificed to the welfare of the larger group known as the nation; or, a more extreme position, that both 'nation' and 'region' are meaningless concepts in welfare terms, and that free market forces not only allocate resources more efficiently but maximise the welfare of individuals. Those who hold different value judgments may demand a different method of handling regional problems.

One alternative solution is to seek a compromise between the pursuit of national efficiency and attention to regional problems, thereby balancing growth and equity considerations. This may involve subjugating independent regional planning to a national decision model, the aim of which is to maximise some index of national economic welfare (e.g. real *per capita* national income) within certain regional constraints. For instance, the model may state that the performance of any region in relation to any particular goal should not fall below a specified level (a **minimum attainment constraint**). Another possibility is that a constraint be imposed on regional growth rates so that the slowest growing region grows at least as fast as the aggregate economy. This is easily inserted into a programming model, though it may be difficult to achieve in practice. For example, assume there are four regions (numbered 1 to 4) with growth rates g_1, g_2, g_3 and g_4. Their weights in terms of

[7] For an attempt to deal with this problem see Koopmans, T.C. and Beckmann, M.J. (1957) Assignment Problems and Location of Economic Activities. *Econometrica*, **25**

income are given by x_1, x_2, x_3 and x_4, where $x_1+x_2+x_3+x_4=1$. We assume that $g_1>g_2>g_3>g_4$. Region 4 is the poorest region, it grows most slowly and hence its growth rate is inferior to the national rate. The aggregate rate of growth G is equal to $(x_1g_1+x_2g_2+x_3g_3+x_4g_4)$. The constraint we wish to impose is that Region 4 grows at least as fast as the nation, in other words that $g_4 \geqslant G$. If we add this constraint to the programme, it becomes $x_1g_1+x_2g_2+x_3g_3+(x_4-1)g_4 \leqq 0$. A third alternative is not to impose direct regional constraints but instead to impose a national constraint on a national planning model where this constraint has desired regional effects. For example, where the depressed regions in the economy are agricultural regions, an appropriate constraint might be a specified relative increase in rural income per head – a national constraint but with considerable regional repercussions.

The drawback of handling regional problems with constraints inserted in national level decision models is that the regional objectives that can be accommodated with this approach may be too broad. A severely depressed region may need to pursue several quite different objectives simultaneously and to deploy an array of policy instruments to deal with them. Although most of these policies may be implementable at the national level, in some cases the responsibility will fall upon regional policymakers and measures will have to be administered at the regional level. What about the potential conflict between national interests and regional objectives in these cases? The answer must be rather a pragmatic one. Although we only require one policy instrument for each objective, there will in most cases be several alternative policies that can be adopted to achieve each goal. In selecting from the different methods available to attain a given objective, we should choose the method that interferes least with the most efficient allocation of resources. In this way conflicts between regional policies and national efficiency can be kept at a minimum. Advocates of regional planning (as opposed to national planners who discriminate between regions to serve national ends) need not be asked to set aside their value judgments or to sacrifice their goals; but they have a duty to pay attention to efficiency criteria when they evaluate investment projects and select policy instruments.

B *Aggregate efficiency and inter-regional equity*

The foregoing analysis has drawn attention to the probability that regional policymakers will have to compromise between the pursuit of national efficiency and inter-regional equity. It has recently been shown how a quantitative trade-off can be made between efficiency and equity objectives.[8] If market forces maximise aggregate output, policies for greater inter-regional equity will reduce total output unless income redistribution can be achieved through lump-sum transfer payments. In practice, the available means of redistribution affect output through their influence on the incentive to work. Thus, conflict is likely between the two objectives and a compromise must then be made between them.

How can this be achieved? We assume a static economy, consisting of two regions. The national population, labour force and capital stock are given. We assume that a homogenous output is produced with the aid of two homogeneous inputs, labour and capital, and that both output and input can be measured in physical terms. We further assume that the output of every region is a function of inputs located physically within the region. With these assumptions, we can obtain isoquants of output for each region in a labour-capital space. Let the production functions have the properties that the marginal productivity of labour and capital >0, and that the marginal rate of substitution diminishes between the inputs. To simplify, we assume that capital in each region is owned solely by residents who own no other capital, and this allows *per capita* income to be derived by dividing the regional output by population. Moreover, if population is a constant multiple of the labour force, loci for equal *per capita* income can be drawn in the same labour-capital space as a set of radiating curves from the origin.

Figure 14.1 shows an Edgeworth box diagram (drawn as a square by representing the capital stock and labour force of Region 1 as percentages of the aggregate capital stock and labour force), with the origins of the two regions in diametrically opposite corners. By drawing isoquants of two regions and adding them for any inter-regional distribution of labour and capital, we obtain isoquants for aggregate output. A map of such isoquants is given in figure 14.1 with the output of each isoquant expressed as a percentage of the point of maximum aggregate output Z which is the competitive equilibrium. This is drawn as an interior efficiency point, a sufficient condition for which with Cobb–Douglas production functions is that

---

[8] Mera, K. Trade-off between Aggregate Efficiency and Inter-regional Equity: A Static Analysis. *Quarterly Journal of Economics*, **81** 658–74

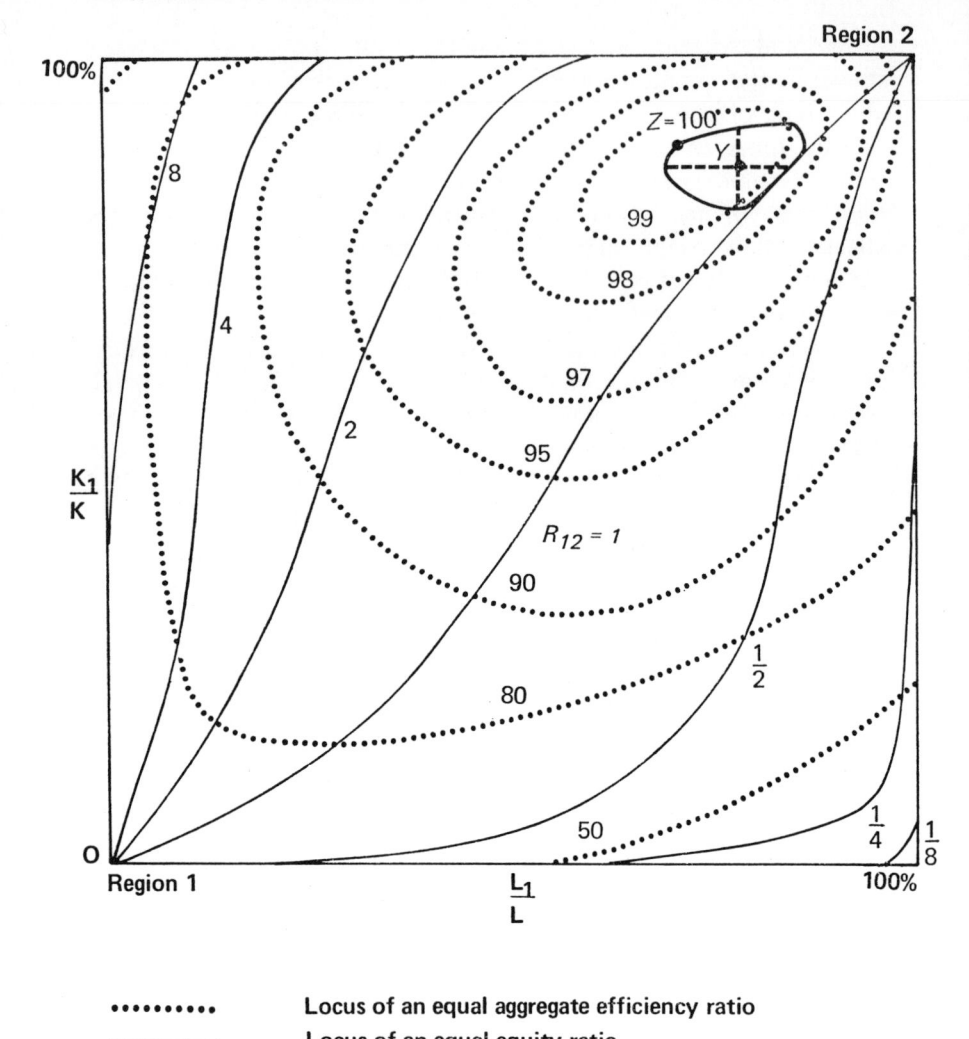

REGIONAL ECONOMICS

Figure 14.1

··········	Locus of an equal aggregate efficiency ratio
————	Locus of an equal equity ratio
▬▬▬▬	Transformation surface with mobile labour and capital
- - - - -	Transformation lines with one mobile and one fixed factor

the two production functions yield decreasing returns to scale. If Z is located near one corner of the box as in figure 14.1 this implies that the production functions of the two regions are different. If the actual distribution of labour and capital between the two regions is at Y, the deviation of Y from Z can be explained by market imperfections.

We can also map how income is distributed between the two regions. The ratio of *per capita* income of Region 1 to that of Region 2 may be called the equity ratio (R_{12}), and loci of equal equity ratios can be derived by superimposing loci of equal *per capita* incomes of the two regions in the same box diagram. Loci of equal equity ratios are a set of curves radiating from the origin of one region and converging into the origin of the other.

When the two box diagrams, relating to total output and the equity ratio, are superimposed, the implications of any regional distribution of labour and capital for efficiency and equity can be seen. The most efficient production point Z is not necessarily on the locus of $R_{12} = 1$. The reasons for this are that the regional distribution of capital ownership may be inequitable and that, even in a competitive equilibrium, rents from irreproducible and immobile factors (land, mines, etc.) are not equal. If Z does not lie on the curve $R_{12} = 1$, a compromise has to be struck between overall efficiency and inter-regional equity. If both labour and capital are redistributable, a transformation surface can be obtained by connecting points which give the maximum attainable aggregate output along every locus of a chosen range of different equity ratios. In figure 14.1 a transformation surface is drawn for a trade-off between maximum efficiency and perfect equity. If only one factor is mobile the transformation surface reduces to a line passing through the initial distribution point Y and parallel to the capital (labour) axis when capital (labour) is mobile. The three alternative transformation surfaces can be redrawn in efficiency-equity space with E measured on the vertical axis and R_{12} on the horizontal axis, where E (the efficiency ratio) is the ratio of the maximum aggregate output for a given value of R_{12} to the unconstrained maximum aggregate output.[9]

Mera shows that with either fixed coefficient or Cobb-Douglas production functions equality of the labour coefficients in the two regional production functions is the condition for a perfect solution, i.e. a distribution of inputs between the regions which satisfies simultaneously both the objectives of efficiency and equity. When there is no perfect solution, achievement of the complete inter-regional equity objective will necessitate some loss in efficiency. The efficiency ratio corresponding to perfect inter-regional equity can be

---

[9] For diagrams of alternative transformation surfaces see Mera, *loc. cit.*, 662, 666, 670, 671 and Table 1, p. 672

expressed as a function of the proportion of population in Region 1 and the ratio of regional *per capita* incomes at the maximum efficiency point:

$$E = \frac{1}{p_{1_z} R_{12_z} + (1 - p_{1_z})}$$

where $p_{1_z} = L_1/L$ and R_{12_z} is the equity ratio, and both are defined at Z, the point of maximum aggregate output.

In the fixed coefficients case, the efficiency ratio is smaller as the relative population size of the richer region at Z is larger. The reason for this is that inter-regional equity can be achieved in this case only by reducing *per capita* income in the rich region towards the level of the poorer region. This is not necessarily so with Cobb-Douglas production functions; an additional factor affecting the efficiency ratio with production functions of this type is the order of homogeneity of production.

The general conclusions drawn from the analysis are not very striking, but then it is the methodology which is important. These conclusions can be summarised as: (1) transformation surfaces between efficiency and equity can be derived if regional production functions are known; (2) the cost of efficiency is greater the wider is inter-regional disparity in *per capita* incomes at the efficiency point; (3) the cost of efficiency is smaller with Cobb-Douglas, where factor substitution is possible, than with fixed coefficient production functions; (4) if Cobb-Douglas functions are more realistic than fixed coefficients, then population redistribution is superior to capital redistribution as a means of achieving inter-regional equity (except in cases where p_{1_z} is relatively small and the degree of homogeneity of the production functions is close to unity).

C *Compatibility of inter-regional goals*

We now present a methodology which enables us to compromise between two regions pursuing a single objective (compatibility of inter-regional goals), though with modifications the technique could be used to handling two objectives in a single region (compatibility of intra-regional goals). The scarcity of resources in the national economy (assumed here to be a system of two regions) makes it impossible to maximise an index of welfare or growth in one region without paying attention to the level reached in the other. We can, however, set up a programme which maximises in one region subject to several levels of attainment in the other region (imposed as a set

POLICY OBJECTIVES AND EFFICIENCY

of constraints); the procedure is then repeated, but now we maximise in the second region subject to certain specified levels attained in the first.

Let us assume that the objective is to maximise gross regional product (*GRP*). We may write the aim of the programme:

1. To maximise: GRP$_1$, subject to GRP$_2 \geq y_1$ or GRP$_2 \geq y_2$ or GRP$_2 \geq y_3$...

We maximise GRP in Region 1, subject to certain target levels in Region 2 being achieved. Next we take a series of target levels for GRP$_1$, and maximise GRP$_2$. We therefore write:

2. To maximise: GRP$_2$, subject to GRP$_1 \geq x_1$ or GRP$_1 \geq x_2$ or GRP$_1 \geq x_3$...

If we plot the results, we obtain what is, in effect a map of production possibilities *ABCDEFGH* as shown in figure 14.2. Each point on the boundary represents some particular combination of levels of GRP in each region with full employment of resources in the system as a whole. The different combinations may be achieved by the implementation of particular policy measures by the government, making resources (labour and capital) flow from one region to the other.

The shape of the curve in the diagram needs a little explanation. It bends back at both ends towards the origin to stress the marked complementarities in inter-regional growth. 'Spillover' effects from regional expansion are assumed to be large, so that relatively high income levels in both regions are more conducive to growth because of the opportunities they present for inter-regional economic intercourse. If, however, we were to maximise GRP$_1$ while holding GRP$_2$ at a very low level, the severe limitations imposed on inter-regional trade would restrain income expansion in Region 1. A second reason why the curve may bend back is the existence of essential *non-transportable* resources located in one but not both regions. It is clear from the diagram that programmes that yield GRP$_1 \geq \bar{x}$ and GRP$_2 \geq \bar{y}$ are preferable to those that fail. It follows that the relevant portion of the curve is the line *CDEF*. All points on this line represent alternative levels of GRP$_1$ and GRP$_2$ that are technically equivalent as optimal, in the sense that no resources are wasted if some point on *CDEF* is chosen. However, the relative productivity of the two regions changes along this line. Between *C* and *D*, for example, Region 2 is more productive than Region 1, since as resources are

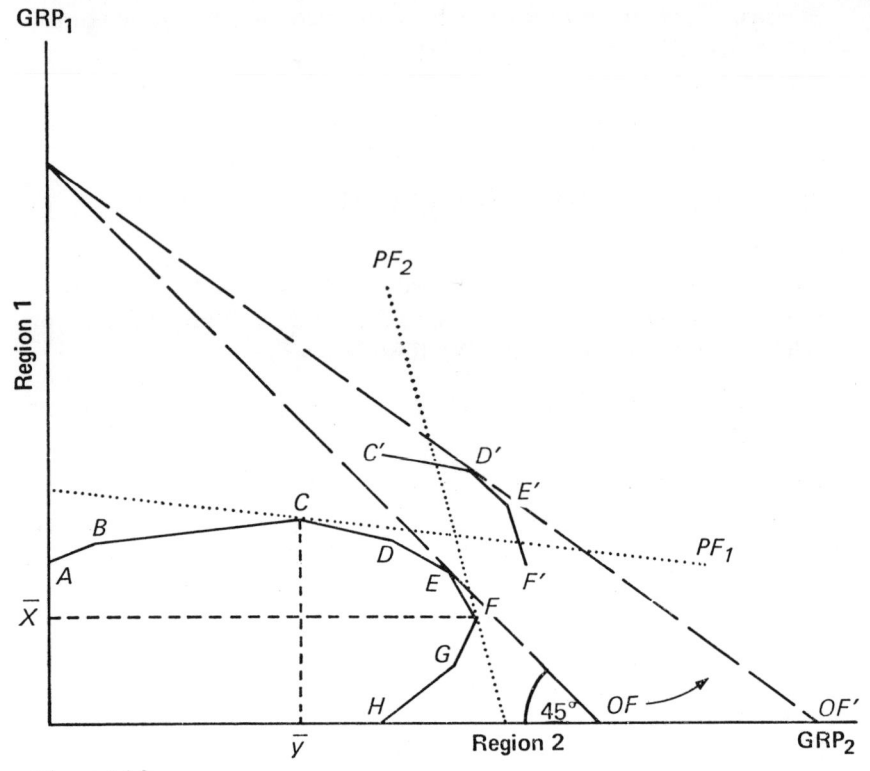

Figure 14.2

transferred from the latter to the former GRP_2 expands much faster than GRP_1 falls; conversely, between E and F, Region 1 is more productive than Region 2.

The policymaker's task is to select the planning programme that is in line with some preferred solution between C and F. The optimal allocation may be guided by the objective function or by society's preference function. Let us assume that the objective function measures short-run social costs and benefits, and that these show that from a social point of view society is indifferent as to whether growth is concentrated in Region 1 or Region 2. The slope of the objective function is therefore 45° (OF) and the optimal programme is E. However, the optimal programme may not be decided by the objective function, but instead by a process of political bargaining or decision-making which implicitly, at least, gives arbitrary weights to the objectives of each region and to national objectives. The result of such a process may be that policymakers lean in favour of one region and against the other. In other words, the nation arbitrates between the views and aims of each region with the result that the planning programme considered optimal is decided not by the objective function (which accords with the national interest by indicating the programme with the highest social benefit/cost ratio) but by a preference function. If the preference function has the slope PF_2, then Region 2 is strongly favoured, and the optimal programme is denoted by F (which maximises GRP_2). A preference function having a slope PF_1, on the other hand, favours expansion in Region 1, and the optimal point is C which permits the maximum possible level of GRP_1.

Even if the programme is determined by the objective rather than a preference function, it may nevertheless be biased in favour of one region. There is no inherent necessity why the objective function should have a slope of 45°. Thus, in figure 14.2, if we consider the long-term rather than the short-term situation, the production possibilities and the objective choices both change. The boundary of production possibilities shifts outwards to $C'D'E'F'$, representing an increase in the stock of resources and/or a rise in productivity over time. It is possible, moreover, for the slope of the objective function to change in the long run. For example, in the long run the social costs of congestion in Region 2 may be very great. Alternatively, assuming $GRP_2 > GRP_1$ and if market forces lead to a widening of inter-regional income differentials, the long-run consequence might be a deterioration in the relative income of Region 1 so great that it imposes a social cost on the nation as a whole. The long-run objective function may, as a result, swing upwards from OF to OF', so that the long-run optimal programme is marked by D'. This means a greater planning emphasis on Region 1 than if the slope of the objective function had remained constant despite the switch from short-run to long-run considerations (in which case the optimal point would have been E'). This conclusion suggests that the long-run planning horizon of policymakers may require a different allocation of resources between regions than either the short-run planning horizon or the private investment horizon (which is also characteristically short run).

3 Regional stabilisation policy

Stabilisation of regional economic activity can be regarded as an important objective in regional policy. There are three different approaches to the problem. Firstly, we could attempt to make weak regions more stable by diversifying their industrial base. But the assumption behind such an attempt, that the amplitude of cycles is narrower in diversified regions, may be false. There may be substantial benefits in specialisation for regions no less than for nations, and these should not be sacrificed lightly. A second possibility is to take steps to shield lagging unstable regions from the restrictive effects of national economic policies. Such measures might include inter-regional interest rate differentials, exempting individuals and firms in certain regions from tax increases and not applying direct controls on bank lending, building licences, etc., to selected regions. However, this approach may seriously weaken the impact of national policies, distort the allocative mechanism or be ineffective because regions cannot be treated as separate watertight compartments.

The third line of attack is more promising. This is a regionally-oriented stabilisation policy based on fiscal measures. It may improve the efficiency of national stabilisation measures, but it is difficult to implement. Inter-regional spillovers of expenditure changes make it very hard for policymakers to assess the precise consequences of their measures. Moreover, in practice, a multi-tier system of fiscal units, each levying taxes and handling individual expenditure budgets, each performing a variety of separate but interrelated functions and each acting independently of one another, make the organisation and administration of a regional stabilisation policy complex and hard to achieve.

As a generalisation, the central government must take full responsibility for a regional stabilisation policy. The causes of regional variations in economic activity are mainly national in origin, and the solutions to the problems resulting from these variations require a nationally-determined regional policy. Local governments lack the necessary financial resources, and firms and individuals can, in extreme cases, avoid the measures of sub-national governments by moving outside their jurisdiction. Attempts by individual regions to cure their own unemployment may lead, because of huge spillovers, to unpaid-for benefits enjoyed by other regions. Most important of all, regions acting independently of each other may implement programmes that result in an excessive increase in aggregate demand. For these reasons, the central government should take control. But local governments may be given some functions to perform under central authority, and can be very useful as administrative organisations responsible for implementing programmes financed by the central government. Moreover, if income within a region increases as a result of the central government's policies this may permit a rise in the level of local government expenditures.[10] Provided that marginal propensities to consume in the private sector are less than unity, local government expenditures will reinforce the stabilisation policies of the central government.

Leaving aside the practical difficulties in the operation of regionally-oriented stabilisation policies, we shall illustrate theoretically the problems that arise in comparing the regional effectiveness of different stabilisation programmes. Attention will be confined to the effects of expenditure changes rather than tax changes. This is partly because of a desire for simplification. If tax changes involve variations in tax rates, then tax yields depend upon the income level in each region. If regional incomes vary, equal tax rate changes would result in different budget changes in each region. A consequential inference is that a desired distribution of income changes among regions would tend to be much harder to control via tax measures than via government expenditures.

Let us assume that employment bears a constant relation to income, so that targets expressed in terms of regional employment can be directly translated into income terms. Let us further assume an elementary system of two regions, Region 1 and Region 2, and employ the simplest form of Keynesian inter-regional trade model. There are no lags and no supply inelasticies (i.e. the effects of income expansion are traced out at constant prices), and no balance of payments constraints are imposed. The model is given by:

$$Y_1 = C_1 + I_1 + G_1 + X_1 - M_1 \qquad (1a)$$
$$Y_2 = C_2 + I_2 + G_2 + X_2 - M_2 \qquad (1b)$$
$$C_1 = m_{11} Y_1 \qquad (2a)$$
$$C_2 = m_{22} Y_2 \qquad (2b)$$
$$M_1 = X_2 = m_{21} (C_1 + I_1 + G_1 + X_1) \qquad (3a)$$
$$M_2 = X_1 = m_{12} (C_2 + I_2 + G_2 + X_2) \qquad (3b)$$

where Y = income, C = consumption, X = exports, M = imports, and I and G, both exogenous, equal investment and government

---

[10] Whether a rise actually takes place will depend on whether local governments operate balanced budgets, and on how their revenue is raised

expenditure. m_{11} and m_{22} are the marginal propensities to consume in the two regions, assumed constant and equal to the average propensities; m_{21} and m_{12} are the respective marginal (=average) propensities to import.

We may outline a number of alternative stabilisation targets. To appreciate whether and how these targets can be achieved, ratios can be drawn up in relation to each target which show how national or regional income is affected by a given change in government expenditures in one or both regions. These ratios can in turn be expressed in terms of the parameters of the model, the marginal propensities to consume and to import. Analysis of particular values for these parameters would then show the policymaker the appropriate regional distribution of expenditure changes required to achieve the chosen target. We can conceive of two different kinds of expenditure programme: the first refers to programmes where the marginal propensity to import from government expenditures is the same as from other expenditures; the second type, which we may call 'local-intensive' expenditure programmes, is where the policy is so designed that all initial expenditure is confined within the region (e.g. expenditures which utilise only locally produced goods and factors), and imports occur only in subsequent rounds of spending in the form of induced consumption. The procedure adopted for alternative targets is summarised in table 5.[11]

Target A, the maximum increase in national employment, does not require any differentiation between regions in government expenditures. It is suitable in cases where the national economy is below full employment but neither region is severely depressed. Target B, maximising employment in one region, is most relevant to stabilisation measures adopted by a single region in isolation. The sub-targets under Target C refer to alternative objectives of a regionally-oriented stabilisation policy. With these targets the regional distribution of employment is the critical factor. Target C (i) calls for an equal increase in employment in both regions, a reasonable aim if both regions are similarly depressed. With Target C (ii) employment expansions in both regions are again required, but policy-makers aim

[11] The following analysis relies on Engerman, S. Regional Aspects of Stabilisation Policy. 7–62, in Musgrave, R.A. (edit) *Essays in Fiscal Federalism* (Brookings Institution, 1965). See also Airov, J. (1967) Fiscal-Policy Theory in an Interregional Economy: General Interregional Multipliers and Their Application. *Papers and Proceedings of the Regional Science Association*, **19** 83–108

Table 5

Alternative regional stabilisation programmes

	(1) targets	(2) relevant ratios	(3) expenditure programmes with imports	(4) 'local-intensive' expenditure programmes
A	$\Delta E_1 + \Delta E_2$	*national income maximisation ratio* $$\frac{dY/dG_1}{dY/dG_2}$$	$$\frac{(1-m_{21})[1-m_{22}(1-m_{12})]+m_{21}(1-m_{12})}{(1-m_{12})[1-m_{11}(1-m_{21})]+m_{12}(1-m_{21})}$$	$$\frac{1-m_{22}(1-m_{12})-m_{21}m_{12}+(1-m_{12})m_{21}m_{11}}{1-m_{11}(1-m_{21})-m_{21}m_{12}+(1-m_{21})m_{12}m_{22}}$$
B	ΔE_1	*regional income maximisation ratio* $$\frac{dY_1/dG_1}{dY_1/dG_2}$$	$$\frac{1-m_{22}(1-m_{12})}{m_{12}}$$	$$\frac{1-m_{22}(1-m_{12})-m_{21}m_{12}}{(1-m_{21})m_{12}m_{22}}$$
C	$\Delta E_1 + \Delta E_2$, where $\frac{E_1}{E_2} = \alpha$ and (i) $\alpha=1$ (ii) $0<\alpha<1$ (iii) $\alpha=0$ (iv) $\alpha<0$	*inter-regional stabilisation 'spillover' ratio* $$\frac{dY_1/dG_1}{dY_2/dG_1}$$	$$\frac{(1-m_{21})[1-m_{22}(1-m_{12})]}{m_{21}(1-m_{12})}$$	$$\frac{1-m_{22}(1-m_{12})-m_{21}m_{12}}{(1-m_{12})m_{21}m_{11}}$$

at increasing employment more in one region than another. Targets C (iii) and C (iv) become relevant when some parts of the country remain depressed while other parts are in an inflationary situation; in C (iii) the aim is to increase employment in one region while holding it constant in the other, and C (iv) demands increases in employment in one region with decreases in the other.

Whether, with respect to each target, expenditure programmes should be concentrated in one region or both and whether programmes should be designed so as to close initial import leakages depend on the values of the parameters (the marginal propensities to consume and to import) given in columns 3 and 4. With Target A it makes no difference whether the expenditure programme involves imports or not. National income will be maximised when expenditures are concentrated in the region with the higher marginal propensity to consume. With Target B and a programme involving imports aimed at increasing Y_1 it is more efficient to make the expenditure in Region 1 if $(1-m_{22})(1-m_{12})>0$; the case for spending in Region 1 is strengthened with a local-intensive programme. The higher the ratio in $C.(2)$ the smaller is the spillover from expenditures made in Region 1 into Region 2. With a programme requiring imports, the ratio as given in $C.(3)$ is higher as m_{21} and m_{22} are smaller and as m_{12} is larger, but it is independent of Region 1's marginal propensity to consume. With a local-intensive programme ($C.(4)$) the spillover is less the smaller are m_{21}, m_{11} and m_{22} and the larger is m_{12}.

The above model can be modified and extended to make it more realistic. For instance, we might introduce lags in consumption and other expenditures behind income. This will affect the time path of policy changes. Thus, at any moment of time a larger percentage of the final income change will have occurred in the region in which government expenditure was made than in any other. The assumption of constant prices could also be relaxed. Now a sufficient increase in aggregate demand will raise prices in the region where expenditure occurs. Unless the demand for local output is price inelastic, this will raise the region's marginal propensity to import and this increase will, assuming that other regions have spare capacity, tend to eliminate unemployment in other regions of the system. In the two region model, the more similar the range of goods produced in both regions and the lower the transport costs, the smaller the increase in prices needed to raise the regional marginal propensity to import.

A final obvious point is that the efficiency of a regionally-oriented stabilisation policy depends on the values of the relevant marginal propensities. This is a question that requires empirical investigation. Here, it is sufficient to point out that Engerman's calculations from a simplified inter-regional input–output table relating to the United States[12] suggested that a high proportion of income increases resulting from a given expenditure injection is concentrated in the region in which it is made, with very limited spillovers. This finding, if it were generally valid, strongly indicates that regional selectivity makes stabilisation policy more efficient. However, the organisational problems and the political constraints involved in implementing such a policy remain immense.

[12] Adapted from Moses, L.N. (1955) The Stability of Inter-regional Trading Patterns and Input–Output Analysis. *American Economic Review.* **45** 803–32

Chapter 15

The strategy of regional policy

1 Alternative strategies for problem regions

A *Introduction*

In the previous chapter we discussed the principles of regional development policies in terms of the advantages and limitations of regional decision models and programming models, the relationship of the pursuit of regional objectives to national efficiency, the problems of inter-regional planning and the rationale of a regional stabilisation policy. Something should also be said about the broad direction of regional policy, particularly about the long-standing controversy of whether problem regions should be dealt with by inducing out-migration of labour or by attracting capital and industry into the region or by a combination of both. At first sight, this appears to switch attention from inter-regional policy framed by the central government in which regional measures are judged on the extent to which they serve national ends to the notion of an economic development programme (or set of measures) for a single region that could be undertaken as easily by regional authorities as by the central government itself. Such an impression is quite false. Regional plans and policies must be conceived with respect to both national and regional goals, and single objective programmes are very rare. If left alone to pursue purely intra-regional objectives, a regional authority would optimise for its own area in a way which might conflict with the legitimate objectives of surrounding regions, for example, by applying measures which limit benefit spillouts but stimulate benefit spillins and cost spillouts. Where central government funds are made available, these may be dissipated in inter-regional competition in which success may reflect the degree of public relations and promotional gimmicks adopted rather than the efficiency of resource allocation. Although sub-national bodies should be encouraged to participate in, and indeed initiate, policies that might improve the economic position of their areas, if only because interest in local area problems might stimulate self-help and internal solutions to their difficulties, the ultimate responsibility must rest with the central government. Thus, a development plan for an individual region geared to a single regional objective, such as raising the level of income *per capita* by a certain percentage, will still need to take account of the national interest, either in the form of parallel national economic objectives in the plan itself or, more usually, as constraints. Accommodating the national interest seems an essential prior assumption for regional policies in a nation state, and if the reader disagrees with this assumption he is likely to dispute much of the analysis which follows.

To define a policy for a lagging region in terms of either encouraging out-migration or attracting in employment is to suggest crude answers to an oversimplified question. It assumes that the regional problem arises solely from local disequilibria in labour markets, and that an effective solution is to shift either population or employment opportunities (or both) so as to equate the supply and demand for labour in each region. But a regional policy may be concerned with objectives other than the elimination of regional unemployment, whether regional (such as raising average income levels or improving the region's economic 'activity mix') or national (such as accelerating the aggregate growth rate or narrowing income inequalities). Multiple objectives are probable, some of which may be non-economic goals such as preservation of open spaces and green belts or high priority may be given to satisfying the locational preferences of individual households. Multiple objectives are difficult to handle with economic analysis alone. Goal formulation may cause more headaches than the design of effective measures,[1] partly because of the difficulties of deciding on objectives, partly because of the potential conflict between them and partly because some goals may be non-economic and difficult to quantify. The advantages of an interdisciplinary approach are very great. These problems probably require the use of systems analysis. This would enable a decision-maker to choose development goals and a definite course of action more rationally, by systematically investigating his proper objectives and

---

[1] W.R.Thompson puts it this way: 'If we wander about in our area development programmes, it is probably as much due to not having picked destinations as to having poor road maps' (p. 83 in Hirsch, W.Z. (edit for C.R.A.) (1966) *Regional Accounts for Policy Decisions*)

comparing, with the aid of quantitative techniques, the costs, effectiveness and risks associated with alternative policies for achieving these objectives. During the analysis additional information requirements would emerge, and these would aid the design of future systems. The complex character of regional problems, conditions of uncertainty, the relevance of non-economic criteria and the probability of limited budget constraints, are all factors which make systems analysis a useful methodology for regional development policy. The technique almost certainly has a great future in regional economics, though its potential has hitherto been little exploited.[2]

Secondly, the simple 'labour-out – capital-in' choice implicitly assumes that all depressed regions face the same difficulties and share common characteristics. But economic conditions in a region may be less satisfactory than the national average for quite different reasons. For example, some regions lag behind the national economy because they are heavily industrialised in old-established stagnating sectors. Their dominant problems may be above-average unemployment, failure to develop sufficient new expanding activities and difficulties in the way of retraining and adapting the labour force. Other regions are problem areas because they rely heavily on primary production and are grossly underdeveloped. Their chief characteristics are likely to be low levels of income per head and a high rate of net emigration. Certain metropolitan regions may grow more slowly than the national average because intensive urbanisation limits population inflow and because a sizeable proportion of their resources has to be diverted into maintaining and replacing obsolete urban capital. Their main features may be traffic and other forms of congestion and the need for urban redevelopment and for overspill areas. The diagnosis of the troubles of these different types of region and the prescription of solutions may alter from one kind of region to another. If out-migration was shown to be the most effective remedy for the problems of one type of depressed region, it does not automatically follow that it is the optimal course of action for others.

Thirdly, the assumption that out-migration or capital flows provide a universal panacea for problem regions may stem from preoccupation with regional differences in unemployment rates. Equally important symptoms of distress may be low activity rates, high rates of out-migration and/or low relative *per capita* income

[2] For a recent attempt see Hoffenberg, M. and Devine, E.J. Influence of National Decisions on Regional Economies. In Hirsch, *op. cit.*, 156–75

levels. Priority given to each symptom may differ from region to region, and with changes in the ranking of priorities it may be necessary to alter the measures applied. For example, it has been argued that planned out-migration is a less effective remedy when a region's problems stem from low activity rates rather than from heavy unemployment.[3] Even more obvious is the absurdity of prescribing out-migration for the region whose main source of worry is a high net emigration rate.

The upshot of these comments is that the case for a general solution applicable in all circumstances is very weak. The problems of every depressed region should be analysed in detail, their main depression characteristics indicated, a list of objectives drawn up and priorities determined, and comprehensive plans formulated and/or individual policy instruments applied which achieve the chosen objectives most efficiently. The decision-making process will vary according to whether agreement is reached on a particular objective and a choice has to be made among alternative means of accomplishing it or whether alternative objectives are to be pursued with limited given means. In the first case, cost-effectiveness studies may be very relevant; in the second, either programming models or systems analysis may be called for. However, having said this, it may be permissible to discuss the relative merits of higher geographical mobility, a location of industry policy and other general solutions provided that we recognise that any final overall assessment cannot dictate the direction of policy in a particular case. Although the risk of over-generalisation is great, these general approaches to a regional policy have been emphasised so much in the literature, and not without considerable confusion, that to neglect them would be a serious omission.

B *The market solution*

A feasible argument is that market forces can take care of regional differences without direct government intervention. Although the emergence of attention to regional problems is a clear sign that market forces have failed to erase all regional differences (in unemployment rates, for example), it might nevertheless be argued that the unrestricted operations of the market mechanism provide the

---

[3] For expressions of this view see Needleman, L. (Jan. 1965) What are We to Do About the Regional Problem? *Lloyds Bank Review*; and Nevin, E.T. (Dec. 1966) The Case for a Regional Policy. *Three Banks Review*

least-cost and a reasonably acceptable solution. Some support for this view may be found in the convergence tendencies in regional *per capita* incomes observed in the United States economy over the last ninety years.

The *laissez faire* case rests on the view that increased national efficiency should be the primary objective of regional development, and that the price system in a market economy is the best available automatic regulatory mechanism for achieving this objective, by inducing the optimal spatial allocation of resources. The justification for this is that man-made regulators can only take limited account of the general interdependence of the space economy as reflected in minute spatial differences in costs, prices and incomes. As Lösch puts it: 'Every individual faces special geographic differences whose controlling influence is attuned to his exact location more finely than any planning could be ... if geographic price differences were to be abolished, or even merely frozen, they would soon have to be replaced by *complete* spatial planning which would face the enormous task of taking into account the effects of thousands of locations upon one another – something that only the play of changing prices has so far been able to do successfully for any length of time'.[4] A second argument for the market solution relates to uncertainty. Because of uncertainties attached to predicting the future, it might be argued that the inevitable gaps between anticipated and realised costs and revenues may be minimised by spreading decision-making as widely as possible among individual firms rather than having it centralised. An objection to this is that strong agglomerating tendencies found in economic activity may be due to the herd instinct more than to independent rational calculations. If this is so, there is no reason why individual forecasting errors should tend to cancel each other out.

Laissez faire in regional development obviously is more excusable in conditions of underemployment. If the economy as a whole operates below the full employment level it is difficult on efficiency grounds alone to argue for regional policy measures. But the presence of unemployment is scarcely a good advertisement for free market solutions. Finally, if the argument that inter-regional differences in capital and direct operating costs of plants are becoming smaller is valid, then it might be argued that the spread of more

[4] Lösch, A. (1954) *The Economics of Location.* 333

information and increased knowledge about geographical cost differentials should induce more firms to go to less favoured regions. However, this view gives too much emphasis to direct location costs. Other determinants – such as market size, communications and the quality of environment – may work against dispersal, especially if sales maximising goals and personal factors influence location decisions.[5]

Although maximisation of private returns to the nation's resources means reliance on the market to determine the regional allocation of investment, the government nevertheless has, in addition to unemployment relief, a lubricating function. Intervention may be necessary to make the labour market competitive, to limit trade union and monopolistic restraints on spatial competition, to reduce resource immobilities and to provide more knowledge. However, the distinction between mere lubrication and active policy measures may become arbitrary, since financial assistance to migrants might be justified as offsetting migration costs (which limit mobility) and even investment incentives to develop in depressed regions might be regarded as a means of outweighing higher risk premiums that restrict free movement of capital. Moreover, changing the structure of relative prices through measures such as regional payroll tax-rebate schemes,[6] is not necessarily inconsistent with market solutions if actual location and migration decisions are left to individual firms and households. On the other hand, since all these latter measures necessitate tampering with the price structure they depart from strictly *laissez faire* principles. But measures of this kind are likely to be supported by those economists who have faith in the price mechanism.

The effectiveness of the market mechanism as a regional allocator is itself open to criticism. The theoretical base for the free market in regional economics lies in general equilibrium theory. But general equilibrium analysis tends to be static rather than dynamic. It rests on marginalist assumptions, whereas in the space economy locational inertia prevents instantaneous adjustments to marginal changes in costs and revenues. Moreover, even if equilibrating tendencies are strong the path of adjustment may be difficult and have harmful

---

[5] See Chapter 4, Section 5

[6] See Clark, C. and Peters, G.H. (March 1964) Steering Employment by Taxes and Rebates. *Town and Country Planning*, **32**; and Clark, C. (October 1966) Industrial Location and Economic Potential. *Lloyds Bank Review*

consequences. The efficacy of market forces depends on the assumption of perfect competition, yet oligopoly and monopolistic elements are common in the space economy; distance may be an effective barrier to competition. In addition, the location decisions of firms and households may be based on irrational grounds and made in the light of imperfect knowledge.

Finally, the *laissez faire* thesis can be attacked if either social benefits are less than private benefits or social costs exceed private costs so that intervention would yield a positive net social rate of return. For example, if government funds for research and development (which are themselves justified on externality grounds) were distributed according to market principles in favour of the most efficient, least cost firms and industries, this may have harmful effects on long-term growth in certain regions. Assuming a relationship between regional R and D expenditures and regional growth, a wide dispersal of government spending on R and D should tend to yield social benefits in excess of any sacrifices in short-run efficiency. Another example is that market forces might lead to such a concentration of economic activities at centres of agglomeration that they give rise to massive social congestion costs.

Apart from theoretical objections, there is the important practical consideration that *laissez faire* may be politically unacceptable. The circumstances in which this may happen are where the free market perpetuates rather than reduces inter-regional inequality. If market orientation and other agglomeration economies outweigh the pull of cheap labour, economic expansion will continue to build up in current high income regions. This is not to challenge the efficiency of the market mechanism but to suggest that the cost of higher efficiency may be intolerably wide regional income disparities. However, the free market does waste resources. For instance, it fails both to obtain the potentially high returns derived from investment in the retraining and migration of mobile workers and to make use of (older) immobile workers whose employment in their domiciliary region involves no opportunity costs. So long as prices are less than perfectly flexible and resources are less than perfectly mobile the effectiveness of the market mechanism will be reduced.

C *Measures to stimulate migration*
There is a tendency for regional economists to prescribe measures either to induce migration out of depressed regions or to attract

capital in as if they were alternative general solutions. In fact, one course of action may be superior in one set of circumstances while the diametrically opposite action may be optimal in another set. The strength of the case for a particular policy depends on the objectives of the policy and on the economic conditions and institutional environment in which it is applied. Thus, if the primary objective of a regional policy was to reduce unemployment or to raise national efficiency planned migration may be more justifiable than if the dominant objective was to narrow inter-regional differences in *per capita* incomes. But even with the latter policy goal, out-migration may raise average income levels in the sending regions in certain circumstances (where migrants are out of work and/or where reduction of the excess supply of labour raises its marginal product).

Measures to stimulate labour migration may take many forms. For example, subsidies for education and retraining improve mobility through their influence on the quality of the labour force, and are often consistent with economic efficiency. Individuals may under-invest in their own education and training because of ignorance, imperfections in the capital market and divergences between private and social rates of return. However, there is a difference between acceptance of the justification for intervention and deciding the level of subsidy. Calculation of the social rate of return on retraining unemployed workers who may be employed elsewhere depends upon a comparison of total social benefits with total social costs, a difficult procedure, especially since some of the benefits may be non-quantifiable. Policymakers may also intervene with direct financial assistance to potential migrants. Such assistance may include travel and removal expenses, initial subsistence allowances to cover the period of a job-hunt and to help with temporary accommodation before the migrant is able to move his family, housing subsidies and allowances to defray other resettlement costs. Because the costs of retraining and moving, along with the uncertainties of finding suitable employment, may wipe out expected income gains, subsidies of this kind may be necessary even though inter-regional wage differentials provide some incentive to migrate. By obtaining estimates of income differentials, the working life span over which the income gains are to be enjoyed, the direct costs of moving and indirect resettlement costs, it is possible to calculate a rate of return on migration which can be compared with competitive rates of return on other kinds of investment. However, migration is not a satisfactory solution if the government can spend a sum equal to the social long-run marginal cost of moving workers from one region to another and raise their levels of living by more than if they migrated.[7] This depends not only on income differentials, moving costs, inter-regional comparisons of social service costs, and each migrant's transfer wage but on the rates of return from industrial investment in the problem regions, and in addition must also take account of all social benefits and costs. The social return from investment in the domiciliary regions may exceed the observed private return because of external economies and/or the inefficiency of local firms.

The argument for inducing labour migration as a solution to regional problems is simple and obvious. The movement of labour from depressed to prosperous regions will create a better balance between regional labour supplies and employment opportunities. The aggregate level of employment will be increased, and total output will rise either for this reason or because labour will have been transferred from low to high productivity industries. Inter-regional income differentials will narrow as excess labour supply is reduced in the sending regions and wage increases are at least slowed down in the receiving regions.[8] Thus, so the argument runs, such a policy is consistent with national efficiency and eliminates the main characteristics of depressed regions (higher levels of unemployment and low incomes).

It is quite true that in some situations these results do not materialise. But the critics of policies to aid migration have too often argued as if their objections had general validity, rather than merely being possible outcomes in particular, probably rare, conditions. In fact, the most serious criticism of migration is social rather than economic. If the satisfaction of the locational preferences of individuals has a high priority among society's objectives and scale of values, then the government is unlikely to frustrate this priority by inducing migration in order to gain marginal increases in efficiency.

The economic arguments against the migration remedy refer to adverse effects in both the destination regions and the regions of origin. The main point with respect to the former is that migrants contribute less in taxes than the marginal social costs of the decision

[7] It is reasonable to assume a preference for not migrating

[8] In a static model the marginal product of labour (and hence wages) will fall in receiving regions. See the analysis in Chapter 12, Section 2, and in Chapter 13

to move. In-migration adds to traffic and other forms of congestion, and raises land rent and business costs. Migrants pay only the average costs of providing public facilities for themselves, despite rising marginal costs. Thus, because public services are not supplied on a user-charge basis, the migrant is encouraged to use them wastefully. Moreover, the migrant with a large family makes a disproportionate claim on public services (for example, demanding costly education services).

These arguments are not convincing. Even if marginal social costs of migration were greater than marginal private costs, this may be outweighed by social benefits. These may be connected with the fact that fewer people are supported by existing services in sending regions and/or the fact that the migrant's productivity is likely to be higher in his new area than the old. If wages are related to marginal value product, there will be a social benefit because the income gain to the region is the average product of the migrants. Of course, it is possible that migration may have unfavourable effects on the distribution of income in the destination region. An increase in employment through immigration will move the region further down the marginal product of labour curve, and, given perfectly competitive labour markets, wages will be depressed. But other sections of the region gain, such as employers of labour. There is a net increase in regional income resulting from migration, and adverse effects on distribution can be offset by corrective fiscal action.

In any event, the whole argument about a divergence between marginal social and private costs of migration is riddled with weaknesses. If migrants fail to pay the marginal costs of social services, this reflects a faulty pricing method and does not suggest that migration is inefficient. In fact, both migrants and indigenous residents will pay the same price, and if this is so there is no subsidy to migrants alone. The large immigrant household may, of course, demand considerable amounts of public services, but in time these claims will decline while the migrant's tax payments continue. Finally, rising marginal costs of services cannot be used as an argument that migration is wasteful. They merely indicate that certain services have less than perfectly elastic supply functions, and therefore suggest the existence of **pecuniary external diseconomies**. To the extent that indigenous residents supply services that have risen in price they gain by migration. On the other hand, these deficiencies in the argument should not be taken to rule out technological external diseconomies as a result of in-migration, such as traffic congestion, air pollution, overcrowding and slums.

If overfull employment exists in prosperous regions, an *a priori* case might be made for in-migration to relieve inflationary pressure. However, it has been argued that such migration would have the opposite effect and would aggravate inflationary tendencies. The grounds for this view are that in-migration into such regions would add more to investment demand than to savings and more to the demand for labour than to supply.[9] But the argument is weak. It is possible that the demand for services by a migrant will *ultimately* raise the demand for labour by more than his own contribution to labour supply. But inflationary tendencies would only be reinforced if this increased derived demand for labour was felt immediately. But increased provision of public and social services for migrants will occur only in the long run; in the short run existing services will simply be used more intensively. The migrants will make an immediate impact on labour supply, while the consequential effects on the demand for labour and capital in new housing, public amenities and social services will show themselves only after a considerable time lag as a stimulus to the region's growth. Inflation will result only in the improbable case where these two effects are felt simultaneously.

As for the sending regions, it is no doubt possible that out-migration may have unfavourable consequences and could depress domestic living standards. Social capital may be underutilised and there may be a rise in its *per capita* burden, excess capacity may develop in private industry, there may be downward multiplier repercussions on local service industries, the quality of the labour force may decline, former investments may be lost through emigration of the educated, and there may be dangers of capital flight. However, far from being general these results are probably seen only in quite narrowly prescribed circumstances. For instance, out-migration may be more than offset by natural increases so that there is no decline in the utilisation of social capital, merely a slower rate of increase in its supply. Moreover, social capital in these regions may be of poor quality needing replacement and/or overutilised so that out-migration simply reduces the pressure on it. As for under-utilised private industrial capital, much of it may be obsolete with no alternative use. Unless it can earn a competitive rate of return in the

---

[9] Needleman, *loc. cit.*, 46–7

long run, national efficiency would have to be sacrificed to maintain and replace it. Furthermore, if the unemployed and their families predominate among the migrants, the fiscal burden of the region for relief and social security benefits will be reduced. Finally, migrants may make remittances from developed to backward regions.

One objection to the migration solution that may be valid stems from the fact that female labour is more tied to a region than male labour. Although, in the long run, households may migrate to maximise the joint income of husband and wife, this is by no means certain. Married women may only desire work for certain periods of their life, and the potential income gains over these periods may be too low to induce migration. Thus, a region may fully employ its male labour force yet contain considerable surplus female labour. This could show itself in below average activity rates. In the circumstances outlined, activity rates cannot be raised by out-migration, so that if raising them is a policy goal it may be necessary to take measures to attract industry into the region.

D *Capital mobility and location of industry policy*
A policy to influence the location of new capital has nowadays a wider measure of acceptance than measures to induce migration. Of course, the two approaches are not inconsistent with each other, and in certain situations the optimal solution for a particular problem region might be a modicum of induced out-migration *and* an inflow of capital and industry. Moreover, movement of both factors was required for steady growth in the models outlined in Chapter 13. Yet the proponents of the 'capital mobility' school rarely accept this logic. For them, depressed regions are to be cured by inducing new industry there. Three aspects of a location of industry policy require discussion. These are the arguments for intervention, the criteria upon which policies should be judged, and the methods available and their relative merits and demerits.

Some of the arguments for intervening in the location of industry are implicit in the earlier discussion. The limitations of the market mechanism provide, at first sight, as much justification for influencing the mobility of capital as for stimulating the mobility of labour. An objection to this statement might be that measures to stimulate migration can be regarded as helping to remove the barriers to perfect mobility (since migrants tend to move from low to high income areas), while subsidies to industry attempt to deflect firms from their freely chosen, and most efficient, locations. This objection is not fully convincing. Reluctance to invest in problem (often peripheral) regions may reflect subjectively high risks and uncertainties rather than lower returns to capital, and subsidies could be excused as providing some cover for these risks. Moreover, central locations may be chosen out of habit rather than reason, so that intervention might be justified as a means of protecting business managers from their own irrationality. There is a widespread impression, not sufficiently tested, that technical changes of the last few decades have reduced the importance of location costs in the overall cost structure in the sense that in many industries plants of optimum size can operate in a wide spread of locations with only minimal differences in production costs. If cost minimisation depends far more on the way in which a factory is operated (i.e. on managerial efficiency) than on where it is sited, then measures to change the location of industry might be excused as involving little departure from the most efficient spatial configuration of production. However, this is at best a permissible apology for intervention rather than an irrefutable argument. Moreover, it has a serious flaw in that it assumes that managerial efficiency and a plant's location are independent of each other. Even if technical production costs are identical at two given locations, if managers attach large 'psychic income' elements to being at one of the locations their efficiency may be adversely affected if they are persuaded to move to the other.

A much stronger argument for intervention is the social benefit derived from using wasted labour resources, in the form of unemployed and non-participants in the labour force who may wish to work if employment opportunities were present. The point is that heavy inducements to migrate may still fail to persuade many unemployed workers to move. Assuming that direction of labour is not feasible in a free society, the only way of employing these truly immobile workers is to create jobs for them where they are. Since their employment will raise national output, the argument is economic not social. The provision of jobs is consistent with efficiency, on condition that the capital necessary for job-creation has not to be diverted from a much higher productive use elsewhere. This argument applies only to unused labour reserves not to under-utilised capital. For instance, if producers in a depressed area have cut back output in response to a fall in demand for their products, the value of their capital is thereby reduced and it is inefficient to subsidise its extended use in order to eliminate excess capacity.[10]

An extension of the above thesis, the economic benefits of utilising immobile labour, is the view that attracting capital into depressed regions will, if the scale of inflow is large enough, also reduce the necessity for migration. Thus, such a policy would satisfy the locational preferences of individuals to a much greater extent than alternatives. This is, of course, a social justification. It may be quite rational, if the objective is to maximise the net satisfaction of individuals in society, to follow this policy even if losses to national efficiency result, though how the gains in satisfaction are to be measured against these losses raises a probably insoluble question. Another benefit sometimes suggested as flowing from reducing migration between depressed and prosperous regions is that this aids 'regional balance', in the sense of bringing the relative population size of regions in the national economy closer together, whereas encouraging migration would lead to a few disproportionately large regions. The whole concept of 'regional balance' is nebulous, but there may be one supportable aspect to the argument. This is that there may be marked complementarities in inter-regional development, so that a system composed of regions of similar size will tend to grow much faster than where one or two regions dwarf the rest. Such complementarities may result from high levels of inter-regional trade and/or inter-regional specialisation.

An argument for location of industry policy frequently urged is that the troubles of problem areas, particularly their slow growth, stem from having an unfavourable industrial composition. The surest way to deal with such regions, it is suggested, is to induce new industries to these areas. Although this reasoning is not necessarily wrong, it suffers from gross over-simplification. In the first place, not all depressed regions are old-established manufacturing areas suffering from decline of their basic industries and, hence, from an out-of-date industrial structure. Some problem regions may be relatively undeveloped, isolated agricultural areas where planned out-migration and some influx of small-scale manufacturing and service activities may be the most appropriate remedies. Secondly, the argument assumes that a region's economic performance is determined by its industrial composition. We have already seen that this

---

[10] The rare exception occurs when production is subject to decreasing marginal costs

is, at best, a half-truth, and that **differential** effects may be more important than **proportional** effects. If a region suffers from unfavourable input–output access for most activities, an influx of new industry will not solve its problems for the new industry will tend to assimilate the depression characteristics of the region as a whole. If out-migration is rejected as a solution for a region of this kind, its problems would have to be handled by much more extensive measures – such as rebuilding its infrastructure, stimulating its adaptability to change, and investment in input–output access improvement. Another point is that, even when conditions are favourable, improving a region's 'activity mix' in order to raise its average income level is predominantly a *long-run* problem; in the short run, the main objective may be to secure full employment which may be achieved more easily by other means, such as subsidies to *existing* industries or aids to migration.

A popular support for a steering policy in regard to industrial location is that this would reduce external diseconomies of congestion in the prosperous, highly urbanised regions. It is argued that the social costs of population concentration in these areas far exceed the private costs, because of general overcrowding and its effects, transport congestion, increased pressure on social services and rising factor prices. As observed above, **pecuniary external diseconomies** do not justify intervention since they are consistent with economic efficiency. But technological external diseconomies of congestion such as traffic congestion and over-extension of resource facilities (e.g. electric power and water) do give rise to social costs.

To accept that these diseconomies exist, however, does not in itself justify intervention in the location of industry. It is difficult to measure these social costs in order that they may be compared with possible benefits sacrificed through persuading firms to relocate. Moreover, some of these external diseconomies arise more from the concentration of people than of industry (of course, both are interconnected). But if the social costs were very heavy, then congested areas might need the export of population as well as industry. This is never entertained in regional policy discussions for the obvious reason that although the movement of population from congested regions to others would relieve congestion, it would not result in net social benefits because the balance of labour supply and employment opportunities would be further distorted. However, this fact suggests that relief of congestion is not primarily an inter-regional problem.

These diseconomies are found mainly in metropolitan areas, and the most effective solution is usually to disperse both households and firms to less congested parts *within* the region by intra-regional planning. Congested cities are found in both depressed and prosperous industrial regions, and it is no solution to this problem to encourage capital to flow out of a metropolitan city in a rich region to a metropolitan city in a poorer region. In other words, technological external diseconomies may justify interference with the free location choice of households and firms, but they do not directly give grounds for inducing *inter-regional* transfers.

A final argument for subsidising capital and industry in problem regions is that revival of such regions may enable firms located there to benefit from increasing returns to scale and external agglomeration economies which would not be present without an initial subsidy. This is a form of infant industry argument, the case for which depends upon the presence of potential external economies and agglomeration economies which become operative only at certain minimum levels of industrial activity. As such, it would appear more applicable to rural regions which have not yet industrialised rather than to mature regions heavily committed to declining basic industries. But there is an economic case for intervention to create a new industrial complex and subsidise its expansion to a level at which investment in other industries becomes profitable (even in a mature region), provided that opportunity cost criteria are satisfied.

Nevertheless, whether a problem region can be revived to grow without aid may depend on its ability to copy the characteristics of growing regions. If the lag of a depressed region is due to policy variables (such as local tax structures), the conditions for revival can be re-created. If its difficulties are due to sociological characteristics within the managerial class (such as loss of drive in old family firms), inducing new industry may be very successful. For example, it may lead to the emergence of a new dynamic entrepreneurial group to run the new industrial complex and to a permeation of their attitudes through to indigenous firms. The problems are more intractable if the failure to grow is due to the absence of internal economies of scale and external agglomeration economies. If industries are carefully selected and if policymakers are willing to provide substantial aid over considerable periods of time, the difficulties are not necessarily insuperable. Nor is it inevitable that investment in these regions yields low returns, though it is probable that high returns are attainable only in the long run.

Apart from the benefits gained from utilising immobile resources, the economic arguments for steering capital and industry are not convincing. Combined with the social arguments, there may be on balance a case for intervention. If this is assumed, the next question is the criteria on which action should be based. In practice, these criteria cannot be divorced from policy objectives. Nevertheless, a few generalisations are possible. Assuming that better conceived regional goals should relate to productivity growth and rising living standards rather than to the absolute growth of employment, output or other aggregate indicators, relative growth in *per capita* output is a more rational criterion of success than, say, a decline in unemployment. Relocations of firms should be evaluated in terms of future income growth in the donating and receiving regions and in terms of demonstration effects and the generation of external economies rather than simply in terms of the number of jobs created and their cost. Thus, for instance, a complete transfer of a plant and its workers may be justified even though it creates few jobs because it may lead to the inflow of more firms.

Another important criterion is that the opportunity cost of an investment, as measured by returns to factors in alternative uses, should be included in evaluation of a subsidy. An exception is where unemployed labour in a depressed region is immobile, and unless employed locally will produce nothing. Thus, in this case, the relevant comparison is not between the net marginal products of capital in both growing and depressed regions but between the net marginal product of capital in the growing region and the total increase to value added in the depressed area (i.e. the gross marginal product of capital).[11]

Application of these criteria suggests the importance of selective inducements rather than blanket indiscriminate aid to all types of firms and all industries. It is inefficient to subsidise the influx of industries into regions with poor input–output access for such

[11] Eckstein takes the contrary view. He argues that the benefits of investment projects in depressed regions would be overestimated if the wiping out of local unemployment was included in the expected gain, since labour would not then become available where needed. But this seems to neglect the above point that some labour is immobile, and would stay unemployed rather than move (Eckstein, O. (1958) *Water-Resource Development.* 33)

activities. Industries which give rise to substantial intra-regional factor receipts and the products of which exhibit high income elasticities of demand may deserve preferential treatment on the grounds that they increase effective demand as well as employ underutilised resources.[12] Similarly, industries exporting a high proportion of their output may be a source of autonomous growth if they can be fostered successfully. Other suggested grounds for selectivity have included emphasis on sectors which minimise capital-output and capital-labour ratios, or which satisfy marginal productivity and marginal growth criteria. But reliance on simple ratios of this kind to guide investment decisions assumes that capital is the only scarce resource and that there are no variations in efficiency by sector.[13] Chinitz has also argued that a discriminatory inducement policy is consistent with efficiency. Assuming a given budget constraint and the availability of information on investment demand elasticities of different investors, the government could maximise the yield from a given overall subsidy by acting as a discriminating monopolist rather than by offering uniform inducements.[14]

Apart from measures to aid migration and reliance on the market mechanism, there is a wide range of instruments available to implement a regional policy directed to the attraction of capital and industry to problem regions. For instance, there are negative restrictive measures. These include direct control on factor movements (rarely applied to labour, more common in relation to capital), direct restrictions on expansion in congested areas possibly supplemented by financial penalties, and regionally differentiated control of bank credit. This latter possibility has not been tried, yet centralised availability of credit is one factor explaining why firms find it easier to expand in centrally placed areas. However, in general, negative controls are not to be recommended. Although of negligible budgetary cost they may hide substantial real costs in terms of sacrifices of national efficiency. A simpler solution may be to offset the agglomeration tendencies of private capital movements by an opposite movement of public funds rather than by direct controls.

[12] Krutilla, J.V. (1955) Criteria for Evaluating Regional Development Programmes. *American Economic Review*, **45**

[13] Rodwin, L. (1963) Choosing Regions for Development, in Friedrich, C.J. and Harris, S.R. (edits) *Public Policy*. Vol. 12

[14] Chinitz, B. (1966) Appropriate Goals for Regional Economic Policy. *Urban Studies*, 3

As for positive measures to influence the location of industry, the options here are even greater. Publicity and provision of information; increasing the supply of basic industrial services, infrastructure and social amenities; investment in education, retraining and natural resource development; direct inducements to firms such as grants, loans or investment incentives favouring capital, or wage subsidies; physical and/or indicative planning, usually on an inter-regional scale; regional discrimination in government contracts and the construction of new government establishments (factories, government departments, R and D laboratories) in depressed areas; regional allocation of public investment projects by cost-benefit analysis and other criteria; regulatory or price-fixing powers in fields such as transport which affect regional location; direction of industry; selection of and stimulus to regional 'growth points'; this list is by no means exhaustive. Some comment on a few of these possible methods may be illuminating.

First, let us consider the relative merits of investment (capital) subsidies and wage subsidies.[15] Wage subsidies are not very suitable for non-industrialised regions, since people in such areas could be employed relatively easily elsewhere. However, in certain circumstances they may be justified; i.e. if the subsidy is offset by a net expansion in output it will not incur a real cost. An investment subsidy, on the other hand, in general induces the use of more capital than is efficient, since if labour is underemployed it is not rational to economise in its use. However, if capital subsidies are favoured, there are certain factors which need to be taken into account in choosing the appropriate type of subsidy. Accelerated depreciation may be a powerful device for encouraging the relocation of a capital-starved firm. Moreover, since firms probably attach considerable importance to high initial inducements to offset the heavy relocation costs, initial investment grants are more effective than continuing subsidies. On the other hand, tax concessions have the merit relative to initial grants that they reward success because firms have to earn profits on the appropriate scale to obtain full benefit. Except in the case of branch factories, this advantage is probably offset by the fact that tax concessions will not do much immediately for a new factory which may not be profitable for several years. A different point stems

[15] The allocative function of wage subsidies is considered separately in more detail. See 2 below

from the fact that the stimulus to relocation often arises in the congested region itself, and site limitations are often the primary cause. Firms when considering relocation place great emphasis on economising managerial time and effort. This favours the first acceptable available site rather than the cheapest, and a strong preference for automatic benefits rather than those requiring long extensive negotiations. Thus, different types of subsidy have conflicting advantages. The preference for a particular form of investment subsidy needs to be decided in the light of the prevailing circumstances rather than by *a priori* reasoning.

The relative advantages of three different kinds of subsidy (labour, capital, and prices respectively) have been compared by Borts within the framework of a simplified model.[16] His aim is to consider the most efficient *short-run* method of securing full employment *within* a region, by comparing the social rate of return from the three types of subsidy. His analysis shows that a wage subsidy is usually preferable to doing nothing, *and is always superior to a capital or price subsidy*.[17] This arises because he measures the cost of a subsidy as a social cost (the output foregone by diverting capital from its most productive use) rather than as a monetary cost, which is merely a transfer. However, his conclusions may be influenced by the assumptions of his model. In particular, his model of a depressed area assumes that the supply curve of labour is perfectly inelastic and that the supply curve of capital is perfectly elastic. Thus, labour is treated as the fixed factor while capital is the variable factor. If these assumptions were altered, we might obtain different results.

Borts's analysis can be summarised as follows. We assume that as a result of an external disturbance the price of a *competitive* industry's output falls in a given region, but that the wage fails to drop. If wages fail to decline, the industry will leave the region unless action is taken, and the region will become depressed. There is thus a discrepancy between the private and the social costs of using labour. The social cost is the productivity of labour in the industry in equilibrium, but the employer has to pay a higher wage than this because the wage decline required by competitive equilibrium is

[16] Borts, G.H. (1966) Criteria for the Evaluation of Regional Development Programs. 183–218 in Hirsch, W.Z. (edit for C.R.A.), *Regional Accounts for Policy Decisions*

[17] Except in the special case of fixed production coefficients, when the rates of return on all three policies are identical

prevented. Three forms of intervention are possible: (1) **a wage subsidy**, that is, the government subsidises employment by paying employers the difference between the new and the old marginal product of labour; (2) a **capital subsidy** with which employers are paid the difference between the competitive rate of return on investment and the return earned after the price decline, assuming that wages remain rigid (this subsidy might take many forms – low interest loans, tax relief or cheap site and factory rents); (3) a **price subsidy** with which output is subsidised by payment of the difference between the new and the old price of output.

He then proceeds to estimate the social rate of return from each of these policies. He evaluates the subsidy relative to the competitive rate of return. He assumes that in the absence of a subsidy, the industry would leave the region; therefore the return to the subsidy is the output of the industry. The cost of the subsidy is the output lost by transferring mobile resources (capital) into the industry, and the sacrificed output is evaluated by the productivity of capital in other uses.

The results are shown in table 6.[18] Policy 1 pays so long as the industry can earn the normal rate of return on capital and also make some contribution to the wage. This will be the case when there is some elasticity of substitution between labour and capital (i.e. when $b>0$). However, in the special case of fixed capital–labour co-efficients (i.e. $b=0$), subsidising labour will not pay if $\dot{P} < -a$. With Policy 2 subsidising the difference between the depressed and long-run competitive return allows the industry to pay the original wage. Except when $b=0$ when $r_1 = r_2$, Policy 2 is always inferior to Policy 1 though it may be preferable to doing nothing. The rate of return on Policy 2 appears the same as on Policy 1 except that X_2 and K_2 refer to a different rate of output and a different stock of capital from X_1 and K_1. The effect of Policy 2 is to raise the capital–labour ratio in order to raise the marginal physical product of labour. The price decline of X is offset by an equi-proportionate increase in the marginal physical product of labour, leaving the marginal revenue product of labour unchanged. Firms are encouraged to use more capital than under Policy 1 because they are led to believe that capital is cheaper and labour more expensive than their correct relative costs.

[18] For the mathematical proofs, see Borts, *loc. cit.*, 209–18

Table 6

Relative efficiency of different types of subsidy

policy	unlimited budget–social rate of return	limited budget–subsidy per job
1 wage subsidy	$r_1 = \dfrac{X_1 P_1 L_o}{P_K K_1 L_o} = \dfrac{r_o}{1-a}\left[1 + \dot{P}(1-b)\right]$	$w_o - w_1 = \Delta P \dfrac{X_o}{L_o}$
2 capital subsidy	$r_2 = \dfrac{X_2 P_1 L_o}{P_K K_2 L_o} = \dfrac{r_o}{1-a}\left[1 + \dfrac{\dot{P}}{1-a}(1+ab-a)\right]$	$\dfrac{\Delta r_K K_2}{L_o} = \dfrac{\Delta P X_o(1+\dot{K})}{L_o}$
3 price subsidy	$r_3 = \dfrac{X_o P_1 L_o}{P_K K_o L_o} = \dfrac{r_o}{1-a}(1+\dot{P})$	$\Delta P \dfrac{X_o}{L_o}$

Key to table 6

X = physical output
P_1 = new lower price
L_o = number of workers
K = capital stock
P_K = price of capital
$\dot{P}$ = percentage change (decline) in output price
$\dot{K}$ = percentage rise in capital stock over initial equilibrium level

r_o = competitive rate of return on capital
r_1, r_2, r_3 = social rates of return on wage, capital and price subsidies respectively
a = share of output paid to labour
b = elasticity of substitution between labour and capital
w = wage

Under what conditions is Policy 2 worth doing?

$$\frac{r_2}{r_o} > 1 \text{ if } \dot{P} > \frac{-a(1-a)}{1+ab-a}.$$

With a Cobb-Douglas production function ($b=1$), this condition becomes $\dot{P} > -a(1-a)$, but with fixed proportions ($b=0$), the condition of the policy being worthwhile becomes $\dot{P} > -a$, which is the same condition applicable to Policy 1, given the same assumption of fixed proportions. Thus, for given values of $\dot{P}$ (which is negative, of course) and a, the larger b is the less profitable is Policy 2; on the other hand, the profitability of Policy 1 rises with b. With Policy 3, both initial output and capital are left unchanged. Policy 3 is better than doing nothing when $\dot{P} > -a$, but it is inferior to Policy 1 except when $b=0$, in which event $r_3 = r_1$. To sum up, when $b>0$, Policy 1 involves withdrawal of less capital from other uses than either Policy 2 or 3. The point is that Policy 1 induces firms to use less capital per worker, while Policy 2 involves an artificial cheapening of capital and Policy 3 implies an artificial rise in the value productivity of capital by subsidising the price of output.[19]

With a limited budget constraint (the previous analysis is based on an unlimited budget), policymakers may have to lower their sights below the attainment of full employment. Their direct concern is likely to be with the maximum number of people who can be re-employed rather than with rates of return on sacrificed output. The subsidy per job is identical with Policies 1 and 3, and both are superior to Policy 2 which requires a larger subsidy by $(1 + \dot{K})$. Moreover, Policy 1 still retains the advantage of involving a smaller withdrawal of capital from alternative uses.

Since the regional problem is not solely a question of how to attract new firms into depressed regions, methods of intervention should not be limited to financial inducements to firms. It will also be desirable to improve the industrial environment of a problem region, and this may require, for example, action to increase the supply of skilled manpower and fostering of points of growth within the region. Government subsidies for education and retraining may be justified by a tendency for declining regions to underinvest in these fields, partly because of fears that the skilled and educated may leave the region, partly because of stringency imposed by falling tax revenues. This latter consideration may also call for subsidies for natural resource development (in an attempt to raise the demand for labour), but underinvestment here could also result from the possibility that resource development projects may overlap regional administrative areas.

If the key to revival in depressed regions lies in the creation of 'growth points',[20] this requires heavy government investment in infrastructure at and around certain locations in these areas and large scale physical planning. The build-up of public investment can generate substantial external economies. If economic growth is primarily a function of the human and social environment, public investment can be used as a stimulus to growth rather than a lagged accommodation to growth. The trouble with growth-point policy is that it is difficult to apply efficiency criteria to investment associated

---

[19] Another advantage of the wage subsidy is that it can be applied to firms worthy of aid which could only borrow profitably at a negative rate of interest, and which consequently could not benefit from loans at less than market, but positive, rates

[20] The meaning of the growth-point concept is discussed in detail later

with it. The public investment required is so extensive that it may not be possible to calculate its social rate of return; such estimates are most easily made when investment occurs in small units. On the other hand, acceptance of growth-point philosophy leads to the rejection of old shibboleths. It involves a reduced emphasis on unemployment since growth points are rarely the highest unemployment zones, the abandonment of blighted areas, and, since interregional migration will be encouraged, a thawing out of frozen population distributions. Moreover, it gives a unifying theme to separate policy measures, such as selective migration inducements, the construction of social capital, and housing and other kinds of subsidies.

2 Wage subsidies, resource allocation and employment

The fact that labour tends to be more immobile than capital suggests that there may be strong pragmatic grounds for looking at methods of providing employment for the out-of-work living in depressed regions without requiring them to migrate. This is especially true in the many cases where the refusal to migrate may be a rational decision for individuals to take. Geographical migration may involve occupational mobility, and the uncertainties and wage levels attached to the new job may be insufficient compensation for the loss of investment in training for the occupation about to be abandoned. Moreover, migration is expensive (transportation costs, delays and costs involved in finding new accommodation, etc.), and the anticipated gain in income from moving – possibly an uncertain gain – may not, when properly discounted, outweigh the actual costs of moving. It must be remembered, of course, that migration costs do not only include money costs. Other intangible costs, difficult to quantify, have also to be taken into account. Of these, the difference between the present and prospective social environments, as shown in a comparison of the outgoing region with the intended destination region, is probably the most important. Most workers including the unemployed would prefer to take a job in their own area, and would attach a 'psychic income' element to this preference. This 'psychic income' differential needs to be transcribed into monetary units to measure the preference of a worker for staying in his own area rather than moving for work to another region.

If, for reasons of this kind, there is a case for attempting to create employment in labour surplus regions, wage subsidies are an obvious method to use. Wage subsidies for a long time received a bad press as a regional policy measure[21] on the grounds that they create inefficiency. It is argued below that a wage subsidy to high wage industries in labour surplus regions, far from distorting resource allocation patterns, actually improves resource allocation by simulating a competitive labour market where market forces have ceased to operate effectively. As we shall see, this is a very different argument from that of favouring a general labour subsidy to all industries in a labour surplus region in order to induce firms to substitute labour for capital. If subsidies were given to labour in all sectors, including capital goods industries, then assuming no change in interest rates the subsidy would also make capital goods cheaper. Other things being equal, there would be no incentive to substitute labour for capital on this ground alone. In a number of special cases factor substitution may be possible: for instance, if the ratio of labour/total costs was much lower in capital goods than in other industries; or if all capital goods were imported into the region from outside. Even in these conditions it is doubtful whether extensive substitution of labour for capital would take place. Existing firms, except when about to re-equip, would be most unlikely to indulge in much substitution. New firms and firms replacing their capital stock will tend to substitute labour for capital in those situations, probably rare, when the production process permits a flexible range of factor coefficients each of which is more or less equally productive.

The alternative role of wage subsidies is to compensate for imperfections in the labour market, and to mitigate adverse effects of wage rigidities – inefficient allocation of labour, unemployment and the enforced migration of people who would much prefer to stay in their locality if they could find a job. If wages were completely flexible, both inefficient allocation of labour between industries and unemployment would be wiped out. Except in areas where the marginal productivity of labour is zero, a wage could be established that would clear the market and mop up all unemployment, just as in a market for goods there will be some price that will clear the available supply. But in modern industrial economies characterised by institutional rigidities and active trade unions wages will be inflexible downwards. The result is that the marginal productivity of

[21] The introduction of a Regional Employment Premium in the United Kingdom illustrates a recent change in ideas on this point

THE STRATEGY OF REGIONAL POLICY

labour will differ among industries and that overall wage levels may not be low enough to absorb the unemployed. The purely competitive market fails to operate. Where wages are rigid, only a system of payroll subsidies can simulate the operation of the competitive market and bring the regional economy nearer to the social optimum.

The general case in favour of such subsidies applies when:

(1) there is a differential between the marginal productivity of (occupationally mobile) labour in different industries because of restricted employment opportunities in the relatively high-wage industries at the prevailing wage levels;

(2) there is unemployment because of restricted employment opportunities at prevailing wage levels in any industry that qualified unemployed workers want to enter.

Thus, regional wage subsidies are called for only in areas where there is unemployment and/or where labour is inefficiently allocated between sectors. The possibility of deriving gain from subsidies depends upon the inefficiency of intra-regional resource allocation.

To understand why this is so, we must recognise that wages have a dual function – to induce the worker to work and to move from low to high productivity sectors, and to allocate labour. The inducement function and the allocation function are not automatically compatible. Apart from the institutional rigidities, wages cannot fall below a certain level otherwise the incentive to work is reduced and some people will prefer remaining idle to coming into employment. Moreover, in regions which are depressed because of large agricultural sectors high wages in manufacturing industry may be necessary to induce transfers of labour from agriculture to industry, and consequently to raise productivity in the region as a whole. The allocation function, however, requires complete flexibility in labour costs to firms. Since the labour force in each firm will tend to be increased until labour cost = marginal revenue product, eliminating unemployment calls for labour cost to be brought into line with marginal revenue product. If there is unemployment at the prevailing wage rate, labour cost must be reduced if the unemployment is to be eradicated. This is the dilemma. Wage levels and inter-industry wage differentials must be high to induce workers into employment and to induce mobility from stagnating to expanding sectors; yet wages (or more precisely, labour costs) must be low to mop up unemployment. The key to the solution lies in the fact that wages are not identical with labour cost. We must drive a wedge between what

REGIONAL ECONOMICS

the worker receives (the wage) and what the entrepreneur pays (his labour cost); payroll subsidies are such a wedge. Thus, the basic objective of a wage subsidy scheme is to reduce entrepreneurial labour cost in high wage industries to a level compatible with an optimal allocation of labour.

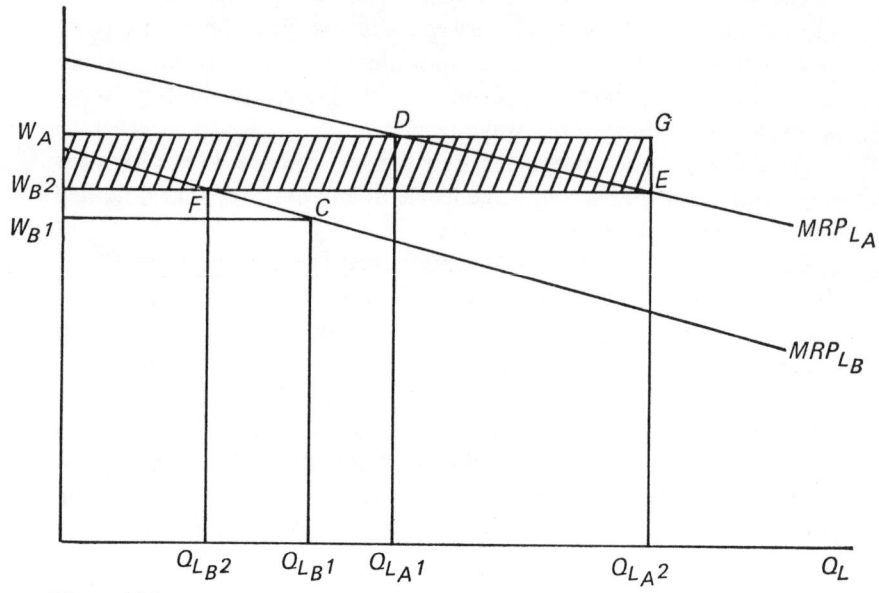

Figure 15.1

This can be illustrated with a simple theoretical model. We assume that a region contains two industries, A and B. Industry A is the high wage industry. Labour is homogeneous, and workers have no preference for either industry except that they prefer a high wage to a low one. The marginal revenue product curves, MRP_{L_A} and MRP_{L_B}, slope downwards in the usual way (figure 15.1). Initially, the wage prevailing in Industry A is W_A and $Q_{L_A}1$ units of labour are employed, while in Industry B the wage level is W_B1 and $Q_{L_B}1$ units of labour are employed. Despite the fact that there is a substantial wage differential between industries ($W_A - W_B1$), a form of quasi-equilibrium reigns. This is because we assume that wages are inflexible in a downwards direction. Workers would still like to move from Industry B to Industry A, but Industry A has absorbed all the labour that it can at the prevailing wage level. $W = MRP$, and the only way in which employment in Industry A could be increased would be for firms to cut wages. The assumption of rigid wages makes this impossible.

What happens if we introduce wage subsidies? Let a lump sum subsidy be paid on each wage bill in Industry A, and assume that this subsidy is sufficient to induce employers in Industry A to expand the industry's labour force to where $MRP_{L_A} = MRP_{L_B}$. MRP_{L_B} will rise as workers leave to transfer to the high wage industry where the demand for labour has increased. In figure 15.1, the subsidy per payroll is equal to $(W_A - W_B 2)$, and the total subsidy paid is $W_A W_B 2EG$. The labour force in Industry A increases from $Q_{L_A} 1$ to $Q_{L_A} 2$, while the labour force in Industry B falls from $Q_{L_B} 1$ to $Q_{L_B} 2$. At the same time, the wage level in Industry B rises from $W_B 1$ to $W_B 2$. The actual wage in Industry A from the point of view of the worker is unchanged and the incentive for workers to move from the low wage to the high wage industry remains so far as employment opportunities permit. The actual wages in both industries differ by the amount of the subsidy. Labour cost to the employer is equal in the two industries. We can identify three main results from the imposition of the subsidy:

(1) there is a net reduction in unemployment – employment increases in Industry A by more $(Q_{L_A} 2 - Q_{L_A} 1)$ than it declines in industry B $(Q_{L_B} 1 - Q_{L_B} 2)$;

(2) there is an increase in regional income because workers have moved from the low productivity sector (Industry B) to the high productivity sector (Industry A);

(3) there is a narrowing of wage differentials $(W_A W_B 1 > W_A W_B 2)$.

All these three effects could be observed if the market solution to the problem of inefficient resource allocation, flexible wages, was allowed to operate. If market forces are ruled out, a subsidy to payrolls in high wage industries works in precisely the same manner.

This is, of course, an abstract static model. If we take into account dynamic considerations, make our assumptions more realistic and consider the practical problems involved, the position becomes less clear-cut. But the principle of wage subsidies and their effects remains the same. However, a few of the difficulties and complications may be mentioned briefly. Subsidies may have to be continued indefinitely, and the level of the subsidy would have to be varied as economic conditions changed. The policymaker would measure the marginal revenue product of labour by the part of the wage bill paid by the employer. Another difficulty in practice is that subsidisation may influence the wage levels prevailing in high wage industries; for instance, it may induce trade unions to step up their wage demands. Furthermore, in a dynamic setting one object of the wage subsidies will be to induce firms in the subsidised industries to move into the depressed regions. But, in the real world, the existence of low labour costs in these industries may not attract incoming firms. Those who favour subsidies of this kind would argue that moderate wage subsidies might induce the location of *new* plants in the region where jobs are needed most and where the net contribution to GNP is greatest, while admitting that they would be unlikely to result in the relocation of existing firms (because of high relocation costs and attachment to traditional commercial channels in their own region). An additional problem is that payment of wage subsidies may constrain the willingness of both individuals and government to invest in education and retraining. Finally, if we relax the assumptions of homogeneity of labour and of no preferences by workers for working in particular industries, the effectiveness of the working of the wage subsidy model will be impaired.

In practice, the financing of wage subsidies creates complications. In the first place, there is no case on efficiency grounds for financing such subsidies by the central government transferring tax funds from other regions. The central government can justify subsidisation – but of vocational training, education, migration and resource development not wage bills. Subsidy programmes of this kind could be supported as a direct attempt to raise the rate of return on human effort. It follows, therefore, that if wage subsidy policies are adopted their financing should be the responsibility of local governments. These governments could tax immobile resources in their area to provide the necessary revenues for the subsidy payments. But how should the revenue be raised? Taxes on property owners might discourage investment; reliance on income taxes might lead to evasion via change of residence or (less likely) the substitution of leisure for income. The main alternatives are a tax on wages (say, a poll tax) or purchase taxes, both of which would hit at the low income household and workers. Whether or not these taxes would be inequitable is not clear, since immobile workers are being taxed only because they refuse to migrate to better employment opportunities elsewhere. Nevertheless, if a payroll subsidy is imposed and financed in this way, and if the measure is effective, a tax on labour to attract low-wage employers is not easily compatible with most people's ideas of a desirable income distribution.

To sum up, there may be serious practical obstacles in the way of adopting a payroll subsidy scheme. In certain sets of circumstances, regional policy objectives may be achieved more easily by using public funds for measures that raise productivity, stimulate investment or assist migration. But the theoretical soundness of wage subsidies, as illustrated in the simple model outlined above, is beyond dispute. A wage subsidy to high wage industries does not destroy the inter-industry wage differentials that may be necessary to induce workers to transfer to more productive industries. At the same time, unless the slopes of the marginal revenue product curves are very odd, the effect of the subsidy will be to increase employment in the region. Despite the widespread popular belief that subsidies always distort the allocative mechanism, these favourable results are achieved precisely because the subsidy on wage bills substitutes for the purely competitive labour market that is made inoperative by institutional rigidities.[22]

3 The growth-point concept

In recent years discussions on regional policy have been improved by introducing the concept of 'growth points'. The focus on specific geographical centres at the sub-regional level has helped to bridge the gap between locational analysis and regional economics. At the same time, it has widened the perspective of policy by looking at regions as meaningful economic entities and by recognising that certain points within a region have greater dynamic potential than others. As a result, regional policy has moved away from the crude prescription of measures for isolated pockets of high unemployment.

Economists have been rather imprecise in defining the concept of 'growth point'. For example, the scale of area to which the concept refers is unclear. Some analysts talk about growth regions. Since, especially in periods of fast overall growth, inter-regional balance is merely an unrealistic limiting case, it is doubtful if the idea of a growth region represents anything new or significant. Comparative advantage and balanced versus unbalanced growth discussions suggest that the concept of a 'leading region' is viable, but this is a rather different phenomenon from the growth point and is probably much more applicable to developing countries. A growth point is a

[22] The case in favour of wage subsidies is argued most cogently by Moes, John E. (1962) *Local Subsidies for Industry*

sub-regional phenomenon. But there is some disagreement as to whether it refers to a whole sub-region or to a concentrated core centre surrounded by zones of influence. The first interpretation stresses homogeneity characteristics while the second emphasises the polarisation flows that link the surrounding zone with the control centre. The latter is almost certainly correct. A basic notion behind the growth point concept is that economic activity tends to agglomerate around certain focal points. The polarisation flows (commodities, factors, services, traffic, communications, etc.) will gravitate within a sub-region towards the control centre (or dominant pole), but because of the costs of moving through space their density will be reduced by distance. If around a focal point we strike a boundary as a locus of points where flows fall off to a minimum critical level, it may be meaningful to describe the area within this boundary as a growth area and the focal point as the growth point.

A second major question is whether a growth point is a natural entity observable in the regional structures of a market economy, or whether it refers to a centre or area where growth is to be deliberately promoted by policy measures. In the latter case a growth point could be created almost anywhere if policymakers were willing to pump in enough resources in the form of public investment on infrastructure and subsidies. But a rational choice of growth points will be based on a comparison of different locations as centres of potential growth, selecting those estimated to have the greatest future potential and repercussionary impact on their surrounding areas. Although natural growth points and artificial ones will initially be very different in the sense that the former are likely to be found at substantial population centres within highly developed regions while the latter may be stimulated in underdeveloped, thinly populated regions, the distinction may be negligible in the long run. If planned growth points are badly chosen, they may require permanent subsidies to keep them viable. If they are selected wisely their rate of expansion will in the future be self-generating, and they will assume the characteristics of natural growth points. Their failure to grow without prior stimulation could be explained by their locational advantages being primarily external economies, justifying public but not private investment. A regional policy based on growth points can therefore be regarded as an *infant area subsidy* policy. A well planned growth point is a potential natural growth point, and the usefulness of the growth point strategy as an approach to regional planning depends on whether or not intra-regional focal centres exist in market economies.

Although the origins of the concept can be traced back to the agglomeration tendencies of the early location theorists, its modern development stems from Francois Perroux's concepts *'pôle de développement'* and *'pôle de croissance'*.[23] Boudeville defines a regional growth pole as 'a set of expanding industries located in an urban area and inducing further development of economic activity throughout its zone of influence'.[24] Regional expansion takes place not so much as a result of cost reductions in existing firms or even an increase in firms in existing industries but because of interaction between key industries at the pole. These industries are called 'propulsive industries', and they form the nucleus of the development pole. They are not necessarily the largest employers of labour, but they are the industries with the greatest direct and indirect impact on regional activity. They tend to be highly concentrated, and usually sell to national markets. They have marked multiplier and polarising effects on the region in which they are situated. They probably draw most of their inputs from within the region, thus retaining a high proportion of increased factor receipts within the region to increase effective demand. At the same time, their products normally have a high income elasticity of demand both within and outside the region, so that the rate of expansion in these key industries will be faster than the rate of increase in national income.

In the expansion of the growth pole Perroux laid stress on induced technical change. The key industry will be advanced technologically, and the effect of its high level of technical efficiency will be to transform other sectors in the region by the force of its example and by the

---

[23] For example, see Perroux, F. (1955) *Note sur la notion de pôle de croissance. Économie Appliquée*, **7**; *Une distinction utile à la politique des pays à croissance retardée: Points de développement et foyers de progrès*. (1959) *Cahiers de l'Institut de Science Économique Appliquée*. Serie F, No. 12; *L'économie du XXe siècle* (1961), Part II, *Les Pôles de croissance*. See also Baillargeon, J-P. *Le Rôle des Pôles dans le Développement: Exposé introductif*. (1961) *Développement et Civilisations*, No. 5; Pottier, P. (1963) *Axes de communication et développement économique. Revue Économique*, **14**; and Aydalot, P. *Note sur les économies externes et quelques notions connexes*. (1965) *Revue Économique*, **16**. For a recent contribution in English see Hansen, N. M. (1967) Development Pole Theory in a Regional Context. *Kyklos*, **20** 709-25

[24] Boudeville, J. (1966) *Problems of Regional Economic Planning*. 11

inter-industry spread of 'disembodied' technical progress. Non-economic variables may also be important. For instance, a high rate of regional expansion may be 'conditional' upon the creation of a 'growth mentality' through the region, a demonstration effect resulting from emergence of the key industry.

This stress on strategic industrial sectors has certain affinities with Isard's industrial complex analysis.[25] An industrial complex is defined as a set of activities at a specific location that are linked by certain technical and production interrelationships. These inter-relationships are such that the industries concerned may operate optimally when clustered together spatially rather than when they trade over a wide area, though complexes may exist with split location patterns or an even more limited degree of spatial interdependence. Although an industrial complex does not necessarily have a dominant propulsive industry as in development pole theory, it places equal stress on economies of agglomeration and concentration.

The industrial grouping aspects of a growth pole can be over-emphasised. The existence of one or two key industries at a given location does not in itself constitute a growth point. What is necessary is not only that there should be rapid growth at that location, admittedly based on the presence of certain growth industries, but that the character of this growth should be such that it induces expansion in the surrounding area. In other words, a description of inter-industry linkages at a given location does not bring out the strategic polarisation effects. In promoting polarisation, a highly developed infrastructure, the supply of services at the centre for the hinterland and the demand for productive factors from the zone of influence may be as important as the concentration of key industries.

Although growth points in an advanced industrial economy will undoubtedly contain growth industries, the underlying idea behind growth points is simply that there is some kind of order and regularity in space as shaped by human, particularly economic, activities. We can conceive of the structure of human settlement as a system of nodes and functional linkages. These nodes are organised into a hierarchical framework, where nodes in each rank of the hierarchy perform a particular set of functions. At the top of the hierarchy there

---

[25] Isard, W., Schooler, E.W. and Vietorisz, T. (1959) *Industrial Complex Analysis and Regional Development* and Isard, W. and Schooler, E.W. (1959) Industrial Complex Analysis, Agglomeration Economies and Regional Development. *Journal of Regional Science*, **1**

will be a dominant node that performs functions that are not supplied by any other centre. Around each centre there will be a zone of influence, called a 'density field' or spatial field, in which we find interaction of many kinds, but especially traffic and communications flows, between the node and the different parts of its field. Because of the friction of space, field densities decline with increasing distance from the centre. Within each region, therefore, we shall find one or several dominant nodes or control centres the rate of growth and functions of which will be the major determinant of the rate of regional expansion. The influence of these nodes will not be felt equally throughout the whole region. Nearby centres, well within the zone of influence, will grow almost as fast as the dominant node itself; distant peripheral areas may stagnate and decline, showing a poorer growth performance than if the nodes were not there. When these 'spread' and 'backwash' effects are averaged out, however, the region's growth is increased by the presence of dominant nodes. It is important to note that this spatial structure will exist, if in an attenuated form, even in a region that is not highly developed industrially.

On the other hand, growth points are more observable in an industrial economy, primarily because agglomeration economies are greater in industry than in other forms of economic activity. In his industrial location theory Weber showed that even with a uniform distribution of materials, labour and demand there was still a tendency for an industry to agglomerate if cost economies could be obtained by merging intersecting market areas into one. Agglomeration results if the fall in production costs associated with it exceeds the increased transport costs between the centre and the peripheral market and supply areas plus the higher rents charged at central locations. In addition to these scale economies, there will be external economies accruing from the close association of several plants in the same industry – co-operative development of technical equipment, specialised optimum scale repair facilities, the presence of a skilled labour pool, savings in overhead costs on energy consumption, transportation facilities, etc. If we then allow interdependence to influence the location of separate industries, we may obtain further economies from concentration of several industries at one location – not only those mentioned above but also scale economies in firms supplying more than one of the concentrated industries with inputs, lower transport costs in input–output transactions, economies in the provision of overhead capital, educational and training institutes, etc.

Since growth points containing industrial complexes are likely to be (or become) substantial population centres, partly because of the market potential and availability of auxiliary services that such centres provide, partly because of entrepreneurial and managerial preferences for sizeable population clusters as site locations, we must also mention urban economies of scale.[26] Certain urban facilities, such as technical colleges and museums, cross the threshold of economic viability at large population size. The question of whether there are economies of scale in the provision of the standard range of municipal functions is an open one, but it is likely that they exist for particular services. Central goods and services of high rank[27] will only be supplied in large population complexes, a tendency that will be reinforced by the fact that maximising demand for such goods and services will require the minimisation of freight and commuting costs.

There is, in fact, a certain parallelism between the relationship of the central place to its complementary region and between the growth point and its zone of influence. Growth points are almost certain to be high ranking central places, and one of the major agglomeration economies may be found in the provision of services to the hinterland. At the conceptual level, however, the two phenomena (growth point and central place) are by no means identical. Central places will be very numerous in a region though arranged in an urban hierarchy, while growth points will be few, in some cases only one within a region. An even more significant difference is that the polarisation flows will be more intense and of a wider character around a growth point than around a central place where commuting flows for shopping, leisure and other services will predominate. To generalise the contrast: the growth of a central place will be sustained by its hinterland; the growth of the zone of influence will be sustained by the growth point.

Another agglomeration economy less frequently discussed[28] refers to communications. Modes of communication (telephone, word of mouth, post, newsprint, research journals and reports, radio and television, etc.) transfer information from one location to another.

[26] These were treated in more detail in Chapter 8
[27] For analysis of these concepts see Chapter 7, Section 2
[28] But see Meier, R.L. (1962) *A Communications Theory of Urban Growth* and the brief discussion in Chapter 7

Consumers require information about availability of goods and prices. Producers require information about demand, competitors' prices, the level of business activity, new techniques and factor availability.

Costs are involved in getting hold of information; these costs depend not only on the communication media used but on the degree of spatial dispersion in economic activity. Although it varies according to the media available, communication costs will normally be lower when production and population centres coincide. This is particularly so since personal contacts are still an important mode of communication in the market place. If a growth point means a set of interrelated industries located in or near a sizeable urban centre, then a growth point is likely to benefit from communications economies.

The major polarisation forces can be lumped under economies of scale and under external economies. These economies arise to a large extent from *indivisibilities*, because in spatial economics we simply cannot treat factors of production and production processes as perfectly divisible. Indivisibilities do not permit proportionality to be maintained between inputs at all levels of output, and result in increasing returns to scale. But the distinction between scale economies and external economies is very difficult to draw. External economies are often regarded as the main factor explaining the agglomeration of production and population. But if we look at so-called external economy effects from the viewpoint of the economy rather than an individual firm or industry, many of them can be reduced to scale economies, or to the existence of indivisibilities (for example, the lumpiness of public investment projects). The growth of specialised services for repair, information, banking and energy consequent upon the expansion at one location of several plants in an industry all come under this head. In this case these specialised activities can only be established at some minimum level of production because of scale economies. Even the availability of schools, other forms of social overhead capital and recreational facilities cannot unequivocally be explained in terms of external economies. The tendency for new plants to be set up at centres where infrastructure of this kind exists is better explained, once again, by indivisibilities and by the high costs of transferring such services from one location to another.[29] The only clear external economies are

---

[29] Bos, H.C. (1965) *Spatial Dispersion of Economic Activity*. 12–13

technical ones – according to which the physical output of a production process is not only dependent on its own inputs but on the outputs and inputs of other production processes – in other words, the inter-industry linkages stressed by industrial complex analysis.

Even leaving aside scale economies and external technological economies, there are other factors that favour concentration at one location rather than dispersion. Certain locations have more desirable characteristics for development than others. They may possess a prolific resource endowment with easily obtainable supplies of raw materials. They may possess favourable topographical features that confer special advantages as industrial sites or as transport nodes. Given the existing pattern of human settlements, some locations will have greater access to markets (i.e. occur at points of high income potential) and high population densities may result in an accessible labour supply. If the region already has a transport network, reflecting the prior development of population centres and markets, some locations will be transhipment points where economies can be gained from breaking of bulk operations and the performance of allied services. Some sites may have specific locational advantages, such as a deep water harbour which is a non-transportable factor that cannot be reproduced elsewhere. Thus, after assessing the locational advantages and disadvantages relating to each site, i.e. input–output access, some sites will emerge with substantial net locational advantages for a specified industry or industries, and agglomeration is likely at such centres.

The forces making for spatial concentration of economic activity are not yet exhausted. The general equilibrium mechanism itself probably has a tendency to centralise industrial activity. The pooling of flows of resources together at a limited number of centres may facilitate a better adjustment of variable proportions in the production process, while in the case of fixed proportions unemployed resources are more likely to be utilised.[30] Where there is a large number of small production centres, they are much more likely to suffer from alternating periods of congestion and capital shortage, on the one hand, and having to pay heavy overhead costs to maintain idle capital on the other. Finally, in industries characterised by certain kinds of market structure and in certain demand conditions, uncertainty about competitors' pricing and other policies may induce

---

[30] Lefeber, L. (1958) *Allocation in Space.* 129–32

firms to locate next to each other, even though the socially optimal location pattern may be dispersion. In location theory, the application of games strategies may quite often result in strong agglomerating tendencies.[31]

When stressing the existence of substantial agglomeration economies, the possibility of diseconomies of scale and external diseconomies should not be forgotten. At some level of population density and/or industrial concentration, the benefits accruing from agglomeration will be outweighed by diseconomies. Predominant among these will be the costs of urban congestion and the overloading of transport facilities. Also, at some city size the *per capita* cost of providing municipal services will rise, though the optimum size may vary significantly from service to service. In addition, the concentration of industries within a limited area may result in rising factor prices (particularly, for labour and land) if factor supply curves are inelastic. The concept of a growth pole or growth point is, therefore, related to some notion, though difficult to quantify, of an optimum size of production and population centre at which maximum advantage is gained from scale and external economies without incurring serious diseconomies of agglomeration. Growth points have a critical minimum size which permits scale economies and promotes development over the growth area as a whole, and an optimum size beyond which net diseconomies are realised. The policy inference is that growth points should not be planned as 'explosive', but instead should be promoted in a way that maximises expansion in the surrounding zone of influence without sacrificing efficiency. Arresting the development of growth points may require direct intervention since congestion costs may fall upon society long before they affect private business. If the optimum size of growth point is reached before the objectives of policy for the region as a whole have been achieved, the correct action is to select a new secondary growth point at considerable distance from the first and promote growth from there.

The above analysis has shown the case (within finite limits) for concentrating economic resources at certain key locations rather than spreading them thinly over a whole region. This case rests upon spatial differentiation in resources, a given uneven distribution of

[31] See Chapter 4.4. Also Isard, W. and Smith, T.E. (1967) Location Games: with Applications to Classic Location Problems. *Papers and Proceedings of the Regional Science Association*, **19**

population and markets that can only be changed in the long run, indivisibilities in production plants and in public investment projects, scale economies in manufacturing, 'central' services and public utilities, and upon external economies of the 'inter-industry linkages' variety. But the growth point concept, particularly its justification as a policy tool, also involves, as we have seen, the hypothesis that centres of agglomeration have zones of influences around them, and that income (or some other indicator) will be maximised in the growth area as a whole by concentrating development at the growth point. This is the argument used to justify disproportionate allocations of public investment for infrastructure purposes at the growth point itself. It is, therefore, necessary to outline briefly some of the inter-relationships between the growth point and its zone of influence (the growth area).

In the first place, the existence of a growth point must involve a certain degree of structural imbalance over the region as a whole. If a growth point means, among other things, a new industrial complex, then this complex will be heavily concentrated in or around the growth point itself. Supplying industries (of raw materials and intermediate goods) already established in the zone of influence will be stimulated by the complex, but even allowing for this there will be marked disparities between the extent of industry in the growth point and in the surrounding area. At greater distances from the growth point, beyond the outer boundary of its zone of influence, income levels may stagnate and areas decline. The growth point philosophy is that such areas are bound to stagnate in any event, and that the structural imbalance that results from concentrating expansion at the growth point will result in higher average incomes *per capita* for the region as a whole. It is this structural imbalance which leads to the polarisation flows that reinforce the growth point.

Secondly, the key industries emphasised in growth pole discussions are, since their function is to accelerate growth within the region, probably 'export' industries (i.e. industries serving national markets). Growth-point theory implicitly draws upon the export-base concept, except that it gives it a further dimension by drawing a geographical division between the export base (key industries at the growth point) and the supplying industries dependent upon it which, though some may form part of the complex at the centre, may tend to be dispersed over the zone of influence. The zone of influence may provide an important service to the growth point by supplying its industries with raw materials and, more generally, with labour. Income received in the zone is raised by receipts from the sale of raw materials and wages earned by commuting workers. Indeed, there is something to be said for equating the growth point with a central labour market and equating the zone of influence with a labour catchment area; one approximate method of plotting the boundary of the surrounding zone is to plot the travel-to-work limits between the zone and the centre.[32]

Thirdly, the growth point will, in turn, service its surrounding area by providing the population of that area with supplies of goods and services that need a high minimum population threshold for viability. Such goods and services will include: physical commodities, such as consumer durables supplied by department or specialist stores; services supplied by the private sector such as the professional services of architects, lawyers and accountants, or entertainment and leisure facilities (theatres, swimming baths, etc.); public services that lend themselves to economies of scale (technical colleges, specialist hospital services, etc.). The importance of these functions will be revealed by data on commuting trips and by examination of the composition of traffic and transportation flows generally.

Finally, the growth point has a socio-economic function – to affect prevailing attitudes to the desirability of economic growth. In regions which are not highly developed and with a slow growth record, one of the objectives of importing an advanced technological industrial complex to the growth point is to transform social attitudes through the zone of influence and to make economic growth there more likely in the future. This is to be achieved by the incentives of higher wages making local workers more productivity-minded and

---

[32] For an alternative model see Goldner, W. (1955) Spatial and Locational Aspects of Metropolitan Labour Markets. *American Economic Review*, **45** 113–28. He argues that the spatial supply of labour is obtained by aggregating the *normal preference areas* of individual workers. A NPA is defined as that geographical area within which an individual is willing to work in normal economic conditions. Differences in preferences and dispersal of residences will lead to overlapping of NPAs. If we aggregate the NPAs of a group of workers we obtain a preference profile. The boundary of the labour catchment area will be found beyond the perimeter of residences at the limit of peripheral workers' NPAs. It is delimited not so much by the physical boundaries of urban areas as by subjective factors i.e. the locational preferences of workers. To the extent that labour supply conditions dictate selection of a growth point, the ideal location will be at or near the peak of the aggregate preference profile

by the growth industries showing local entrepreneurs the possibilities of growth and highlighting the existence of investment opportunities. In some cases growth points will be developed in old-established stagnating industrial regions. Here, their socio-economic role is that the influx of new entrepreneurial talent may dispel the pessimistic expectations of indigenous businessmen and educate them to a higher level of technology and to employ new production and management techniques generally. A highly concentrated enclave of technically advanced, fast growing industry may result in accelerated development through the zone of influence via its effect on the expectations patterns and behaviour of the indigenous population. The little empirical work done on this aspect of the relationship between the growth point and its surrounding area suggests that this may be more a hope than an inevitable part of the relationship.[33]

Conclusions

In summary, agglomeration economies make concentrations of production and population more efficient than dispersal. These economies include increasing returns to scale within the firm, external technological economies, and economies of scale in the supply of urban services. Thus, even in a free market economy we find unbalanced growth spatially. Industrial activity, establishments supplying public utilities and other services that require a high population threshold for viability, and population expansion itself will cluster around certain focal points. The operation of market forces will have selected these focal points because they have special locational advantages – access to raw material sources or markets, unique non-transportable facilities, or favourable topographical features. These growth centres have influential effects on economic activity in the region where they are located. Their expansion may divert activity from peripheral areas which may lose population and fail to gain a proportionate share of capital and entrepreneurial talent, but from the point of view of the region as a whole this diversionary tendency will be more than offset by induced economic expansion in the zones of influence surrounding each centre. These induced benefits will include provision of employment for the zone's population and markets for its input–supplying and primary industries.

---

[33] James, B.G.S. (1964–5) The Incompatibility of Industrial and Trading Cultures: A Critical Appraisal of the Growth-Point Concept. *Journal of Industrial Economics*, 13 90–4

The assumption behind growth-point analysis as a planning tool is that the agglomeration that proves profitable for the private investor and entrepreneur also results in benefits to society as a whole (especially in the sense that the region is better off than if economic activity were dispersed). This assumption is more reasonable if we recognise that there are limits to the build-up of activity at the focal points, i.e. that there is some optimum size beyond which net diseconomies emerge.

In a dynamic framework, there will be at any period of time embryonic growth points that will develop in the future if aggregate economic growth and population expansion continue. If policy-makers aim to accelerate growth in lagging regions, their task must be to choose the potential growth points in these regions before market forces bring them into existence. Although regional planners may create growth points out of nothing if enough resources are available, a rational selection will choose centres with locational advantages and conditions conducive to population expansion. It is arguable that the function of regional planning in this sphere is merely to anticipate the market. Once the efficiency of growth points is accepted, most individual regional policies fall into place. Social overhead capital may be concentrated at growth points by allocating them a disproportionate share of public investment; they may also be given preferential treatment in housing programmes, local authority subsidies, etc. Selective aid to migrants may be used to encourage migration *within* the region towards the designated centres. If these steps are taken, inducements to private industry can afford to be non-selective within the region since the infrastructure and availability of services would naturally draw industrialists to the growth points.

The advent of growth points (or growth poles) as an element in regional planning strategy reflects a parallel development in the theory of regional economics. Although location theory has a long ancestry and location analysts obviously treated distance factors explicitly, the early development of regional economics proper was devoid of spatial content. Regional economics began as an amalgamation of macroeconomics (theory of income determination) and international trade theory.[34] Regions were looked upon as homogeneous units without intra-regional spatial differentiation. In effect, they

---

[34] For instance, Ohlin, B. (1933) *Interregional and International Trade*. Also the Metzler-type analysis (*Econometrica*. 1950) described in Chapter 10

could be treated for analytical purposes as points. More recently, it has been recognised that understanding of inter-regional relations can be improved by emphasis on spatial differences *within* regions. This recognition accounts for the interest developed in *intra*-regional as well as inter-regional flow analysis (*polarisation analysis*); metropolitan economics, central place theory, and urban hierarchy studies; agglomeration tendencies in location theory, industrial complex analysis and reconciliation of input–output analysis with location theory; the structure of regional labour markets, transport networks and nodes, and the spatial diffusion of innovations and 'growth-mindedness'; and, above all, gravity potential models. The rationale behind growth-point analysis is largely based on some of these analytical concepts and techniques. To this extent, the growth-point concept represents an important step forward in the integration of spatial and regional economics.

Bibliography

This bibliography lists the books and articles referred to in the notes plus other works which were helpful in the germination of the ideas in this book. It is not intended to be a comprehensive bibliography on regional economics. In particular, empirical work with no theoretical implications has been excluded.

Books
ALONSO, W. (1964) *Location and Land Use: Towards a General Theory of Land Rent.*

ARTLE, R. (1959) *Studies in the Structure of the Stockholm Economy.*

BALASSA, B. (1962) *The Theory of Economic Integration.*

BARNA, T. (edit) (1963) *Structural Interdependence and Economic Development.*

BECKMANN, M.J. (1968) *Location Theory.*
— and MARSCHAK, T. (1956) *An Activity Analysis Approach to Location Theory.* Cowles Foundation Paper, No. 99.

BERRY, B.J.L. (1967) *Geography of Market Centres and Retail Distribution.*

BOGUE, D.J. (1949) *The Structure of the Metropolitan Community.*
— and BEALE, C.L. (1961) *Economic Areas of the United States.*

BORTS, G.H. (1961) *Regional Cycles of Manufacturing Employment in the United States, 1914–53,* N.B.E.R.
— and STEIN, J.L. (1964) *Economic Growth in a Free Market.*

BOS, H.C. (1965) *Spatial Dispersion of Economic Activity.*

BOSKOFF, A. (1962) *The Sociology of Urban Regions.*

BOUDEVILLE, J.R. (1966) *Problems of Regional Economic Planning.*

BRAZER, H.E. (1959) *City Expenditures in the United States,* N.B.E.R.

REGIONAL ECONOMICS

BUNGE, W. (1962) *Theoretical Geography.*

CHAMBERLIN, E.H. (1956) *The Theory of Monopolistic Competition.* 7th edition.

CHAPIN, F.S., Jr, *Urban Land Use Planning.* 2nd edition.
— and WEISS, S.F. (edits) (1962) *Urban Growth Dynamics.*

CHENERY, H.B. and CLARK, P.G. (1959) *Interindustry Economics.*

CHINITZ, B. (edit) (1964) *City and Suburb: The Economics of Metropolitan Growth.*

CHIPMAN, J.S. (1950) *The Theory of Inter-Sectoral Money Flows and Income Formation.*

CHISHOLM, M.D.I. (1962) *Rural Settlement and Land Use: An Essay in Location.*

CHRISTALLER, W. (1966) *Central Places in Southern Germany.* Translated by C.W. Baskin.

DEAN, W.H. (1938) *The Theory of Geographic Location of Economic Activities.*

DICKINSON, R.E. (1964) *City and Region.*

DUNCAN, O.D. *et al.* (1960) *Metropolis and Region.*

DUNN, E.S., Jr. (1954) *The Location of Agricultural Production.*

ECKSTEIN, O. (1958) *Water Resource Development.*

FEDERAL RESERVE SYSTEM (1955) *Record of Conference on the Inter-regional Flow of Funds.*

FFORDE, J.S. (1956) *An International Trade in Managerial Skills.*

FIREY, W. (1947) *Land Use in Central Boston.*

FRIEDMANN, J.P. and ALONSO, W. (1964) *Regional Development: A Reader.*

GIBBS, J.P. (edit) (1961) *Urban Research Methods.*

GOODRICH, C. (1934) *Migration and Economic Opportunity.*

GREENHUT, M.L. (1963) *Microeconomics and the Space Economy.*
— (1956) *Plant Location in Theory and Practice.*

HAAVELMO, T. (1954) *A Study in the Theory of Economic Evolution.*

HAGGETT, P. (1966) *Locational Analysis in Human Geography.*
HALL, P.G. (edit) (1966) *Von Thünen's Isolated State.*
HANNA, F. (1959) *State Income Differentials, 1919–54.*
HAWLEY, A.H. (1950) *Human Ecology.*
HIRSCH, W.Z. (edit) (1963) *Urban Life and Form.*
— (1964) *Elements of Regional Accounts.*
— (1966) *Regional Accounts for Policy Decisions.*
HIRSCHMAN, A.O. (1958) *The Strategy of Economic Development.*
HOCHWALD, W. (edit) (1961) *Design of Regional Accounts.*
HOOVER, E.M. (1937) *Location Theory and the Shoe and Leather Industries.*
— (1948) *The Location of Economic Activity.*
— and VERNON, R. (1959) *Anatomy of a Metropolis.*
HOYT, H. (1939) *The Structure and Growth of Residential Neighbourhoods in American Cities.*

ISAAC, J. (1947) *Economics of Migration.*
ISARD, W. (1956) *Location and Space-Economy.*
— (1960) *Methods of Regional Analysis.*
— and CUMBERLAND, J.H. (edits) (1961) *Regional Economic Planning: Techniques of Analysis for Less Developed Areas.* O.E.C.D.
— SCHOOLER, E.W. and VIETORISZ, T. (1959) *Industrial Complex Analysis and Regional Development.*

JEROME, H. (1926) *Migration and Business Cycles.* N.B.E.R.
JOHNSON, H.G. (1958) *International Trade and Economic Growth.*

KUENNE, R.E. (1963) *The Theory of General Economic Equilibrium.*

LEFEBER, L. (1958) *Allocation in Space: Production, Transport and Industrial Location.*
LEONTIEF, W.W. (1966) *Input–Output Economics.*
LÖSCH, A. (1954) *The Economics of Location.*
LOWRY, I.S. (1964) *A Model of Metropolis.*

MARGOLIS, J. (edit) (1966) *The Public Economy of Urban Communities.*

MAYER, H.M. and KOHN, C.F. (edits) (1959) *Readings in Urban Geography.*

MCCRONE, G. (1969) *Regional Policy in Britain.*

MCKENZIE, R.D. (1933) *The Metropolitan Community.*

MEADE, J.E. (1961) *A Neo-Classical Theory of Economic Growth.*

MEIER, R.L. (1962) *A Communications Theory of Urban Growth.*

MEYER, J.R. et al. (1965) *The Urban Transportation Problem.*

MOES, J.E. (1962) *Local Subsidies for Industry.*

MUSGRAVE, R.A. (1959) *The Theory of Public Finance.*

MYRDAL, G. (1957) *Economic Theory and Under-Developed Regions.*

NATIONAL BUREAU OF ECONOMIC RESEARCH (1957) *Studies in Income and Wealth.* Vol. 21 *Regional Income.*

NEUTZE, G.M. (1965) *Economic Policy and the Size of Cities.*

NOURSE, H.O. (1968) *Regional Economics.*

O.E.C.D. (1965) *Wages and Labour Mobility.*

OHLIN, B. (1933) *Interregional and International Trade.*

PARK, R.E. et al. (1925) *The City.*

PERLOFF, H.S. and DODDS, V.W. (1963) *How a Region Grows.*

— DUNN, E.S., Jr., LAMPARD, E.E. and MUTH, R.F. (1960) *Regions, Resources and Economic Growth.*

PFOUTS, R.W. (edit) (1960) *The Techniques of Urban Economic Analysis.*

QUINN, J.A. (1960) *Human Ecology.*

RATCLIFF, R.V. (1949) *Urban Land Economics.*

REISSMAN, L. (1964) *The Urban Process: Cities in Industrial Societies.*

REYNOLDS, L.G. (1951) *The Structure of Labour Markets.*

ROMANS, J.T. (1965) *Capital Exports and Growth among U.S. Regions.*

SCHALLER, H.G. (edit) (1963) *Public Expenditure Decisions in the Urban Community.*

SCITOVSKY, T. de (1958) *Economic Theory and Western European Integration.*

SHRYOCK, H.S., Jr. (1964) *Population Mobility within the United States.*

SIMPSON, P.B. (1953) *Regional Aspects of Business Cycles and Special Studies of the Pacific North West.*

SIRJAMAKI, J. (1964) *The Sociology of Cities.*

SPENGLER, J.J. and DUNCAN, O.D. (edits) (1956) *Demographic Analysis.*

— — (1956) *Population Theory and Policy.*

THOMPSON, W.R. (1965) *A Preface to Urban Economics.*

TIEBOUT, C.M. (1962) *The Community Economic Base Study.*

UNITED NATIONS (1953) *The Determinants and Consequences of Population Trends.*

— (1954) *World Population Conference.* Vol. II.

UNIVERSITIES – N.B.E.R. (1961) *Public Finances: Needs, Sources and Utilisation.*

VICKREY, W.S. (1964) *Microstatics.*

WARNTZ, W. (1959) *Toward a Geography of Price: A Study in Geo-Econometrics.*

WEBER, A. (1929) *Theory of the Location of Industry.* Translated by C.J.Friedrich.

WEIMER, A.M. and HOYT, H. (1960) *Principles of Real Estate.*

WEINTRAUB, S. (1956) *Price Theory.*

WHITMAN, M. VON N. (1967) *International and Interregional Payments Adjustment: A Synthetic View* (Princeton Studies in International Finance, No. 19.

WILLHELM, S.M. (1962) *Urban Zoning and Land Use Theory.*

WILLIAMS, A. (1962) *Public Finance and Budgetary Policy.*

WINGO, L., Jr. (1961) *Transportation and Urban Land.*

ZIPF, G.K. (New edn 1965) *Human Behaviour and the Principle of Least Effort.*

Articles

Abbreviations

A.E.R.	American Economic Review
A.S.R.	American Sociological Review
Eca.	Economica
E.J.	Economic Journal
Em.	Econometrica
J.A.I.P.	Journal of American Institute of Planners
J.A.S.A.	Journal of American Statistical Association
J.P.E.	Journal of Political Economy
J.R.S.	Journal of Regional Science
L.B.R.	Lloyds Bank Review
O.E.P.	Oxford Economic Papers
P.P.R.S.A.	Papers and Proceedings of the Regional Science Association
Q.J.E.	Quarterly Journal of Economics
R.E. & S.	Review of Economics and Statistics
R.E.S.	Review of Economic Studies

ACKLEY, G. (1942) Spatial Competition in a Discontinuous Market. *Q.J.E.* **56**.

AIROV, J. (1963) The Construction of Interregional Business Cycle Models. *J.R.S.* **5**.

— (1967) Fiscal Policy Theory in an Interregional Economy: General Interregional Multipliers and their Application. *P.P.R.S.A.* **19**.

ALONSO, W. (1967) A Reformulation of Classical Location Theory and its Relation to Rent Theory. *P.P.R.S.A.* **19**.

ARTLE, R. (1963) Public Policy and the Space Economy of the City. in L. Wingo (edit.), *Cities and Space*.

AYDALOT, P. (1965) *Note sur les économies externes et quelques notions connexes*. Revue Économique. **16**.

BAILLARGEON, J.P. (1961) *Le Rôle des Pôles dans le Développement: Exposé Introductif*. Développement et Civilisations. **5**.

BAUMOL, W.J. and IDE, E.A. (1956) Variety in Retailing. *Management Science*. **3**.

BECKMANN, M.J. (February 1957) On the Distribution of Rent and Residential Density in Cities. Paper presented at Yale University.

BERRY, B.J.L. and GARRISON, W.L. (1958) Recent Development of Central Place Theory. *P.P.R.S.A.*

BHAGWHATI, J. (1966) The Pure Theory of International Trade: A Survey. In *Surveys of Economic Theory*. Vol. II American Economic Association and Royal Economic Society.

BIRD, R.M. (1967) Regional Policies in a Common Market. In *Fiscal Harmonisation in Common Markets*. Vol. I: *Theory* (C.S. Shoup (edit)).

BJORK, G.J. (1968) Regional Economic Adjustment: United States, 1880–1950. *O.E.P.* **20**.

BORTS, G.H. (1960) The Equalisation of Returns and Regional Economic Growth. *A.E.R.* **50**.

BOWSHER, N.N., DAANE, J.D. and EINZIG, R. (1957) The Flow of Funds between Regions of the United States. *P.P.R.S.A.* **3**.

BRONFENBRENNER, M. (1939–40) The Keynesian Equations and the Balance of Payments. *R.E.S.* **7**.

BUCHANAN, J.M. and MOES, J.E. (1960) A Regional Countermeasure to National Wage Standardisation. *A.E.R.* **50**.

CHINITZ, B. (1966) Appropriate Goals for Regional Economic Policy. *Urban Studies*. **3**.

CHIPMAN, J.S. (1950) The Multi-Sector Multiplier. *Em.* **18**.

CLARK, C. (October 1966) Industrial Location and Economic Potential. *L.B.R.*

— and PETERS, G.H. (March 1964) Steering Employment by Taxes and Rebates. *Town and Country Planning*. **32**.

DACEY, M.F. (1966) Population of Places in a Central Place Hierarchy. *J.R.S.* **6**.

DEVLETOGLOU, N.E. (1965) A Dissenting View of Duopoly and Spatial Competition. *Eca.* **32**.

DUNCAN, O.D. (1959) Service Industries and the Urban Hierarchy. *P.P.R.S.A.* **5**.

EASTERLIN, R.A. (1958) Long Term Regional Income Changes: Some Suggested Factors. *P.P.R.S.A.* **4**.
— (1960) Regional Growth of Income: Long Term Tendencies. In *Population Redistribution and Economic Growth, United States, 1870–1950*. Vol. II. *Analyses of Economic Change*, by S.Kuznets, A.R.Miller and R.A.Easterlin.

EMMER, R. (1957) Influences on Regional Credit Expansion. *P.P.R.S.A.* **3**.

ENGERMAN, S. (1965) Regional Aspects of Stabilisation Policy. In *Essays in Fiscal Federalism*. R.A.Musgrave (edit).

ENKE, S. (1942) Space and Value. *Q.J.E.* **56**.
— (1951) Equilibrium among Spatially Separated Markets: Solution by Electric Analogue. *Em.* **19**.

FETTER, F.A. (1923–4) The Economic Law of Market Areas. *Q.J.E.* **38**.

FLEISCHER, B.M. (1963) Some Economic Aspects of Puerto Rican Migration to the United States. *R.E. & S.* **45**.

FOURAKER, L. (1955) A Note on Regional Multipliers. *P.P.R.S.A.* **1**.

GARBARINO, J.W. (1954) Some Implications of Regional and Industrial Differences in Unemployment. *Western Economics Association.*

Geographia Polonica. (1964) Methods of Economic Regionalisation. **40**.

GOLDNER, W. (1955) Spatial and Locational Aspects of Metropolitan Labour Markets. *A.E.R.* **45**.

GUPTA, S.P. and HUTTON, J.P. (1968) Economies of Scale in Local Government Services. *Royal Commission on Local Government in England.* Research Studies No. 3.

GUTHRIE, J.A. (1955) Economies of Scale and Regional Development. *P.P.R.S.A.* **1**.

GUTTENBERG, A.Z. (1960) Urban Structure and Urban Growth. *J.A.I.P.* **26**.

HÄGERSTRAND, T. (1952) The Propagation of Innovation Waves. *Lund Studies in Geography*, Series B. *Human Geography.* No. 4.
— (1966) Aspects of the Spatial Structure of Social Communication and the Diffusion of Information. *P.P.R.S.A.* **16**.

HAIG, R.M. (1926) Toward an Understanding of the Metropolis. *Q.J.E.* **40**.

HAMMER, C. and IKLÉ, F.C. (1957) Intercity Telephone and Airline Traffic Related to Distance and the 'Propensity to Interact'. *Sociometry.* **20**.

HANSEN, N.M. (1967) Development Pole Theory in a Regional Context. *Kyklos.* **20**.

HARRIS, C.D. (1954) The Market as a Factor in the Localisation of Industry in the United States. *Annals of the Association of American Geographers.* **44**.

— and ULLMAN, E.L. (1945) The Nature of Cities. *Annals of the American Academy of Political and Social Science.* **242**.

HARTLAND, P. (1949) Interregional Payments Compared with International Payments. *Q.J.E.* **63**.

HARTMAN, L.M. and SECKLER, D. (1967) Toward the Application of Dynamic Growth Theory to Regions. *J.R.S.* **7**.

HERBERT, J.D. and STEVENS, B.H. (1960) A Model for the Distribution of Residential Activity in Urban Areas. *J.R.S.* **2**.

HIRSCH, W.Z. (1959) Expenditure Implications of Metropolitan Growth and Consolidation. *R.E. & S.* **41**.

HOOVER, E.M. (1936–7) Spatial Price Discrimination. *R.E.S.* **4**.

HOTELLING, H. (1929) Stability in Competition. *E.J.* **39**.

HUFF, D.L. (1961) Ecological Characteristics of Consumer Behaviour. *P.P.R.S.A.* **7**.

HUGHES, J.T. (1967) Economic Aspects of Local Government Reform. *Scottish Journal of Political Economy.* **14**.

HYSON, C.D. and HYSON, W.P. (1950) The Economic Law of Market Areas. *Q.J.E.* **64**.

INGRAM, J.C. (1959) State and Regional Payments Mechanisms. *Q.J.E.* **73**.

ISARD, W. and FREUTEL, G. (1954) Regional and National Product Projections and their Interrelations. In *Studies in Income and Wealth.* Vol. 16 *Long Range Economic Projection.* National Bureau of Economic Research.

— and PECK, M.J. (1954) Location Theory and International and Interregional Trade Theory. *Q.J.E.*

— and SMITH, T.E. (1967) Location Games: with Applications to Classic Location Problems. *P.P.R.S.A.* **19**.

— and SCHOOLER, E.W. (1959) Industrial Complex Analysis, Agglomeration Economies and Regional Development. *J.R.S.* **1**.

— and WHITNEY, V.H. (1949) Metropolitan Site Selection. *Social Forces.* **27**.

ISBELL, E.C. (1944) Internal Migration in Sweden and Intervening Opportunities. *A.S.R.* **9**.

JAFFE, A.J. and WOLFBEIN, S.L. (1945) Internal Migration and Full Employment. *J.A.S.A.* **40**.

JAMES, B.G.S. (1964–5) The Incompatibility of Industrial and Trading Cultures: A Critical Appraisal of the Growth Point Concept. *Journal of Industrial Economies.* **13**.

KISH, L. (1954) Differentiation in Metropolitan Areas. *A.S.R.* **49**.

KOOPMANS, T.C. and BECKMANN, M.J. (1957) Assignment Problems and Location of Economic Activities. *Em.* **25**.

KOSLOWSKI, J. and HUGHES, J.T. (1967) Urban Threshold Theory and Analysis. *Journal of the Town Planning Institute.* **53**.

— — (1968) Threshold Analysis – An Economic Tool for Town and Regional Planning. *Urban Studies.* **5**.

KRUTILLA, J.V. (1955) Criteria for Evaluating Regional Development Programmes. *A.E.R.* **45**.

LERNER, A.P. and SINGER, H.W. (1937) Some Notes on Duopoly and Spatial Competition. *J.P.E.* **45**.

LEVEN, C.L. (1964) Establishing Goals for Regional Economic Development. *J.A.I.P.* **30**.

LOMAX, K.S. (1943) Expenditure per Head and Size of Population. *Journal of the Royal Statistical Society.* **106**.

MAKOWER, H., MARSCHAK, J. and ROBINSON, H.W. (1938–40) Studies in the Mobility of Labour. *O.E.P.*

MALISZ, B. (1969) Implications of Threshold Theory for Urban and Regional Planning. *Journal of the Town Planning Institute.* **55**.

MERA, K. (1967) Tradeoff between Aggregate Efficiency and Interregional Equity: A Static Analysis. *Q.J.E.* **81**.

METZLER, L.A. (1950) A Multiple Region Theory of Income and Trade. *Em.* **18**.

MEYER, J.R. (1966) Regional Economics: A Survey. In *Surveys of Economic Theory*. Vol. II. American Economic Association and Royal Economic Society.

MILLS, E.S. and LAV, M.R. (1964) A Model of Market Areas with Free Entry. *J.P.E.* **72**.

MORONEY, J.R. (1967) The Strong-Factor-Intensity Hypothesis: A Multisectoral Test. *J.P.E.* **75**.

— and WALKER, J.M. (1966) A Regional Test of the Heckscher–Ohlin Hypothesis. *J.P.E.* **74**.

MORRILL, R.L. (1963) The Development of Spatial Distribution of Towns in Sweden. *Annals of the Association of American Geographers*. **53**.

— (1968) Waves of Spatial Diffusion. *J.R.S.* **8**

MOSES, L.N. (1960) A General Equilibrium Model of Production, Interregional Trade and Location of Industry. *R.E. & S.* **42**.

— (1958) Location and the Theory of Production. *Q.J.E.* **72**.

— (1955) The Stability of Interregional Trading Patterns and Input–Output Analysis. *A.E.R.* **45**.

MUNDELL, R.A. (1957) International Trade and Factor Mobility. *A.E.R.* **47**.

MUTH, R.F. (1961) The Spatial Structure of the Housing Market. *P.P.R.S.A.* **7**.

NEEDLEMAN, L. (January 1965) What are We to Do about the Regional Problem? *L.B.R.*

NEFF, P. (1949) Interregional Cyclical Differentials. *A.E.R.* Papers **39**.

NEVIN, E.T. (December 1966) The Case for a Regional Policy. *Three Banks Review*.

NORTH, D.C. (1955) Location Theory and Regional Economic Growth. *J.P.E.* **63**.

OKUN, B. and RICHARDSON, R.W. (1961) Regional Income Inequality and Internal Population Migration. *Economic Development and Cultural Change*. **9**.

OLIVERA, J.H.G. (1967) Is Free Trade a Perfect Substitute for Factor Mobility? *E.J.* **77**.

OLSEN, E. (1965) Regional Income Differences within a Common Market. *P.P.R.S.A.* **14**.

PAPPENFORT, D.M. (1959) The Ecological Field and the Metropolitan Community: Manufacturing and Management. *American Journal of Sociology.* **65**.

PARRY LEWIS, J. and TRAILL, A.L. (1968) The Assessment of Shopping Potential and the Demand for Shops. *Town Planning Review.* **38**.

PEACOCK, A.T. (1965) Towards a Theory of Interregional Fiscal Policy. *Public Finance.* **20**.

PERLOFF, H.S. (1957) Interrelations of State Income and Industrial Structure. *R.E. & S.* **39**.

PERROUX, F. (1955) *Note sur la notion de pôle de croissance. Économie Appliquée.* **7**.

POLAK, J.J. (1955) The Post-War International Cycle. In E. Lundberg (edit), *The Business Cycle in the Post-War World.*

POTTIER, P. (1963) *Axes de Communication et développement économique. Revue Économique.* **14**.

PREDOHL, A. (1928) The Theory of Location in its Relation to General Economics. *J.P.E.* **36**.

PRATT, R.T. (1967) Regional Production Inputs and Regional Income Generation. *J.R.S.* **7**.

PULLEN, M.J. (1964) Transport Costs and the Disappearance of Space in the Theory of the Firm. *Yorkshire Bulletin of Economic and Social Research.* **16**.

RAHMAN, M.A. (1963) Regional Allocation of Investment. *Q.J.E.* **77**.

RAVENSTEIN, E.G. (1885) The Laws of Migration. *Journal of the Royal Statistical Society.* **48**.

REDLICH, F. (1953) Ideas, Their Migration in Space and Transmittal Over Time. *Kyklos.* **6**.

REILLY, W.J. (1929) Methods for the Study of Retail Relationships. *University of Texas Bulletin.* No. 2944.

REINER, T.A. (1965) Sub-National and National Planning: Decision Criteria. *P.P.R.S.A.* **14**.

RODGERS, A. (1957) Some Aspects of Industrial Diversification in the United States. *Economic Geography*. **33**.

RODWIN, L. (1950) The Theory of Residential Growth and Structure. *The Appraisal Journal*. **18**.

SAMUELSON, P.A. (1948) International Trade and Equalisation of Factor Prices. *E.J.* **58**.
— (1949) International Factor Price Equalisation. *E.J.* **59**.
— (1952) Spatial Price Equilibrium and Linear Programming. *A.E.R.* **42**.

SIMON, H.A. (1959) Theories of Decision Making in Economics. *A.E.R.* **49**.

SINGER, H.W. (1936) The 'Courbes des Populations', A Parallel to Pareto's Law. *E.J.* **46**.
— (1938) A Note on Spatial Price Discrimination. *R.E.S.* **5**.

SIRKIN, G. (1959) The Theory of the Regional Economic Base. *R.E. & S.* **41**.

SJAASTAD, L.A. (1962) The Costs and Returns of Human Migration. *J.P.E.* Supplement 70.

SMITH, D.M. (1966) A Theoretical Framework for Geographical Studies of Industrial Location. *Economic Geography*. **42**.

SMITH, V.L. (1963) Minimisation of Economic Rent in Spatial Price Equilibrium. *R.E.S.* **30**.

SMITHIES, A. (1941) Monopolistic Price Policy in a Spatial Market. *Em.* **11**.
— (1941) Optimum Location and Spatial Competition. *J.P.E.* **49**.

STEWART, J.Q. (1947) Empirical Mathematical Rules Concerning the Distribution and Equilibrium of Population. *The Geographical Review*. **37**.

STONE, J.R. (1960) A Comparison of the Economic Structure of Regions Based on the Concept of Distance. *J.R.S.* **2**.

STOUFFER, S.A. (1940) Intervening Opportunities: A Theory Relating Mobility and Distance. *A.S.R.* **5**.

STRODTBECK, F.L. (1949) Equal Opportunity Intervals: A Contribution to the Method of Intervening Opportunity Analysis. *A.S.R.* **14**.

TAKAYAMA, T. and JUDGE, G.C. (1964) Equilibrium among Spatially Separated Markets. *Em.* **32.**

THOMAS, M.D. (1964) The Export Base and Development Stages Theories of Regional Economic Growth: An Appraisal. *Land Economics.* **11.**

THOMPSON, W.R. (1961) Locational Differences in Inventive Effort and their Determinants. In *The Rate and Direction of Inventive Activity.* National Bureau of Economic Research.

TIEBOUT, C.M. (1956) Exports and Regional Growth. *J.P.E.* **64.**

— (1956) A Pure Theory of Local Expenditures. *J.P.E.* **64.**

ULLMAN, E.L. (1962) The Nature of Cities Reconsidered. *P.P.R.S.A.* **9.**

— (1953) Regional Development and the Geography of Concentration. *P.P.R.S.A.* **4.**

VINING, R. (1948) The Region as a Concept in Business Cycle Analysis. *Em.* **16.**

— (1949) The Region as an Economic Entity and Certain Variations to be observed in the Study of Systems of Regions. *A.E.R.* Papers 39.

WASSERMAN, G. (1967) The French Regional Accounting Framework: An Alternative to the Keynesian Approach. *Bulletin of Oxford University Institute of Economics and Statistics.*

WEBBER, M.M. (1964) The Urban Place and the Nonplace Urban Realm. In M. M. Webber (edit), *Explorations in Urban Structure.*

WENDT, P.F. (1958) Economic Growth and Urban Land Values. *The Appraisal Journal.* **26.**

— (1957) Theory of Urban Land Values. *Land Economics.* **33.**

Name Index

Airov, J., 281, 382
Alderson, W., 73
Alonso, W., 121, 124, 130, 137, 143, 145, 149
Andrews, R.B., 165
Arrow, K.J., 289
Artle, R., 127, 128
Aydalot, P., 417

Baillargeon, J-P., 417
Balassa, B., 225, 253, 262, 301
Baskin, C.W., 156
Baumol, W.J., 95, 136, 137, 194
Beale, C.L., 225
Beckmann, M.J., 124, 125, 137, 371
Berry, B.J.L., 160
Blumenfeld, H., 165, 168, 169
Bogue, D.J., 171, 225
Borts, G.H., 4, 277, 342, 348, 350, 354, 405, 406
Bos, H.C., 2, 421
Boskoff, A., 162, 171
Boudeville, J.R., 368, 417
Bowsher, N.N., 262
Brazer, H.E., 188, 198
Bronfenbrenner, M., 263
Browning, H.L., 183
Brownlee, O.H., 210
Burgess, E.W., 146

Cao-Pinna, V., 239, 241
Chamberlin, E.H., 21, 25, 81, 85, 86
Chenery, H.B., 238, 239, 240, 289
Chinitz, B., 177, 188, 403
Chipman, J.S., 281, 286
Christaller, W., 156, 159, 160, 163, 164
Clark, C., 340, 391

Clark, P.G., 238
Cohen, K.J., 95
Cox, R., 73
Cumberland, J.H., 234, 237, 239
Curtis, E.T., 165
Cyert, R.M., 95

Daane, J.D., 262
Dacey, M.F., 160, 182
de Scitovsky, T., 262, 263, 264, 265
de Torres Martinez, M., 239
Deane, P., 234
Delwart, L., 342
Devine, E.J., 388
Devletoglou, N.E., 84, 85
Dodds, V.W., 342
Domar, E.S., 9, 321, 323, 324, 331, 335, 339
Dorau, H.B., 119
Dorfman, R., 361
Duesenberry, J.S., 308
Duncan, O.T., 164, 174, 179
Dunn, E.S., Jr., 336, 343, 345, 346, 348, 356

Easterlin, R.A., 348, 353, 356
Eckstein, O., 402
Edgeworth, F., 373
Einzig, R., 262
Ely, R.T., 119
Emmer, R.E., 262
Engerman, S., 281, 382, 385
Enke, S., 18, 24, 25, 28

Ferguson, C.E., 81
Fetter, F.A., 25, 83
Fforde, J.S., 319
Firey, W., 146

Fisher, A.G.B., 340
Friedrich, C.J., 403

Gajda, R.T., 227
Garbarino, J.W., 277
Garrison, W.L., 160
Garvin, W.W., 361
Geronymakis, S., 234, 237
Gibbs, J.P., 149, 165, 183
Goldner, W., 425
Gordon, R.A., 308
Greenhut, M.L., 8, 20, 24, 28, 81, 88, 91, 98, 104, 108, 109, 110, 111
Gupta, S.P., 198
Guttenberg, A.Z., 119, 122, 123, 146, 155

Haavelmo, T., 295
Hägerstrand, T., 312
Haig, R.M., 119, 120, 121, 137, 148
Hall, P.G., 120
Hammer, C., 134
Hanna, F., 348
Hansen, N.M., 417
Harris, C.D., 146, 153, 154
Harris, S.R., 403
Harrod, R.F., 9, 321, 323, 324, 331, 335, 339
Hartland, P., 262
Hartman, L.M., 322
Hawley, A., 123, 124, 149
Heckscher, E., 287, 290, 291, 294
Herbert, J.D., 126
Hinman, A.G., 119
Hirsch, W.Z., 1, 171, 188, 198, 231, 388, 405
Hitchcock, F.L., 18
Hochwald, W., 231, 233, 342
Hoffenberg, M., 388
Hoover, E.M., 21
Hotelling, H., 8, 25, 81, 82, 84, 86, 87, 88
Hoyt, H., 146, 150, 151, 165
Huff, D.L., 135

Hughes, J.T., 179, 198
Hurd, R.M., 120
Hutton, J.P., 198
Hyson, C.D., 25, 83
Hyson, W.P., 25, 83

Ide, E.A., 136, 137
Iklé, F.C., 134
Ingram, J.C., 262, 263
Isaac, J., 298
Isard, W., 5, 8, 45, 49, 54, 56, 57, 103, 104, 111, 132, 178, 199, 200, 234, 237, 239, 251, 280, 281, 361, 364, 418, 423
Isbell, E.C., 299

James, B.G.S., 426
Johnson, H.G., 326
Judge, G.C., 18

Kish, L., 149, 172
Koopmans, T.C., 18, 371
Kozlowski, J., 179
Krutilla, J.V., 253, 403
Kuenne, R.E., 6, 102, 239, 240
Kuznets, S., 348

Lampard, E.E., 336, 342, 345, 346, 348, 356
Lasuen Sancho, J.R., 239
Launhardt, 1n.
Lav, M.R., 33, 160
Lefeber, L., 8, 103, 104, 111, 112, 113, 114, 115, 116, 292, 370, 422
Leontief, W.W., 238, 239, 290, 346
Lerner, A.P., 8, 25, 85
Leven, C.L., 234, 239, 361
Lewis, J. Parry, 133
Lomax, K.S., 198
Lösch, A., 8, 69, 70, 72, 73, 74, 75, 76, 81, 91, 96, 104, 105, 107, 108, 110, 111, 390
Lowry, I.S., 126
Lundberg, E., 280

INDEX

Malisz, B., 179
March, J.G., 95
Mattila, J.M., 165
McKenzie, R.D., 133, 171
Meade, J., 332
Meier, R.L., 175, 420
Mera, K., 373, 375
Merton, R.K., 313
Metzler, L.A., 9, 254, 256, 281, 427
Miller, A.R., 348
Mills, E.S., 33, 160
Minasian, J.R., 289
Minhas, B.S., 289
Moes, J.E., 415
Moroney, J.R., 290, 291
Morrill, R.L., 165, 312
Moses, L.N., 239, 385
Mundell, R.A., 287, 288
Musgrave, R.A., 188, 203, 212, 281, 382
Muth, R.F., 336, 342, 345, 346, 348, 356

Needleman, L., 389, 396
Neff, P., 277
Nevin, E.T., 389
North, D.C., 225, 250, 336

Ohlin, B., 103, 287, 290, 291, 294, 427
Olsen, E., 294
Ozga, S.A., 322

Pappenfort, D.M., 173, 174
Pareto, A., 182, 288
Park, R.E., 146
Peacock, A.T., 234
Perloff, H.S., 336, 341, 342, 345, 346, 348, 356
Perroux, F., 417
Peters, G.H., 391
Pfister, R.L., 262
Pfouts, R.W., 165, 168
Phelps Brown, E.H., 322

Polak, J.J., 280, 281
Pottier, P., 417
Predohl, A., 104

Quinn, J.A., 122

Ratcliff, R.V., 119
Redlich, F., 312
Reilly, W.J., 132, 133, 134, 166
Reissman, L., 171
Rodwin, L., 152, 403
Romans, J.T., 333, 336, 348
Rosenstein-Rodan, P.N., 370
Ruggles, N.D., 233
Ruggles, R., 233

Samuelson, P.A., 15, 18, 24, 25, 203, 285, 287, 288, 361
Schaller, H.G., 194, 211
Schnore, L.F., 171
Schooler, E.W., 418
Seckler, D., 322
Simon, H.A., 93, 99, 101
Simpson, P.B., 281
Singer, H.W., 8, 21, 25, 85, 182
Sirjamaki, J., 171
Sirkin, G., 248
Smith, D.M., 59
Smith, T.E., 423
Smith, V.L., 18
Sodenblum, S., 342
Solow, R.M., 289, 361
Spengler, J.J., 179
Spivey, W.A., 361
Stein, J.L., 4, 342, 348, 350, 354
Stevens, B.H., 126
Stewart, J.Q., 39, 73, 299
Stone, J.R., 234, 235, 239, 246
Stouffer, S.A., 299

Takayama, T., 18
Thomas, M.D., 336
Thompson, W.R., 1, 165, 177, 185, 187, 312, 387

REGIONAL ECONOMICS

Tiebout, C.M., 165, 194, 204, 206, 207, 250, 336
Traill, A.L., 133

Ullman, E.L., 146, 153, 154, 227, 312, 315

Valavanis-Vail, S., 290
Vickrey, W.S., 211
Vietorisz, T., 418
Vining, R., 225, 226
Von Thünen, J.H., 29, 120

Walker, J.M., 291
Walras, L., 6, 41, 103, 116, 223

Warntz, W., 38, 39, 74, 157
Webber, M.M., 176, 314, 315, 319
Weber, A., 8, 45, 49, 54, 56, 104, 419
Wehrwein, G.S., 119
Weigmann, H., 104
Weimer, A.M., 146
Wendt, P.F., 125, 126
Whitman, M.Von N., 262
Whitney, V.H., 132
Willhelm, S.M., 146
Williams, A., 213
Wingo, L., 120, 123, 137, 139

Zipf, G.K., 182, 299

Subject Index

accelerator: in business cycles, 281–6; and growth, 322n.
accessibility, 119, 124
accounts, regional: 231–46; income and product, 234–7; input-output, 237–46; and theory, 231–2; value of, 231–4
addivity assumption, 238
agglomeration economies: 6, 19, 33, 35, 38, 157, 164, 180, 211, 293, 311, 316, 318, 392, 423, 426; exhaustion of, 355; in gravity models, 135–6; and growth, 348–9, 352, 401; in Hotelling analysis, 83–4; to minimise risks, 93; underestimation of by Lösch, 108; in Weberian theory, 45, 56, 419
agricultural commodities, prices of, 39
agricultural regions, applicability of central place theory to, 164
allocation branch of government, 189, 191
attraction: and repulsion among activities, 153; of retail establishments, how to measure, 134
autonomous investment, 256

backwash effects of growth, 348–9, 419
balance: equation in accounts, 244; in growth, 321–2, 415; lack of, due to growth points, 367, 424; regional, 399
balance of payments: banking system and, 264; capital market and, 265; of a city, 170; factor flows and, 268–9; fiscal influences on, 267–8; and growth, 327–8, 331; income effects on, 266–7; influences on, of a region, 259–62; mechanism of adjustment, 262–70; price effects and, 266; of regions compared with nations, 262, 269–70; smoothness of adjustment in, 270; sticky wages and, 266
base ration. *See under* economic base
Baumol–Ide model, 136–7
behavioural theories of location, 95–100
bid price curves, 130–2
blight, urban, 194
business cycles: 9, ch. 11; alternative approaches to, 275–81; damped, 285; empirical analysis of, 280–1; inter-regional multiplier-accelerator, model, 281–6

capital: goods and base theory, 253; goods industries, location of, 72; labour ratio, 290, 350, in USA, 291; market and balance of payments, 265–6; mobility of, 304–10; output ratio, 322–35 *passim*; stock, 283
cash grants: 212, 213; unconditional, 213–15; specific, 215–17
central government: and budget functions, 188–92; financing of urban government services by, 212–17; responsibility for regional policy, 368–9, 386–7; role in regional accounts, 235; and

447

central government—*cont.*
stabilisation, 380–1; subsidies, 414
central place theory: 156–68; according to Christaller, 156–9; criticisms of, 162–5, 420; generalised, 160–2; and hierarchy, 161–2; and number of places, 158–9
Chamberlin: and competition, 21; treatment of locational interdependence, 86–7
Chicago, 173
city: business location within, 129–32; region, 228–9; optimum size, 178; size, & urban growth, 176–85; and changes in urban hierarchy, 163. *See also under* Urban
Clark–Fisher hypothesis, 340
classical economists, 1, 5
Cobb–Douglas production function, 373, 375, 376, 407
collusion among sellers, 36, 37
communications: 311; nodes, 314, 420–1; theory of urban growth, 175–6
community: choice of, 9, 203–8, 218; participation potential, 178, 200–1
comparative advantage, 290
complementary region, 157, 158
concentric zone hypothesis, 146–50, 155
concept of a region, 223–31
Condorcet paradox, 368
congestion: in cities, 64, 98, 388; influence on location, 66, 99
constraints: of indifference, 85; in linear programming models, 362–3; on number of regions, 224; in regional policy, 372, 387
construction, 279
consumer: durables, 279; goods,

location of, 72; preferences, 203–8
consumption function, 137, 226, 283
contiguity of regions, 224
convergence of *per capita* incomes: 347–57; empirical evidence on, 356–7
cost curves: average in long run, 20; space, 59–69, 79–80, parallel between, and non-spatial curve, 60–2, scope for empirical testing of, 68–9, shape of, 61, 63–5, virtues of, approach, 68–9; total, 96–7
costs: basic, 60, 63; of friction in urban structure, 119–23; locational, 60, 63; in Löschian theory, 106; marginal, 21, 109, 114, 115, constant in Hotelling's analysis, 82, high, in locational interdependence, 86, shape of, 88; migration, *see under* migration; spatial differences in, 89
criticality studies, 170
cross-hauling, 38
curvilinear transport curve, 44, 49, 53–4

decision models, 358–61
decisions of urban governments, 194–6
decomposable system, 284
demand: cone, Löschian, 69–72, modified spatial, 72–7, overlapping, 78; curve, homogeneous in Lösch's theory, 69, departures from homogeneity of, 73–4, kinked, 34, in residential market, 138–45 *passim*; shape of, in spatial oligopoly, 34–5; functions for trade, 290; in space, 20
demonstration effect, 158

Department of Applied Economics, Cambridge, 234
Descartes' ovals, 26
diffusion of knowledge through space, 102, 294, 310–16
discrimination, price, in space, 20–4, 38, 90
dispersion in space: 19–41; of buyers, 28, 34; in duopoly, 84–5; fiscal implications of, 193–4; in locational interdependence, 86–7, 90; of sellers (Von Thünen case), 29–30
distance variables: in regional income models, 270–3. *See also under* space
distributed facilities, 122
distribution branch, 189, 190
disutility of moving, 301
diversification, 177, 276, 380
dominance, 171, 172, 173
dual, the, 18, 365
duopoly, 35–6, 81–5

economic (export) base: of a city, 165–70, Blumenfeld's critique of, 169–70, composition of, 167, low predictive power of, 168, measures of, 167–8; of a region, 225–6, 247–54, criticisms of, 250, 251–4, as a cyclical tool, 277–9; theory of growth, 336–9, compared with Harrod–Domar model, 339
economies of long hauls, 44, 77
economies of scale: 6, 61, 65, 157, 163, 186, 192, 293, 363, 370, 401, 422; in innovation, 315; in urban government services, 196–203, 218, 420, empirical evidence for, 198n.
elasticity of demand: 19, 34, 37, 70, 73, 74, 75, 78; constant, 20; cross, 90; income, for land, 124, for political participation, 197, and resource transfers, 345; in locational interdependence, 27; affected by transport costs, 23; zero, 82, improbability of, in duopoly, 85
elasticity of substitution, 62, 406
electric analogue as a solution to spatial pricing problem, 17–18
embodied technical progress, 311
environmental preferences, 99, 100
equal tax treatment of equals, 192
equality doctrine, 3, 349
equilibrium: conditions of, in Heckscher–Ohlin model, 290, in spatial price theory, 16; of demand and supply for land, 139–40; growth, 321–36, 349; in Lefeber's model, 111–16; level of investment, 309; in open economy, 263; in regional income, 273
equity between regions: 4, 10, 365–6, 371–2; trade-off with efficiency, 371, 372–6
expenditure: 282, 381–4; functions in regional income models, 255; of urban governments, 186
exponents in gravity models, 134–5
exports: autonomous, in base models, 248; and business cycles, 278; endogenous, in input–output analysis, 239; as linear functions of prices, 16; surpluses and regional growth, 325, 327–8
external economies: 80, 187, 315, 363, 401, 419–20, 421–2; difficult to measure, 92; and diseconomies, 395–6, 400, 401; and growth points, 423
extraneous variables in decision models, 358–61

449

factor mobility: 3, 9, ch. 12; and balance of payments, 268–9; and general equilibrium, 287–95, 320; imperfect, 293–4; and regional growth, 323, 329–30, 350–4, 397
factor price equalisation, 287–9, 292–3, 294, 347, 353
feedback effects, 253
final demand in input–output accounts, 243, 245, 246
financing: of urban government expenditures, 192, 208–19; of wage subsidies, 414
fiscal: influences on balance of payments, 267–8; problems in urban economy, ch. 8; residue, 196. *See also under* stabilisation
flows: of capital, 309. *See also under* savings; polarised, 227, 228, 230
f.o.b. pricing, 19, 21, 28, 29, 33, 37, 71, 76, 107
free trade: 349; as a substitute for factor mobility, 288
freight absorption, 34, 37
friction: cost minimisation, 119–23, Guttenberg's version of, 122–3; of space, 5, 119

games theory, 36, 423
general equilibrium analysis: 6, 103, 116, 223, 295, 370–1, 391, 422; and factor mobility, 287–95, 320; not applicable to space economy, 101; and spatial price analysis, 41
goals: 360, 386–7, 402; of the firm, 95; inter-regional compatibility of, 376–9; in the location decision, 90–100 *passim*; ordering of, 368–9; regional, and conflict with national, 10, 365–72
gradient: around city, 147; of land values, 148–9

grants, cash: 212, 213; specific, 215–17; unconditional, 213–15
gravity models: 8, 39; low predictive power of, 135; and migration, 299; and regional macroeconomics, 270–4; of retail location, 132–6, 137
Greenhut's general theory, 108–11
growth: in regions, ch. 13, and national compared, 321; urban, 8, ch. 7, rates and migration, 300, variations in rates, 177, 181
growth points: integrate location theory and regional economics, 427–8; as natural entities, 416; origins and concept of, 417; and regional policy, 10, 408–9, 415–28; socio-economic role of, 425–6
growth pole, 417, 418

hierarchical marginal good, 162
homogeneous regions, 224–7
horizontal equity, 196
household demand spatial equilibrium schedule, 140, 142
households, location of, 121, 137–45
human ecology: and concentric zone theory, 147; and minimum friction costs hypothesis, 122; and urban growth, 170–5

impact evaluation, 232, 233
imports: in accounts, 232, 235, 240, 244; of capital, 335; functions in regional income models, 255; leakages, 257; marginal propensity to, 251, 252, 267, 268, 272, 384; replacement of, 250, 337; in urban base theory, 169
income: 3, 9, 354, 356–7, 376, 387; and diffusion of innovation, 313; effects on balance of payments, 266–7; primary and secondary

income—*cont.*
  effects of expansion in, 259–60; level of, in cities, 188; and population, 39–40; potential, 78, 422; property, unequal distribution of, 294, 354; psychic, 91, 94, 100, 110, 200, 318; and residential spatial structure, 150–1; rising, and urban government activity, 187; spillovers, 233, 377, 380; and urban structure, 126
income determination models in regions, 9, 254–6, 282, 381–2
indecomposable system, 284
indeterminacy: of Lösch demand cone, 72; of satisficing models, 100
indivisibilities, 370, 421
industrial complex analysis, 418, 422, 424
industrial structure: 9; in cities, 181; and cycles, 275–7; and growth, 342–7; and policy, 399–400
industries: key, 417, 424; propulsive, 417–18; regional and national, 366–7; to be subsidised, 402–3
inertia: in location, 87, 93, 100, 115–16; of managers, 296
inflation and migration, 396
input–output access, 345–6, 422
input–output models: 9, 385; role in accounts, 237–46; in urban structure, 128
institutional rigidities in Lefeber's theory, 115
instrumental variables, 358–61 *passim*
interdependence: between growth rates and social climate, 318; among incomes, 225; in location, 8, 25, 81–90, 98, 109, 111, 422, Lösch's neglect of, 69, 108, summary of factors in, 87–90, with two producers, 81–5, with three or more producers, 85–7; in multiple region system, 254; among nodes, 227–8
interest rate: 302–4; analogy to transport rate, 5, 49; and capital market, 305; and growth, 332, 335
intermediate: demand, 243; goods, 115
international trade: and interregional trade, 287–95 *passim*; relationship with regional economics, 2
inter-regional: approach to cycles, 279–80; factor flows, and balance of payments, 268–9, and growth, 350–4, and policy, 397; multiplier 256–9, accelerator model of regional cycles, 281–6; neglect of, growth in export base theory, 337; relations and space, 428; trade, models, 102–3, stability of coefficients, 239–40
intervening opportunities model, 299
intra-regional resource allocation: and efficiency, 411; and growth, 354
invasion-succession, 148
investment: autonomous, 256; in comparative statics model, 304–9; in cycles, 279; dynamic, 310; social, 365, 408–9, 427
isoquants, 61, 61n., 287

'Keynesian cross', 249

labour: catchment area, 166, 425; cheap, site, 58; female, 397; migration, 295–304, role of internal, 295–7, theoretical models of, 298–304; as a non-transportable factor, 113; orientation, 56; participation rates, 294, 328–9, 354; pools as an influence on location, 64, 99, 176; supply inelastic in old regions, 355; unused, reserves as a justification for policy, 398

laissez faire in regional policy, 390–2

land use, spatial structure of, 145–55

land values: 120, 122; Hawley's theory of, 123–4; Wendt's theory of, 125–6

learning by doing, 311

Lefeber's general theory, 104, 111–16

Leontief's input–output models, 238

Lerner–Singer's treatment of locational interdependence, 85–6

linear: input functions, 238; market assumptions in location, 82–4; rent-distance functions, 148–9

linear programming: 3; and general theory, 104–5, 112; method of finding spatial price equilibrium, 18; model of residential development, 126; planning, 360, 361–5

local government and triple budget function, 188–92

localised raw materials, 45

location: ch. 4; divisible, in Lefeber's theory, 115; end point, 44, 53; and equilibrium, 52–3, 105–6, 109–10, 112, 114–15, in duopoly, 81–4, of an urban firm, 129–32; general theory of, ch. 5, 6, obstacles to, 101–4; and growth, 346; of industry policy, 397–409; least cost, 80, 89; median, 84; moves long drawn out, 4; optimum, 2, 38, 58, 91; rents defined, 112; and technical change, 4, 92, 398; and transport costs, ch. 3; triangle, 45, 47–9, 54; weight, 45

Lorenz curve, 163

Löschian theory: 69–72; criticisms of, 73–4, 91, 107; as a general theory, 104, 105–8

lubrication, 391

managerial mobility, 316–20

marginal: cost, 21, 86, 109, 114, 115, constant, 82, of migration, 395; efficiency of investment and cost of funds, 306–10 *passim*, 352; product, 114, 289, 306, 352; productivity theory of migration, 298; propensity to import, 251, 252, 267, 268, 272, 273, 382, 384; propensity to spend, 257, 260–1, 267, 268, 273; rate of return, 305; rate of substitution, 61n.; revenue 20, 21, 96, 109, 412–13, 415

marginalism: 3; inapplicable to space economy, 102

margins, spatial, to profitability, 63–4, 65, 66

market areas: 25, 26, 36, 37, 75, 103, 106–7; as derived by Lösch, 69–70; shape of, 32–3, 107, 108, 160

market: central, and price analysis, 30–2; equilibrium for urban land, use 140, 142; forces, 3; orientation, 94, compatible with revenue maximisation, 98; sheltered, 83: no, solution to level of public expenditures, 203; solution to regional problems, 389–92

material index, 45–6, 48

material orientation, 19, 43, 46, 98

maturity hypothesis of regional growth, 355–6

merit wants, 191

metropolitan influence, 172, 174

microeconomics: relation to location theory, 3, 60–2, 68, 92; analogy between bid price and indifference curves in, 130

migration: costs, 207, 295, 296, 301, 302, 303–4, 393, 409; effects of, 293, 394–5, 396; and goals, 369; and growth, 328–9, 350–2; of labour analysed, 295–304; measures to induce, 388–9, 392–7; propensity coefficient, 303–4; between towns, 208; and urbanisation, 165

minimum attainment constraint, 371

mobility: of capital, 304–10; costs of, 207, 393; of managers, 316–20 and regional policy, 397–409; spatial, between urban communities, 203–8

monopolistic competition in space, 32–3

monopoly in space, 20–4

multi-level fiscal system, 189

multi-plant firms and regional accounts, 234

multiple nuclei hypothesis, 153–5

multiplier: 417; -accelerator model, 281–6, and growth, 322n.; base, 251–2; and business cycles, 278–9; inter-regional, 256–9

multiproduct plants, implications for location theory, 92

neoclassical growth model, 331–6, 339

net economy curves, 199–200

new entry in Greenhut's model, 109, 111

nodal regions, 227–9, 230

nodes: and growth points, 418–19; as locations, 99, rare in Lösch's theory, 108

non-economic factors: and growth, 349; in location, 2, 3, 94; in migration, 296, 301, of managers, 318–19; and urban structure, 146

non-transportable resources, 112–13, 377, 422

objective function, 361–2, 378, 379

objectives. *See under* goals

oligopoly in space, 24, 34–6, 98

opportunity cost, 309, 366, 402

optimum: city size, 178; community size, 204–5; Pareto, 288; population concept, 298–9; urban unit, 197, 202

Pareto optimum, 288

participation rates, 294, 328, 354

pecuniary external diseconomies, 395, 400

perfect competition, 287, 288, 366, 369–70

personal: considerations in location, 94, 99; contacts as a locational influence, 90, 97

phantom freight, 38

planning: 4, 119, 152–3; functions of, 121; growth point as a tool, 416, 427; region, 229

points, regions as, 7, 13, 428

polarisation analysis, 227, 228, 230, 416, 420, 428. *See also under* nodes

pôle de croissance, 417

pole of growth, 417–18. *See also under* growth points

policy: broad direction of, 386–9; instruments, 403–4, 408–9; location of industry, 397–409; market solution, 389–92; measures to promote migration, 392–7

polygon, locational, 46, 53, 54

population: concentrations as low cost points, 61; growth and regional development, 321–35

453

population—*cont.*
passim; as an influence on location, 72–4, 76–7, 79, 90, 422; retail model based on, 128; as a source of demand, 19, 33; uneven density, 226–7; uniform density, 69
potential: gross economic population, 39–40, 73–4, 157n.; income, model, 127–8; population, 39, 73, 76, 78
preference: environmental, 99, 100; of firms, 131; function, 367–8, 378–9; of households, 143, 203–8, 399; normal, area, 425n.
price-ratio lines, 50–3
prices: agricultural, 39; basing point, 24, 36, 37, 38, 90; commodity, 287–95 *passim*; constant, in stabilisation policy model, 384; delivered, free, 37, uniform 24, 36, 90; discrimination, 20–4, 38, 90; flexibility, 266; in linear programming models, 364; between regions, 3; shadow, 114; in space, ch. 2 *passim*, 390; stability, 36
primal, 365
product, supply and demand space and time potential, 40–1
production functions: 112, 116, 331, 352; Cobb–Douglas, 373, 375, 376, 407; identical, 287; in regions, 289, 293, 294; in USA, 289–90
production possibilities, 377, 379
profit maximisation: 8, 42, 77–81, 105, 106, 109–10; assumptions of, in spatial analysis, 91–3; of urban firm, 120
programming: model, 360–1, 361–5 *passim*; quadratic, 18; region, 229
pure competition, 19, 20, 21

radial sector theory, 150–3, 155

range of a good, 157, 158, 161
rank size rule: 82; criticisms of, 183–4
rate deficiency grant, 213
rectangular hyperbola, 141, 144
regional macroeconomics: 7, 226, 427; limitations of, 270–1
Reilly's law of retail gravitation, 132–3
rent: 128, 129, 138; as item in costs of friction, 119; minimisation, 18; Von Thünen's theory of, 120
resale possibilities limit discrimination, 24
research and development, 392, 404
residential: development and radial sector hypothesis, 150–1; equilibrium, Wingo's model of 137–45; land values, 123
residentiary sector in export base theory, 337
resource scarcities, 361
retail: location of, establishments, 132–7; models, 128, Baumol–Ide, 136–7
revenue: marginal, 20, 21, 96, 109; maximisation, 78, 95–8, as a location goal, 96; space, 76–9, 80–1; total, 96
risks, 301, 307
rival sellers as a constraint on monopoly, 24
rural locations, advantages and disadvantages of, 64n.

Samuelson–Enke spatial price analysis, 13–18, 24–5
Samuelson multiplier-accelerator model, 285
'satisficing': as a goal, 98–9; implications of, 99; models, 98–100; operational weakness of, 100
savings: 304, 307, 308, 325, 327, 334–5; income ratio, 293, 304

scale: economies. *See under* economies of scale; of plant as an influence on location, 97, 98; of region, 223–4, 338–9
security motive in location, 93
sector theory of growth, 340–1
share analysis, 344
shift analysis: 344; proportional and differential, 344–5, 400
short-circuiting of central market, 32
social capital, effects of migration on, 297
social wants, 191
socio-economic: determinants of growth, 312, 317; function of growth point, 425–6
sociological interpretations of urban growth, 170–6
space: neglect of in regional economics 1–5, 7; preference, 94, 143; social, 171
spatial: differences in benefits from services, 202; margins to profitability, 63–4, 65, 66, 69; mobility between communities, 203–8; price equilibrium, 13–18, conditions of, 16; structure within cities, 119–55
spread effects of growth, 348–9, 419
S-shaped curve describing innovation, 312–13
stabilisation: branch, 189, normally left to central government, 190–1; built-in, 267; policy, 379–85; targets, 382–4
stability: in Greenhut's analysis, 110; of growth process, 339, 347–57 *passim*; in Hotelling, 83–4; of regional system, 256
stage of development of region, 253
statistical deficiencies, 4
strong factor intensity hypothesis, 290

structural coefficients: of decision model, 360; of multiplier-accelerator model, 285
subsidies: effect on location, 66–7; types of, 404–5; of wages as an aid to policy, 409–15; of wages, capital and prices compared, 405–8
substitution: between labour and transport costs, 56–8; of one input for another, 62, 67–8, 406; between transport costs and rent, 139–45 *passim*
suburbs, flight to, 9, 180, 188
supply areas, 29
supply of entrepreneurship, 317
systems analysis and planning, 387

taxes: 267, 380, 381, 391, 414; effect on location, 66–7; from government services, 195, 209, 211; indirect, allocation to region, 234
technological change: 332, 333, 334, 355; embodied, 311; impact on location, 4; spatial diffusion of, 310–16
telephones as index of centrality, 163
terminal costs, 44, 77
tertiary industries, role of, 340–1
threshold: cost analysis, 179; of demand in central place theory, 157, 161
time: elements in location decision, 93, 97; in general theory, 101; and innovation, 312; path, of cycles, 284, of policy changes, 384; role of, in economics, 1, 2; in spatial price variations, 40
trade: balanced, 16–18, 19, 273; free, 349, in space, 13, as a substitute for factor mobility, 288; inter-regional, 102–3, 239–40

455

transfer payments, 267
transformation: curves in Lefeber's analysis, 113–14; lines, 50–3; surface, 372–6 *passim*
transhipment points, 45, 153, 422
transport costs: as an aid to monopolist, 42–3; as a deduction from demand, 22; and demand cone, 74–5; and growth points, 422; as an influence on market area size, 20, 26, 70–1; and location, ch. 3, 65; and marginal costs, 88; minimum, 43–4, in Weber, 45–9; and prices in spatially separated markets, 13–18; and space cost curve, 63; substituted for labour costs, 56–8; and transport rate, 5, 49; in Wingo model, 138–9; zero, 2, 3, 103, 287, 292
transport: and conditions of equilibrium, 114–15; distinction between transportable and non-transportable resources, 112–13; inputs, defined, 49, role in Isard's theory, 49–56, 111; in Lefeber's theory, 112, 116, and criticisms of Lösch and Isard, 111; neglect of in Greenhut's general theory, 111; network and concentric zones, 150; orientation in Weber, 56; routes, 3, 55; system, 145, and friction costs, 122–3
trend-cycle relationship, 277
trip distribution indices, 127
triple budget function and local government, 188–92

ubiquities, 45, 46
unbalanced regional system, 230
uncertainty: 358, 390; and capital market, 307; and location decision, 89, 92, 102; and migration, 301

unemployment: and base models, 253–4; and migration, 297
uniform distribution of resources, 64, 69
urban: concepts of, structure, 145–55; economic base, 165–70; fraction, 184; fringe, 173; growth, ch. 7; hierarchy, 182–3, 418, deviation index, 184, and innovation, 313–14, 319, in UK, 183; large units, advantages of, 201–2; locations, advantages and disadvantages of, 64, 69, 79; public economy, ch. 8; realms, 176, 314–15, 318; size ratchet, 177; spatial structure, 8, ch. 6, friction cost minimising models, 119–23, other models of, 123–8; time budget, 175; transportation, 186–7
urbanisation indices, 163–4
urbanised nuclei, 172
user charges: 194, 195, 209–11; advantages of, 209; obstacles in the way of, 210–11

vertical dispersion of location, 42

wages: allocative function of, 411; flexibility, 3, 410, lack of, 266; and migration, 296, 297; subsidies, 10, and regional policy, 406–8, 409–15
Warntz's method of studying spatial price variations, 38–41
Weber's location theory, 45–9, 56
weight loss in production, 46, 53, 64, 98
weight triangle, 45–7
Wingo's model of urban residential equilibrium, 137–45

workplace, separation of residences from, 9, 193

zone of influence, 180, 228, 416, 418–19, 424–5, 426

zones: in concentric zone hypothesis, 147–8; in multiple nuclei theory, 154; in radial sector model, 151–2
zoning restrictions, 121